COGNITIVE PROCESSES

LYLE E. BOURNE, JR.
University of Colorado

ROGER L. DOMINOWSKI
University of Illinois, Chicago Circle

ELIZABETH F. LOFTUS
University of Washington

PRENTICE-HALL, INC., ENGLEWOOD CLIFFS, NEW JERSEY 07632

Library of Congress Cataloging in Publication Data

Bourne, Lyle Eugene
  Cognitive processes.

  Bibliography.
  Includes index.
  1. Cognition. 1. Dominowski, Roger L.,
joint author. II. Loftus, Elizabeth F.,
joint author. III. Title.
BF311.B64   153.4   78–16953
ISBN 0–13–139634–X

PRENTICE-HALL SERIES IN EXPERIMENTAL PSYCHOLOGY
James J. Jenkins, Editor

© 1979 by Prentice-Hall, Inc., Englewood Cliffs, New Jersey, 07632

Printed in the United States of America

10 9 8 7 6 5 4 3 2 1

Prentice-Hall International, Inc., London
Prentice-Hall of Australia Pty. Limited, Sydney
Prentice-Hall of Canada, Ltd., Toronto
Prentice-Hall of India Private Limited, New Delhi
Prentice-Hall of Japan, Inc., Tokyo
Prentice-Hall of Southeast Asia Pte. Ltd., Singapore
Whitehall Books Limited, Wellington, New Zealand

CONTENTS

chapter four

chapter five

chapter six

chapter seven

chapter eight

chapter nine

chapter ten

chapter eleven

PREFACE

THIS BOOK HAS ITS ORIGINS in another text, *The Psychology of Thinking*. Some time ago, we considered a revision, but felt *The Psychology of Thinking* had become out of date and no longer reflected the field as it is today. Also, we perceived a need for a single, contemporary volume which provides adequate textual material for the undergraduate course in cognition. Once discussions began, however, we quickly realized that revising the earlier text would not be sufficient; major changes were needed. The outcome is a brand new book.

A decade ago, the field of learning, memory, and cognition was in a state of transition. The essentially behavioristic establishment faced a serious challenge from a new mentalism. The mentalists were gaining strength, while the behaviorists seemed to be on the defensive. Since that time, the field, which has become commonly known as cognitive psychology, has changed considerably. The confrontation between old and new seems to have passed, or at least become more mellow. The traditional theme is no longer behavioristic in character but rather mentalistic. In this book, we have tried to provide a portrait of current views of cognitive processes. While there are many references to the basic, research literature for those who desire detailed information, our fundamental goal is to make the study of cognitive processes understandable to the undergraduate student.

Many different activities come under the heading of "cognitive processes," and we have tried to cover the field broadly. As a guiding orientation, we have adopted the perspective of human beings as information-processing systems. We have focused on issues and phenomena which best illustrate how people process and utilize information in trying to accomplish various goals.

We begin our coverage with a brief history of the field, reflecting the changes that have occurred in psychologists' views of cognition in the last half century. After setting the stage for the contemporary scene, we discuss the basic processes of attention and the storage and retrieval of information over the short and the long term, these processes representing the core of cognition. An understanding of these fundamental ideas allows us to consider more complex matters such as the acquisition and the use of general knowledge, the relation between language and thought, concept learning, problem solving, and reasoning. The study of cognition has taken on increasing scope over the last decade. With this maturity has come a significant literature on the development of cognitive processes in human beings and the application of cognitive psychology to the "real" world. We cover these matters in the final chapters of the book.

The authors of a text are not the only contributors to the final product. We would like to express our special appreciation to Bruce R. Ekstrand, one of the authors of *The Psychology of Thinking*. We are indebted to James J. Jenkins for his critical comments, suggestions, and encouragement. Lawrence Kurdek contributed very useful library research concerning cognitive development. For their assistance in typing the manuscript and obtaining permission, we are grateful to Suzanne Reissig, Donna Behnke Partyka, and Janice Hastings. Finally, we would like to thank the many researchers whose work is essential to this or any other text.

L. E. B. Jr.

R. L. D.

E. F. L.

INTRODUCTION

outline

THIS BOOK CONCERNS ITSELF WITH the capabilities and limitations of the human mind. While the study of cognitive processes has always been a part of psychology, it is only relatively recently, say, over the last 15 years, that truly significant progress has been made. It is the purpose of this book to describe that progress, to inform the reader of the present state of the science, and to set the stage for some of the significant problems that remain to be solved.

Cognitive psychologists approach their discipline from a basically scientific perspective. There is a tendency among them to view the human mind as a calculational device, albeit somewhat imprecise and error-prone. In this book, we adopt a model of the human mind as a system for processing information. We begin in this chapter by laying out a general framework along these lines which we hope will prove useful in studying the substantive topics of later chapters.

As a starting point, let's consider what the human mind can accomplish. You will find the following cases most unusual; nonetheless they are real-life examples of what the human mind can do if pushed to the extreme. They not only challenge psychologists to study and understand human cognition, they also represent the kind of processes that a complete science of cognition must eventually deal with.

SOME CAPABILITIES OF THE HUMAN MIND

A MENTAL CALCULATOR

I. M. L. Hunter (1968) described the unusual powers of rapid mental calculation possessed by Professor A. C. Aitken, a distinguished mathematician at Edinburgh University. He gives the following example. Professor Aitken is asked to express the fraction 4/47 as a decimal. In Hunter's words, "He is silent for 4 seconds, then begins to speak the answer at a nearly uniform rate of 1 digit every three-quarters of a second. '0–8–5–1–0–6–3–8–2–9–7–8–7–2–3–4–0–4–2–5–5–3–1–9–1–4, that's about as far as I can carry it.' The total time between the presentation of the problem and this moment is 24 seconds. He discusses the problem for 1 minute and then continues the answer at the same rate as before 'Yes, 1–9–1–4–8–9, I can get that.' He pauses for 5 seconds. '3–6–1–7–0–2–1–2–7–6–5–9–5–7–4–4–5–8, now that is the repeating point. It starts again at 085.

So if that is 46 places, I am right' " (p. 341). This is indeed a remarkable performance! One might rightly wonder whether any other human being is capable of such mental "gymnastics." Hunter's report gives the impression that Aitken has a computer for a brain and can grind out answers to arithmetic questions of this sort with little conscious effort. Actually, a more intense study of what it is that Professor Aitken is doing reveals a much more ordinary basis. Professor Aitken has no unusual memory capacity nor is he more intelligent than everyone else. The fact is that he knows how to perform numerical calculations in his head about as well as any person who has ever lived. This ability is largely acquired and rests upon a broad knowledge of number facts and highly developed manipulative skills that can be performed mentally on those number facts.

A CALENDAR CALCULATOR

Seemingly incredible calculational skills are not restricted to individuals with intense training or high intellect. They sometimes crop up in otherwise low scoring individuals. Extreme cases of this sort have been labeled *idiot savant* (wise idiot). An example is reported by Scheerer, Rothmann, and Goldstein (1945). They describe an 11-year-old boy, L., who was very poor as a student and could not get along in school. His intelligence test score fell technically within the mentally retarded range (IQ = 50). Judging from his schoolroom behavior, he appeared to be limited in both intellectual and social skills. Some of his cognitive accomplishments, however, were truly remarkable. He could listen to an unfamiliar piece of music and then reproduce it by ear on a piano. He could add together two-digit numbers about as rapidly as they could be read to him. His memory for names, places, and dates seemed inexhaustible.

Probably his most impressive skill was calendar calculation. Given any person's birthdate, he could immediately say on what day of the week it fell during the previous year. He could name the day of the week for any date beginning with the year 1880, and could give the date for the second Tuesday in April, 1940, or the last Thursday in December, 1934. Not only were his answers to these and similar questions virtually immediate but also his recall of the birthdates of real people was almost perfect. Cases such as these present intriguing riddles for cognitive psychology to solve. Unfortunately, the number of such cases is small and there has been little opportunity to study them scientifically in detail.

A MNEMONIST

A. R. Luria (1968) wrote a fascinating account of a man, S., who had a truly fantastic memory. Luria studied the man carefully over a span of many years. In the course of his work, Luria discovered that S. could remember volumes of information of a variety of sorts after a brief and seemingly effortless examination. Further, he seemed able to store the material for any length of time and recall it at will. The basis of this remarkable memory seemed to be in S.'s unusual but profound use of mental imagery. To quote Luria, "When S. read through a long series of words, each word would elicit a graphic image . . . since the series was fairly long, he had to find some way of distributing these images of his in a mental row or sequence. Most often (and this habit persisted throughout his life), he would 'distribute' them along some roadway or street he visualized in his mind. . . . Frequently he would take a mental walk along that street . . . slowly . . . 'distributing' his images at houses, gates, and in store windows. . . . This technique of converting a series of words to a series of graphic images explains why S. could so readily reproduce a series from start to finish or in reverse order; how he could rapidly name the word that preceded or followed one I'd selected from the series. To do this, he would simply begin his walk, either from the beginning or from the end of the street, find the image of the object I had named, and 'take a look at' whatever happened to be situated on either side of it" (Luria, 1968, pp. 1–33). Mnemonics, the devices people use to enhance their memories, constitute an important topic in contemporary psychology. We are beginning to understand how people utilize imagery and other mental processes to ensure the stable representation of experiences in memory. People who are extremely good at mnemonics, like Luria's S., have perfected systems of remembering by rote an amount of material which would, on the surface, seem impossible. It has been shown in the cognitive psychology laboratory, however, that with sufficient practice, many individuals can approximate the same level of performance.

SHORT- AND LONG-TERM MEMORY

We will be concerned in this book with the distinction cognitive theory commonly makes between short-term and long-term memory. Short-term memory refers to holding information that is necessary only for some immediate use, for example, looking up the telephone number of the local service station and remembering it only long enough to dial. Long-term memory refers to the capacity to store information for activities that may occur at some unspecified time in the future. There is evidence to suggest that all information must pass through short-term to long-term memory; that is, we must process new information in some immediate sense before it is in a form suitable for more permanent representation. Older people often report difficulty in storing new information in long-term memory. It is often observed that a senile person can recall events in his life that happened before senility set in, but his memory bank seems closed to new inputs.

Certain types of brain damage appear to create a similar memory deficit. Milner (1966) describes a study of a young man who had lost part of his temporal lobes and hippocampus in a brain operation. Prior to the operation, his IQ was 104, about normal. After the operation, he tested at 118, significantly above normal. There are reasons for this change, but the point is that the operation did *not* result in a reduction of intelligence. This individual could remember events in his life prior to the operation as well as anybody. However, nothing that happened to him after the operation seemed to stick in long-term memory. Says Milner, "Ten months before I examined him, his family had moved from their old house to one a few blocks away on the same street. He still has not learned the new address, though remembering the old one perfectly, nor can he be trusted to find his way home alone. He does not know where objects constantly in use are kept; for example, his mother still has to tell him where to find the lawn mower, even though he may have been using it only the day before. She also states that he will do the same jigsaw puzzle day after day without showing any practice effect, and that he will read the same magazines over and over again without finding their content familiar" (1959, p. 49). The man described his own life as "like waking from a dream" and not really remembering where he was or how he got there. He remarked that, for him, every day is alone in itself. It is as if today is continually pushed out of his short-term memory, one item at a time, and tomorrow never comes and could not be remembered even if it did.

What is striking about this patient is that he can remember events that happened before brain damage, but events that occurred after the operation are retained but for a brief period of time. The theoretical conception of memory as having both short-term and long-term storage helps us to interpret this kind of result. Apparently, whatever else the brain damage did, it obliterated those processes which are responsible for the transfer of information from short- to long-term storage. How neurological processes provide the underpinning for this transfer process is currently an issue of intense experimental examination by cognitively oriented biological psychologists.

FLASHES OF INSIGHT

What we have discussed so far falls mainly under the heading of rote or reproductive performance. Neither the feats of Professor Aitken or of the calendar calculator L., remarkable though they are, can qualify as insightful or creative. By what process does creativity occur? This is another problem of intense interest to cognitive psychologists. Sometimes what is called creative is accomplished mainly by dint of hard, plodding work. *War and Peace* was not written overnight nor did the ideas occur to Tolstoy in an immediate burst of insight. Rather, the writing of this masterpiece involved long, agonizing, and highly imaginative toil. But sometimes, creative solutions to a problem do seem to occur in a single instant. It is said that Friedrick Kekulé solved the chemical problem of the arrangement of carbon and hydrogen atoms in the compound benzene while dreaming. To quote Findlay (1965): "In 1865, Kekulé, then Professor of Chemistry at Ghent, was engaged one evening in writing his textbook, but his thoughts were elsewhere. 'I turned my chair to the fire and dozed,' he relates. 'Again the atoms were gambolling before my eyes. This time the smaller groups kept modestly in the background. My mental eye, rendered more acute by repeated visions of this kind, could now distinguish larger structures, of manifold conformation; long rows, sometimes more closely fitted together; all twining and twisting in snake-like motion. But look! What was that? One of the snakes had seized hold of its own tail, and the form whirled mockingly before my eyes. As if by a flash of lightning I awoke'; but the picture Kekulé had seen of the snake which had seized its own tail gave him the clue to the most puzzling of molecular structures, the structure of the benzene molecule, for which Kekulé suggested a closed ring of six

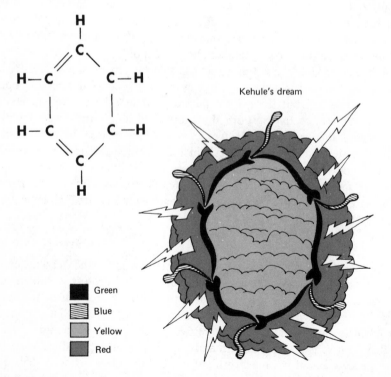

Structure of the
Benzene molecule

Kehule's dream

■ Green
▨ Blue
□ Yellow
■ Red

FIGURE 1–1.

carbon atoms, to each of which a hydrogen atom is attached" (pp. 39–40). The solution occurred to Kekulé in a moment of insight. His dream, not his waking activities, was the immediate antecedent of his idea about the benzene ring, which has turned out to be one of the most important discoveries in all of organic chemistry.

How does one establish the conditions for insightful solutions? Some suggestions are beginning to appear in the research of cognitive psychologists. If the proper set of conditions could be discovered, think of the importance this would have for all the creative work that remains to be done.

MIND OVER MATTER

There have been numerous reports of cases in which an individual demonstrates extraordinary control over his own bodily functions. You have heard of the Indian yogi who can sleep on a bed of nails. Another yogic practice is to sit in a tub and voluntarily draw water up into the lower intestine to cleanse it. At the Menninger Foundation, an Indian yogi voluntarily threw his heart into fibrillation—that is, he made it beat at about 300 beats per minute—for 17 seconds. At this rate the heart will not pump any blood, and so his pulse disappeared. Reports of such unusual actions have been largely ignored in the scientific literature but are now being looked at intensely by cognitive psychologists because of the rapidly developing field of biofeedback research.

If an instrument is used to inform a person exactly what some part of his body which is normally inaccessible to consciousness is doing, the person often can find ways of changing and controlling the activity. For example, if the activity of a single muscle fiber is electronically amplified and displayed either visually or in auditory form, the subject can learn to relax or to activate the fiber. Likewise, if a sound is used to indicate when an alpha rhythm appears in the electronic recording of brain activity (EEG), many subjects seem to be able to learn to decrease or increase the amount of their alpha rhythm. The essence of biofeedback techniques is that they make available to consciousness information that is ordinarily not present. Having that information, people can try various strategies to see what effects they have on the "involuntary" process. A person can thus achieve cognitive control over his bodily activity, essentially what we mean by mind over matter.

MAN AS A SYSTEM FOR PROCESSING INFORMATION

How can we understand these various kinds of cognitive performance? Today's cognitive psychologist faces the enormous task of explaining phenomena such as these in scientific terms. In the recent past an information-processing approach to these questions has yielded some progress; it continues to offer the most promising framework for further research.

How people behave is largely dependent on the information they have available. We adopt a theme for this book, common among contemporary cognitive psychologists, to the effect that a human being, or better the human mind, is a system that processes information. We shall give a brief introduction to that system in this section, hoping to lay the groundwork for further elaboration in subsequent chapters. The presentation at this point is not meant to be definitive but only to provide a useful background for understanding what is to come as well as the examples we discussed at the outset. We make no attempt to be technical. There are, to be sure, precise and formal ways to define information and the processes a person carries out on information. At this point, we shall be content to be general, imprecise, and commonsensical in our description.

The information a person has to work with at any moment comes from three sources: (1) his circumstances, which will include some focal stimulus; (2) his memory wherein resides information about past experiences and functional skills; and (3) the feedback he receives as a consequence of action, information which derives partly from sensing one's own movements and partly from the reaction of one's social and nonsocial environment. It is possible, of course, to include feedback stimuli as a subset of circumstances, and thereby talk in terms of two kinds of informational input. There are some qualitative distinctions, however, between information which is contingent on performance and information which is not, so we prefer to maintain the distinction.

STAGES OF INFORMATION PROCESSING

Information takes time to be processed. During processing, information may pass through several stages, each with its own characteristics, limitations, and parameters. Let's trace the stages as portrayed in Figure 1-2.

SENSORY MEMORY.   If information is to be effective, it must first be registered perceptually. That is to say, a person must see, hear, feel, or otherwise sense the information. There is evidence to the effect that under some circumstances the impression left by sensory experience may persist in all its complexity within the organism, either at the receptor level or in the brain, for a short period of time. Sensory memory is something different from an afterimage which follows a prolonged or intense stimulus. It appears to be a true form of memory although quite primitive. The two major characteristics of this memory are high capacity and fast decay. That is to say, the system will record for some period of time a nearly exact replica of the event that occurred in the environment. However, the period

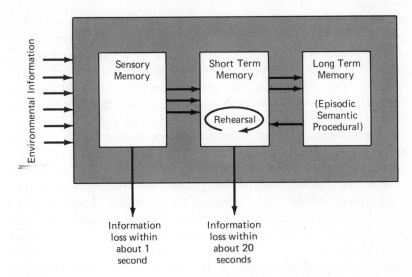

FIGURE 1–2. A schematic representation of the information-processing system.

of time is fairly brief and, if the information is not converted to some more durable form, it will quickly be lost.

Even at the level of sensory storage, certain complicated information-processing activities take place. We see in sensory storage the first evidence of attentional processes. While the sensory system is capable of registering a vast amount of information, those events which are the focus of attention are registered with greatest clarity. The focus of attention can be determined by either peripheral factors, for example, the brightest or loudest or most salient event, or by central factors, those aspects that make an event the one we expect or want to perceive. Further, the process of pattern recognition is initiated during sensory storage. Although the entirety of information stored in sensory memory is itself meaningless, the persistence of images in this mode allows the process of identification and recognition to begin. In order for an image to be recognized, of course, it must be understood in light of previous experience. The process of coming to identify, name, or otherwise recognize an image begins with perception but often involves more than just the persistence of the stimulus itself. Finally, if the event that has occurred is to be retained in any sense, it must be converted to a more durable form—that is, it must be encoded for later stages of processing. But this brings us to the next topic.

SHORT-TERM MEMORY.   For greater durability, the sensory image must be converted to a more memorable form, what we call the process of encoding. There is no general agreement on how encoding is accomplished or about the form it takes. Some hypothesize that encoding is largely a matter of converting experience to words, at least in human beings. Others suggest that the encoding may be image-like in nature, retaining many of the characteristics of the sensory experience. Still others assume an abstract representation which is neither verbal nor image-like. We shall discuss these issues later. In any case, encoded information is more durable than pre-processed information and can be passed from sensory storage into short-term storage.

Short-term memory, like consciousness, seems to be what we are aware of at any given moment. It is an active form of memory, often referred to as working memory, whose capacity is rather limited. Evidence suggests that we can hold in short-term memory only something on the order of 7 (plus or minus 2) items of information at any given time. Thus, short-term memory is easily overtaxed and is generally thought to admit only those items to which we strictly attend. In addition, a continual flow of information to short-term memory necessitates that some items will be replaced by incoming items. Furthermore, even if there were no significant interference, items would fade out in time if not further processed. The limited duration of short-term memory is evident in the example of looking up and dialing a telephone number. Usually we experience no lasting memory for the number once the dialing operation is complete.

To keep information alive in short-term memory, we must engage in rehearsal. Rehearsal seems to have primarily two functions, first to maintain information over a time period, and second to convert or elaborate information in short-term memory into an even more durable form so that it can be transferred into long-term storage. Milner's (1966) study indicates that the transfer processes have a specific neurological base.

LONG-TERM MEMORY. Information that is processed into long-term storage can pass from consciousness and still be remembered. The form this information takes, still a subject of theoretical debate, is highly durable. It has been argued that information which once achieves long-term storage is never really forgotten. Whether or not that is the case, long-term memory is certainly more permanent than any of the other forms of memory, and its capacity is virtually infinite. Until or unless an individual encounters certain organic problems, for example, brain damage, he seems capable of memories that last throughout his lifetime.

Many different kinds of information are represented in long-term memory. The distinction among episodic, semantic, and procedural memories takes note of these differences. Episodic memory is the ability to recall one's personal history. Facts of this sort have both a temporal and a spatial marking and are recalled less for their substance and more in terms of the context of their occurrence. Semantic memory has to do with one's knowledge of the world—the facts and concepts a person knows, without necessarily knowing how or when he acquired them. This is one's repository for meanings in the world. Finally, procedural memory has to do with one's skills. This is the memory for "knowing how" as opposed to "knowing that." This is the repository for what one can do with facts, concepts, and episodes as opposed to what those entities are. There is much more to be said about the content of long-term memory and its organization. It is an interesting and fascinating topic that we will discuss in detail later on.

USING INFORMATION

Thus far we have traced how environmental information, whether performance-contingent (feedback) or not, becomes represented in memory. Having a memory completes the picture of informational input in any circumstance. Thus, whatever one's present circumstances, his reaction will be governed by an interaction of input from environmental and internal sources. But performance cannot be characterized as a simple reaction to external or internal events. There is considerably more to human behavior. There are other processes involved in making use of available information. Human beings have the ability to go beyond the specifics of a situation and to react in a more expansive and general sense. We outline some of these processes in Figure 1-3.

CONSTRUCTIVE PROCESSES. Usually when we are asked to describe an experience or to explain what we remember of a story or chapter we have read, our response is not simply a reproduction of the original experience. Performance in such circumstances is partly constructive. Some specifics of the experience are remembered, to be sure, but these are typically just fragments. Ordinarily there is a necessity to fill in the gaps so as to make connections between these fragments. The connections are constructed, primarily on the bases of one's general knowledge of the world—that is, a person's understanding of the circumstances—and one's skills of inference. Remembering one or a few things allows us to induce or deduce what other things are likely to have happened. Thus, performance in the current situation is a product of how the current situation is sensed, what recollections one has of previous similar circumstances, and one's ability to construct alternatives for behaving which are sensible (inferable) from these two informational inputs.

CONCEPT FORMATION. One kind of inductive process, called concept formation, is basically a classification device. Early in life, for example, we encounter many different people who are nevertheless alike in that they form a category clearly distinguishable from nonpeople. Likewise, we encounter different types of animals and learn to classify them as dogs, cats, or birds. Later in life, categories become more complex, so that we begin to understand what is meant by furniture, professions, religions, and the

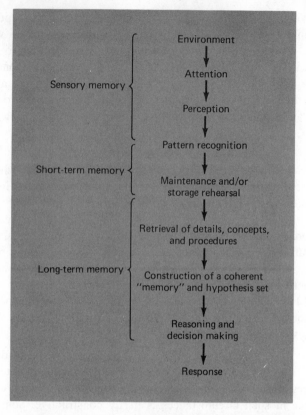

FIGURE 1–3. Flow of sequentially organized processes with corresponding theoretical structures leading from environmental input to response.

like. We learn not only that items go together but the reasons for their going together. This process of concept formation affords some economy for memory and for behavior in the sense that, in most circumstances, instances of the same category can be treated identically and need not be distinguished. In most theories of semantic memory, concepts, not individual instances, are the basic content elements. We use the knowledge of concepts in a variety of kinds of performance, as later chapters will explain.

REASONING. But the mind is not simply an inductive device. It also works in a deductive way. That is to say, we can use our knowledge of the world for making decisions about what must logically be the case given the circumstances. If all A's are B's and all B's are C's, then it is logically (deductively) true that all A's are C's. Although the mind is subject to certain nonlogical operations, the use of reasoning and deduction is one way we have of predicting our own or others' behavior from fragmentary memories of previous events.

OTHER PROCESSES. There are other high-level cognitive processes of which the mind is capable. Among them are problem solving and decision making. We have covered enough, however, to illustrate the general point. The human mind can be described as an information-processing system, and human behavior is a consequence of such processing. The processing that occurs depends on but is not wholly determined by informational input from the environment and from memory. Information represents the elements on which our skills operate to calculate possible and sensible forms of behavior. We use these general notions throughout the remainder of the book as a guide to studying and understanding the cognitive behavior of man.

A BRIEF HISTORY

Contemporary psychologists are engaged in an intensive search for the scientific principles of human cognitive processes. Even as recently as the nineteenth century, however, most philosophers generally accepted the idea that formal logic represented the laws of thought. Logic was supposed to reveal, in some sense, the essence of human reasoning. It was obvious, of course, to logicians and psychologically oriented philosophers that, in their behavior, human beings exhibited all sorts of violations of logic. This in itself would seem to disprove any theory that identified thinking with logic. But many nineteenth-century philosophers and psychologists conceived of human beings dualistically—that is, in terms of independent mental and bodily functions. There was, therefore, no reason to expect that bodily action would correspond strictly to logical mental processes. Thus, although reason and logic might be violated by a given person's acts, the operations of the human mind were still presumed rational.

Once the enterprise of scientific psychology began to function in earnest, during the latter part of the nineteenth century, it became clear that the dualistic philosophy was a hindrance to scientific progress. It was rejected so violently in some quarters that the concept of the mind itself was thrown out as illegitimate and nonscientific. Contemporary psychology has accepted a more middle-of-the-road position, assuming a unity, a cohesion, and a continuity of behavior involving both symbolic activity (the mind) and bodily movement.

One could trace the history of the study of cognitive processes as far back as Aristotle and the roots of associationism. We have chosen, however, to shorten our treatment and to emphasize primarily developments in America during the twentieth century. The reader who is interested in a more extensive history can consult an earlier textbook on thinking (Bourne, Ekstrand, & Dominowski, 1971) or the extensive history of psychology written by Chaplin and Krawiec (1974). Let us begin, however, with a methodological discovery made during the mid-nineteenth century which has had a profound impact on contemporary cognitive psychology.

TIMING MENTAL EVENTS

From the notion of a personal equation employed by astronomers to correct for individual human differences in the temporal recordings of celestial events came the development of mental chronometry (Boring, 1950), a system for calibrating the time characteristics of the mind. F. C. Donders, a Dutch psychologist, constructed the system on the assumption that the duration of mental events can be computed from the difference between simple reaction time and the speed of reaction in situations which require some intervening process or processes. For example, to measure discrimination time, an experimenter should determine both the speed of reaction to a single stimulus, such as light onset (simple reaction time), and the speed of reaction in a similar task wherein the subject must respond to only one of two or more stimuli. In the second task, it is assumed

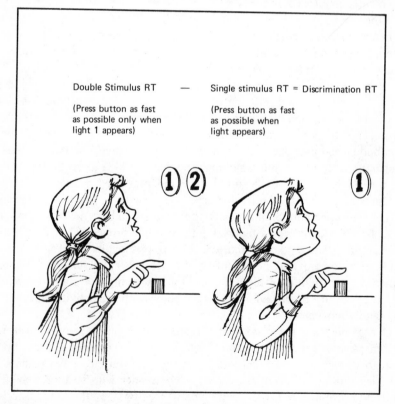

Double Stimulus RT — Single stimulus RT = Discrimination RT

(Press button as fast as possible only when light 1 appears)

(Press button as fast as possible when light appears)

FIGURE 1–4. Timing mental events, here, discrimination, according to Donders.

that the subject has to discriminate between the stimuli before responding. Only after such discrimination could he respond properly. If one assumes that the second task involves all that is involved in the first task plus discrimination, then it follows that the time for discrimination is the difference between the speeds of reaction in the two tasks (see Figure 1-4). By similar reasoning, procedures can be designed for measuring mental events other than discrimination, such as choice, association, judgment, and the like.

This technique has been criticized over the years, largely on the grounds that adding components to the simple reaction time situation might do more than simply introduce another step in the chain of mental events; that is, the effect of additional components may be to change the task substantively. Then, too, the nature of the task, as described to individual subjects during preliminary instruction, might establish an expectation which involves uniquely different response mechanisms. These criticisms were so impelling that mental chronometry fell into disuse during the first half of this century. Recently, thanks largely to new methods introduced by Sternberg (1966), mental chronometry has been revitalized. As we shall see, today it represents a widely used technique for the analysis of mental events.

WILLIAM JAMES

No history of psychology would be complete without some acknowledgment of the work of William James. James contributed broadly to the discipline, and, despite the fact that his significant publications appeared before the turn of the century, his works are still popular and remarkably contemporary. James would hardly qualify as an empirical researcher; he did no experiments of consequence. He was more an innovator, a theorist, and a systematist. His position, set forth in his *Principles of Psychology* (1890), is neither structuralist, evolutionary, nor process-oriented, and yet it contains a little of all these and more. He conceived of mind as an array of functions, of consciousness as a dynamic stream of interacting events (with no rigid structure), and of psychology as the study of adaptive processes—before any of these ideas were popularized by the functionalist school in America. As a pragmatist, James attempted to explain both behavior and consciousness through a conception of the mind as a biological organ whose functions are used to contend with a hostile environment. Except for its greater intricacy and complexity, the mind, according to James, is no different from other organic structures, such as the heart or the lungs, which play vital roles in the functioning of the whole organism. The human mind has merely evolved to a point where its functions are more versatile and pervasive than any other single organ.

James was the first to offer a truly scientific theory of memory. To remember, according to James, is to think about something which was previously experienced but which was not being thought about immediately before. James distinguished between primary memory, that which we are aware of and which is the focus of current attention, and secondary memory, or memories of great duration held at an unconscious level. This distinction, remarkably similar to the contemporary concepts of short-term and long-term memory, is clearly anticipatory of modern developments.

FUNCTIONALISM

Functionalism gained prominence in psychology under the influence of John Dewey at the University of Chicago just before the turn of the century. Functionalism was never a cohesive system, but rather represented a protest against the German school of structuralism founded by Wilhelm Wundt. The protest addressed primarily structuralism's insistence on the exclusive study of consciousness and the elements of the mind through introspection. Functionalism's identity with Chicago was short-lived, as it quickly spread to other American universities with formal psychology programs. Its substance was taken from principles of William James as embellished by the insights and empirical findings of John Dewey, his students and colleagues.

SIGNIFICANCE OF CONSCIOUSNESS. Functionalists identified and defined some of psychology's most significant problems. For example, obvious as it might be to the modern student that learning is one of the most basic processes in human life, it was not accorded any major role in behavior by psychologists prior to the 1900s. Functionalists were not constrained by the artificiality of early scientific psychology. They did not dispute the importance of human consciousness and mental life. They did, however, deemphasize consciousness in favor of a direct interest in behavior per se. Consciousness was treated by the functionalist as a mediator between environment and performance. This principle, coupled with the general idea that function and purpose of mind and behavior were the matters to be explained, meant that the last vestiges of dualism, the separation of mind and body, had been laid to rest.

John B. Watson assisted greatly in the latter process. Watson was as thoroughly convinced that mind had no place in psychology as Wundt was that mind was the only important subject matter. To Watson, evidence accumulating at the turn of the century on the nervous system meant that the mind as such could be completely replaced by a biological substructure of behavior. *Mind* and *consciousness* became "taboo" words in Watson's vocabulary, replaced by movement—the only datum of psychology; introspection as a method yielded to objective observation. Within ten years after Watson had taken his degree under the functionalists at Chicago, the pendulum had swung to its opposite extreme: a new school of behaviorism was founded in which mind and consciousness were ruled out of the psychological laboratory. But that is part of another story which will be picked up shortly.

DEWEY AND PROBLEM SOLVING. John Dewey took a position with respect to goal-oriented thinking that approximates the one adopted in Chapter 8 of this book. According to Dewey (1910) the problem-solving process is a multistage affair describable as follows: (a) recognition of a problem or a "felt difficulty"; (b) location and definition of the problem or the isolation of its relevant features; (c) formulation of possible alternative solutions; (d) mulling over or reasoning through the various possibilities to determine the most likely one; and (e) testing the selected solution. One clearly recognizes in this analysis the major elements of cognition—conceptual behavior, coding, language, problem solving, decision making, and the like—which are the primary topics of discussion in this text.

LATER FUNCTIONALISM. As mentioned, functionalism was not long limited to Chicago. Another early locus for functionalists and their research was Columbia University where, around 1900, Cattell, Woodworth, and Thorndike came together.

E. L. Thorndike (1898) pioneered the experimental study of animal behavior and intelligence. From his observations of how animals escape from puzzle box confinement (by pressing levers, pulling strings, scratching ears, or the like), Thorndike came to the conclusion that problem solving, at least in lower animals, proceeded on the basis of overt trial and error. There appeared to be no reasoning underlying the process of discovery exhibited by his animals. There were marked individual differences in the speed with which subjects reached the solution to the problem, but no indication that they saw through the problem or solved it in a purposeful, insightful fashion. Further, on subsequent presentations of the same problem to the same subject there was little indication of immediate recall of previous solutions.

Thorndike's interpretation emphasized response and motor factors involved in learning and problem solving. Trial and error, according to Thorndike, is to be found in the overt muscular activity of the organism. Perceptual, symbolic, and central processes play little or no role in his interpretation of problem solving. Later researchers claimed that the nature of the experimental situation and the problems selected by Thorndike prevented his animals from behaving in any way other than trial and error. That is, Thorndike had, by and large, required responses, such as pulling a string, which were unfamiliar to his subjects at the outset and thus forced them not only to discover the response but actually to learn to make it within the problem situation. If Thorndike had instead elicited familiar responses to novel stimuli, the chances of an insightful, rational solution rather than blind fumbling and trial and error might have been enhanced. In addition, Thorndike's tasks, according to some critics, disguised the relevant relations the subject had to perceive and understand before the problem could be solved insightfully. For example, in those cases where the animal had to pull a string to release a latch on the door to the confining box, the string-latch attachment could not easily be seen. Allowing the subject to perceive the relevant features of the problem might conduce, some argue, to insightful problem solving.

Nonetheless, Thorndike himself was convinced that animal behavior was not mediated by ideas or symbolic processes. Responses are linked and made directly to the stimulus situation as it is sensed by the subject. Because experiments with human subjects often yield similar results, he was led to believe that essentially the same learning principles were fundamental among all species. Thorndike's critics have granted that his simple laws may be necessary in an account of complex human behavior, but have strongly questioned their sufficiency.

BEHAVIORISM

Whereas functionalists admitted the data of consciousness into their theoretical system, Watson, the behaviorist, did not. For the functionalist, behavior (generally equated with the organism's movement) was important as an indicator of the underlying state and process of the organism's mind. Such an idea is not inconsistent with the current view of cognitive psychology. For the early behaviorist, however, action, movement, or behavior itself was the focus of attention, the primary datum. Depending on the extremity of his stand, a behaviorist might consider consciousness to be either inaccessible, unimportant, irrelevant to psychology, or nonexistent. In any case, he would claim that there is no point in trying to understand consciousness when the real data of psychology are open, observable, and available to direct measurement and investigation. Vague references to cognitive states are excess baggage, according to Watson's position. Knowledge of the regularities of organismic movement is all that one really need be concerned with.

WATSON ON THINKING. It is difficult at first to resolve the extreme Watsonian position with the crassly apparent fact that much of animal and human behavior is symbolic and without gross motor accompaniments. But it was not so much that Watson denied the existence of implicit events. He merely refused to conceive or speak of them as mentalistic entities, such as images, feelings, associations, and the like. Rather the behaviorist translated states of consciousness into miniaturized behaviors. Feelings, images, thoughts were conceptualized as units of covert physical behavior, which if we knew when, where, and how to look for them would be found to be just as recordable and reliable as the grosser forms of movement. According to Watson, we would eventually discover that much of what is considered in mentalistic terms as "thinking" is in reality hidden motor activity.

Words are responses we have learned to apply to objects and events in the environment. They can be called symbols in the sense that they stand for or represent things which they themselves are not. We can then "think" of these objects or events in terms of their verbal counterparts. When we "think to ourselves" about them, we are merely suppressing the overt verbal responses to the point where they become difficult or impossible for others to detect. But, with sensitive recording and measuring apparatus, we should find evidence of them in minute laryngeal movements. Thus, according to Watson, much of what we call thinking is subaudible speech. If there is thought, there must be physical representation of it somewhere within the organism. Behaviorism is said to espouse a peripheral, or motor, theory of thinking, in which the important activities are muscular or glandular rather than central or ideational.

EXPERIMENTS ON THE MOTOR COMPONENTS OF THINKING. Many experiments have provided evidence on the interplay between symbolic activity and movement. Jacobson, who interestingly enough was trained by the structuralist Titchener at Cornell University, reported a series of experiments in the late 1920s and early 1930s on the thinking–acting relationship. Jacobson developed a technique for physically relaxing human subjects. Introspective reports from subjects indicated that mental activity generally diminished in quantity with relaxation. Subjects reported that inner speech and imagery were typically impossible in a state of deep relaxation. When these subjects were instructed to imagine or think of certain events or actions, however, their thoughts were almost invariably accompanied by patterns of electrical activity recorded from particular muscular loci associated with the imagined process. For example, when a subject was instructed to think of flexing his right forearm, electrical signs of muscular activity were picked up from that arm but not from other locations (see Figure 1-5). When asked to imagine the Eiffel tower in Paris, electrodes on the subject's brow gave evidence of incipient, up–down scanning movements of the eyes. Jacobson's results seem clearly to indicate that specific patterns of muscular activity accompany and correlate with the content of thought processes. From this he drew the conclusion that thought was movement and that thought and muscular relaxation were incompatible.

Later, Max (1937) conducted a study of muscular activity in the limbs of a group of mutes who had learned to converse through a sign language. Records of electrical activity in the hands and arms were taken during

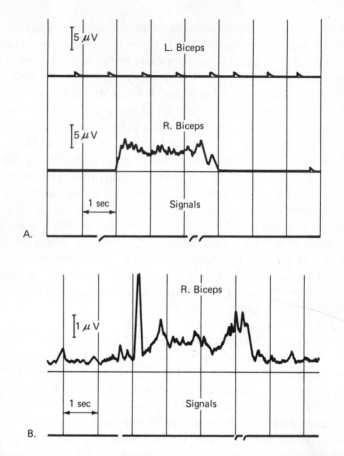

FIGURE 1–5. *A.* Electromyographic recording from right arm flexor muscle when the subject is instructed to bend his right arm at the elbow at the sound of a click and to relax at the sound of a double click. Significant rise in electrical activity occurs in the right arm only.
B. Identical recording when the subject is instructed to imagine bending the right arm at the elbow. Results are similar in A and B except microvoltage in imagining is about one-fifth the level of actual bending. (Note difference in voltage scale in A and B.) (From E. Jacobson, "Electrophysiology of mental activities and an introduction to the psychological process of thinking" F. J. McGuigan, & R. A. Schoonover, (Eds.) The psychophysiology of thinking. New York: Academic Press, 1973. Courtesy of the author and Academic Press, Inc.

both sleep and waking hours. Such activity generally decreased during sleep but there were occasional bursts which were apparently associated with dreams. Max tried waking subjects during bursts and during periods of relative quiet, asking them whether they were dreaming. In some 85 to

90 percent of cases, subjects replied affirmatively upon being wakened during bursts and negatively during quiet. While working on simple problems of arithmetic, roughly 85 percent of deaf-mute subjects showed muscular activities in the hands while only 30 percent of normal individuals did. Finally, there is the evidence of Schilling (Boring, 1950) that speech-like movements, for example, activity in the lips or throat, occurring during silent reading, facilitate the understanding of the material being read.

AN EVALUATION. It seems likely that there are muscular (especially subvocal) correlates to thinking. It might be that mental activity is in some sense dependent on a certain level of muscular tonus. Even today, there is a large group of psychologists who argue that thinking can be reduced and explained in terms of its physiological, especially motor, underpinnings (McGuigan & Schoonover, 1973). But the evidence has not been sufficient to convince the majority of psychologists that thought and action are identical or that thought can be completely represented by patterns of peripheral activity. The muscular activity recorded in the above-mentioned experiments might, in fact, be merely an overflow phenomenon; that is, as thinking occurs, its neurological correlates develop and send weak signals to respond to the muscles and glands. Peripheral organs are thereby activated during thinking, but comprise no essential part of it. This description represents the antithesis of behaviorism. An intermediate position might be closer to the truth, however, such as one which allows for facilitative support of thinking provided by some (optimal) level of muscular tonus but also admits to the important role of central events in the ongoing process.

GESTALT PSYCHOLOGY

Another form of protest against structuralism was Gestalt psychology, which emerged at about the same time as behaviorism but advanced a quite different viewpoint. The fundamentals of this system are almost entirely the product of three men, Max Wertheimer, Kurt Koffka, and Wolfgang Köhler, who were colleagues briefly in the early years of this century in Frankfurt, Germany. When all three founders immigrated to the United States, they brought with them the notions of Gestalt psychology. Like the other schools we have outlined, Gestalt psychology attempted to deal with the full range of psychological inquiry. Only a summary of its contributions to a study of thinking will be attempted here, however.

The name Gestalt is a German word with no precise English equivalent. It is usually translated as "organized whole" or "configuration." The name captures the essence of the Gestalt protest against structuralism. Gestalt psychologists argued that psychological experience neither consists of nor is compounded by static, discrete, and denumerable elements that come and go in time, but rather comprises an organized but dynamic and ever changing field of events which interact or mutually affect each other. When an organism experiences its environment, so the argument goes, it does not perceive or react to individual elements, but rather to the whole configuration of forces. *Properties of the whole psychological field are different from the simple sum of its parts.* These properties merge from the combination and interaction of parts. Gestalt psychology can be characterized as anti-elementaristic; sensations, perceptions, images, associations, reflexes, and the like are not accepted as meaningful psychological units. To understand psychological processes, one must consider a system of stimulation in which the alteration of any part can affect all other parts.

To illustrate the argument, Gestalt psychologists often cite the example of such perceptual phenomena as apparent movement. It is well known that if two lights are properly spaced and blinked on and off with appropriate timing, one continuous light moving from side to side is seen, rather than two discrete, alternating stimuli. The experience of apparent movement, which is the principle underlying moving pictures, is surely different from what one would expect from a simple perception of two contributing parts alone.

GESTALT DESCRIPTION OF THINKING.   The processes involved in thinking from a Gestalt point of view can be described as follows. A problem is said to exist when there are unresolved tensions or stresses resulting from interaction of some perceptual and memory factors in the individual's environment. The word *stress* is used in Gestalt theory as a hypothetical construct but is said to involve a competition of forces as in actual physical stress. Thinking occurs as the stresses work themselves out, thus forcing certain organismic activity. Past experience with related problems is no guarantee of solution. The solution seemingly arises from the stresses in the problem as perceived, just as apparent movement arises under appropriate viewing conditions. Thinking, then, is a process resolving field stresses. But solution, of course, does not always occur, at least not immediately. The problem solver might have to restructure the environment, that is, look at it from several angles, before the interactions of events forces a clear picture of the solution. Further, he might require external direction in order to readjust a system under tension. When the proper way of looking at the problem is achieved, however, a solution appears almost automatically. Recall the sequence of events leading to Kekulé's solution for the benzene molecule. This is a prime example of thinking and problem solving by insight. Clearly, there is a strong relation between thinking and perception. They are governed, according to Gestalt theory, by essentially the same principles, the major difference being that thinking goes on at a more symbolic (or internal) level and is less under the control of external events.

EXPERIMENTAL WORK. The most influential Gestalt research on thinking was that of Köhler who, during the years just prior to and during World War I, studied the performance of captive apes in a variety of problematic situations. As an example, there were several problems in which the animal was required to use one or more sticks as tools to rake in food that was out of reach beyond the bars of his cage. Köhler observed considerable activity among his subjects that might be called overt trial and error, in Thorndike's sense. Fundamentally, however, Köhler's conclusions are the antithesis of Thorndike's. Rather than acquiring some useful habits over a series of experiences with the given problem, Köhler's subjects almost invariably undertook the proper behavior or response sequence leading to solution after insight into the problem. Köhler reported that his subjects might hit upon a solution to a problem accidentally, but, once having seen the problem in its proper perspective, could repeat the solution without hesitation on subsequent occasions.

Wertheimer's research into thinking consisted of little more than a few demonstrations of the importance for learning of "seeing through" or understanding a task. Wertheimer's contention, which has been fairly well borne out in later, more substantial experiments, was that rote learning, if possible at all, is vastly inferior to learning based on an understanding of the organization, meaning, and applicability of the material studied, especially insofar as later use in transfer and retention situations is concerned.

Duncker (1945), a latter-day Gestalt psychologist, also contributed significantly to the study of thinking. Some of his work was concerned with the different perspectives and types of reorganization that are required for the production of insight into a problem's solution. His more influential work, however, dealt with *functional fixedness,* a form of mental set which reduces the tendency to use a given object in a necessary way as a result of some prior function which that object has served. We shall have more to say about this phenomenon in later discussions (see Chapter 8), for it is an interesting and unresolved empirical issue today.

A GESTALT THEORY OF FORGETTING. Gestalt psychologists approach the study of memory from the side of perception. Memory, according to the Gestaltists, is a well organized whole but is subject to essentially the same dynamic processes as is perception. The perception of the whole dominates the perception of the parts and makes them conform as far as possible to a well-formed structure. Likewise the memory trace of an event assumes a unitary, highly configured form, perhaps even more rigid than the original event. A tendency toward unification acts, at a subconscious level, on the memory trace of the event, exerting unifying pressure on the parts so that they closely conform to the generalized form of the whole.

From this theory, certain predictions can be made. For example, a picture, as remembered, should be a "better figure" than it appeared when originally seen; that is, it should be more symmetrical and freer from irregularity. Second, a picture or a story should become better and better with the lapse of time. Third, an event should never be truly forgotten although it might merge with other remembered events and no longer be identifiable with its original perception.

Wulff (1922; translated, 1939) undertook an experiment on memory for pictures in order to obtain evidence on this theory. Sometime after an irregular or asymmetrical nonsense figure had been shown, the subject was requested to draw it from memory. Changes in the reproduced figure were classified by Wulff under three headings, *leveling, sharpening,* and *assimilation.* Leveling means that the reproduced figure lacked certain detail contained in the original figure; sharpening refers to the accentuation of some part or feature of the original figure; and assimilation means that the figure was normalized, that is, made to look like a more familiar object. All three trends, which are illustrated in Figure 1-6, are consistent with expectations from a Gestalt theory.

The results obtained by Wulff were later seized upon by Bartlett (1932) and shown to be almost entirely the same as results on the retention of

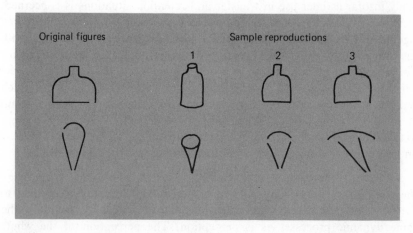

FIGURE 1–6. Fictitious examples of the forgetting processes observed by Wulff (1939). The subject first studies several original figures. Later he draws what he remembers having seen. Reproductions tend to be more normal (assimilated, Column 1), to be smoother and more symmetrical (leveled, Column 2), and sometimes to accent irregularities (sharpened, Column 3).

stories. In addition to the three categories of error identified by Wulff, Bartlett observed tendencies to extrapolate or to go beyond the original picture, story, or event. Bartlett theorized that memory is really a *constructive* not a reproductive process. According to Bartlett, the subject retains from any experience the general form of the original, as a schema, and some of the detail. At the time of retention he draws upon the retained schema and detail, but also upon his general stock of ideas, knowledge, and interests so as to round out a consistent picture. Thus, the reproduction corresponds only roughly to the original event.

AN EVALUATION. Undeniably, Gestalt psychologists have contributed significantly to our knowledge of symbolic processes. Their insistence on the fundamental importance of perception or the original encoding of an event, on insight as a principle of learning, on mental set as a factor controlling problem solving, and on memory as a dynamic process have all influenced contemporary cognitive psychology. There is little evidence to refute any of these principles.

Throughout this century, experimental psychology in the United States has been firmly in the grip of behaviorism, which views the organism mechanistically, that is, reacting more or less automatically to the various sources of external stimulation. The doctrine of behaviorism stripped animal and human subjects alike of any "higher mental processes." Gestalt psychology was a healthy neutralizer of that point of view. But Gestalt principles were never developed in any explicit or formal way. The behaviorists argued that it is difficult if not impossible to generate predictions about what should happen in experiments or in the real world from Gestalt theory. Without formalization and predictive power, Gestalt theory could achieve only limited prominence in the science of psychology. Nonetheless, Gestalt theory helped to establish a more balanced and realistic view with respect to complex human behavior than would have been possible through a strict behaviorism alone.

SUMMARY

We have described briefly some of the more influential points of view in the history and development of the psychology of cognitive processes. Each has supplied significant information, either through its emphasis on a particular but otherwise neglected facet of the problem or by its method of collecting and analyzing data. We have witnessed marked changes in the predominant research orientation, from an emphasis on images and other classifiable mental events to the analysis of behavior and its underlying processes. The major schools of psychology have disappeared. The modern psychologist typically leans in the direction of one or another orientation, but it has become increasingly apparent that no single point of view centering on a select set of simple principles can account for the vast and varied knowledge presently available. Ultimately, it will probably take some composite theory, which borrows the better ideas from a variety of theories, to provide a successful summary and organization of what we know. In subsequent chapters, we shall see how the more valid principles of early psychology have persisted and become incorporated into contemporary theory.

AIMS AND PLAN OF THE BOOK

This book aims to provide a resume of what psychologists know or speculate about human cognitive processes. The approach is not exhaustive, but rather emphasizes a selected set of examples. We hope to sample and to integrate sufficient information, however, to provide the reader with an understanding of the way scientific psychology conceptualizes one of its most important problems and the degree to which it is capable of contributing to the understanding of it.

We conceive of human beings as information-processing systems. Our first goal will be to describe this system in detail and to review some evidence that makes it a tenable framework for organizing what we know. Our description will begin where the flow of information begins, that is, with attending to and sensing external input. We will follow the flow of information through processes of sensory memory, pattern recognition, short-term memory, and long-term memory. At all stages of information processing, we will be concerned with such questions as, How is the information encoded and organized? What are the possibilities of informational loss (forgetting)? What operation is the subject conducting upon available information? Perhaps the most important topic that such a discussion will get us into is the question of how information is understood and represented in memory and the extent to which performance based on what we remember is a reproductive versus a constructive matter.

Once the details of the system are worked out in Chapters 2 through 4, we will proceed to discuss some of the more complex uses of the system. In Chapters 5 through 9, we review the empirical evidence and theory in psychology which relates to the topics of language, text comprehension, concept formation, problem solving, and reasoning. We wish to consider in detail how language and thought interact. Some psychologists have argued that language in one form or another is the essence of human thought. Recall Watson's idea that thinking in human beings is subvocal speech. Others, for example, Piaget (see Flavell, 1963), have argued just as strongly that thought is more abstract and must precede the use of language. Whatever the case, it is clear that thought and language are closely intertwined and can mutually affect their superficial or surface manifestation. We will deal with concept formation from both a structural and a process-oriented point of view. Much of the more traditional research and theorizing has been aimed at understanding processes by which concepts are formed and used. This research has neglected very important questions about the mental representation of concepts. More recent work on the structural aspects of concepts eventually will lead to a clearer portrayal of the processes involved. Problem solving and reasoning are in part connected to constructive aspects of memory. They both involve making use of facts and skills that have been acquired under other circumstances for purposes of effecting some suitable conclusion in a novel situation. In Chapter 10, we try to summarize the facts about cognitive development. We trace those changes in cognitive abilities which are correlated with age and experience, in an effort to show how the mature system for processing information unfolds from the primitive, rudimentary behavioral repertoire characteristic of human beings at birth.

The last chapter was the most fun to write. It introduces no new substantive material. Rather it is our effort to give some life to the formal discipline of cognitive psychology. We discuss in this chapter some of the applications and practical implications of the principles of cognitive science. We want to show that knowing these principles can make a difference in your life. Despite the relative recency of basic research in cognitive psychology, many of its applications are readily apparent. We have selected only a few for discussion, merely to give a flavor of the possibilities. We hope that our examples will be sufficient to interest some of our readers in further work toward an applied cognitive psychology.

chapter two

ACQUISITION OF NEW INFORMATION

outline

SOME PSYCHOLOGISTS REGARD an Intelligence Quotient (IQ) score above 150 as equivalent to genius level. Scores above a level of 200 are just about unheard of, but a figure of 210 has been attributed to Kim Ung-Yong of Seoul, South Korea, who was born on March 7, 1963. Kim spoke four languages (Korean, English, German, and Japanese), and performed integral calculus at the age of 4 years 9 months on television in Tokyo on "The World Surprise Show" on November 2, 1967.

Unless you had read about Kim in *Guinness' Book of Records,* or learned about him in some other way, the preceding paragraph probably conveyed a good deal of information. The first time you are presented with new information about any topic, you may remember only bits of it. But, were you repeatedly to come across the information, you would begin to remember more and more. In other words, we can talk not only about the *acquisition,* or initial learning, of new information but also about its *retrieval* (or reproduction) at some later time after a period of *retention.* The three distinct components involved in acquiring knowledge, namely acquisition, retention, and retrieval, will be dealt with repeatedly throughout the next several chapters of this book.

THE HUMAN INFORMATION-PROCESSING SYSTEM

We begin this chapter by laying out a relatively simple overview of how the human memory system operates. A number of different psychologists have advanced this theory in one form or another, but the theory has been described in its most complete form by Atkinson and Shiffrin (1968, 1971). It is important to realize that the ideas we present here are simply one framework in which we can view the way that human beings acquire, retain, and retrieve information. The view we present is a convenient one for thinking about memory, although it is by no means universally accepted by psychologists.

The basic structural features of the system are three memory stores, which are called the *sensory memory, short-term memory* and *long-term memory.* Figure 2-1 represents a schematic view of the system; the three major memories or repositories of information are represented as boxes, whereas the arrows in the figure represent the flow of information from one memory to another. To get an idea of how the system works, suppose that

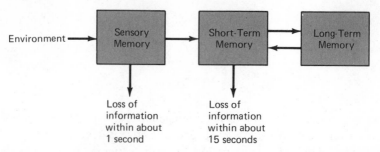

FIGURE 2–1. A schematic view of the human information-processing system.

you see or hear the piece of information "Kim Ung-Yong has an IQ of 210." This item first enters the system via one of the sense organs, for example, the eyes or ears. It is then received by sensory memory, a memory which holds a nearly literal record of the sensory image. In other words, this memory accepts all sensory information in a fairly complete form, but it does not hold that information for very long. Rather, information decays quickly, in most cases in less than a second or so. However, information may be preserved for longer than a second by quickly transferring it to another memory, short-term memory.

Short-term memory is really a working memory, a place where conscious mental processes are performed. It has several major characteristics which we outline here and discuss in some detail later in this chapter. First, it is of limited capacity, that is, it cannot hold very much information simultaneously. Second, information from this memory will decay and be gone completely within about 15 seconds, unless one does something to prevent this decay. Constant attention to or rehearsal of the information can serve to maintain it indefinitely. As human beings, we can decide which information we want to rehearse or devote attention to depending on our personal needs. Thus, if we hear "Kim Ung-Yong has an IQ of 210" and want to remember the name of the person, we could rehearse "Kim Ung-Yong," shifting attention away from the part of the message that concerned the level of his IQ.

Long-term memory is the final component of the memory system. It is the memory that holds the vast amount of information we have learned in the past, along with rules for processing that information. It holds our name and the names of our friends, it holds words and their meanings, it holds the experiences we have had. We speak of information becoming a part of long-term memory by being copied from short-term memory. It is believed that the longer an item is in short-term memory, in other words, the more we think about it, the better chance it has of getting into long-term memory where it will then be more or less permanently available. As we rehearse some new fact or some new piece of information, then, it is being transferred to long-term memory. Sometimes this process is referred to as memorization. If we are repeatedly presented with information about a person named Kim, or about a new toothpaste called Tserc which is purportedly better at preventing cavities, we might now have these names tightly secured in our long-term repository of information.

Suppose now that we are called upon to retrieve some piece of information from long-term memory. For example, we are standing at the counter of our local drugstore, desiring to buy a tube of toothpaste, and need to give a brand name to the druggist who is waiting to serve us. According to the theory, we would first check short-term memory for the name, and, if we did not find it there, we would begin searching long-term memory. Retrieving information from long-term memory essentially consists of transferring the information back to short-term memory where we can then consciously deal with it. Once the name of the toothpaste, Tserc, is transferred from long- to short-term memory, we can produce it verbally. Of course, when the druggist hears the name Tserc, that name passes through his sensory memory to short-term memory, and eventually enters long-term memory. Once the name is comprehended, the druggist will, via short-term memory, presumably make an appropriate response such as handing over a tube of Tserc, and perhaps remarking, "That'll be 79 cents."

This concludes our brief sketch of the human information-processing system and how it operates. We have outlined skeletally how new information goes from the sense organs to long-term memory and becomes a part of our repository of general knowledge. In this and the next two chapters we describe some of the experiments that have been performed by cognitive psychologists to illuminate the properties of the system. We begin by focusing on how we *acquire* new information in the first place. How does a new stimulus enter the system and get into long-term memory? In Chapter 3 we discuss what happens to information that is *retained* in long-term memory. Finally, in Chapter 4, the emphasis is on how we *retrieve* information that has been residing in long-term memory. At this point let us emphasize again that there are several ways to view this tripartite distinction between sensory, short-term, and long-term memory. Some psychologists have conceptualized three separate memory systems, like three boxes in which one can store information and transfer it from one to the other. Others have hypothesized three types of processing. Sensory memory representations are relatively unanalyzed, short-term memory representations are much better analyzed, and finally long-term memory representations are interwoven with other items in long-term memory. Despite these differences, the tripartite distinction is a conventional one in the literature that carries over to the methods used by investigators of short-term memory versus those used by analysts of long-term memory. Because the problems addressed by each group of researchers are essentially different, the tripartite distinction is a useful way to organize a textbook. Although we may talk at times as if we view information as passing from one box to another, it is important to remember that the overall theory can be viewed in other ways.

SENSORY MEMORY

Vast amounts of information impinge upon our sense organs at any given moment, a fact which is true no matter whether we are walking down a busy street or quietly reading a magazine. This information initially enters what we have called a sensory memory. Actually we should have referred not to a single sensory memory but to "sensory memories" since there are several sensory memories, each corresponding to a different sensory modality. Thus, visual information entering the system through the eyes is initially placed in a visual sensory memory, called "iconic memory"; auditory information entering the system through the ears is initially placed into an auditory memory, called "echoic memory." Other sensory memories correspond to the other modalities—to taste, touch, and smell—but since most of the research on this early stage of processing has studied visual and auditory phenomena, we will confine our discussion to these activities.

SPERLING'S EXPERIMENTS

Earlier we asserted that the sensory memory accepts a large amount of information in a fairly complete form, but does not hold that information for very long. What evidence do we have for this assertion? The classic experiments performed by Sperling (1960) as part of his doctoral dissertation provide us with an answer. Beginning with the simple question, How much can be seen in a single brief exposure?, Sperling showed that people could see much more than was formerly believed. Before Sperling's work had become known, psychologists had performed numerous studies in which arrays of items, such as that shown on the left side of Figure 2-2, were briefly presented to a subject in a tachistoscope (a device for presenting visual stimuli very, very briefly). Whether the array contained 8 or 12 or 20 items, most subjects could report only four or five, and this number was thought to be the "span of apprehension"—all that a person could see in a single glance. Despite the fact that most subjects could recall only a few of the letters from the array, they insisted that they had actually seen more letters than they had been able to report. Some claimed that they had seen virtually all of the letters but, as they were reporting the first four or five, they forgot the others.

In the pre-Sperling experiments, subjects were asked to report *all* the

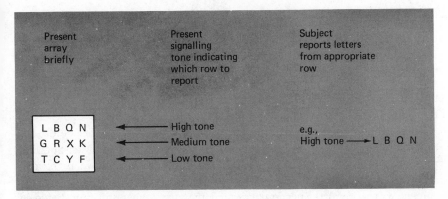

FIGURE 2–2. Sperling's (1960) partial report technique.

letters they could remember from an array, a procedure termed the "whole report" procedure. But this procedure clearly did not give a true picture of what a subject could perceive, since many of the items perceived were apparently forgotten during actual recall. Sperling's innovation was to devise a "partial report" procedure, as illustrated in Figure 2-2. Subjects were briefly presented with a 12-item array (say, 3 × 4 letters). But, instead of having to report all the letters in the array, they were required to report only a single four-letter row. By means of a signal occurring immediately after the array was turned off, the subjects were told which row to report. A high-pitched tone indicated that only the top row was to be reported; a medium-pitched tone meant only the middle row; and a low-pitched tone meant only the bottom row was to be reported. For each array, the row the subject was required to report from was selected randomly so that the subject had no way of knowing beforehand which row he was going to have to report. An important aspect of this procedure is that the tone was presented *after* the letters had been turned off.

Using the partial report procedure, Sperling was able to estimate the total number of letters the subject must have had available at the instant the array was turned off. He did this in the following way. For a 12-item array, for example, the subject, on the average, was able to report about three out of four letters per row. Because the subject did not know in advance which row he was going to have to report, this must have meant that he had three letters available from each of the rows. The total number of letters estimated to be available was, therefore, three rows times three letters per row, or nine letters in all. This value is about twice as large as the earlier estimate of four or five letters obtained with the whole report procedure. The logic of Sperling's procedure is similar to the logic of a professor who gives an objective examination to his students. If a student can answer three out of four test questions correctly, the professor assumes that the student knows about three-fourths of all the material covered in the course, even though not all of it was covered on the test.

To reiterate, Sperling's important finding indicates that the span of apprehension does not accurately measure the amount of information that subjects are able to perceive. Further, Sperling's work confirms the idea that during a brief visual presentation people are able to see more than they can ultimately report.

If, as Sperling showed, people have a brief image that fades before all of it can be reported, it is natural to ask how long this image lasts. Sperling provided an answer to this question by varying the time between the offset of the array and the presentation of the tone indicating which row the subject was to report. Sperling reasoned that the longer the time between the offset of the array and the tone, the more the image would have faded, and the fewer items the subject would be able to report. His results confirmed this reasoning and indicated that after a delay of about 1 second nearly the entire image had deteriorated. This can be seen in Figure 2-3, for an experiment in which subjects saw arrays containing nine letters.

To summarize, Sperling's work rounds out our picture of the visual sensory memory, indicating first that much of the visual information presented to the eye is perceived and second that it enters a sensory memory but decays within about a second. Similar experiments have been performed with auditory material and have been highly successful in uncovering the existence of "echoic memory." One main difference between the two memories seems to be the length of time it takes for information to

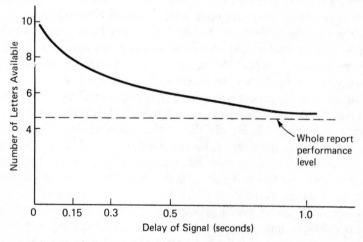

FIGURE 2–3.   In a partial report situation, the number of letters available declines as the signal to report is delayed. (After Sperling, 1960. Reprinted by permission of the author and American Psychological Association.)

decay; here the echoic memory seems to have somewhat of an advantage (Darwin, Turvey, & Crowder, 1972).

PATTERN RECOGNITION

As we have seen, information decays from sensory memory rather quickly, but not all information need necessarily decay. Some of it may be transferred from sensory memory to short-term memory by means of a process we term *pattern recognition*. This process essentially consists of "recognizing" a physical pattern in the sensory memory as representing something meaningful. Exactly how this process is accomplished is still not completely understood, but a more detailed discussion of it may be found in Moray (1969). What is important for the purposes of this chapter is that a human being has some control over which information is transferred and which is not. By deciding what to devote *attention* to, we decide what to transfer.

ATTENTION

What is attention? William James put it most eloquently when he said:

> Every one knows what attention is. It is the taking possession by the mind, in clear and vivid form, of one out of what seem several simultaneously possible objects or trains of thought. Focalization, concentration, and consciousness are of its essence. It implies withdrawal from some things in order to deal effectively with others. (James, 1890, pp. 403–404)

We can only focus on, concentrate on, or be conscious of a few things at once, despite the rumor that Julius Caesar could dictate four letters while writing a fifth (James, 1890). When an activity is so well learned that it takes very little effort, we can engage in other activities at the same time. Thus, most people can walk and carry on a conversation and perhaps even eat an ice cream cone, all at once. But if the task is more difficult, such as driving in a blizzard, it may require our complete attention and simultaneous conversation may be impossible.

Attention seems to require active, conscious processing, and we are limited in our capacity for attentional processing. For example, we usually have to work consciously at retrieving material from memory, or listening to one speaker while ignoring others. Moreover, we seem to be limited in our capacity to attend simultaneously to more than one task in much the same way we are limited in our ability to think about several problems at the same time. Thus, attention is associated with the conscious, active processing required, for example, whenever we perceive some event and then remember it later on.

In the following pages we attempt to convey the current level of understanding of attentional processing. The emphasis is on contrasting views rather than attempting a theoretical synthesis. Psychologists' views about attention are changing rapidly as the available data base grows, and we have attempted no more (and no less) than to point out major lines of inquiry. We begin by considering the problem of definition.

Definition of Attention

The study of attention dates from the very beginnings of psychology as a scientific discipline (for example, Kulpe, 1904; Titchener, 1908; Wundt, 1874.) Although attentional concepts have been central to much psychological research and theory, few phenomena have so consistently defied definition. Recently, Berlyne (1974) has offered a definition which seems descriptive of much current research and theory. Berlyne proposes that attention refers to "processes or conditions within the organism that determine how effective a particular stimulus will be" (p. 124). This definition reflects a primary concern with central, cognitive factors in attention, rather than peripheral mechanisms such as the orienting reflex. These peripheral mechanisms are only "attention" in the limited sense that certain stimuli are effective while others are rendered ineffective by their failure to excite receptors. It is probably best to interpret Berlyne's definition as one that specifies some of the conditions under which we can identify attentional processes. However, it does not exhaust the meaning of the concept "attention." The reason is that attentional processing may occur in the absence of any specific, observable stimulus. We may have a thought, for example, that causes us to turn our attention in a certain direction.

Attributes of Attention

There are different aspects to attention which we can appreciate by citing a number of different ways in which the effectiveness of an external stimulus can vary. First, there are fluctuations in the influence which the overall environment has on our behavior. This aspect of attention is variously described as alertness, attentiveness, or *vigilance*. The precision with which observable behavior reflects variations in external events can vary to greater or lesser degrees. For example, a student may be alert to classroom activities, or may attend instead to internal events such as memories of last Friday's date, or less pleasantly, a current agonizing stomach ache. A driver may be vigilant in the specific task by attending to traffic signals and to other automobiles, or may daydream about some future engagement. Of course, the degree of vigilance can and does fluctuate over a period of time.

Second, there are fluctuations in how control of behavior is distributed among features of the environment. *Distribution* of attention can vary from concentrated to diffused. A currently important distinction is between focused and divided attention. The student may concentrate more or less exclusively on what the instructor is saying, or attention may be shared between the instructor and a friend. The driver may focus attention on informational signals when approaching a critical, dangerous intersection in a strange city, whereas attention may be more diffuse on the open highway.

Vigilance and distribution have been called the *intensive* aspects of attention. They refer to the "amount" of attention, and ultimately relate to the capacity of the system to handle large amounts of information over relatively long periods of time.

A third distinction is that fluctuations occur in which aspects of the environment control behavior. This refers to the *selective* or directive aspect of attention. Attention is directed toward and selective of a particular aspect of a complex stimulus or to a particular region of space. The student may selectively attend to what the instructor is saying, what is written on the blackboard, or to what an adjacent friend is doing. The driver may, when first approaching an intersection, "look for" only large green or white signs and ignore for the most part yellow signs which do not convey the information needed. Furthermore, after locating a green sign, the driver will then attend to the informational content of the sign and not its color. In short, we are blessed with a system that can isolate one property of a stimulus object, causing other properties to be ignored, or at least to be processed less completely.

Vigilance, distribution, and selection are all functional aspects of attention, but they are not independent of each other. Any given situation usually involves all three aspects. For example, in focusing attention on the instructor the student is simultaneously regulating the distribution of attention and selecting for processing one aspect of the environment. However, the vigilance function is involved in maintaining a sufficient level of arousal or alertness throughout the class period. Nevertheless, these distinctions allow us to isolate various aspects of attention over an extended period of time. For example, in studies of the distribution of attention we are investigating the capacity of the system for information processing, and in selective attention studies we are concerned with the abstraction ability of the system.

A Quick History of Attention

While the very earliest efforts in attention involved almost exclusively visual stimuli, the auditory modality has dominated most of the research responsible for the revival of interest in attentional functions. However, current studies seem once again to be focusing on visual attention. The implicit assumption has been that the same central mechanisms and processes mediate attention functions for all perceptual modalities, and intersensory experiments are beginning to appear which test this basic assumption (for example, Triesman & Davies, 1973; Shiffrin & Grantham, 1974).

VISUAL ATTENTION. Attention research is usually traced to the pioneering work early in this century of Kulpe (1904), who established that when one attribute of a tachistoscopically presented, multidimensional stimulus is emphasized by instruction to the subject before stimulus presentation, the report is more accurate for the emphasized than for the unemphasized dimensions. Thus, if stimuli are presented which differ in terms of color and size, and color is emphasized, then subjects will be more accurate on color than on size. Kulpe interpreted this "set" effect as reflecting a "tuning" of the perceptual apparatus by instruction, such that the emphasized dimension of the subsequent stimulus is actually *perceived* more clearly. Later, Harris and Haber (1963) disagreed with Kulpe's interpretation, arguing that the reason people are more accurate on emphasized dimensions is because they are encoded (stored) first when the greatest amount of stimulus information is available. In other words, it appears that when a stimulus is first presented and information is available in sensory memory, a person can attend to whichever (emphasized) aspects are desired. Other aspects that are reported later, when the image has faded, are thus recalled less accurately.

AUDITORY ATTENTION. Interest in visual attention was maintained at a moderate level from Kulpe's time, but the real impetus for the current explosion of interest in problems of attention came from work in auditory attention during the 1950s. At this time the development of new paradigms and theoretical perspectives provided the basis for a fruitful reformulation of attentional problems. Two experimental paradigms were introduced: The *split-span* task and the *shadowing* task.

Broadbent (1954) introduced what has come to be called the split-span task—a memory span experiment in which the to-be-recalled material is split between a person's two ears. In a typical split-span experiment, two digit series are presented over headphones, with one series being fed to the left ear and a different series to the right ear (see Figure 2-4). For example, "7, 3, 4" is presented to the right ear, and simultaneously "2, 1, 5" is presented to the left ear. Subjects are better at recalling digits by ear than at recalling by order of presentation (that is, "7, 2, 3, 1, 4, 5"). Broadbent interpreted this difference in recall to mean that the two ears function as channels of information, that the different physical locations for the two messages are preserved in a short-term sensory memory prior to receiving the additional processing necessary for recalling them. In other words, while the subject is recalling "7, 3, 4," the digits presented in the other ear

FIGURE 2–4. Subject in a typical split-span experiment. He listens to two series of digits, then recalls both.

must have been stored somewhere, and that somewhere is what we have been calling sensory memory. Attention operates to determine which channel gets recalled first. Switching attention between channels requires considerable time, and performance is poorer when recall by presentation order is required because more attentional switching is involved. While attention is being switched between channels information is decaying and is thus less and less available.

About the same time as Broadbent's work with the split-span task, Cherry (1953) introduced the experimental task known as *shadowing*. In a typical shadowing experiment, a subject wears headphones and listens to two messages, one presented to each ear. The subject's task is to listen to only one of the messages and to repeat the words in the message as he hears them (or to *shadow* the message). He is to ignore the other message. (See Figure 2-5.) Most subjects can comfortably tune out the message they are not supposed to attend to and shadow the other one. Some investigators have asked whether anything can be remembered from the unattended message, and the usual finding is that people remember very little. For example, Moray (1959) found that even when English words were repeated as many as 35 times in the unattended message, subjects did not remember them. However, occasionally a subject will remember hearing his own name. This latter finding repeats in a laboratory situation what many of us have experienced in a real-life situation. It is known as the

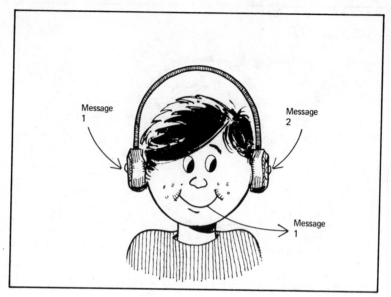

FIGURE 2–5. Subject in a typical shadowing experiment. He listens to two different messages, repeating one aloud and ignoring the other.

"cocktail party phenomenon." When a person stands in the midst of others at a crowded cocktail party carrying on a conversation, it is usually easy to concentrate on that conversation. If the person hears his own name from a different conversation, attention may be diverted momentarily. This is a good example of what William James meant when he said that attention "implies withdrawal from some things in order to deal effectively with others." We withdraw from the conversation in which we are engaged so that we can attend to the one in which our name has been mentioned. This example suggests that we attend to what interests us, what is pertinent to us, what is meaningful for us. Naturally, though, what is interesting to one person may not be so for another person.

Drawing largely on data from split-span and shadowing tasks, Broadbent (1958) formulated his now famous filter theory of attention. Briefly, Broadbent proposed a model that introduced the concept of selective attention. He argued that upon presentation of a stimulus, information—in an essentially unlimited quantity—is held very briefly in sensory memory. But only some of this information reaches short-term memory. Selective attention determines which information will survive. Broadbent conceived of selective attention as a filter that lets only certain types of information pass on to short-term memory. Only information that is coming from the right channel will pass. In other words, only information from, say, the left ear, or only information from the female (rather than the male) voice, passes the filter and is processed. Information from the wrong channel, for example, from the to-be-ignored right ear, is rejected. Put another way, Broadbent's filter is a device that selects information along physical dimensions of the stimulus. The popularity of Broadbent's theory is attested to by the scores of investigators who attempted (successfully) to disconfirm it. Among the first instances of such disconfirming data was that provided by the work of two Oxford undergraduates, Gray and Wedderburn (1960) who in their "Dear Aunt Jane" task modified the split-span procedure to divide two messages of different semantic categories between the two ears. For example, "Dear, 5, Jane" was presented to one ear and simultaneously "3, Aunt, 4" was presented to the other ear. Their subjects were now no better at recall by ear than by order of presentation. Gray and Wedderburn concluded that Broadbent was wrong in assuming selection to be possible only along physical dimensions. Subjects can also select for processing along dimensions of meaning when such cues are available in messages.

Many interesting and important theoretical accounts were developed during this period. For a detailed treatment of this research, see the accounts presented by Norman (1976), Massaro (1975), and Anderson (1975).

Some Recent Developments in Attention

It is obvious that there are many activities which do not seem to require any appreciable amount of attention. For example, walking does not usually affect our ability to carry on a simultaneous conversation, even though walking surely requires complex processing of information, involving, for example, the analysis of feedback concerning the perceptual consequences of our movements. This implies that information processing cannot be a strictly serial affair, but must involve something like simultaneous processing of many sources of information. A further implication is that the amount of attention we must give to some task will depend upon the degree to which the task is habitual or automatic. When we first learned to ride a bicycle, the task required so much attention that it was probably difficult, if not impossible, to carry on a conversation. Once bicycle riding became habitual, it was possible to do many other things, such as munch on an apple or carry on a decent conversation, at the same time. These realizations have resulted in a view of attention as something that can be allocated to different tasks simultaneously. In other words, much of the current work focuses on our ability to divide our attention. The work of Richard Shiffrin is an example of this recent line of investigation.

Shiffrin and Gardner (1972) attempted to determine if attention can be directed toward a particular location in the visual field, and if the system is limited in its capacity to process information from more than one location. Visual locations are taken to be information channels in the same way that ears have been considered, and therefore, this work illustrates how concepts developed from work in auditory attention have been applied to visual attention. The general method used by these investigators may be called the *simultaneous-successive paradigm*. In all conditions subjects are presented with a fixed array of stimuli occurring in different locations (channels). On each trial, one of the stimuli is one of a limited number of alternative targets. For example, the key stimulus might be the letter F or the letter T. Location and identity of the target item varies randomly from trial to trial. The subject's task is to identify the target and its location on each trial. In the simultaneous condition, all stimuli are presented at the same time. Thus, the subject might see:

O F

O O

The correct answer is that an F occurred in the upper right corner. In the successive condition, the stimuli are presented in rapid temporal succession, in a known order. Thus, with successive presentation the subject can focus attention on each location as it occurs, and should perform better than with simultaneous presentation where attention must be distributed among all locations.

Shiffrin and his colleagues have consistently failed to find differences between simultaneous and successive conditions. This has led Shiffrin (1975; Shiffrin & Geisler, 1973) to conclude that selective attention during perceptual processing is not possible, that the perceptual system operates automatically, without subject control, to encode stimuli and pass the results to short-term memory. Shiffrin has developed a theory in which attention has its effects post-perceptually. For him, attention determines what we do with the information once it is in short-term memory.

There exists at present much controversy on the subject of attention and where it comes into play. It is thus not yet possible to draw clear conclusions. However, most of the theoretical frameworks that have appeared agree in one sense: they include a role for something we have been calling short-term memory. We now turn to this topic.

SHORT-TERM MEMORY

IS THERE REALLY A SHORT-TERM MEMORY?

Long before the modern-day cognitive psychologists were even born, William James proposed a dichotomous view of memory. He postulated one component, primary memory, which is analogous to short-term memory, and a second component called secondary memory, analogous to long-term memory. But what was the evidence for this dichotomy? What advantage did it have over a unitary theory?

The evidence did not really begin to mount until the 1950s. Certain laboratory findings provided striking evidence in favor of the dichotomous view, and subsequently observations in a clinical setting with actual patients provided additional support. What follows is one example of each of the classes of evidence.

Laboratory Evidence

Using a procedure called free recall, it is possible to provide support for the distinction between short- and long-term memory. In a free recall experiment a subject is presented with a list of unrelated words, one at a time. Some time later, he is asked to recall as many of the words as possible, in any order. Figure 2-6 shows a typical result: the curve is called a *serial position curve*. It is simply the probability of recalling a word as a function of the order in which the words were originally presented. Thus, the first word presented to the subject occupies the first serial input position, no matter whether or when the subject recalls it. It is clear from Figure 2-6 that the probability of recalling a word is strongly dependent on when the word was presented to the subject. Words from the early part of the list are recalled well, a phenomenon referred to as the *primacy effect*. Similarly, words from the end of the list are recalled well, the *recency*

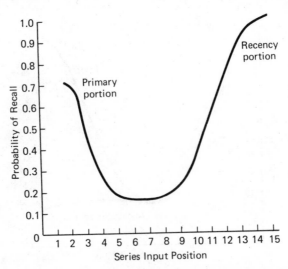

FIGURE 2–6.   Results of a typical free-recall experiment: the serial-position curve. (From Loftus & Loftus, 1976, p. 36. Courtesy of Lawrence Erlbaum Associates, Inc.)

effect. The words from the middle portion of the list are recalled relatively poorly.

While the primacy effect is an important one, it is the recency effect that is of interest to us in distinguishing short- and long-term memory. Those psychologists who believe in a unitary system of memory would claim that the reason for the recency effect is that the closer a word is to the end of the list, the most recently it has been encountered, thus the less likely it is to have been forgotten. By way of contrast, proponents of the dichotomous view would offer a different explanation for recency. Their assertion is that the closer a word is to the end of the list, the higher is its probability of being in short-term memory when the recall test begins, and that words still in short-term memory are recalled extremely well.

To distinguish the two explanations, consider a variation on the usual free recall procedure. After the list of words has been presented, suppose the subject is asked to spend 30 seconds performing a distracting arithmetic task, and then to recall the words. The recall of this second group of subjects can be compared with that of control subjects who begin their recall immediately after the list has been presented. The unitary view would have to argue that all words in the list have a greater chance to be forgotten after 30 seconds of arithmetic, and are recalled more poorly than words in the control condition. Words from the end of the list would still be recalled somewhat better than words from the middle. On the other hand, the dichotomous view would hold that the arithmetic task would enter short-term memory and interfere with recall of the entire word list, such that

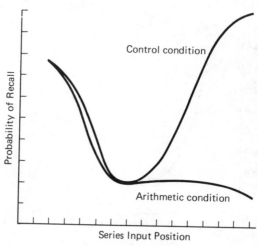

FIGURE 2–7. Prediction of a dichotomous view of memory in a modified free-recall experiment. (From Loftus & Loftus, 1976, p. 36. Courtesy of Lawrence Erlbaum Associates, Inc.)

words from the end of the list would be recalled no better than the words from the middle. This experiment has been done in two independent laboratories, and both provide data similar to that in Figure 2-7 supporting the dichotomization of memory into two separate functions (Postman & Phillips, 1965; Glanzer & Cunitz, 1966).

Clinical Evidence

A neuropsychologist, Brenda Milner (1966), has written extensively about her patient, H. M. who came to her with a severe case of epilepsy. At that time it was common practice to remove certain portions of the human brain in order to cure the epilepsy. Indeed the operation did cure the patient's epilepsy, but subsequently it was discovered that the operation had a devastating side effect—it interfered with normal memory functioning.

H. M. was given many memory tests. He was very good at recalling events that had occurred before his operation. He knew his initials, his address, the alphabet, all about the Depression, and so on. He also could carry on a conversation reasonably well and remember new information for limited periods of time, as long as he could rehearse it. But it was discovered that he could not learn anything new. If he were told a new piece of information, he would forget it before 5 minutes had elapsed. It seemed that H. M. had an intact long-term memory and his short-term memory seemed usual, but he could not transfer any new information from short- to long-term memory. Whatever mechanism was responsible for this transfer had apparently been destroyed by the operation.

SHORT-TERM MEMORY: AN INTRODUCTION

Suppose now that we have attended to a particular piece of information and it has entered short-term memory. What fate awaits it? Earlier in this chapter we pointed out that information is forgotten from short-term memory quite rapidly, unless a person does something (like rehearse) to prevent that forgetting. Most of us have had the experience of looking up a telephone number and then forgetting it before it could be dialed. If the number is rehearsed out loud we can usually retain it long enough to dial. An important question for cognitive psychologists is this: Without rehearsal, how long does it take for information to be forgotten from short-term memory? As we will see, the research conducted by Brown (1958) and by Peterson and Peterson (1959) has indicated that when rehearsal is prevented, forgetting from short-term memory occurs within about 15 seconds. Two other important questions regarding short-term memory are (1) How much information can it hold? and (2) How do we retrieve information from it?

An experimental procedure used to study forgetting from short-term memory is called the Brown-Peterson paradigm, after the psychologists who developed the technique. It is shown in Figure 2-8. On each trial in the experiment, a subject is presented with a string of three consonants, such as BKG. Following the consonant trigram, a retention interval passes, ranging from 0 to 18 seconds. In order to prevent the subject from rehearsing the trigram, he is required to perform a fairly difficult mental arithmetic task during the interval. The task is counting backward by threes from a three-digit number. At the end of the interval, the subject recalls the trigram.

Figure 2-9 shows how probability of recall of the trigram is related to retention interval. Notice that if the trigram is tested immediately (that is, after a retention interval of zero) then recall is nearly perfect. At longer intervals, however, memory performance drops rapidly until at an interval of about 15 seconds, the trigram is recalled only about 10 percent of the time. At intervals longer than 15 seconds, performance does not drop below this level, so that 10 percent is thus the asymptotic performance level.

Let's now discuss this experiment in terms of the major components of the information-processing system. First, the trigram is presented, and information about it passes through sensory memory into short-term memory. Additionally, some of the information gets into long-term memory. During the retention interval, information is lost from short-term memory

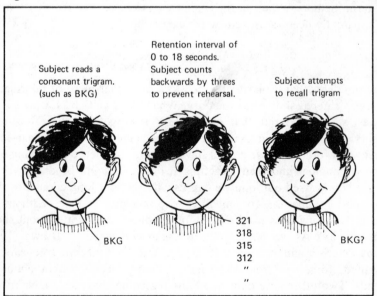

FIGURE 2–8. The Brown-Peterson paradigm for studying forgetting.

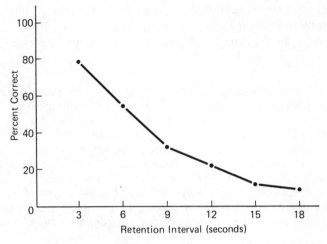

FIGURE 2–9. Short-term retention function for trigrams. (Adapted from Figure 2 in Peterson & Peterson, 1959. Reprinted by permission of the author and American Psychological Association.)

so that by 15 seconds forgetting is complete. However, at intervals longer than 15 seconds, subjects are occasionally correct (10 percent of the time); they are apparently responding from the bit of information that was transferred to long-term memory.

CAPACITY OF SHORT-TERM MEMORY

Suppose we present a person with some new information and ask the subject to recall it immediately. Presumably the information reaches short-term memory and a verbal response is made based on the contents of that memory. If the information consists of two letters, M and N, most people could repeat them back accurately. However, if the information consisted of a longer string of, say, 14 letters—G S P T U W X L Z M A O R B—most people could not report them accurately. The reason is that short-term memory has a limited capacity. George Miller's (1956) masterful summary of experimental work in this area is entitled "The Magical Number Seven, Plus or Minus Two." Miller showed that short-term memory seems capable of holding about seven items regardless of their size. He coined the term "chunk" to refer to the items that short-term memory holds seven of. The exact definition of a chunk is somewhat elusive, but it might best be characterized as a stimulus that has some unitary representation in long-term memory, for example, a letter—such as B—or a digit. The letters Y P P A H constitute five chunks, but in reverse order the word *happy* is a single chunk. This reasoning can be taken somewhat further; a phrase like "kick the bucket" can be thought of as a chunk because it, as an idiom, has a unitary representation in long-term memory.

Miller believed the capacity of short-term memory to be seven chunks. His classic paper begins:

> *My problem is that I have been persecuted by an integer. For seven years this number has followed me around, has intruded in my most private data, and has assaulted me from the pages of our most public journals. This number assumes a variety of disguises, being sometimes a little longer and sometimes a little smaller than usual, but never changing so much as to be unrecognizable. The persistence with which this number plagues me is far more than a random accident. There is, to quote a famous senator, a design behind it, some pattern governing its appearances. Either there really is something unusual about the number or else I am suffering from delusions of persecution. (1956, p. 81)*

He was speaking about the number seven. Other investigators, for example, Mandler (1967), have argued that seven is too large; the capacity of short-term memory is probably four or five. Whatever the precise capacity, there is agreement that short-term memory is severely limited in the number of items it can hold.

Murdock performed a large number of studies to investigate the nature of the limitation in short-term memory capacity (for example, see Murdock, 1968, 1974). In one experiment, subjects were presented with a list of 10 words and had to recall them. In some instances they were to begin recall with the first words on the list and in other cases they began with the last words on the list. If required to begin with the first words, subjects usually recalled the first, second, and third word with high accuracy, plus a few additional words. If required to begin with the last words, subjects usually recalled the last few words, then whatever others they could dredge up from memory. In both cases, the average number of words recalled varied between 4.6 and 5.2, indicating that despite the fact that a subject can shift his concentration to one part of the list or another, the overall memory capacity remains about the same.

RETRIEVAL FROM SHORT-TERM MEMORY

An experimental paradigm that has been enormously useful in examining short-term information retrieval was developed in the mid-sixties by Sternberg (1966, 1967, 1969). The task is shown in Figure 2-10. A subject is first read or shown a string of items called the *memory set,* consisting perhaps of letters or digits, which he places in his short-term memory. Next, he presses a button that initiates the presentation of a single item, called the *test item.* The subject's task is to report whether the test item was or was not a member of the memory set. Thus, if the memory set consists

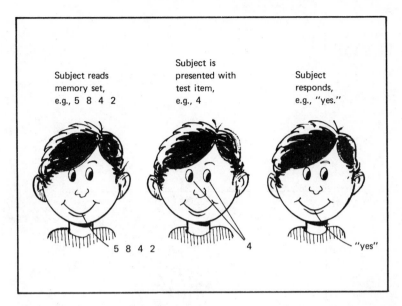

FIGURE 2–10. Sternberg's paradigm for studying retrieval from short-term memory.

of the digits 5 8 4 2, and the test item is 4, the correct response would be *yes*. If the test item were 6, the correct response would be *no*. Usually the response is made by pressing a button, one corresponding to *yes* and the other to *no*. The subjects are asked to respond as quickly as they can, but to avoid errors. Since the error rate is usually very low (less than 5 percent), the experimenter is primarily interested in how fast the subject responded, or the *reaction time* between the appearance of the test item and the subject's response.

This basic paradigm has been used to investigate a fundamental question concerning how information is retrieved from short-term memory. Are the items in short-term memory examined one at a time (serial processing) or are they examined all at once (parallel processing)? To answer this question, Sternberg varied the size of the memory set, or the amount of information in short-term memory, in order to see whether reaction time was affected. He reasoned that if a parallel search is conducted, then the number of items in short-term memory should not have much effect on reaction time. Conversely, if a serial search is conducted, then the number of items should have an éffect; the more items in the memory to be searched, the longer the search should take. The two predictions are shown in Figure 2-11.

Figure 2-12 shows the results of Sternberg's experiments. Because the curve rises, Sternberg reasoned that a serial search was being conducted and accordingly postulated the following model of how a subject accom-

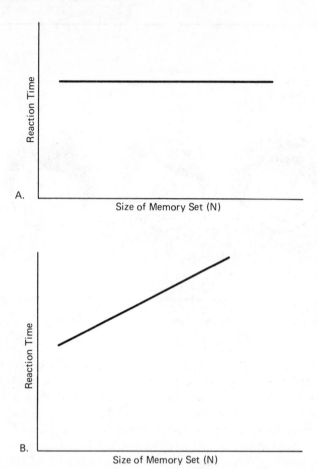

FIGURE 2–11. Possible results in a Sternberg task:
A. Results predicted by a parallel search model.
B. Results predicted by a serial search model.

plishes this task after memorizing the memory set. First, the test digit is read and encoded. This stage is assumed to take e milliseconds. Next the encoded form of the digit is successively compared with each member of the memory set. For each member, the subject determines whether the test item matches the member. Assume the time to make a single comparison is c milliseconds and the time for N comparisons is cN. In the final stage, the subject determines whether or not a match was found, and responds *yes* or *no* accordingly. Assume it takes d milliseconds to make this decision and execute the response.

The total time it takes a subject to respond (RT) should be simply the sum of the times for each of the three stages.

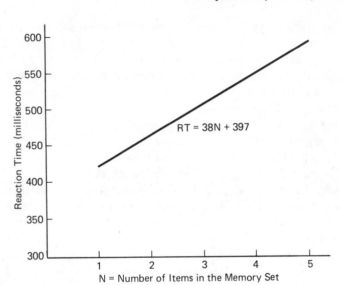

FIGURE 2-12. Results of the Sternberg (1966) experiment. (Adapted from Figure 1 in Sternberg, 1966. Copyright by American Association for the Advancement of Science.)

$$RT = \text{Stage 1} + \text{Stage 2} + \text{Stage 3}$$

or

$$RT = e + cN + d$$

or, rearranging,

$$RT = cN + (e + d)$$

In general, we can express a linear function relating two variables, x and y, as:

$$y = ax + b,$$

where a is the slope of the function and b is the y intercept of the function. The function in Figure 2-12 is such a linear function, then, where reaction time is predicted to be a function of memory set size (N) with a slope equal to c and a y intercept equal to $(e + d)$. From the data in Figure 2-12, we can calculate the slope c, which happens to be about 38 msec per item. The intercept $(e + d)$ is about 397 msec. Putting together Sternberg's model with his data, then, we conclude that it takes about 38 msec to make a single comparison and about 397 msec to encode the stimulus, make a decision, and execute the response.

Another theoretical question that concerned Sternberg was whether the serial search was *exhaustive* or *self-terminating*. An exhaustive search is one in which the subject examines every item in the memory set before deciding whether the test item is a member of the set. In a self-terminating search, the process stops as soon as the subject determines that the test item is a member of the set. No further comparisons are conducted. Sternberg answered this question by comparing the reaction times for a *yes* response to those for a *no* response.

Both the exhaustive and the self-terminating models predict the same *RT*s on a negative trial. This is because in order to make a negative response, the subject must compare the test item with every item in the memory set. He must determine that it matches none of them.

However, the exhaustive and self-terminating models have different implications for the positive *RT*s. For some of the positive trials the matching item will be toward the end of the memory set, for others toward the beginning. On average, then, only half (actually $(N + 1)/2$) of the possible comparisons need be made for a memory set of size Z. Thus, the self-terminating model predicts that when a positive response is made, the total time for the comparison stage is less than it would be for a negative response. The slope of the *yes* function should be half that of the *no* function.

Sternberg found that both *yes* and *no* reaction times yield the function shown in Figure 2-12. The slopes were equal, indicating that in both cases the subject performs an exhaustive search rather than a self-terminating one. Thus even when a match is found between the test item and a memory set item, the subject apparently continues to compare the test item to the rest of the memory set items. Why this seemingly inefficient strategy? One possibility is that the comparison process is an extremely rapid one and that the decision process takes much longer. Efficiency would thus dictate doing all the comparisons and making one decision rather than making a decision after each comparison.

Sternberg's work has had a profound impact on the field. Not everyone has agreed with his theoretical interpretation yet at the same time hundreds of psychologists have used his paradigm. In addition, at least one model has appeared which treats the Sternberg task in terms of a serial, self-terminating process (Theios, Smith, Haviland, Traupmann, & Moy, 1973). Another possibility is a parallel model with a limited amount of processing capacity (see Townsend, 1972). This latter model assumes that the items are examined simultaneously, but since processing capacity is limited, it must be distributed over all the items to be processed. With a small number of items in the memory set, each one can be processed quickly; however, large memory sets result in longer processing times. Thus, the limited-capacity parallel model predicts that *RT* increases with memory set size.

While the battle over what is the correct theoretical interpretation proceeds, hundreds of variations on the Sternberg experiment have appeared since the publication of the original studies. For example, Clifton and Tash (1973) used the basic procedure, but instead of digits subjects memorized sets of words. Some of the words contained six letters and one syllable (for example, *street*) while others contained three syllables (for example, *memory*). The usual reaction time functions were obtained for these materials, and for simple sets of letters. The experimenters found that the type of material in the memory set did not affect the slope of the *RT* function. The fact that the slopes were all equal indicates that comparison time depends on neither (1) the visual length of an item nor (2) the amount of time it takes to say an item.

One factor that does affect search rate, however, is the correspondence between the memory set and test item modality (Chase & Calfee, 1969). Modality simply refers to how the event is presented, visually, verbally, or whatever. In one experiment, subjects either saw or heard the test item. The results were straightforward. When the memory set and test item occurred in the same modality, each comparison took about 50 msec, which is similar to the 38 msec figure observed by Sternberg. However, when the memory set and the test item were in different modalities, the comparison time averaged 65 msec per item, representing about a 30 percent increase. These experiments were performed to shed light on the format in which the memory set is stored; however, this puzzle has not been completely resolved.

TRANSFER FROM SHORT- TO LONG-TERM MEMORY

REHEARSAL

When we rehearse information, as when we repeat a telephone number to ourselves, two things happen. First, rehearsal serves to keep the information in short-term memory for as long as we continue rehearsing. Second, rehearsal may also effect a transfer of information from short-term to long-term memory. As we shall see, these functions may involve two different types of rehearsal. First, however, consider some empirical evidence for the role of rehearsal and its function as an information-transfer mechanism.

We begin with the experiments by Rundus (Rundus & Atkinson, 1970; Rundus, 1971), who presented his subjects with a list of words for later recall. The subject's job was to rehearse out loud any word he wished during the presentation of the list, while a tape recorder kept track of what the subject said. So, the first word in the list might be "hoof," and the subject might say out loud "hoof, hoof, hoof . . . ." The second word might be "kindness" and the subject might then rehearse "hoof, kindness, hoof, kindness . . ." and so on. Rundus then asked the subject to recall all of the words he could remember in any order he wished. The results are very clear: The more times a word was rehearsed, the more likely it was to be recalled later on.

Subsequent experiments indicated that there may be more than one way to rehearse new information. Craik and Lockhart (1972), for example, suggested that there are at least two major types of rehearsal. They called the first type "maintenance rehearsal," by which they meant merely repeating the material without thinking about it. Maintenance rehearsal may allow indefinite maintenance of the material in short-term memory, but it may not cause any of the material to be transferred to long-term memory. The second type of rehearsal has been termed "elaborative rehearsal" and is thought to involve taking the new information and doing something with it. That something might include creating an elaboration of some sort, for example, associating to it, trying to image it, trying to relate it to other things that are known. In this way information is transferred to long-term memory.

The two types of rehearsal are quite distinct; in fact subjects find it easy to switch between the two types if they are instructed to do so (Bjork, 1975). Further, there is other evidence to support the distinction. Consider an experiment by Craik and Watkins (1973). Presented with a long list of words, subjects were instructed that when the list ended they were to report the last word in the list that began with some particular letter, say P. Because the subject does not know how many P words will be in the list, he must maintain in short-term memory any given P word that occurs until it is replaced with another P word. Thus, suppose the subject hears, "Table,

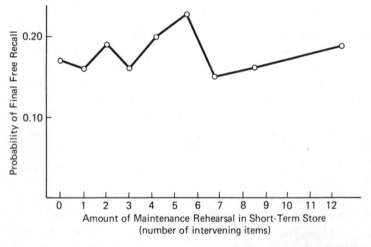

FIGURE 2–13. Results of the Craik and Watkins (1973) experiment: Probability of final free recall as a function of maintenance time. (Adapted from Craik & Watkins, 1973. Courtesy of Academic Press, Inc.)

pen, horse, king, pit, apple, pond. . . ." The subject must maintain *pen* until it is replaced with *pit,* which is maintained until it is replaced with *pond.* In this way the amount of time a subject maintains any given word in short-term memory can be manipulated. At some point the subject will be asked to report the last P word in the list, and for the above example the subject would respond "pond."

To the subject's surprise, after receiving several such lists, an unexpected final free recall test is given. Figure 2-13 shows the probability of correctly recalling a given word as a function of the length of time the word has been maintained in short-term memory. The curve is nearly flat. Thus a word that was maintained for a considerable length of time is not recalled any better than a word that was only briefly maintained. How do we reconcile this result with Rundus' postulate of a relationship between rehearsal and probability of correct recall? The answer is that rehearsal does not automatically lead to transfer of information into long-term memory. If the rehearsal is of the shallow, "telephone" variety—like the type we perform to keep a new telephone number in mind from the time we get it until it can be dialed—little will be transferred to long-term memory. If the rehearsal is of the deep, elaborative type, as when we try to set up meaningful connections among the items we are trying to remember, much can be transferred. Watkins and Watkins (1974) have confirmed these notions.

ORGANIZATION

It turns out that although the term *elaborative rehearsal* is relatively new, it has been studied over the years under the general label of "organization." One of the best ways to learn new material or to help someone else learn it is to organize it, and by organization we mean try to make it fit into some preexisting logical framework, try to relate it to something we already know. There are many different ways to accomplish this goal. For example, one can weave a list of words into a story, with the result that the list is much easier to remember than it would have been by forced memorization (Bower & Clark, 1969). One can improve recall of pairs of objects by imagining a mental scene or mental picture in which the two objects are interacting in some way (Bower, 1972). One can improve recall of all sorts of different material by use of mnemonics.

A mnemonic is a technique or "memory trick" for organizing information so that it can be more easily remembered. When we learned the number of days in each month, we learned "Thirty days hath September, April, June and November. . . ." Instead of having to remember the individual number of days in each month, as by memorizing January—31, February—28, March—31 . . ., we now have a single rule (in fact, a chunk). As a second example, one of the authors relied on the phrase "ladies prefer men" to remember the order of the avenues Lexington, Park, and Madison while traveling west in New York City. Another enormously powerful mnemonic is called the method of loci: various items that a person wants to remember are imagined to be located in different physical locations (or loci). Recall that this was a favorite technique of Luria's subject S. who was described in Chapter 1. With the method of loci, items are recalled by visualizing each of the locations and "plucking" the object from it. The basics underlying the method of loci can, as Norman points out, best be appreciated by considering an anecdote about the Greek poet Simonides first told by Cicero in his *De oratore:*

> *At a banquet given by a nobleman of Thessaly named Scopas, the poet Simonides of Ceos chanted a lyric poem in honour of his host but including a passage in praise of Castor and Pollux. Scopas meanly told the poet that he would only pay him half the sum agreed upon. . . . A little later, a message was brought in to Simonides that two young men were waiting outside who wished to see him. He rose from the banquet and went out but could find no one. During his absence the roof of the banqueting hall fell in, crushing Scopas and all the guests to death beneath the ruins; the corpses were so mangled that the relatives who came to take them away for burial were unable to identify them. But Simonides remembered the places at which they had been sitting at the table and was therefore able to indicate to the relatives which were their dead. . . . And this experience suggested to the poet the principles of the art of memory of which he is said to have been the inventor. Noting that it was through his memory of the places at which the guests had been sitting that he had been able to identify the bodies, he realised that orderly arrangement is essential for good memory. (1976, pp. 136–137)*

It is clear that mnemonics are extremely useful, and rigorous laboratory experiments have been conducted to confirm their usefulness.

SUMMARY

We began our exploration of how new information is acquired by noting that from the environment it is first placed into sensory memory. Sensory memory is thought to hold a large amount of information—essentially most of what impinges on a given sense organ. Information decays quickly from this memory. A portion of the information in sensory memory is transferred to short-term memory via the process of pattern recognition, which is simply the process of attaching meaning to a sensory pattern. The decision of which information to transfer out of sensory memory and which to let decay is the phenomenon of attention. Once we decide to attend to some parts of the stimulus, those parts can be transferred into short-term memory. Short-term memory is thought to be limited in capacity—it holds about seven chunks, where a chunk is anything with a unitary representation in long-term memory. Forgetting from this memory occurs within about 15 seconds unless the information is rehearsed. If it is rehearsed it can be maintained in short-term memory indefinitely and some of it can be transferred to long-term memory. While still somewhat of a controversial issue, there is at least some evidence that information in short-term memory is retrieved via a sequential, exhaustive search.

chapter three

RETENTION
IN LONG-TERM MEMORY

outline

EVERYONE OF US IS ABLE (most of the time) to recognize the faces of our friends, familiar foods, the voices of people we know. In fact, we all have a great deal of information in long-term memory, information which—as we saw in Chapter 2—was processed with the aid of such techniques as rehearsal, organization, and elaboration. The capacity of long-term memory is virtually unlimited—at least we know of no human being (except perhaps brain-damaged patients) whose long-term memory was "overstocked," preventing him from learning new information. We begin this chapter with a review of the types of information that are retained in long-term memory, and follow that review with a discussion of forgetting.

TYPES OF INFORMATION IN LONG-TERM MEMORY

SEMANTIC INFORMATION

Long-term memory holds *semantic* information, by which we mean information about meaning. In fact, it has been argued that the dominant, most important mode of representation in long-term memory is semantic (Anisfeld & Knapp, 1968; Grossman & Eagle, 1970), a conclusion which is partially based on experiments that utilize a *false recognition* procedure. In a typical experiment of this sort, a subject sees a list of words that might include, for example, the word *car*. Later, he is given a new list of words and must distinguish between those he saw before and those he did not. Usually, a subject is much more likely to think that he saw the word *auto*, *vehicle*, *Pontiac*, or even *train*, which are semantically related to *car*, than to think he saw *tar* or *cat*, which look or sound like *car* but are not related in meaning. The content of long-term memory is a topic that is currently being reexamined, however, and new findings indicate that other types of information in permanent storage may be just as important as semantic information.

VISUAL INFORMATION

Evidence is mounting that picture-like codes can be stored in long-term memory. This may seem obvious because of the sometimes vivid images that we all have the ability to generate; however, cognitive psychologists have debated the point. Imagine going to your refrigerator for a drink; imagine opening the door; imagine reaching for a bottle of lemonade; now go to the freezer for an ice cube. Is the freezer compartment at the top or at the bottom? Are the ice trays on the left or on the right? You can practically "see" this in your mind's eye. Isn't this proof enough that we have picture-like representations in long-term memory?

Allan Paivio has done extensive work in the area of visual, as compared to verbal, information in long-term memory. He has found, for example, that when people form images of stimulus materials, they can usually remember those materials better than others who merely verbally code the material (Paivio, 1971). More recent experiments (Paivio, 1975) have provided evidence that visual as well as verbal codes are being used in long-term memory, a position which has come to be known as the *dual-coding hypothesis*. The hypothesis is best stated by Paivio himself:

> *Verbal and nonverbal information are represented and processed in functionally independent, though interconnected, cognitive systems. . . . One system, the imagery system is presumably specialized for encoding, storing, organizing, transforming, and retrieving information concerning concrete objects and events. In brief, it represents our knowledge of the world in a form that is highly . . . analogous to perceptual knowledge. . . . The other (verbal) system is specialized for dealing with information involving discrete linguistic units and structures. Independence implies, among other things, that the two systems can be independently accessed by relevant stimuli: the imagery system is activated more directly by perceptual objects or pictures than linguistic stimuli, and conversely in the case of the verbal system. Interconnectedness simply means that nonverbal information can be transformed into verbal information, or vice versa. (1975, p. 635)*

To capture the flavor of the experiments Paivio designed to lend support to the dual-coding hypothesis, note the pictures and printed names in Figure 3-1. Cards such as these were shown to subjects, who were asked to judge which member of the pair was conceptually larger. The time it took the subject to respond was recorded. Paivio reasoned as follows. If long-term memory (LTM) contained only information stored in the semantic (or verbal) mode, then subjects should take longer to respond to pictures than words, since pictures would have to be translated into words before the judgment could be made. If, on the other hand, LTM contained a visual code then pictures would take no longer since they could be accessed directly from memory. Paivio also varied whether the pairs were congruent or incongruent, that it, whether relative sizes of the objects pictured corresponded to their actual sizes (compare the two cards in Figure 3-1). Paivio reasoned that if LTM contained a visual code, a conflict would be created by the incongruent pairs that would slow the subjects down. In-

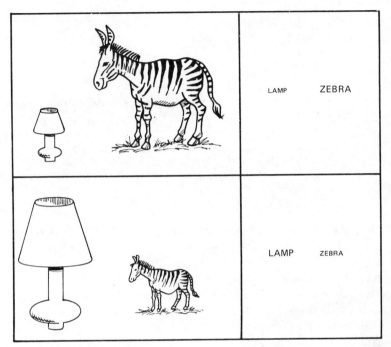

FIGURE 3–1. The pairs on the top are congruent while those on the bottom are not. (After Paivio, 1975. Courtesy of Psychonomic Society.)

congruence in the verbal pairs, however, should not create a problem, since they would first be translated into their verbal equivalents. The results supported the existence of visual codes by showing that subjects responded to incongruent pictures more slowly than congruent ones, whereas word pairs were responded to equally quickly whether they were incongruent or not.

Visual Versus Verbal Codes

In order to shed some light on the distinction between a verbal and a visual code, Bahrick and Boucher (1968) performed an experiment in which subjects looked at drawings of common objects, such as the cup pictured in Figure 3-2A. Some subjects were instructed to label the drawings as they studied them, others were not. After a delay of either 1 minute or 2 weeks, the subjects were given two tests. The first was a recall test in which they listed the objects in any order they wished; the second was a multiple-choice recognition test like the one shown in Figure 3-2B.

The results are fairly clear-cut, and show a large difference between the recall (verbal) and the recognition (visual) tests. For the recall test, labeling the picture increased the performance on the immediate test, but

A. Target cup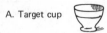

B. Multiple choice recognition test

FIGURE 3-2.   Stimuli used in the Bahrick and Boucher (1968) experiment. (Adapted from Figure 1 in Bahrick & Boucher, 1968. Reprinted by permission of the author and American Psychological Association.)

did not help performance when the test was delayed for 2 weeks. By contrast, labeling the picture had no effect on the likelihood that a subject was correct on the recognition test, whether immediate or delayed.

Bahrick and Boucher also looked at the effect of labeling on the type of *incorrect* response subjects made; responses could be similar to the target or quite dissimilar (see Figure 3-2B). Labeling did *not* cause subjects to choose a more similar incorrect alternative. Furthermore, subjects who chose correctly on the recognition test (or who chose a similar incorrect alternative) were not necessarily more likely to have earlier recalled the object correctly. In other words, recall performance was in no way related to recognition performance. This result, and the fact that labeling (verbal) did not help recognition (visual), has been used to support the notion that the storage of labels and the storage of picture-like images involve independent memorial systems.

Different Kinds of Visual Codes

Imagine yourself getting up from reading this book and walking to the refrigerator to get an apple for a snack. Now imagine that you are *watching* yourself, say from the other side of the room, accomplish the same sequence of acts. The images you have in these two instances would clearly have a different perspective. In one case you would have a good "view" of the shoes on your feet, in the other case you would not. In one case the details of the apple should "appear" larger than in the other. That images can assume different perspectives in relation to the subject prompted an unusual experiment reported by Abelson (1975).

The subjects in this experiment read a 68-sentence story about a person strolling out of a hotel and down the street a block or so. All subjects were asked to close their eyes and "imagine, as best and as vividly as you can, along with what you hear." But some subjects were told to imagine themselves being the main character in the story (the Self subjects). Other subjects (the Balcony subjects) were asked to imagine themselves watching from a fourth-floor hotel balcony. A control group was not instructed on the vantage point for the images.

While the subjects were imagining this stroll down the street, they also imagined several different kinds of details. "Far visual" details, such as a sign over a bank, were those that could best be seen from a distance, whereas "near visual" details, such as a wristwatch, were more clearly observable from close range. The subjects were also asked to imagine "body sensation" details such as drinking hot coffee. Twenty minutes after hearing and imagining the story, all subjects were given a cued recall test. Table 3-1 presents the mean proportions of the three different types of details correctly recalled by the Self and Balcony subjects. As might be expected, relative to the Self subjects, the Balcony subjects performed better on the recall of far visual details, whereas the reverse was true for the recall of body sensation details. The two groups were equal in their recall of near visual details. While on the one hand it might be expected that the Self subjects would perform better on these details, in actuality Balcony subjects sometimes reported "floating down" off the balcony from time to time to get a better "look" at a detail that was otherwise too small to imagine clearly.

In discussing the results, Abelson reminds his readers that all subjects were told to *imagine* what they heard. Thus, it cannot be argued that some subjects were oriented toward visual information and others toward some other type of nonvisual information. All that was different between the groups of subjects was the vantage point from which they did their imagining. For Abelson the results not only support the existence of nonverbal codes in long-term memory, but may even suggest the existence of different forms of nonverbal codes, depending upon the point of view of the listener. One processing mode might be best for one vantage point, and another mode might be best for another vantage point. These modes would then have different consequences for what a subject most readily remembers. Abelson called his speculation "theory-boggling" for, if true, it seriously complicates the task of a theorist attempting to understand the use of visual codes in long-term memory.

TABLE 3-1. MEAN PROPORTIONS OF CORRECT RECALLS OF DETAILS IN ABELSON (1975).

| | Type of detail | | |
	Far visual	*Near visual*	*Body sensation*
Self	.42	.62	.66
Balcony	.59	.61	.51

In addition to semantic and visual information, LTM appears to store phonetic or acoustic information as well. Many experiments have pointed to this conclusion; we briefly consider one by Bruce and Crowley (1970). These investigators presented subjects with a list of words, many of which were phonetically related to each other, for example, *gain, pain, sane,* and *vein.* The key words could either occur consecutively at the beginning and end of the list, or be distributed throughout it. Phonetically related words were later recalled significantly better than control words which did not bear a relation to each other; however, this was true only if the phonetically related words occurred at the beginning and end of the list. This result indicates that when the phonetically similar words were presented consecutively, subjects noted the similarity and improved their performance accordingly. In another condition, subjects were presented with semantically related words, for example, *apple, peach, orange,* which could appear consecutively at the beginning or end of the list, or nonconsecutively throughout the list. Subjects recalled these words better than control words *no matter where the words appeared in the list.* This final result suggests that the semantic information is more readily seized upon than is phonetic information, or that it is more likely to be accessed in the situation being studied here.

Long-term memory also apparently contains codes that correspond to taste and olfaction as well as to motor knowledge. We must have these, for how else could we recognize the taste of an orange or the smell of fresh roast coffee? How else could we remember how to ride a bicycle? Examples such as these attest to the wide variety of types of information that can be stored in long-term memory. It is difficult to rate them in terms of importance, but clearly visual information ranks somewhere near the top of the list. The prevalence and variety of visual images have made *imagery* a topic that has captured the attention of cognitive psychologists around the world.

IMAGERY

WHAT IT IS ABOUT AND WHAT IT CAN DO

When we construct a mental image, we are experiencing a sensation in the absence of any external stimulus. Yet, like external stimuli, images can be visual, tactual, auditory, gustatory, or olfactory. Thus, if we imagine the appearance of a box of popcorn, how it feels when we pick up a handful, how it sounds when we munch it in the movies, how it tastes in our mouth, and how it smells, we are experiencing a variety of images in the absence of an actual box of popcorn. For the most part cognitive psychologists have confined themselves to visual images and our discussion of imagery will follow that lead.

Earlier in this chapter we discussed the work of Paivio (1971, 1975) who put forth the dual-coding hypothesis: Both images and verbal codes exist in LTM. We also learned that when people form images of stimulus materials they remember them better than when they simply rehearse the material, or verbally process it in some way. Evidence to support this contention comes not only from Paivio but from other researchers, for example, Bower and Winzenz (1970), who used a *paired associate task* in their study of imagery. Subjects were presented with pairs of words such as *piano–cigar* and were instructed to learn the pairs so that when the first member was presented alone (*piano*), the second member (*cigar*) would be recalled. Some subjects were told to learn the pairs by simply repeating them over and over. Others were either presented with or made up for themselves a sentence in which the first member was the subject and the second member was the object, for example, *The piano was burned by the cigar.* Still others were told to visualize an interaction between the objects denoted by the words (in other words, to use imagery). In this condition a subject might imagine a cigar on top of a piano. Subjects performed best in the imagery condition. Their recall was next best in the sentence conditions and worst in the condition in which learning was accomplished by rote repetition.

Do the objects really need to be interacting in the images? Does it help if the images are bizarre? These issues were addressed in a study by Wollen, Weber, and Lowry (1972). Their subjects were asked to perform a paired associate learning task like the one used by Bower and Winzenz. With each pair subjects were shown images of the two objects; either in a bizarre relationship or not, and either interacting or not. Thus, for each pair of objects, one of four pictures was possible. These possibilities are shown in Figure 3-3. Performance in each case was to be compared to the performance of control subjects who learned the word pairs without the aid of a drawing.

Wollen et al. found the important factor was whether the objects interacted. If the objects interacted performance was better than if not. Bizarreness did not help performance, and in fact relative to the control group, the group that had looked at bizarre drawings performed somewhat worse. While these later studies are important in showing the types of imagery that facilitate memory, the real value of the work of Paivio and others is in demonstrating that the mere process of creating images or viewing pictures dramatically increases recall.

We came across the topic of imagery in Chapter 2 when we discussed mnemonics, particularly the *method of loci*. Recall that this method involves placing distinct visual images of items to be remembered in various

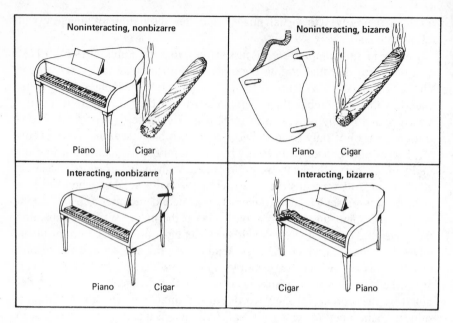

FIGURE 3–3. Examples of the four kinds of drawings that accompanied the word pairs presented in the Wollen et al. experiment. (After Wollen, Weber & Lowry, 1972. Courtesy of Academic Press, Inc.)

mental spatial locations. The to-be-remembered items are retrieved by moving through the spatial locations mentally. The method of loci works extremely well, as Groniger (1971) has shown. Subjects were told about the method of loci and were asked to work out a spatial image that was familiar to them and had 25 distinct locations in it. They were then given a deck of 25 cards and told to learn them in a specific order. Control subjects were not told about the method of loci; they were told to learn the deck however they wished. Most later admitted to using rote rehearsal. After relatively long retention intervals of 1 and 5 weeks all subjects returned for testing. As was expected the imagery group outperformed the control group. The former recalled 92 percent of the cards after 1 week and 80 percent after 5 weeks; the control group recalled only 64 percent after 1 week and a mere 36 percent after 5 weeks.

Clearly imagery is a powerful aid to memory. This fact has been used to support the notion that visual information must be stored in LTM, but *how* is it stored? Before we address this issue, we consider some recent, exciting work on mental rotation.

Mental Rotation

We know from examining our own personal experience that it is possible to conjure up new images in our minds. We can imagine a professor walking around with a copy of this book on her head even though we have never

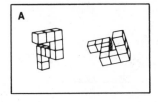

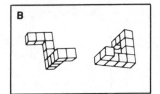

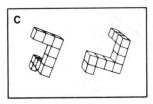

FIGURE 3–4. Determining whether one of a pair of figures can be rotated into the other. The A pair: A rotation on the plane of the page. The B pair: A rotation in the third dimension. The C pair: The task cannot be completed. (Adapted from Figure 1 in Shepard & Metzler, 1971. Copyright by American Association for the Advancement of Science.)

actually seen this combination. To study how mental images are generated and manipulated is extremely difficult, however, because images are simply not accessible to direct observation. Recently, though, a series of ingenious experiments by Shepard and his co-workers demonstrated that such studies are possible.

In one study (Shepard & Metzler, 1971), subjects looked at pairs of figures constructed to possess several special properties. The A pairs are identical except one has been rotated on the plane defined by the surface of the page. The B pairs are identical except one has been rotated on the plane perpendicular to the surface of the page (that is, rotated in the third dimension, back into the page). The C pairs are not identical. The two figures look similar, but one cannot be rotated so that it exactly corresponds to the other.

A, B, and C type pairs were presented to the subject at various angles, and his task was to indicate whether the two members were the same (identical, as in A and B) or different (as in C). Reaction time was recorded.

Imagine an A pair in which one member was rotated only slightly from the other. These would look very similar. However, if one member were rotated 180 degrees from the other, that member would appear to be upside down. The angle of rotation was one of the major variables of interest in this experiment. The reasoning was that if a subject must actually "mentally rotate" one figure into the other in order to respond that they are identical, it ought to take longer to respond when the angle of rotation is

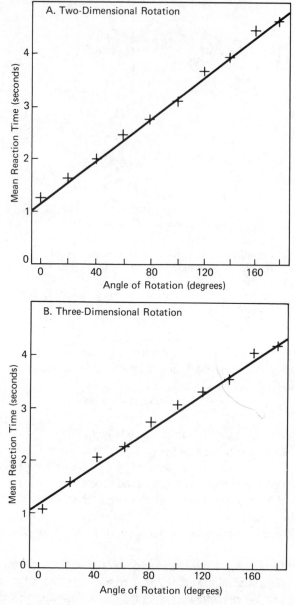

FIGURE 3–5. Subjects take longer to respond to pairs of stimuli (such as those shown in Figure 3–4) when the angle of rotation is large rather than small. (Adapted from Shepard & Metzler, 1971. Copyright by American Association for the Advancement of Science.)

large. As we can observe in Figure 3-5, when the angle was very small (close to 0 degrees), subjects took an average of 1 second to respond; however, for 180-degree rotations they took more than 4 seconds.

Two points are worth mentioning. The relationship between mean reaction time and angle of rotation is a linear one, which means that mental rotation proceeds at a fairly constant rate. That rate is about 60 degrees per second. Second, the data are almost identical for both the A (two-dimensional) and the B (three-dimensional) rotations. In other words, subjects perform equally fast and accurately on both of these types. We might have thought that rotating back into the third dimension would be more difficult, but these data contradict that supposition. The experiment as a whole provides rather impressive evidence for a remarkable ability to rotate objects in the mind's eye.

More details of mental rotation were provided by Cooper and Shepard (1973), who presented subjects with letters or digits, such as R or Я, and instructed them to press one button if the stimulus was normal and another button if it was a mirror image. As in the study with complex block figures, the stimuli could differ from the usual upright position by a rotation. Figure 3-6 shows some of the orientations for a normal letter R and for its mirror image. Notice the symmetry in the stimuli in Figure 3-6. The 60-degree normal R is titled slightly clockwise from the 0-degree normal R, whereas the 300-degree normal R is tilted slightly counterclockwise. It turns out that subjects sometimes rotated clockwise and sometimes counterclockwise, depending on the particular stimulus that faced them.

In earlier experiments, subjects' response time had varied directly with the magnitude of an object's deviation from the normal vertical, upright position. According to Figure 3-7, however, the longest reaction times were

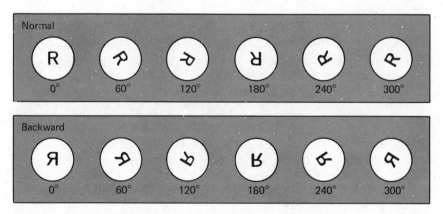

FIGURE 3–6. Subjects had to decide whether a given stimulus was normal or a mirror image of normal. (After Cooper & Shepard, 1973. Courtesy of Academic Press, Inc.)

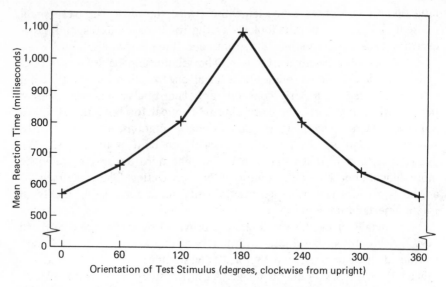

FIGURE 3–7. The orientation of a character, such as R, influenced the time it took a subject to respond whether the character was normal or a mirror image of normal. (After Cooper & Shepard, 1973. Courtesy of Academic Press, Inc.)

obtained when the stimulus was upside down (180 degrees from vertical). Apparently, then, subjects do not simply rotate the representation in a clockwise fashion until it reaches the upright position and then decide if the character is normal or a mirror image. Rather, they decide whether to rotate clockwise or counterclockwise, complete the rotation, and then make their decision.

These results provide compelling evidence that people can rotate mental representations in their minds. The techniques allow us to measure approximately how quickly people can perform these rotations and further indicate that people have some control over the direction of their rotations.

THEORIES OF HOW IMAGES ARE STORED

Most of the theories that discuss how images are stored in memory can be classified into one of three categories: Picture-analogy theories, symbolic representation theories, and surface representation theories. The first category appears to be the most common.

Picture-Analogy Theories

When a person looks at a picture, certain mental data are processed. Picture-analogy theories claim that images are processed in the same way. Some variations of the theory actually assume that when a person uses imagery to memorize some verbal material, that material is converted to mental pictures which are stored and later retrieved (Bugelski, 1970). Others have assumed that images are capable of being analyzed and scrutinized much like pictures during perception (Hebb, 1968). Paivio's view is similar, although for the most part he has focused his attention on the difference between images and verbal representation. Bower (1972) and Neisser (1972; Neisser & Kerr, 1973) have also espoused positions which fall into this category, believing that images resemble percepts in at least some significant ways. Yet none of these theories has really explained why imagery is such a powerful facilitator of memory. None has detailed how images are constructed. None discusses how information is retrieved from images.

Symbolic Representation Theories

Unlike the picture-analogy theories, this class of theories posits that the representations underlying images are not different from those underlying verbal material. Both representations resemble descriptions. In the words of Simon, "all internal modalities employ basically the same kinds of structure for storage; their differences are differences in organization" (1972, p. 201). Most of the proponents of this class of theories have attempted to embody their theory in a working computer simulation (for example, Anderson & Bower, 1973). A computer simulation is a computer program that is written to instruct a computer to mirror the cognitive behavior of a human being. Thus both image and verbal representation would be encoded in the common language of the computer program.

These theories also have their limitations. Usually the simulations concern very limited, highly specific tasks. They leave much of what we know unaccounted for.

Surface Representation Theories

The argument of this class of theories is that images are derived from some underlying long-term representation, but the nature of that representation is left unspecified. Images are thought to be generated in short-term memory, and once generated, their surface can be analyzed—perhaps by processes that are similar to those used in visual perception. Pylyshyn (1973) and Kosslyn (1975) have both developed this view.

In addition to believing that people generate images from some underlying representation and then process the surface of the image, Kossyln claims that we can create an image "in the same general way a computer program can produce a picture on an oscilloscope screen" (p. 368). Relatively small images would thus be difficult to inspect. In his 1975 experiments, Kosslyn found this to be so. For example, in one study subjects were to imagine a rabbit standing either next to an elephant or next to a

FIGURE 3–8. When a person *images* a rabbit, the rabbit is usually smaller if imaged next to an elephant rather than next to fly.

fly. In the first condition, the bulk of the image would probably be taken up with the elephant, leaving little room for the image of the rabbit. In the second condition, however, the rabbit image can be larger (see Figure 3-8). In this latter case, one might expect that subjects would take less time to use their image to verify that a rabbit has some property, say ears. Kosslyn found what he expected—that it took people more time to evaluate an animal when the subjective image of it was small rather than large. Conversely, it takes people longer to construct large images than to construct small ones.

While Kosslyn is far from outlining a complete theory of how information is represented in and later retrieved from visual images, he has provided useful information for what must be contained in any such theory.

Our discussion of the types of theories of imagery has been brief. Unfortunately the issue is far from being resolved. We will return to the general topic of how information is represented in long-term memory again in Chapter 4. If you as readers find yourselves somewhat frustrated that no final answers are forthcoming, you are not alone. Cognitive psychologists have been battling this one out for years and will continue to do so. Perhaps we won't really know how information is represented in images for another fifty years. On the other hand, at least we are now beginning to understand something about how images *function,* even if we do not fully understand how they are *structured.*

FORGETTING FROM LONG-TERM MEMORY

Forgetting is a common experience for all of us. This probably accounts for the stupendous success of Lorayne and Lucas' *The Memory Book,* which swept the country in 1974 in hardback and again in 1975 in paperback. *The Memory Book* is a practical book filled with techniques to help you remember speeches, playing cards, grocery lists, and other types of things that you do not want to forget. It advertises that "you can remember all the things that make the vital difference in your everyday existence, eliminating the unnecessary loss of so much knowledge and information that should be yours to keep and use forever" (1975, p. 1). These techniques work for some people, largely by helping to organize and elaborate upon material in the same way that mnemonic devices do (see Chapter 2). But why are they needed in the first place? What causes forgetting?

INTERFERENCE THEORY

One theory of why people forget events they have experienced is that other events prevent the original one from being remembered. In other words, events interfere with each other in memory. Since most of us are fairly active human beings, it is likely that we encounter numerous events that potentially interfere with others we may wish to remember.

If this position is correct, then we ought to be able to eliminate forgetting by eliminating interfering events. One way to accomplish this might be to have people go to sleep immediately after learning some new material. This is exactly what was done in a classic experiment performed over 50 years ago (Jenkins & Dallenbach, 1924). Only two subjects were used, each of whom had to learn lists of nonsense syllables under various conditions. In some cases they learned the lists and immediately afterwards went to sleep. In other cases, they learned the lists and then carried on with their normal activities of eating, studying, swimming, or whatever. After either 1, 2, 4, or 8 hours the subjects were asked to recall the material they had learned. (In the sleep conditions, the subjects were awakened at the appropriate times.) The resulting forgetting curves are shown in Figure 3-9. For all retention intervals, recall was better after sleep than after being awake. After eight hours of being awake subjects could remember only about one nonsense syllable, whereas after eight hours of sleep they recalled nearly six. Jenkins and Dallenbach said of their results, ". . . forgetting is not so

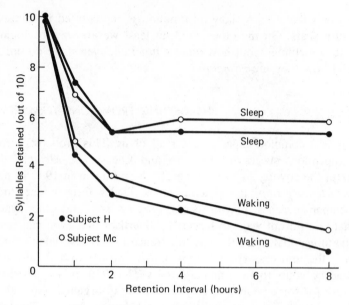

FIGURE 3–9. Amount of material remembered after sleep and waking conditions. When subjects sleep after learning some new material their retention is superior. (After Jenkins & Dallenbach, "Ovliviscence during sleep and waking" American Journal of Psychology, 1924. Courtesy of University of Illinois Press)

much a matter of the decay of old impressions and associations as it is a matter of the interference, inhibition, or obliteration of the old by the new" (p. 612). Since the original experiments, many succeeding investigators have replicated the basic superiority of the sleep over the awake condition for remembering (for example, Ekstrand, 1967, 1972).

If we stop to examine the interference theory of forgetting, we find that it actually consists of two subtheories. One, *proactive interference* (sometimes called *proactive inhibition,* and denoted PI), refers to forgetting that is caused by interference from material learned previously. The other, *retroactive interference* (sometimes *retroactive inhibition,* denoted RI), refers to forgetting caused by information learned afterward. These two types of interference are illustrated in Figure 3-10.

Retroactive Interference

After we have learned something, other things presented to us during the retention interval produce forgetting of that original learning. Experiments that have been conducted on RI have used this basic paradigm:

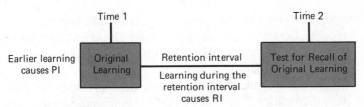

FIGURE 3–10. Interference theory. At Time 1, some material is learned. After a retention interval, the material is tested for recall at Time 2. Material learned before Time 1 produces proactive interference (PI), whereas learning occurring during the retention interval produces retroactive interference (RI).

EXPERIMENTAL GROUP	Learns information A	Learns information B	Recalls information A
CONTROL GROUP	Learns information A	No new learning	Recalls information A

Both the experimental and control group learn some new information, A, and later attempt to recall that information. The experimental group learns some additional information, B, during the retention interval, while the control group does not. As you might expect, the experimental group has a much harder time recalling information A. This is as interference theory would have it; the finding indicates that B serves to disrupt or interfere with the retention of A.

Representative data pertaining to retroactive interference were reported by Briggs (1957). Briggs demonstrated a basic fact about RI; the amount of interference depends upon the number of trials with an interfering list of material. In his study, subjects learned two lists comprised of adjective pairs. In the language of our basic paradigm, we can consider the first list to be information A and the second to be information B. Experimental subjects were given either 2, 4, 10, or 20 trials on the interfering list. The control subjects were not given an interfering list or they received 0 trials on the interfering list. Briggs measured the amount of RI for each condition by a formula called relative retroactive interference. The measure takes percent correct for the control group, minus percent correct for the experimental group, all divided by percent correct for the control group. In other words:

$$\text{Relative RI} = \frac{\text{control group percentage} - \text{experimental group percentage}}{\text{control group percentage}}$$

This formula expresses interference as a percentage of control group learning. By so doing, the formula takes into account the difficulty of the original information and allows relative RI in one situation to be compared to relative RI in another situation.

To see how this formula is actually used, we apply it to the data from one of Briggs' conditions. In this particular condition, experimental subjects who received extensive interfering material (20 trials) correctly recalled only 43.8 percent of the original material, whereas control subjects who received no interfering material correctly recalled 94.4 percent of the original material. Applying the formula for relative RI,

$$\frac{\text{Control }\% - \text{Experimental }\%}{\text{Control }\%} = \frac{94.4\% - 43.8\%}{94.4\%} = 54\%$$

Figure 3-11 shows a relative RI function for subjects who learned the original material extremely well. After no intervening material, subjects showed no retroactive interference. After 10 trials of intervening material, they showed about 60 percent retroactive interference. Finally, after 20 trials, they showed over 70 percent retroactive interference. Briggs also measured relative RI for subjects who had not learned the material as well. His results are qualitatively similar: Interference is positively related to the amount of practice on an interfering list.

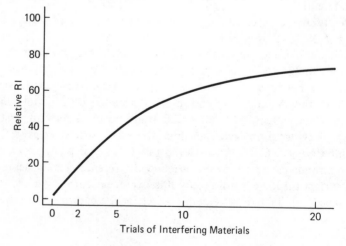

FIGURE 3–11. Relative retroactive interference as a function of the amount of interfering material. (After Briggs, 1957. Reprinted by permission of American Psychological Association.)

When we learn some new material, things that we have learned previously can also produce forgetting of that new material. Experiments that have been conducted on proactive interference, or PI, have used this basic paradigm:

EXPERIMENTAL GROUP	Learns information B	Learns information A	Recalls information A
CONTROL GROUP	No prior learning	Learns information A	Recalls information A

Both groups learn information A and then recall that information. However, prior to that learning, the experimental group learns some other material, whereas the control group does not. As may be expected from interference theory, the experimental group has more difficulty recalling information A than does the control group.

An experiment reported by Underwood (1957), but conducted by Archer, nicely shows the effects of amount of prior learning on the learning of new material. The subjects learned lists of adjectives, and then attempted to recall them one day later. Then they learned a new list and recalled it one day later. This procedure continued until nine lists had been learned and recalled. As Figure 3-12 shows, performance is initially fairly good (71 percent of the adjectives from List 1 are recalled correctly); but it declines steadily so that subjects are recalling only 27 percent from List 9.

By the systematic investigation of proactive interference Underwood was able to provide a key that would unlock an interesting mystery. The mystery was this: The great psychologist Ebbinghaus, inventor of the nonsense syllable, taught himself syllables and then attempted to recall them. He did this with hundreds of lists, and usually found that he was able to recall only 35 percent of what he had initially learned. On the other hand, the typical college student of the 1940s who learned a list of nonsense syllables and was tested one day later, could recall 80 percent of the items (Underwood, 1948a, b, 1949). How could the performance of a college student who had learned only a single list so far outweigh the performance of the great memorizer Ebbinghaus? Reflecting upon this question, Underwood noted that a key difference between Ebbinghaus and the college students was that the former had learned hundreds of lists while the latter had learned only a single list. Thus, when Ebbinghaus tested himself, his recall was preceded by the learning and recall of many, many prior lists. It was these prior lists that produced the decrement in his performance. In the words of the unraveler of this mystery:

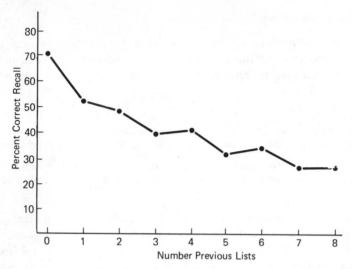

FIGURE 3–12.   As the number of prior lists learned and recalled increases, performance declines. Thus proactive interference, due to prior lists, increases. (After Underwood, 1957. Reprinted by permission of the author and American Psychological Association.)

> *. . . we give the subject a second list to learn and test him on this 24 hours later. This time his performance is not quite so good as it was [for the first list]; he forgets more than 20 percent. We go on in the same way with a third list, a fourth, a fifth and so on. . . . Plotting his successive performances on a graph, we find a startlingly sharp rise in his rate of forgetting. . . . In the case of the 20th list, 24 hours after learning it he has forgotten 80 percent of the items* (Underwood, 1964, p. 5).

Thus, Underwood accounted for the seemingly disparate performance of Ebbinghaus versus the college students. By demonstrating that students' recall drops from 80 percent on the first list to 20 percent on the twentieth list, he vindicated what had seemed to be Ebbinghaus' rather modest performance of 35 percent after exposure to hundreds of lists. The point should be clear: How much new material we can remember strongly depends on the activities we have engaged in before that new learning took place. Prior learning can interfere extensively with current learning.

Theoretical Basis for Interference Theory

Several hypotheses have been proposed to account for RI and PI. One of the most prevalent views proposes that the two types of interference are due to extinction or unlearning, while two other views rest heavily on the notion of competition.

EXTINCTION AND UNLEARNING.   The well known work of Pavlov (1927) and his followers on classical conditioning forms the basis of one of the major hypotheses about interference. As most students learn in introductory psychology, Pavlov used a paradigm in which he paired a *conditioned stimulus* (for example, a bell) with an *unconditioned stimulus* (for example, food). After the two had been paired a number of times, the conditioned stimulus came to elicit the *conditioned response* of salivation. As long as the bell is usually followed by food, salivation occurs at the time the bell rings.

Suppose the bell were presented without the food. If this happened continually, the conditioned response, salivation, would gradually decline, and soon it would not appear at all. This phenomenon is called *extinction*. We can also observe another phenomenon within this paradigm, called *spontaneous recovery*. If a response has been extinguished over a period of time and we once again present the conditioned stimulus (bell), the conditioned response (salivation) will spontaneously reappear. The longer the interval between the last extinction trial and the new presentation of the conditioned stimulus, the stronger the conditioned response. We say that the response has spontaneously recovered.

With this background material under our belts, we can better understand the extinction or unlearning explanation of RI and PI. Consider a typical RI with a paired associate experiment. The term A–B will be used to refer to a paired associate list in which stimulus terms are taken from a set A and response terms from a different set B. Thus the A terms might be adjectives and the B terms might be a set of digits, so that "Happy–3" might be a typical member of the AB list. An A–C list would be constructed by using as stimuli the same A terms as were used in the A–B list, but the responses would now be taken from set C. If C consisted of a different set of digits, "Happy–8" might be in the A–C list.

Suppose a subject first learns an A–B list. Next he learns an A–C list. Finally, the subject is required to respond to an A term with a B term, for example, to respond to the word *happy* with the digit 3. As we already know, it is likely that a subject who has had the A–C interpolated learning will perform worse on this final test than a control subject who has not. Further, the more time and effort the subject expends on the A–C list, the poorer his performance on the final (A–B) test. This situation is directly analogous to Pavlovian theory: During the learning of the A–C list, the B responses to A stimuli are extinguished because they are elicited but not reinforced.

Similarly, the proactive interference experiment is explicable within a Pavlovian framework. In the PI experiment a subject first learns an A–B list, then an A–C list. Finally, he must recall the C terms in the presence of the A terms. As we know, a subject performs worse on the final A–C list than a control subject who has not learned the original A–B list. Furthermore, as the period of time between the initial A–C learning and the final A–C test is increased, the subject becomes progressively worse at emitting correct C responses and occasionally recalls some of the earlier learned B responses. In the language of Pavlovian conditioning, we assume that between the initial A–C learning and the final A–C test, some of the original B responses undergo spontaneous recovery and interfere with the recall of the C terms.

The extinction or unlearning hypothesis has perhaps one overriding weakness (Adams, 1976). Its principles have been taken from the area of animal learning and may have very little to do with the way human beings process and retain verbal material. Future research will show the extent to which concepts derived from animal work can be extended to human verbal behavior. Perhaps we have overextended them.

RESPONSE COMPETITION.   Another explanation of interference effects is in terms of response competition (McGeoch, 1942). It holds that two or more interfering responses compete at the time a subject is attempting to recall one of them; the strongest of them wins out. Thus, if a subject learned an A–B list containing the pair "Happy–3" and subsequently learned the A–C pair, "Happy–8," both responses would be "connected" to the adjective *happy,* but the digit 8 might be stronger since it was learned more recently. If sufficient time passed between the learning of "Happy–8" and the final test, the other response, "3," might increase in relative strength. Thus the actual response a subject makes might come from either the to-be recalled list or from the interfering list, depending on which was stronger at the time. One problem with this explanation for interference is that it predicts that when a subject makes an error, the error will come from the interfering list. In the previous example, if the subject were supposed to remember "3" and erred, his erroneous response would be "8." Unfortunately for the survival of the response competition theory, research showed that errors did not take on this predicted form (Melton & Irwin, 1940).

RESPONSE-SET INTERFERENCE.   A somewhat different "competition" theory has been called response-set interference (Postman, Stark, & Fraser, 1968). Rather than postulating that individual responses compete with each other, this view proposes that whole sets of responses compete with each other. If a subject learns an A–B list, all of the B terms would compete with all of the C terms to which the subject was subsequently exposed. More specifically, when a subject learns an A–B list, all of the B terms are readily available or activated. During A–C learning, the C terms become activated and the B terms are temporarily inhibited. If we test on A–B immediately after A–C learning, retroactive interference will be observed since the C terms will still be more strongly activated. As time passes between A–C learning and A–B recall, it will become harder and harder for subjects to differentiate between the B and the C terms. Note that unlike the relearning hypothesis, this hypothesis does not assume that A–C learning causes a *weakening* of the A–B responses. It assumes that the B responses become harder to generate and eventually harder to distinguish from C responses.

A further assumption of this view is that under special conditions there will be no RI. One such special condition is when a subject is asked not to recall the B terms, but merely to recognize which ones matched the A terms. Since the subject in this situation is not asked to differentiate the B from the C terms, he should experience no retroactive interference. This prediction was empirically supported by results of Postman and Stark (1969), which indicated that subjects have difficulty generating or retrieving B terms (after A–C) learning, but experience no difficulty associating those terms with their proper A terms.

Support for these notions comes from recent work on proactive interference in which subjects retain material for very short periods of time. Recall the Brown-Peterson paradigm from Chapter 2. A subject was presented with three letters, such as BLP, and then, after a period of counting backwards by threes, attempted to recall the item. As the period of counting backward was increased from 0 to 18 seconds, the subject's ability to recall the item declined. In 1970, Wickens performed a Brown-Peterson experiment using—in addition to three consonants—three words and three numbers as to-be-recalled items. For the words, he stipulated a retention interval of 20 seconds, for the consonants and numbers, 10 seconds. On the first trial, performance was reasonably good for all three types of material (see Figure 3-13). But performance declined rather rapidly on subsequent trials, exhibiting the usual buildup of proactive interference. An explanation in terms of response-set interference would seem to apply, since as a subject is given more trials, more items are stored in memory, and there should be a greater difficulty is discriminating the items of one trial from the items of the other trials.

At this point, Wickens (1973) went one step further in his thinking and proposed the phenomenon of "proactive interference release" or *PI release*. In a PI release study, a subject might receive three Brown-Peterson trials with numbers as stimuli and suddenly, on trial 4, he receives three words. When the type of item is suddenly changed like this, a dramatic reduction in proactive interference is observed. For example, Figure 3-14 illustrates the results of Wickens' (1973) experiment in which subjects were given four Brown-Peterson trials. On the first three trials, however, the type of item differed from one group of subjects to another. Some subjects

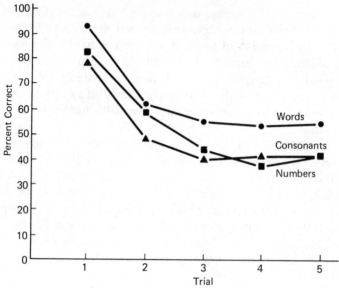

FIGURE 3–13. Proactive interference in short-term retention as a function of the number of single items learned and recalled. Curves for three types of verbal material are shown. (After Wickens, 1970. Reprinted by permission of the author and American Psychological Association.)

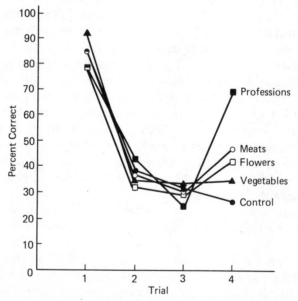

FIGURE 3–14. Effects on proactive interference of shifting to a common category, fruits, as a function of category on the first three trials. (After Wickens, 1973. Courtesy of Psychonomic Society.)

were given vegetables, others were given flowers, still others were given meats or professions. On trial 4, however, all subjects were given the names of three fruits to recall, for example, peach, grape, orange.

Notice in Figure 3-14 that for control subjects who had been instructed to recall fruit names on trials 1 through 3, PI continued on trial 4—that is, performance continued to decline. By contrast, if trial 4 was a switch from professions, a category totally unrelated to fruits, performance took on a dramatic improvement—what Wickens termed a release from PI. Switching from categories that somewhat related to the fruit items presented on the test trial yields an intermediate degree of release. This result jibes nicely with the response-set interference hypothesis. Apparently, recall is high for the completely different category because it is easy to differentiate those items from previously presented items. There is likely to be very little response-set interference.

Interference Theory: A Final Note

It looks as if learners do not disassociate Behavior B from Situation A when required subsequently to learn Behavior C in Situation A. We are . . . left with the idea that two different behaviors can be associated with a single stimulus. . . . How does the learner decide when to emit B and when to emit C when Stimulus A is presented? (Martin, 1971, p. 320)

Martin's question has still not been adequately answered. Although we understand a great deal about the interference paradigms, and even have some tentative hypotheses to explain behavior observed in these paradigms, resolving the inconsistencies in experimental findings and uncovering the actual mechanism of interference will require much more work. This point has been made by two of the leading proponents of interference theory, Postman and Underwood: "the most urgent task is the resolution of the many inconsistencies and apparent contradictions in the rapidly growing body of experimental findings" (1973, p. 37). Modern-day cognitive psychologists continue to work on this task.

CONSTRUCTIVE PROCESSES

Much of the experimentation we have been discussing involves the use of relatively simple verbal materials, for example, memory for strings of letters, nonsense syllables, or individual words. Interference theory seems to provide a reasonable explanation for why people have difficulty remembering material of this sort. But what about the more complicated sort of forgetting that we are more likely to encounter in our everyday lives?

The classic experiment on natural language, one type of real-world forgetting, was performed by Bartlett (1932). In some experiments, Bartlett used the method of *serial reproduction:* A complex story was read by one subject, who told it to another, who in turn told it to another, and so on. In other experiments, Bartlett used the method of *repeated reproduction:*

THE WAR OF THE GHOSTS

One night two young men from Egulac went down to the river to hunt seals, and while they were there it became foggy and calm. Then they heard war-cries, and they thought: "Maybe this is a war party." They escaped to the shore, and hid behind a log. Now canoes came up, and they heard the noise of paddles, and saw one canoe coming up to them. There were five men in the canoe, and they said:

"What do you think? We wish to take you along. We are going up the river to make war on the people."

One of the young men said: "I have no arrows."

"Arrows are in the canoe," they said.

"I will not go along. I might be killed. My relatives do not know where I have gone. But you," he said, turning to the other, "may go with them."

So one of the young men went, but the other returned home.

And the warriors went on up the river to a town on the other side of Kalama. The people came down to the water, and they began to fight, and many were killed. But presently the young man heard one of the warriors say: "Quick, let us go home: that Indian has been hit." Now he thought: "Oh, they are ghosts." He did not feel sick, but they said he had been shot.

So the canoes went back to Egulac, and the young man went ashore to his house, and made a fire. And he told everybody and said: "Behold I accompanied the ghosts, and we went to fight. Many of our fellows were killed, and many of those who attacked us were killed. They said I was hit, and I did not feel sick."

He told it all, and then he became quiet. When the sun rose he fell down. Something black came out of his mouth. His face became contorted. The people jumped up and cried.

He was dead.

SUBJECT'S REPRODUCTION

Two youths were standing by a river about to start seal-catching, when a boat appeared with five men in it. They were all armed for war.

The youths were at first frightened, but they were asked by the men to come and help them fight some enemies on the other bank. One youth said he could not come as his relations would be anxious about him; the other said he would go, and entered the boat.

In the evening he returned to his hut, and told his friends that he had been in a battle. A great many had been slain, and he had been wounded by an arrow; he had not felt any pain, he said. They told him that he must have been fighting in a battle of ghosts. Then he remembered that it had been queer and he became very excited.

In the morning, however, he became ill, and his friends gathered round; he fell down and his face became very pale. Then he writhed and shrieked and his friends were filled with terror. At last he became calm. Something hard and black came out of his mouth, and he lay contorted and dead.

FIGURE 3–15. (From Bartlett's War of Ghosts, 1932. Courtesy of Cambridge University Press.)

A subject studied the story and was later asked repeatedly to reproduce it. The most famous of his stories is a legend called "The War of the Ghosts," about a tribe of North American Indians, and it is reproduced in Figure 3-15. Also in this figure is a sample subject reproduction which illustrates many of the things that Bartlett observed. The subjects' reproductions tend to be shorter, more concrete, and more modern in phraseology. Subjects distorted the stories so that they fit into their own cultural conceptions of what is logical and conventional. Unfamiliar terms dropped out in their recall. For example, the name of the town, Egulac, does not appear in the subject reproduction in Figure 3-15. In discussing his results, Bartlett offered the notion that subjects form abstract representations, or mental "schemas," of stories they read. These schemas are assimilated into the subject's existing knowledge, beliefs, and emotions. The process of assimilation itself results in the kinds of changes that Bartlett observed. Put differently, when subjects hear a story for the first time, they usually do not remember portions of it which do not fit in with their existing LTM structure. Further, they change certain items to become more familiar and coherent. Without substantial modification, a straightforward interference theory would have difficulty explaining these "constructive" changes.

Constructive changes also appear when a person attempts to remember largely visual material that has been experienced in the past. This has been demonstrated in the classic study by Allport and Postman (1958) in which subjects saw the illustration shown in Figure 3-16. As can be seen, the illustration shows several people on a subway car, including a black man

FIGURE 3–16.   Original figure in Allport and Postman (1958).

with a hat and a white man with a razor in his hand. Using the method of serial reproduction, where one subject describes the picture to another, who describes it to another, and so on, these investigators found that the razor tended to migrate in memory from the white man to the black man. One subject reported, "This is a subway train in New York headed for Portland Street. There is a Jewish woman and a Negro who has a razor in his hand. The woman has a baby or a dog. The train is going to Deyer Street, and nothing much happened" (1958, p. 57). Something more than simple interference is at work here. In this case, we see that subjects' stereotypes (for example, "blacks are more violent") are affecting what they perceive and recall.

When we try to remember complex verbal or visual material that we have been exposed to, constructive errors are commonly observed. We can usually recall a few facts, and using these facts we can construct other facts that probably happened. We make inferences. From these probable inferences we are led to other "false facts" which might have been true. To paraphrase C. S. Morgan (1917), we fill up the lowlands of our memories from the highlands of our imaginations. This process of using inferences and probable facts to fill up the gaps in our memories has been called *refabrication,* and it probably occurs in nearly all of our everyday reports of events that we have observed. We supply these bits and pieces, largely unconsciously, to round out fairly incomplete knowledge.

SUMMARY

This chapter has dealt with several aspects of information as it is retained in long-term memory. First, of the several forms of information stored in long-term memory, the most commonly researched are semantic information and visual information. We are able to use this information to generate images, and the structure and function of these images has captured the attention of modern-day cognitive psychologists.

We know, for example, that visual imagery can help people remember things better. Thus, if a person must learn to associate two words, for example, *dog–shoe,* performance is superior when an image is constructed, such as an image of a mangy dog holding a dirty tennis shoe in its mouth. We also know that it is possible for people to manipulate their mental images. Images can be rotated to the right, tilted to the left, or turned completely upside down, and the speed of these manipulations can be measured. While many theories have been advanced for how images are stored, there is still very little agreement on this question.

Another topic we dealt with in this chapter is forgetting from long-term memory. Interference theory was shown successfully to account for a good deal of our forgetting behavior. According to this theory, forgetting of information is caused by interference from material learned previously (proactive interference) and also by interference from material learned afterward (retroactive interference). Interference theory cannot explain it all, however. Empirical work with more naturalistic materials, such as films of real events, has revealed that constructive processes also play a role in producing systematic changes in information while it is retained in long-term memory.

GENERAL KNOWLEDGE
AND ITS RETRIEVAL

outline

SUPPOSE YOU WERE ASKED for the name of the first and only president of the United States to be elected for a fourth term. If you cannot recall the name immediately, let us offer a hint. He beat Wendell Willkie when running for a third term. Who is he? Need another hint? He beat Thomas Dewey when running for his fourth term in November, 1944. Have it? A final hint? His initials are FDR. At this point, if not earlier, you have probably realized that the president was Franklin D. Roosevelt. Even if you did not retrieve his name initially, it is clear that the name was in your memory all the time, for you were able to retrieve it later with the proper hints. The feelings that we sometimes get when attempting to retrieve a forgotten item have been eloquently captured by William James:

> *Suppose we try to recall a forgotten name. The state of our consciousness is peculiar. There is a gap therein; but no mere gap. It is a gap that is intensively active. A sort of wraith of the name is in it, beckoning us in a given direction, making us at moments tingle with the sense of our closeness, and then letting us sink back without the longed-for term. (1890, p. 251)*

RETRIEVAL CUES

When we were searching for the first president to run for a fourth term, some hints were more helpful than others. If we had been told that the person was a man, this would have been no help at all, since to date all U.S. presidents have been men. But when told that his initials were FDR, retrieval of his name became easy.

Endel Tulving has performed numerous experiments demonstrating the power of providing proper retrieval cues. In one study (Tulving & Pearlstone, 1966) subjects read a list of category names (such as animals and fruits) along with one or more instances of the category (for example, horse and peach). The subjects' task was to remember only the instances, not the category names. Later, half the subjects were handed a blank sheet of paper while the other half were handed a sheet containing all the category names. All subjects had to write down as many instances from the original list as they could remember. As Figure 4-1 shows, subjects given the category names as cues recalled more instances. This was particularly

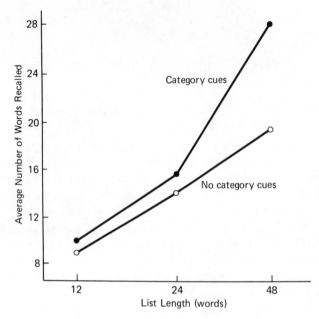

FIGURE 4–1.   Average number of words recalled as a function of list length in the Tulving-Pearlstone (1966) experiment. More words were recalled when category cues were provided than when they were not. (After Tulving & Pearlstone, 1966. Courtesy of Academic Press, Inc.)

true in the condition when subjects were given a list of 48 items, or 12 categories of four words each. Those who were given category cues recalled about 30 words on the average, but the control group recalled only about 20 words. At a later time, the control group was supplied with the category names, and these subjects were now able to recall about 28 words from the list. Those extra eight or so items must have been stored in the memory, but they could not be retrieved without a special retrieval cue. In other words, they were *available* in memory, but not *accessible*. The situation is analogous to that of a student who attempts to find a particular book in the library, only to discover that the card indicating its location is missing. The book is available, but it cannot be accessed. Providing the missing card, like providing the proper retrieval cue, is one of the best ways to facilitate retrieval.

Later work in Tulving's laboratory further revealed the power of the retrieval cue (Tulving & Thomson, 1971, 1973). There are circumstances in which a person can even fail to recognize a word he has recently learned, but, with the right retrieval cue, he can recall it. A typical experiment is illustrated in Figure 4-2. Subjects saw a list of word pairs, such as pretty-BLUE, in which the left-hand, lower-case word is the cue and the right-

Stage 1:
A subject learns a list of
paired words and must
remember the words
on the right

Cue words	To-be-remembered words
whistle	BALL
pretty	BLUE
noise	WIND
fruit	FLOWER
country	OPEN
	etc.

Stage 2:
The subject is shown a list
of words and is asked to free
associate to those words;
after free association the
subject circles any words
that he remembers as being
on the list he originally
learned

lake:	boat	cool	blue
eat:	food	fruit	flower
fast:	car	woman	race
soft:	down	bed	skin
clean:	bath	living	soap
night:	day	open	sky
		etc.	

Stage 3:
The subject is given the cue
words from the original list
and must write down the
corresponding to be
remembered words

country	*open*
fruit	_____
bath	_____
noise	_____
	etc.

FIGURE 4–2. A three-stage experiment by Tulving and Thomson (1973). (After Tulving and Thomson, 1973. Reprinted by permission of the author and American Psychological Association.)

hand, capitalized word is to be remembered later. After the capitalized words were studied, the subject performed a free association test in which he was given a different list of stimulus words, and had to write down a number of words that he thought of as associated with the stimulus words. If the subject wished to include in his free associations any recently seen words, he was allowed to do so. To give an example, suppose the subject had been given the italicized words on the left as stimuli, and he responded with the words on the right in his free association:

eat	food, fruit, flower, picnic, lunch
lake	boat, fish, swim, water, cold, blue
clean	bath, living, soap, mister, dirty

When the free association test was finished, the subject was asked to circle those words in his free association that he recognized as being on the list of previously memorized words. So, if he recognized *blue* on his free association responses to *lake* as having been a word he had memorized earlier, he would so indicate. Many previously memorized words were included in the free associations, but only about 25 percent of them were recognized as having been previously memorized. Thus, subjects performed poorly on the recognition task. However, when the subjects were subsequently shown the cue words from the original list and asked to recall the memorized words, over 60 percent of the memorized words were recalled. In other words, subjects *recalled* many words that they had failed to *recognize* moments earlier. Once again, retrieval cues are instrumental in eliciting a desired word from a subject. Here we have the unusual case in which a retrieval cue for a word is more effective than seeing the entire word itself spelled out.

TIP-OF-THE-TONGUE PHENOMENON

When you attempted to recall the name of the first president to run for a fourth term, perhaps there was a moment in which the name was almost there, you almost had it, but not quite. We say it is on the "tip of the tongue." Suddenly, "Franklin Roosevelt" rises to your consciousness. What sort of search and evaluation processes go on in the mind when this sort of thing happens to us?

This question motivated Brown and McNeill (1966) to develop a technique for producing the tip-of-the-tongue (TOT) state. They presented subjects with definitions for uncommon English words and instructed subjects to attempt to produce the proper word to fit the definition. For example, a subject might be given the definition "a navigational instrument used for measuring angular distances" in an attempt to get him to produce the word *sextant*. The definitions for other difficult words, such as *nepotism, ambergris, caduceus,* and *sampan,* were also used. Some definitions which may produce a tip-of-the-tongue state are presented in Table 4-1. (You might take a look at these definitions, first to give yourself a first-hand feeling for the TOT state and, second, just on the off chance that one of these definitions will appear on your Graduate Record Examination!)

Subjects indicated that a tip-of-the-tongue state had been produced by raising their hands. A graphic description of this mentally painful state has been provided by Brown and McNeill:

> . . . *the signs of it were unmistakable; he would appear to be in mild torment, something like the brink of a sneeze, and if he found the word his relief was considerable. While searching for the target, the subject told us all the words that came to his mind. He volunteered the information that some of them resembled the target in sound but not in meaning; others he was sure were similar in meaning but not in sound. The experimenter intruded on the subject's agony with two questions (a) How many syllables has the target word? (b) What is its first letter? . . .* (1966, p. 326)

TABLE 4–1. Some Definitions Used to Produce a Tip-of-the-Tongue State. (The Correct Words Are Given Below.)

1. A fanatical partisan; one who is carried away in his pursuit of a cause or object.
2. Lying on one's back, with the face upward.
3. Selecting, choosing doctrines or methods from various sources, systems, etc.
4. A conciliatory bribe, gift, advance, etc.
5. An instrument having 30 to 40 strings over a shallow, horizontal sounding box and played with picks and fingers.
6. A hiding place used by explorers for concealing or preserving provisions or implements.
7. To clear from alleged fault or guilt; to absolve, vindicate, acquit, or exonerate.

Words corresponding to definitions.

1.	Zealot	5.	Zither
2.	Supine	6.	Cache
3.	Eclectic	7.	Exculpate
4.	Sop		

Over 200 tip-of-the-tongue states were produced in the experiment. During the state, other words came to mind. Most often these words were similar in sound to the correct word (*secant* instead of *sextant, saipan* instead of *sampan*), but many were similar in meaning (*leucasis* instead of *caduceus*). Perhaps the reason that words tended to be similar in sound is because the subjects' task required that the word be pronounced. With both similar sound and similar meaning guesses, the subjects knew that these were not quite correct, but felt they were close. There were other patterns observed in the type of incorrect guesses that subjects produced; similar sounding words contained the same number of syllables as the correct word over 60 percent of the time, and the initial letter sound was guessed correctly over half of the time.

The TOT data show that partial information about both the sound and the meaning can be retrieved before complete access to the word is possible. (This, of course, runs counter to the alternative view that assumes that once a person locates an item in memory, the entire item becomes accessible—see Kintsch, 1970, for example.) When a person is in the TOT state, he can apparently retrieve bits of the sought-for item, but cannot gain access to all of it.

How must long-term memory be organized to permit TOT behavior? Brown and McNeill suggested first that a word is located in some location, and further that its location contains information both about its sound and about its meaning. For this reason, most words can be retrieved from LTM either by sound or by meaning. For example, I can give you the word *umbrella* and ask you for its meaning, or I can give you the meaning "item used for protection against rain" and ask you to give me the word. Stored with each word were thought to be associations, or marked pathways, to other words also located in LTM. Thus, when given a particular definition, a subject might come up with the target word or he might produce a word that meant something similar. For Brown and McNeill, then, LTM consisted of a large set of associated storage locations, with each location containing information related to a single word or a single fact. Since their initial investigation, perhaps hundreds of studies have been performed to shed light on how our general knowledge is structured and retrieved. Many major theories have been proposed.

Before turning to these theories, which will constitute one of the major topics in this chapter, consider briefly a very different approach to and analysis of the tip-of-the-tongue phenomenon.

Freud's Analysis of TOT

Sigmund Freud once told a story of how he strove to recall the name of the master artist who painted the imposing frescoes of the "Last Judgment" in the dome of Orvieto. Two names—Botticelli and Boltrafio, both well-known artists in their own right—continued to intrude on his thoughts. But, as Freud well recognized, neither was the creator of the "Last Judgment." The situation Freud describes thus fits well into what we have been discussing as the tip-of-the-tongue phenomenon.

Freud's tip-of-the-tongue state occurred while he was riding with a stranger in a carriage bound for Herzegovina, a region south of Bosnia in central Yugoslavia. The story goes as follows. Freud told the stranger that he knew of a doctor in whom Turkish patients placed a great deal of confidence. Whenever this particular doctor admitted that he could not save a patient, it was common for relatives of the patient to say, "Sir (Herr Doktor, in Freud's native German), what can I say. I know that if he could be saved, you would save him." During the conversation, Freud remembered that his doctor friend had also told him that Turks value sexual pleasure highly and appear to be more concerned about losing their sexual potency than about dying. Freud felt, however, that he could not express this thought in polite conversation with a stranger, which is perhaps understandable given the Victorian times. In addition, he felt uncomfortable thinking about the theme of death and sex, for he had recently heard, while visiting the town of Trafoi, that one of his former patients had committed suicide because of a prolonged, incurable sexual problem. So Freud switched the topic to traveling in Italy and it was at that time that he found himself unable to recall the creator of the "Last Judgment"—Signorelli.

Freud's own analysis of his tip-of-the-tongue state relied heavily on the concept of repression, or the conscious pushing out of awareness of uncomfortable thoughts. Freud wanted to forget about death and sexuality, thoughts which were connected with the words Trafoi and Herr Doctor. Thus he repressed those words. By association, he also repressed Signor, the Italian word for Herr or Sir. In attempting to recall the name of the artist, then, he picked up pieces from the conversation with his companion —*Bo* from the region, Bosnia, *elli* from the artist's name, and *traffio* from the town Trafoi. This combination of parts led to the compromise responses, Botticelli and Boltraffio, both of which were, of course, incorrect.

Comparing the approaches of Freud and of Brown and McNeill, an important distinction emerges. Freud was interested in studying individual people, and from these case histories he hoped to establish general principles. Brown and McNeill, on the other hand, utilized statistics in order to establish those general principles of behavior. Many of Freud's ideas are compatible with the principles established in the laboratory, but Freud's emphasis was different. Freud was much more interested in the motives and needs, the experiences and fantasies of each individual whom he observed (including himself). Most experimental psychologists have not been concerned with the individual; rather data are collected from large numbers of subjects, and theories are constructed that are meant to encompass almost all human beings. We now examine some of those theories.

SEMANTIC MEMORY

EPISODIC VERSUS SEMANTIC MEMORY

In 1972, Endel Tulving's *Organization of Memory* was published, one chapter of which articulated an important distinction between *episodic* and *semantic* memory. In Tulving's words:

Episodic memory receives and stores information about temporally dated episodes or events, and temporal-spatial relations among these events. . . . (p. 385)

Semantic memory is the memory necessary for the use of language. It is a mental thesaurus, organized knowledge a person possesses about words and other verbal symbols, their meaning and referents, about relations among them, and about rules, formulas, and algorithms for the manipulation of these symbols, concepts, and relations. (p. 386)

In other words, episodic memory contains information about our personal life experiences; it contains information which is associated with a particular time or place. The information that I was in Boston on my last birthday is episodic, as is the information that the words *horse* and *clock* were presented to me in a psychology experiment last Tuesday. Semantic memory contains information that is not associated with a particular time or place, such as the fact that a horse is a type of animal.

Tulving conceived of episodic and semantic memory as two information-processing systems that (1) selectively receive information from perceptual and cognitive systems, (2) retain various aspects of that information, and (3) transmit that information when it is needed. The two systems are thought to differ in terms of the type of information that is stored, the conditions and consequences of retrieval, and possibly their vulnerability to interference.

Tulving never doubted that the two systems would be heavily dependent upon one another. Clearly this interdependence exists, as the following situation highlights. Suppose that you witness an automobile accident that is highly complex and sudden. You are then asked a series of questions about the accident. Although this is an "episodic" situation, the knowledge contained in semantic memory influences your memory and the way you answer questions about the accident. This was demonstrated in a recent experiment (Loftus & Zanni, 1975) in which college students watched a film of a traffic accident and then answered questions about it. Some of the students were asked questions containing an indefinite article (for example, "Did you see a broken headlight?"), whereas other students were asked questions containing a definite article (for example, "Did you see the broken headlight?"). There was no broken headlight in the film, and yet subjects who were asked the "Did you see *the* . . ." question produced many more *yes* responses, indicating false recognition of an object that did not exist.

The reason this happens is simple: When asked a question using the definite article, a person who is familiar with the semantic rules governing the use of *the* is likely to infer that the object was, in fact, present. After all, we use the definite article when we are referring to a particular object, and we use the indefinite article when we refer to any member of a class of objects. This information about the use of the words *the* and *a* is contained in most people's semantic memories. (Our semantic memories of course contain information about traffic accidents in general.) The fact that people will answer a question about something they have witnessed differently depending on how the question is worded illustrates something important: A person's semantic knowledge can influence his report of an event he has actually experienced. The indication is that semantic memory and episodic memory depend highly on each other, a relationship that is nicely illustrated in Figure 4-3.

Because previous chapters have concentrated heavily on episodic memory, the rest of this chapter is about semantic memory. It focuses on the

Episodic memory

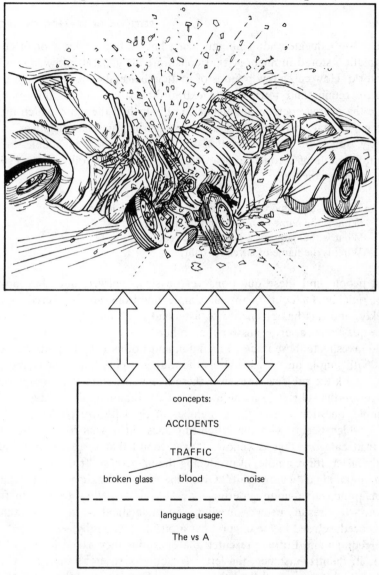

Semantic memory

FIGURE 4–3. Episodic and semantic memory are interdependent.

structure of the information contained in our semantic memory and on the way in which we retrieve and use that information.

The well-educated adult human being has perhaps billions of pieces of information stored in memory that constitute his general knowledge about the world. How can a few pounds of matter that make up the human brain acquire, retain, and retrieve this extraordinary amount of information? While the average person might not be able to find the word which means "a navigational instrument used for measuring angular distances" very quickly, much of the information in our memories is available to use within a couple of seconds of search time. Answer the following questions as quickly as you can:

1. What is the name of a state beginning with the letter M?
2. What is the name of a state in the Northeast?
3. What is the name of a fruit that is red?
4. What is the name of a yellow fruit?

Most people find these questions very easy to answer, and they answer them quickly. Of course, not all simple questions are answered equally quickly, and this has given rise to a second question: What factors make some questions easier to answer than others?

To investigate these issues, Freedman and Loftus (1971) presented subjects with simple questions such as the four just posed, and measured how long it took the subjects to answer these questions. Note that the questions all require the subject to name a member of some delimited category. For example, question 1 asks for a member of the category of states (of the U.S.) which begins with the letter M. Question 4 asks for a member of the fruit category that is yellow. It was found that subjects were significantly faster, for example, in producing the name of a "fruit that is yellow" than in naming a "yellow fruit." Given that natural English language habits favor an adjective–noun ordering—we talk about yellow fruits, not fruits yellow—this result seemed puzzling. To understand it we must examine the procedure used in the experiment a bit more carefully.

Freedman and Loftus presented the questions they asked in one of two ways. In the first instance, the letter (or other restrictor) was shown first, followed by a pause and then the category. For example, the letter M was shown, followed soon afterward by the category *state*. The subject could respond with Minnesota or Massachusetts, among other possibilities. Reaction time was measured from the time "state" appeared until the subject made his response. When the letter restrictor came first, as soon as the category *state* appeared, the subject had to do three things:

1. Find the place in memory where information about *states* is stored—that is, "enter" his *states* category
2. Retrieve the relevant information from the category
3. Produce a response

Suppose that we let the time to enter the category (step 1) be called t_1. Further, we refer to the time to find an instance (step 2) as t_2 and the time to produce a response (step 3) as k. Then the total time to produce a correct response (RT_1) when given a stimulus such as "M–state" is:

$$RT_1 = t_1 + t_2 + k$$

Now let us look at the second method of presentation Freedman and Loftus used, namely, presenting the category before the letter. In this mode, *state* would be presented, followed by a pause and then the letter M. Reaction time for these items was measured from the presentation of M until a response was made. When the category is presented first, however, it is possible for a subject to enter the category (step 1) during the interval between *state* and M. In other words, it is possible for him to complete step 1 *before* his reaction time is measured. Thus, the time to complete step 1, or t_1, is not included in the total measured reaction time, which then becomes:

$$RT_2 = t_2 + k$$

We are now in a position to obtain an estimate of the duration of t_1, the time to enter the category, by a simple substraction—$RT_2 - RT_1$. The value for t_1 obtained by Freedman and Loftus was 250 msec, or a quarter of a second. The existence of this observable time difference led these investigators to postulate a two-step theory of retrieval, support for which has been observed in subsequent experiments.

One Retrieval Influences Another

If you were asked for the product of 8×13, it might take you a few seconds to produce the correct answer, 104. But, if a couple of minutes later you were again asked for the product of 8×13, you could probably produce the answer much more quickly than you did the first time. The answer is somehow more accessible; in this case you might not have to go through the same calculations again. Similarly if you were asked for the name of the psychologist who performed the classic experiments on the sensory register, you might think a moment before responding "George Sperling." If asked a few minutes later, the name would be readily available. It is evident, then, that we can very quickly find a piece of information that we have recently produced.

It is also apparent that a piece of information is easier to produce if we have recently retrieved a *related* piece. Collins and Quillian (1970), for example, presented sentences such as "A canary is a bird" and subjects determined whether they were true or false. Prior exposure to one sentence, it was found, reduced the reaction time to a second sentence in which the same noun appeared as the subject. For example, prior exposure to "A canary is a bird" reduced the time subjects took to verify other sentences about canaries, such as "A canary is yellow."

This sort of facilitation has also been experimentally observed when subjects are first asked to name one member of a category and soon thereafter a different member of the same category (Loftus, 1973; Loftus & Loftus, 1974). You yourself may have exhibited this phenomenon when you were asked earlier in this chapter to name a red fruit and then a yellow one (although you would probably not have been aware of it since the total reaction times are so short). To use one of our previous examples, subjects are asked to respond first to "state–M" and then to "state–C." The second and all later responses usually follow much more quickly than the first. Why should this be?

One possible explanation is that the first retrieval activates one or more memory locations, in other words, increases the accessibility of one or more locations. Information retrieval from these activated locations would then be easier when the second retrieval is attempted. Thus, presentation of the category *fruit* apparently activates not only the memory location representing a specific sub-category (for example, red fruit) but also such nearby locations as "yellow fruit," "green fruit," and so on. Since locations cannot

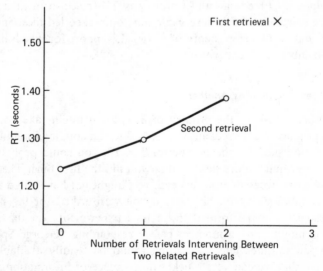

FIGURE 4–4. (After Loftus, 1973. Courtesy of University of Illinois Press)

remain activated forever, it is reasonable to assume that this greater accessibility decays rather rapidly. This leads to the prediction that as we increase the time between the two retrievals, or we increase the number of different, unrelated retrievals, we should reduce the facilitating effect. Figure 4-4 confirms this prediction. The figure displays data obtained in an experiment in which subjects were instructed to produce a member of a category and, after zero, one, or two intervening retrievals, were asked for a different member of the same category. Subjects asked to produce a response from a category not previously elicited took an average of 1.52 seconds. By contrast, however, they produced that same member in 1.21 seconds if they had named a different member on the previous trial; in 1.29 seconds if there was an intervening, unrelated response; and in 1.38 seconds if there were two intervening responses. These results show clearly that if we ask a person to name a member of a category and soon thereafter he names a different member, facilitation occurs. This facilitation declines gradually as we increase the time or number of intervening items between the two retrievals, indicating that the memory locations are becoming deactivated.

Retrieval and Structure

We have just presented some data that are illustrative of how we retrieve very simple, well-learned information from our store of general knowledge. However, before we can postulate a complete theory about how this information is retrieved, we must have some idea about how it is structured in memory. An analogy will make this point clear. Suppose you are spending the weekend at the home of a friend who will be out of town. Before leaving, your friend tells you to help yourself to whatever you need. Getting ready for bed, you realize that you need a towel to dry your face and some sheets with which to make up the bed. You go to retrieve these things from the linen closet and discover that it contains only old rags. Disturbed at the prospect that you must go to bed with a wet face and sleep under scratchy blankets with no sheets, you stop at the refrigerator for a snack. Inside, you see a pile of sheets. Your friend neglected to tell you that he likes a cold bed and therefore keeps his sheets in the refrigerator. (As long as this fictional story has been designed to illustrate a point, you may speculate on where the friend kept his towels and why old rags filled the linen closet.) The point of this analogy is that in order to retrieve something we need to know how it is stored. Similarly, in order to theorize about a retrieval process, we need to know something about the structure from which we are retrieving. We turn now to some models of semantic memory and see how both structure and retrieval are accomplished within them.

In this section we will discuss three models of semantic memory, each of which focuses on the representation and retrieval of word meanings. Taken together, these models illustrate well the kinds of assumptions that theorists have made about semantic memory. We should mention that these are only some of the more recent ideas about the organization of semantic memory. A stimulus for much of this work can be found by going back to the early 1950s when Bousfield (1953) described a phenomenon called *category clustering.* In Bousfield's experiments, subjects studied a 60-word list composed of 15 members of each of four categories. The categories of animals, names, professors, and vegetables were used. Bousfield found that even when the words were presented randomly, subjects recalled them in clusters according to category. This finding, as well as others obtained during this period, indicated that the memory does organize information in some way and that people draw upon this organization when they learn and recall a new list of words.

Network Models

In a paper entitled "Retrieval Time from Semantic Memory," Collins and Quillian (1969) postulated that the items stored in semantic memory are arranged in a giant network and connected to each other by links. A portion of such a network is shown in Figure 4-5. The concepts in this system are hierarchically organized into logically nested subordinate–superordinate relations. Thus, the superordinate of *canary* is *bird,* and the superordinate of *bird* is *animal.* The system is thought to be economical in the sense that a property characterizing a particular class of objects is

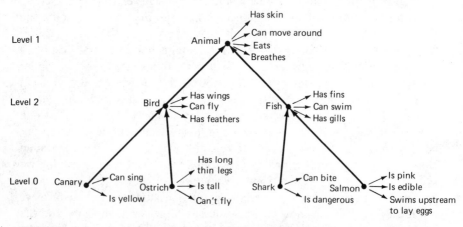

FIGURE 4–5. A portion of a hierarchically organized memory structure. (After Collins & Quillian, 1969. Courtesy of Academic Press, Inc.)

assumed to be stored only at the place in the hierarchy that corresponds to that class. This assumption has been called, not surprisingly, the assumption of "cognitive economy." To illustrate, a property that characterizes all birds, such as the fact that they have wings, is stored only at *bird*. It is not stored with each of the different types of birds, even though they all typically possess wings.

If information is organized into a hierarchical structure, how is it retrieved from that structure? To answer this question, Collins and Quillian presented subjects with simple statements, such as "A canary can sing," "A canary is a bird," "A canary is pink," or "A canary is a fish." The subjects had to decide whether the statement was true or false, and their reaction time (*RT*) was measured. The subject in each statement was always a concrete noun from the lowest level of a hierarchy similar to the one depicted in Figure 4-5.

All statements presented to the subjects were then classified according to the semantic level at which the information needed to answer the item is stored. For example, for "A canary eats," the information "eats" is stored with *animal,* two levels from *canary.* Similarly, the information "has wings" is stored one level away, while "can sing" is stored zero levels away. Collins and Quillian predicted that subjects would take longer to answer questions when the information needed was located two levels away than when it was located only one or zero levels away. This prediction is borne out, as can be seen in Figure 4-6. Why do subjects take longer to retrieve information that is several levels away? Collins and Quillian's explanation was simple. In order to determine whether "A canary is yellow" the subject must first enter the level in memory that corresponds to *canary* and here is stored some information, such as the fact that canaries are yellow. Thus, the question can be answered relatively quickly. To determine whether "A canary can fly," the subject still enters memory at *canary* but does not find any information there concerning whether canaries can fly or not. Because a canary is a bird, however, the subject moves up a level to *birds* where the information he needs is stored. Thus, since a canary is a bird and birds can fly, the question can now be answered in the affirmative. Of course, the extra step of moving up the hierarchy to the bird level takes time, and thus the question takes somewhat longer to answer. A similar analysis explains why it takes people even longer to determine that a canary eats. This statement requires that the subject move up an additional level in the hierarchy to *animal* in order to find the needed information. Because a canary is a bird, and a bird is an animal, and animals eat, it can be concluded that a canary eats.

A closer inspection of Figure 4-6 reveals that it takes on average somewhere between 75 and 90 msec longer to respond to a level 1 statement than to a level 0 statement, and an additional 75 to 90 msec to respond

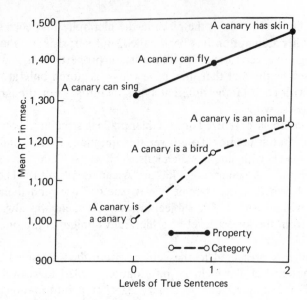

FIGURE 4-6. Reaction time taken to answer questions about various nouns and their properties and category membership. (After Collins & Quillian, 1969. Courtesy of Academic Press, Inc.)

to a level 2 statement. This may represent the time to travel from one level of the hierarchy to the next level. Another inference from the data is that it takes about 200 milliseconds to search through the properties stored with a particular concept. This inference is based on the approximately 200 msec difference in times between those statements which ask about properties (for example, "a canary can fly") and those which ask about category membership (for example, "a canary is a bird").

OTHER NETWORK MODELS.   The hierarchical network model proposed by Collins and Quillian is perhaps the best known model of semantic memory. Since its initial publication, other, far more ambitious efforts in this domain have appeared. In fact many of them are really large-scale theories of meaning and memory (such as those by Anderson & Bower, 1973; Kintsch, 1974; and Norman & Rumelhart, 1975), including much more detail and encompassing far more data than the original network model we have just discussed. For example, in the model developed by Anderson and Bower, called "HAM" for Human Associative Memory, long-term memory is viewed as a vast collection of locations and associations among them. However, the basic component of the model is a "proposition," an entity which is akin to an English sentence but much more abstract. Propositions are envisioned as representing not only linguistic information, but also visual scenes and other sorts of nonlinguistic information. HAM and the other large-scale theories are extremely complex, and will not be discussed here. They have already been systematically reviewed by Anderson (1976).

EVALUATION OF THE COLLINS AND QUILLIAN MODEL. The original Collins and Quillian paper stimulated a plethora of investigations on semantic memory. The modified Collins and Quillian model (1972b) provided the first detailed description of how information is represented and retrieved. As Smith (1976) points out, it was sufficiently attractive to be adopted by other semantic-memory researchers (among others, Freedman & Loftus, 1971) and even incorporated wholesale into a more general theory of language comprehension (Rumelhart, Lindsay & Norman, 1972).

However, evidence against its core assumptions soon began to mount. The assumption that noun concepts are organized hierarchically was crushed by studies in which statements involving immediate superordinate concepts sometimes took longer to verify than those involving distant superordinates (see Rips, Shoben, & Smith, 1973). According to the original model, a person should verify the statement "A collie is a mammal" faster than "A collie is an animal," since in a logical network *mammal* would be closer to *collie* than *animal.* Yet people do not. Similarly, people take longer to verify that "a cantaloupe is a melon" than to verify that "a cantaloupe is a fruit," even though *melon* is logically closer to *cantaloupe* in a semantic hierarchy.

The cognitive economy assumption also fell on hard times with the experimental results of Conrad (1972). Collins and Quillian's assumption was:

Information true of birds in general (e.g., can fly, have wings and have feathers) need not be stored with the memory node for each separate kind of bird. Instead, the fact that "A canary can fly" can be inferred by finding that a canary is a bird and that birds can fly. By storing generalizations in this way, the amount of space required for storage is minimized. (1972a, p. 118)

Conrad tested this assumption by choosing level 3 properties and varying the level of the subject of the statement. (Recall that Collins and Quillian used level 0 subjects, and varied the level of the property.) For example, she used "A shark can move," "A fish can move" and "An animal can move," which use increasingly higher-level subjects. If "can move" is stored only with *animal,* it should take subjects longer to verify "A fish can move" than "An animal can move" and longer still to verify that "A shark can move." Conrad failed to find a difference in reaction times that corresponded to the number of levels separating a subject and a property.

In another study, Conrad asked subjects to describe a canary, a bird, an animal, and other concepts to be used later on. She then tabulated the frequency with which various properties were mentioned. She found that the properties frequently associated with canary (such as its being yellow) were those presumed to be stored directly with *canary*. She thus hypothesized that *property frequency* rather than hierarchical distance is what determines retrieval time, and she conducted an experiment to test this hypothesis. In her experiment both noun-property association (or frequency) and hierarchical distance were manipulated. She found that verification time decreased as the associative relation between the noun and property became stronger, but it did not vary consistently with the hierarchical distance (in terms of number of levels) between the noun and the property. Figure 4-7 illustrates her results. Note that strong associates, such as in "An orange is edible" are verified quickly even though orange and edible were presumed by Collins and Quillian to be separated by two levels.

Another problem with Collins and Quillian's model is that it does not readily explain how statements are disconfirmed. How does a person decide that an anteater does not have pages? In their 1972a paper, Collins

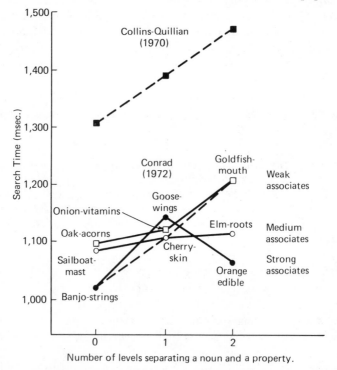

FIGURE 4–7. Search time depends on the strength of association between a noun and a property, and not on the number of levels separating the noun and property. (Data of Conrad, 1972 are compared with those of Collins and Quillian, 1969. Courtesy of the American Psychological Association & Academic Press, Inc.)

and Quillian introduced the *extraneous-path hypothesis* to account for dis-confirmations. It states that when a subject finds a promising clue, he will check that clue out, which, of course, will consume time. If asked whether "a canary is blue" he might note that some birds are blue, and be slowed by this "extraneous path." The statement "a collie is blue" would not produce the same problem since there are no dogs which are blue. The extraneous-path hypothesis was tested in an experiment in which subjects were timed while they responded to plausible false statements such as "A tiger has a mane" or "A St. Bernard is a cat" and implausible false statements such as "A leopard is a snail" or "An elephant has a bill." The plausible statements are the ones which might cause the subject to trace out an extraneous path to check out a promising lead. For example, "A tiger has a mane" might be slowed by the clue that lions have manes and tigers are similar to lions. Collins and Quillian's results are shown in Figure 4–8. Note that overall implausible statements are disconfirmed much more quickly than plausible ones. Furthermore, the implausible category statements were rejected about 300 msec faster than the plausible ones, whereas the property statements were rejected about 100 msec faster. This experiment constituted at least a first step toward understanding how false state-

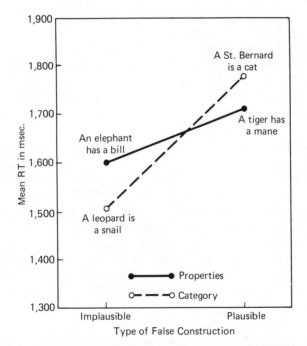

FIGURE 4–8. Subjects are faster to disconfirm both category and property statements that are implausible than to disconfirm plausible statements. (After Collins & Quillian, 1972a. Courtesy of John Wiley & Sons, Inc.)

ments are disconfirmed, but much work remained to be done. The fact that Collins and Quillian did not have a tidy theory to account for disconfirmation is not as serious a criticism as the fact, discussed previously, that ample counterevidence to the specific assumptions of the model was accumulating. Some of the charges were responded to in a later paper by Collins and Loftus (1975), to which the interested reader can turn.

Set-Theoretic Models

One alternative to the network models of semantic memory has been termed the set theoretic model, because it treats semantic memory as if it consisted of a huge number of sets of elements. One set may include all instances of dogs; thus collie, boxer, and sheepdog would all be members of this set. Sets can also include attributes of a concept, for example, the information that dogs bite, bark, wag their tails, and occasionally fetch sticks. Similarly another set might include exemplars of the *bird* category, such as robins, sparrows and parrots; while another set includes the attributes of birds, such as the fact that they have wings and feathers. In short, concepts are represented in semantic memory as sets of information.

A two-stage model of Meyer (1970), called the predicate intersections model, is an example of a set-theoretic model. Here Meyer assumes that memory consists of sets of attributes. Thus, *collie* is represented by a set of the defining attributes of a collie and *dog* by the defining attributes of dogs. To decide whether a collie is a dog, a person must decide whether every attribute included in *dog* is also an attribute included in *collie*. Of course, the process for this example would be very rapid indeed, for we are hardly aware of making a great number of decisions when we verify a simple statement such as "A collie is a dog."

Before elaborating on the role of these sets of attributes in Meyer's model, consider the task faced by his experimental subjects. The subject sits in front of a display screen where he is shown sentence frames such as "All ——— are ———" or "Some ——— are ———," depending on which experimental condition he is in. A few moments later the blank spaces are filled in with the names of two semantic categories, which we will refer to as S and P (for subject and predicate). For example, S might be collies and P might be dogs, resulting in "All collies are dogs" for some subjects and "Some collies are dogs" for others. The subject responds to these sentences by pressing one of two buttons to indicate whether they are true or false. Before reading further, can you predict whether "All" statements or "Some" statements would be faster, and why?

If you predicted that "Some" statements would lead to faster responses than statements using "All," you correctly predicted Meyer's result. What model can account for this finding? Meyer's predicate intersections model,

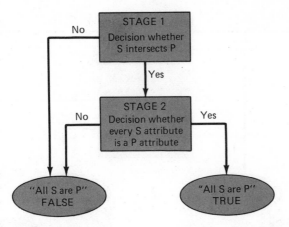

FIGURE 4–9. Meyer's two-stage model for verifying or disconfirming "All" statements. (After Meyer, 1970. Courtesy of Academic Press, Inc.)

involving two stages, does a reasonable job of explaining the Some-All difference as well as other more complex observed results. The model is shown in Figure 4-9. For statements of the form "All collies are dogs," the subject first looks through the names of all the categories that overlap, or intersect, or have some members in common with the P category (*dog,* in this case). In doing so the subject might find boxers and collies, but also animals and living things, among other possibilities. All of these have some members that are also dogs. If the search through these names produces an instance which is also a member of the S category, the two categories are said to intersect, and the first stage of the process ends with a "match." The search might not produce a match for the S category, however, and the subject would produce a negative response. "All S are P" would be disconfirmed at the end of the first stage.

Given that some member of S intersects P, the second stage of the process is then executed. At this stage the subject must decide whether every attribute of the P category is also an attribute of the S category. In our example, to decide whether "All collies are dogs," a subject must determine that the two categories intersect and then determine that every attribute of *dog* is also an attribute of *collie.*

Turning now to Figure 4-10, we can see what the model predicts will happen with "Some" statements. These involve only the decision as to whether the S category intersects the P category, that is, whether collies and dogs have at least one member in common. If so, the subject can respond *true,* for some collies (at least one) are indeed dogs. If not, the subject responds *false.* It should be clear why the model predicts that "All" statements take longer to verify than "Some" statements: "Some" state-

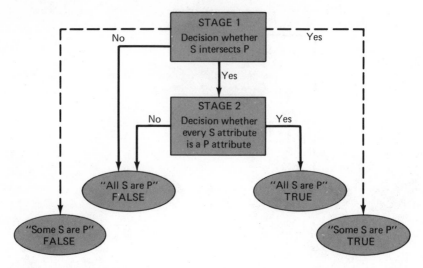

FIGURE 4–10. Meyer's two-stage model for verifying and confirming "Some" statements and "ALL" statements. (After Meyer, 1970. Courtesy of Academic Press, Inc.)

ments require only one stage to be executed for verification whereas "All" statements usually require two.

Meyer's model makes another prediction having to do with disjoint statements, where the subject and predicate concepts denote mutually exclusive sets. "Some collies are gems" and "Some collies are stones" are examples of disjoint statements. The two examples we have cited share a subject term but differ in their predicate terms; further, *stones* is a larger category than *gems*. According to Meyer's model, both statements will be disconfirmed in the first stage; by extension of the theory, however, the search for the "stone" sentence should take longer than that for the "gem" sentence—since there are more intersecting categories to be searched when the predicate category is large rather than small. The reasoning is that with "stones" one must search through everything required by "gems" (for example, rubies, diamonds, emeralds) plus all the non-gem stones. Meyer (1970) performed an experiment to test what he termed the category-size effect. In the experiment, the category size of the predicate, P, was manipulated. Although it is usually difficult to measure the exact size of a category, Meyer got around the problem by using relative category size. That is, if one category is contained in another, then the latter must be larger than the former. This is the case with dogs and animals, with gems and stones, and so on. Meyer found the time to respond either *true* or *false* increased with the category size of P. Of course, Collins and Quillian (1969) also observed a category-size effect ("A collie is a dog" is verified faster than "A collie is an animal"), but they explained their results in terms of differential search times through a semantic network. For all investigators, the category-size effect became an accepted fact of life, an effect to be explained by anyone building a model of semantic memory.

EVALUATION OF THE PREDICATE INTERSECTIONS MODEL. On the positive side of the coin, the predicate intersections model had an edge over the Collins and Quillian network model in that the former more easily dealt with disconfirmations. In Meyer's model, "Some" statements are disconfirmed after a single stage whereas "All" statements may require that both stages be executed. For Collins and Quillian the category-size effects for false statements posed a much greater problem. A second plus for Meyer's model is that it was subsequently successfully extended to account for the verification of statements containing negatives, such as "Some collies are not stones" (see Meyer, 1975).

A serious problem for the model, however, is presented by recent findings that run counter to its critical predictions. We have seen an example of one such prediction, namely, that "Some collies are dogs" will be confirmed faster than "All collies are dogs." In Meyer's experiment, the "Some" statements were presented in one block of trials and the "All" statements in a different block of trials. When Rips (1975) randomly intermixed "Some" and "All" statements rather than presenting them in separate blocks, the advantage of "Some" over "All" statements, in terms of reaction time, disappeared. The fact that Meyer's model cannot explain the disappearance of this critical effect seriously discredits it.

Another difficulty with the model is that like the original Collins and Quillian model it has no easy way of explaining why some instances of a category can be verified faster than others. That is to say, why are people faster to verify that "a robin is a bird" than to verify that "a chicken is a bird"? This result has been observed often enough to know it is reliable (among others, Rips, Shoben & Smith, 1973; Rosch, 1974). Any model which follows the logic of set relations and which makes no differentiation among members of a category will certainly have difficulty with this observation.

One final difficulty with the model arises from our natural language use of "hedges." Hedges are linguistic modifiers that are used to qualify statements that we make about things we encounter in the world. "Strictly speaking" and "technically speaking" are hedges. "Technically speaking, a chicken is a bird" illustrates the use of a hedge in a sentence. It means something like "A chicken isn't a very good example of a bird, but it actually is a bird." "Loosely speaking, a bat is a bird" is another hedge, which means something akin to "A bat is a little like a bird, but it is not really a bird." How can the set-theoretic model explain our easy use of such hedges? The bat category and the bird category have no members in common, no overlap, no intersection; if Meyer's model is correct, how could anyone verify a hedged statement such as "Loosely speaking, a bat is a bird"? Some of these considerations led to the proposal of the feature-comparison model to which we now turn.

The Feature-Comparison Model

Like the set-theoretic model, the feature-comparison model proposed by Smith, Shoben, and Rips (1974) assumes that the meaning of any item in semantic memory can be represented as a set of semantic features. These are thought to vary continuously in the degree to which they define category membership. At one extreme there are features which are essential to the meaning of the item, and these are known as *defining features*. At the other extreme, there are features that are not essential, but are descriptive of the item. These are referred to as *characteristic features*. Although the features are thought to vary continuously in their degree of "defining-ness," we can select an arbitrary cutoff point to separate the defining features from the less important characteristic features. As we shall see, the feature-comparison model gives greater emphasis to the defining features.

Using the word *robin* to illustrate these two kinds of features, we single out the defining features that robins are living, they have feathers and wings, and they also have red breasts, since these characteristics must be present. Of course, robins are also undomesticated and harmless, and they like to perch in trees. These features are associated with robins, but they are not necessary to define the concept. When a subject is asked to decide whether an instance is a member of a category (for example, whether a

Concepts		
	Robin	Bird
Defining features	Is living Has feathers Has a red breast — — —	Is living Has features — — — —
Characteristic features	Flys Perches in trees Is undomesticated Is smallish — —	Flys — — — — —

FIGURE 4–11.   The meaning of a concept is defined in terms of semantic features. The higher on the list a feature is, the more essential it is for defining the concept. (After Smith, Shoben, and Rips, 1974. Reprinted by permission of the author and American Psychological Association.)

robin is a bird), the feature-comparison model assumes that the sets of features corresponding to the instance and the category are partitioned into two subsets corresponding to the defining and characteristic features. Figure 4-11 gives an example of this partitioning for *robin* and *bird*. Note the difference in features between a category name such as *robin* and its superordinate, *bird*. Since the superordinate is more abstract and general, it will have fewer defining features; or, conversely, in addition to all the defining features of *bird, robin* will have some of its own unique ones. Thus, the more general the category, the fewer defining features it will have.

In an attempt to provide experimental evidence for the notion of semantic features, Rips et al. (1973) collected subjects' ratings of how closely related each of several instances was to its category name. For example, subjects rated how closely related *chicken, duck,* and *robin* were to each other and to their superordinate, *bird*. If two items are closely related, it can be said that there is a small distance between them. Very sophisticated computer programs (for example, a "multidimensional scaling program") exist which can transform subjects' ratings into actual distances. These distances can then be plotted in a two-dimensional graph format which represents a subject's "cognitive" space.

Consider the two-dimensional spaces derived from subjects' ratings of items in the *bird* and *mammal* categories (see Figure 4-12.) It is assumed that when subjects initially rated the closeness of various concepts, they used the semantic features of the concepts that were contained in memory.

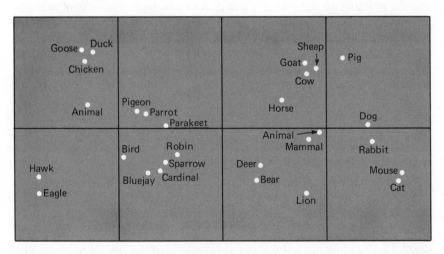

FIGURE 4–12. Two-dimensional spaces derived from subjects' ratings of the relatedness of members of the categories birds (left) and mammals (right). (From Rips, Shoben, & Smith, 1973. Courtesy of Academic Press, Inc.)

The more features that two concepts had in common, the greater the judged relatedness. This being the case, an examination of the two-dimensional spaces should reveal the semantic features that subjects used in making their relatedness judgments. When Rips et al. examined the *bird* space in Figure 4-12 they noted that such large birds as hawks and eagles were at one end of the horizontal axis whereas the small birds were at the other end. Similarly in the *mammal* space, deer and bear and other large mammals are at one end while small animals such as mice and rabbits appear at the other end. The vertical dimension in both the *bird* and *mammal* spaces seems to reflect the extent to which the animals preyed upon others. It was thus termed the "predacity" dimension. Wild mammals are at the bottom whereas farm animals are at the top. Similarly predatory birds like hawks were separated from tame birds such as ducks and chickens. The consistency of the dimensions in the *bird* and *mammal* spaces has been used to support the notion that these dimensions indicate something about semantic features that subjects are using in their relatedness judgments. It appears that the relatedness judgments were based on semantic features dealing with the size and predacity of the creatures being compared.

USING THE FEATURE MODEL.   How does a person decide whether a robin is a bird? The process of verifying whether an instance is a member of some particular category is shown in Figure 4-13. Like Meyer's predicate intersection model, this is a two-stage model. The first stage involves a comparison of both the defining and characteristic features of the instance and the category to determine the degree to which the two sets of features are similar. If the two sets are highly similar, the subject responds *true*. If the two sets of features have very little correspondence or very low similarly, the subject can respond *false* immediately. But, if there is an intermediate level of similarity between the two sets of features, a second stage must be executed. In this second stage, the subject compares only the defining features of the instance and the category. If all of the defining features of the category are also defining features of the instance, then a *true* response can be made. If all of the features do not match, the statement is false.

It must still be determined how well the feature-comparison model accounts for the findings in the semantic memory literature. We consider several major findings. First, it has been shown that some instances of a category are verified faster than others. More typical instances (of, say, *birds*) such as robins are responded to faster than less typical ones, such as chickens, a phenomenon which has been termed the *typicality effect*. The feature-comparison model explains this effect by assuming that if the instance to be verified is highly typical of the category, then the two will share a large number of both defining and characteristic features. During

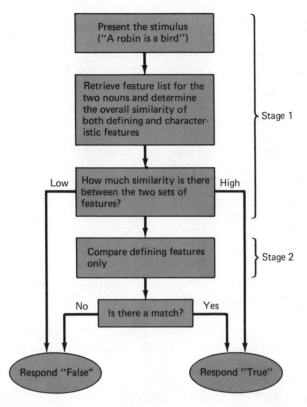

FIGURE 4-13. The feature-comparison model for the verification of such statements as "A robin is a bird." (After Smith, Shoben, & Rips, 1974. Reprinted by permission of the author and American Psychological Association.)

Stage 1 it will be discovered that the instance and the category have a great number of overlapping features, and thus the subject can make an immediate response without executing Stage 2. Instances which are atypical, on the other hand, will not have much overlap with the category in terms of characteristic features. For these instances, Stage 2 will need to be executed, and the time to respond will accordingly be longer. In short, typical instances are verified faster because they may require only Stage 1 processing, whereas atypical instances require the execution of two stages.

The feature-comparison model can also explain the category-size effect; or the finding that subjects can verify "A canary is a bird" faster than they can verify "A canary is an animal." If one simply assumes that the features of *canary* overlap more with those of its immediate superordinate *bird* than with those of its less immediate superordinate, *animal,* the category-size effect reduces to a relatedness effect. In the *bird* case, Stage 2 processing is more likely to be omitted, and this causes RT to be quicker. According to this reasoning if one could find a large category that was more related to *canary* than a smaller one, subjects would be faster with the larger category. This appears to be the case when we compare reaction times to "A dog is a mammal" and "A dog is an animal." From the two-dimensional *mammal* space in Figure 4-12 we see that *dog* is more related to *animal,* and, as we have shown, subjects are quicker to verify that a dog is an animal. In other words, it may be relatedness and not category size that counts. In fact the effects of both typicality and category size are thought to result from the same mechanism—overall number of features in common between the instance and the category.

The model can also account for some of the more perplexing results that have been observed with false statements. "A table is a bird" can be disconfirmed more quickly than "A bat is a bird." In general, it takes less time to disconfirm a statement if the instance and category are completely unrelated than if they have some relation to each other (Rips, 1975; Smith et al., 1974). The feature-comparison model handles this finding with the simple idea that unrelated statements can be disconfirmed by the first stage whereas the related statement needs two stages for disconfirmation.

In addition to doing a reasonably good job at accounting for both the category-size and typicality effects, and for false statements, the feature-comparison model can also handle the fact that we might agree with the hedged statement, "Loosely speaking, a bat is a bird," whereas we would not want to agree flatly that "A bat is a bird." The phrase "loosely speaking" indicates that the instance which follows possesses many of the characteristic features of the category. Bats possess many characteristic features of birds. But, when it comes to defining features, this similarity disappears. The defining features of the instance are not equivalent to those of the category. A person who hears "Loosely speaking, a bat is a bird" and is asked whether he would agree with this statement, executes a two-stage retrieval process. In the first stage, he determines that bats and birds do possess many features in common, and in the second stage he determines that bats do not possess all the defining features of birds. Consequently, the person should find it reasonable to agree that "Loosely speaking, a bat is a bird," because many of the characteristic features are held in common. He would not be likely to agree with the flat statement, "A bat is a bird," because, if he is knowledgeable, he relies on the fact that the defining features of the two concepts do not completely match. In a typical reaction time experiment, subjects are under a good deal of time pressure and will occasionally agree with the statement "A bat is a bird." Why does this happen? The explanation is that when pressured, subjects will occasionally omit Stage 2 and make a fast *true* response on the basis of Stage 1 processing. This is expected since Stage 1 processing indicated a large overall number of overlapping features between bats and birds.

"Technically speaking, a chicken is a bird." This statement illustrates another hedge in use, and is one most people would confirm. The hedge is handled by the model by assuming that "technically speaking" is used when an instance has the defining features of the category but not very many of the characteristic features of that category. A chicken is certainly a bird, since it possesses the defining features of birds. It has wings, it has a beak, etc. However, it does not have the characteristic features of a bird (that is, it doesn't fly or sing; it's much larger than average). Thus, it is a bird, technically speaking. Another example that has been bandied about is this: "Esther Williams is a regular fish." Can you explain how the feature-comparison model would handle this hedged statement?

EVALUATION OF THE FEATURE-COMPARISON MODEL. Perhaps this model's greatest strength is its ability to account for many of the major findings in the semantic memory literature by means of a single principle, namely, that similarity of features will aid in the case of a confirmation and hinder in the case of a disconfirmation. That is, a statement such a "A robin is a bird" will be verified quickly because of the higher featural similarity between the instance and category; on the other hand, a statement such as "A bat is a bird" will be disconfirmed slowly for the same reason. Further, it escapes the problems of a model that follows the logic of class relations, since it allows for degrees of category membership. Some members of the category are "better" members than others (Rosch, 1974), and these stereotypic members will be dealt with more easily.

The feature-comparison model is not without problems, however. For one thing, the distinction between defining and characteristic features has the inherent difficulty that there is no feature that is absolutely necessary to define some concept. To illustrate, if a bird loses its wings, does it cease to be a bird? If the feathers are plucked from a peacock, does it stop being a peacock? Can a chair still be a chair with only three legs? Most people would answer these questions in the affirmative. Further, most people have difficulty deciding whether any particular feature you can name is a defining or a characteristic feature of some concept. Is "having a cover" a defining feature of books? What if a friend ripped the cover from this book, would you still call it a book? While Smith and his colleagues postulated the existence of degrees of definingness, assuming that features are more or less defining, the distinction between defining and characteristic features has been said to be somewhat artificial.

Perhaps a more serious problem for the model is that it cannot explain a result observed by Glass and Holyoak (1975) on disconfirmation times.

They found cases in which false statements containing similar nouns were disconfirmed *more* quickly than false statements containing less similar nouns. For example, people can disconfirm the statement "Some chairs are tables" faster than the statement "Some chairs are rocks," even though chairs and tables are more similar to each other than chairs and rocks. According to the feature-comparison model, this should not happen; the nouns *chairs* and *rocks* have almost zero features in common and the subject should disconfirm quickly. The nouns *chairs* and *tables* do have features in common (both are pieces of furniture) and therefore it should take somewhat longer to disconfirm a statement about these two nouns, since Stage 2 must be executed. Thus, the feature-comparison model predicts a result the opposite of which has been observed experimentally. These observations led Glass and Holyoak (1975) to propose a new theory, called the marker search model. Its assumptions about representations are rather complex, and the interested reader is referred to their article for both a discussion of the theory and a more detailed critique of the feature-comparison model.

SUMMARY

We have discussed three kinds of models of semantic memory: network models, of which the Collins and Quillian model is an example *par excellence;* set-theoretic models, exemplified by Meyer's predicate intersections model; and feature models, of which the feature-comparison model is an example. In many ways, the models are similar to each other. Each offers a theory for how information is represented in semantic memory and how we retrieve information from that representation. The models differ dramatically, however, in their general assumptions about semantic representations and how these representations are used to verify or disconfirm simple statements. In the network model, concepts are defined by the total set of their relations to other concepts. These relations include subordinates and superordinates as well as attributes. In the predicate intersections model, concepts are represented by their intersections with other concepts. In the feature-comparison model, concepts are represented as sets of features that are relatively unstructured but weighted by their degree of definingness.

The three models can explain a great number of the findings in the semantic memory literature, although their specific strengths and weaknesses differ. For example, some of the models have an easier time than others handling the data on disconfirmations.

The three models also differ in terms of the data they attempt to explain. The predicate intersections model and the feature-comparison model were designed to account for data collected from subjects who performed highly specific tasks. These tasks included the verification of statements about category membership ("A robin is a bird") or attribute possession ("A robin has wings"). While network models also concern themselves with these data, they are capable of handling a large number of tasks involving cognitive processing. For example, the large-scale network theories of Anderson and Bower (1973) and of Norman and Rumelhart (1975) attempt to deal with forgetting, perception, learning, and other behaviors.

Changes in the field of semantic memory are continually occurring. New theories and new data are challenging the old. The study of interdependence of semantic and episodic memory is one important new development. Smith (1976) has pointed to other new directions, for example, the notion that a statement might not be simply true or false, but might be "probably true" or "probably false." That is, a person's conclusion about a statement might actually be only probabilistic rather than absolute. Another direction is toward the development of "hybrid" models that are actually a summation of two or more existing models. All this activity serves to make the area of semantic memory one of the most exciting areas being investigated in cognitive psychology today.

chapter five

LANGUAGE AND THOUGHT

outline

IN THE EARLY 1970s twin daughters were born to Mr. and Mrs. Thomas Kennedy. The girls, named Grace and Virginia, uttered only gibberish and so were thought for many years to be severely retarded. Grace called Virginia "Cabengo," while Virginia called Grace "Poto." While the two were playing with their dollhouse, Grace was observed to say to Virginia, "Dug-on, haus you dinkin, du-ah." Virginia replied, "Snup-aduh ah-wee die-dipana, dihabana." For the first 17 months of their lives, the girls uttered no sounds, and then these bizarre ones. They were put in a school for the mentally retarded. Soon their teachers began to realize that something was wrong, and at age 6 the girls were sent to a hospital in California. Fortunately, speech therapists who examined the girls at the hospital discovered that Grace and Virginia had developed their own private language and were actually very bright six-year-olds. The girls spoke to each other in "idioglossia" or twin speech. One of the therapists noted that, "Development of this kind of language has been found to occur in very rare instances among twins who have had no other contact with other children. There is very little in the medical literature about it" (*Seattle Times,* July 25, 1977, p. 2).

The therapists say the girls actually have three languages in addition to their own. They comprehend English and German (their mother's native language), and they learned quickly, during therapy, to use sign language. Their own language is a complete mystery to the therapists and others who have tried to translate it but the two girls communicate exceptionally well with it.

What is interesting about this true story is that due to their extremely strange language, the parents of Grace and Virginia, and their doctors and nurses, decided the girls were retarded. Is there really such a relationship between a person's language and his ability to think? In the case of the twins, a false conclusion was reached. The girls were certainly not retarded; quite the opposite, they were rather bright. What then is the relationship between language and thought? To address this issue properly, we need a few basics.

LANGUAGE

One type of information which is part of our long-term memories is our knowledge of language. In fact, our general knowledge about the components and rules of language is probably one of the most basic and im-

FIGURE 5–1.   These girls developed their own language, intelligible only to themselves. Others decided they were retarded, since they could not communicate. (Wide World Photos)

portant parts of our semantic memories. For instance, we know that there is a letter *q* and another letter *t,* but in English they cannot appear next to one another; *qt* is not an acceptable combination in English (except perhaps as the name of a tanning lotion), since *u* must always follow *q.* One exception to the rule pertaining to *q* and *u* occurs when *q* appears as the last letter of a proper name, such as in *Iraq.* Similarly, we know that there are rules for the order of the letters *i* and *e:* "*i* comes before *e,* except after *c,* or in words sounding like *ay* such as *neighbor* and *weigh.*" (There are some w*ei*rd exceptions to this rule.) So our long-term memories contain not only the letters of our alphabet, but also the rules which allow some kinds of sequences to occur and prohibit others from occurring. Exceptions to the rules must also be stored, usually on an individual basis.

Why have a section in this book on language? One reason that our language system is so important and worthy of study is that it influences so many of our nonlanguage behaviors. We can see this by examining the behavior of cultures that speak entirely different languages. The Arabs, for example, have about 6000 different ways of naming camels (Thomas, 1937). The Hanunoo people in the Philippine Islands have a name for each of 92 varieties of rice (Brown, 1965). And, for the people of Liberia who speak the Bassa language, the color spectrum is differentiated in a strikingly different way (see Figure 5-2 and Gleason, 1961). Clearly the language we speak influences the way we *talk* about an experience, but does

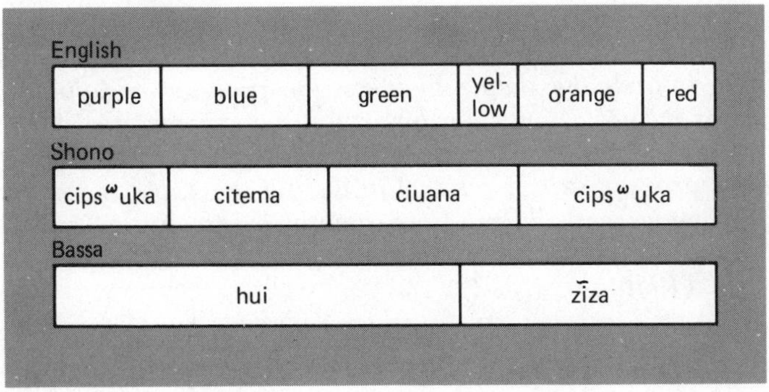

FIGURE 5–2.   Verbal labels for the spectrum of visible wavelenths in three different languages. (From an Introduction to Descriptive Linguistics, Rev. Ed. by H. A. Gleason. Copyright 1955, 1961 by Holt, Rinehart and Winston. Reprinted by permission of Holt, Rinehart and Winston.)

it influence the way we *think* about that experience? Does the Arab see differences in varieties of camels that we cannot see? Can the speaker of Bassa tell the difference in color between a plum and a head of lettuce? The question of whether the language one speaks controls the manner in which he perceives and understands the world has intrigued social scientists for nearly as long as the twentieth century is old.

LINGUISTIC RELATIVITY

Linguistic relativity or *linguistic determinism* is the hypothesis that a person's language determines how he thinks and perceives his world. Although it was proposed as early as the eighteenth century by Johann Herder and was later extended by Wilhelm von Humboldt and Edward Sapir, it is now most closely associated with the name Benjamin Lee Whorf (1956). Whorf had quite an unusual background for an anthropological linguist: he studied chemical engineering at M.I.T. and spent most of his working life with the Hartford Fire Insurance Company—while pursuing linguistics as a hobby on the side. His hobby was pursued with vigor; he spent time studying Mayan hieroglyphics and modern Aztec, as well as American Indian linguistics. From this effort came his view of linguistic relativity, or, as it is sometimes called, the *Whorfian hypothesis*. The essence of this view is that the structure and semantics of the language a person speaks play a determining role in the nature of his thinking. A passage in Whorf's own words, taken from a collection of Whorf's writings, gives a clear indication of the importance he placed on the role of language in thought:

. . . the background linguistic system (in other words, the grammar) of each language is not merely a reproducing instrument for voicing ideas but rather is itself the shaper of ideas, the program and guide for the individual's mental activity, for his analysis of impressions, for his synthesis of his mental stock in trade. Formulation of ideas is not an independent process, strictly rational in the old sense, but is part of a particular grammar and differs, from slightly to greatly, as between different grammars. We dissect nature along lines laid down by our native languages. (1956, pp. 212–213)

In support of his hypothesis, Whorf marshalled evidence from his studies of American Indian languages, particularly Hopi. He noted that the various languages "dissect nature" using differing numbers of words for describing what English describes with only one word. As an example, consider this finding: "We have the same word for falling snow, snow on the ground, snow packed hard like ice, slushy snow, wind-driven flying snow, —whatever the situation may be. To an Eskimo, this all-inclusive word would be almost unthinkable; he would say that falling snow, slushy snow, and so on, are sensuously and operationally different, different things to contend with; he uses different words for them and for other kinds of snow" (1956, p. 216). But it was not only the lexical differences which he thought were important; it was what they indicated about people's views of their environment. For example, he claimed that English, by dividing sentences into two basic components, the noun phrase and the verb phrase, seems to emphasize a distinction between objects or things and actions or events. Some Indian languages, however, appeared not to make such a distinction. Whorf has argued that this distinction in English guides our thinking about the real world such that we are highly prone to analyze experience into things and actions, an analytical method foreign to the Hopi Indians whose language makes no such distinction.

The notion that reality was a kaleidoscopic flux of impressions and language a system laid out like a grid to organize those impressions was very popular indeed. Further, the belief that structural differences between two languages will be paralleled by nonlinguistic cognitive differences in the speakers of those two languages, and that this structure strongly determines a person's world view, was enormously congenial to many psycholinguists during the 1950s. But how should the idea be properly tested? they asked. Were Whorf's data sufficient? No one disputed the fact that there were differences in vocabulary among languages. But do these differences influence the world outlook of the people speaking them? Just because Arabic has more names for camels than English, does it follow that speakers of Arabic see differences in camels that English speakers cannot see?

Not necessarily. One might hypothesize that speakers of diverse languages see the world in the same way, but that certain concepts are simply more easily expressible in some languages than in others. In support of the alternative view is the observation that new words are invented as they are needed. For example, we certainly could have comprehended the idea of an astronaut long before the word was coined, although at that time we might have called one "a person who travels outside the earth's atmosphere." Similarly, if the American culture suddenly depended as heavily on camels as that of the Arabs, we can be sure that new words would enter the American vocabulary, words that would code all of the important distinctions among camels. If camels were important to us, we would be communicating about them often, and we would want a highly differentiated vocabulary to facilitate this communication. We have seen this sort of thing happen in the technological realm over the last 100 years. Americans probably now have more words for talking about automobiles than the Hanunoos have for talking about rice. Clearly the Hanunoo people know more about rice than we do, talk about rice more than we do, and think about rice more than we do. In looking at different kinds of rice, they will obviously be more aware of the differences than we would be, not necessarily because of the language they speak, but because of the knowledge they possess. Similarly, we have more knowledge about Chevrolets and Cadillacs, and are more aware of their differences.

The verbal behavior of the Arabs with respect to camels and that of the Eskimos with respect to snow is clearly different from ours, but do these linguistic differences correspond to differences in nonlinguistic behavior? Whorf's purely linguistic data do not address this issue, but the research of Brown and Lenneberg (1954) does. Much of what follows draws heavily on an excellent summary of this work by Roger Brown (1976).

A Test of Linguistic Relativity

The classic experiment of Brown and Lenneberg (1954) seemed at the time to support the notion that there are indeed differences in nonverbal behavior that can be traced to language differences. These investigators attempted to measure the ease with which colors can be linguistically coded in English. Their subjects looked at numerous color patches and attempted to give each color a name. *Name* was defined as "the word or words one would ordinarily use to describe the color to a friend" (1976, p. 131). For some colors, subjects responded with single common color words, like *blue*, quickly and with little variation. For other colors, the names were given more slowly, with great variation. One subject might use a modified word (such as *light green*), another might use a low-frequency term such as *aqua*. Colors named rapidly and easily (usually those with short names, like *blue*) and for which there was high agreement among subjects on the appropriate name were said to be high in codability. Measuring the codability of colors constituted the first phase of the experiment.

In the second phase, subjects were shown patches of four different colors and, after a delay, were asked to pick out these four colors from a set of 120 different colored patches. Highly codable colors (those easily named during phase 1) were recognized most accurately. This was especially true when a long delay preceded the recognition test.

Consider the subject's task in this experiment. First, he is exposed to four colors, which he probably names according to his own perception of them. Later, during the recognition test, he searches the array of 120 patches for colors that he would name exactly as he named the four original colors. Thus, if he had labeled one of the original colors *pale blue,* he would search the entire array until he found one that would also fit the label *pale blue.* Brown and Lenneberg's conceptualization of the task thus consisted of two steps: (1) derive distinctive names for the color exemplars; and (2) find colors that match the *distinctive names* that were stored in memory. From this the conclusion follows that those colors which are difficult to name (uncodable) are the same ones that are difficult to remember.

This study shows in its first phase that some color experiences are easier to encode in English than others; in its second phase, it purports to show that this linguistic difference does in fact correspond to a nonlinguistic difference, namely, the ability to recognize colors from memory. In general, if you have a single word that encodes all the relevant information of an experience, you will be able to remember that experience more easily than if you have a multiple-word encoding that in addition probably did not encode all the attributes necessary to recognize that experience. What is important is whether all the information necessary to solve the problem at hand is in the linguistic response. Coding a color as *pink* is useful only if you have to differentiate it from among a series of blues, yellows, and greens. But if the matching array contains 19 different shades of pink, then recognition memory will undoubtedly be poor.

By way of summarizing, the Brown–Lenneberg work on color coding indicated to its originators that within a language different colors are differentially codable and that this can influence the accurate recognition of colors. Languages differ in the ease with which various colors can be coded, and these language differences are reflected in the retrieval behavior of the speakers. Thus, a relationship between linguistic structure and cognition had been shown to exist but it had not been proven that the structure had actually *caused* the cognition.

Further Testing of Linguistic Relativity

Brown and Lenneberg were presuming that if they had performed their experiment on some other language community, different codability scores would have been produced for the same array of colors, and that the recognition scores of these other communities would correspond directly to their various codability scores. The presumption was quite reasonable at the time. Suppose that instead of using colors the experiment were performed with 92 varieties of rice. One could use both Hanunoo and American subjects who could be shown four varieties of rice for study, and then asked to recognize the four from among the 92. Obviously (we think) the Hanunoo would outperform the American at this task, not simply because the American would have to use multiple-word encodings (for example, small brown grains with dark spots) but also because the Hanunoo encodings would contain all the relevant information, whereas the American encodings might not. At the time of recognition, the American may find two grains that are small and brown with dark spots. These two may differ in shape, something which the American did not include in his encoding. The single words of the Hanunoo would encode all of the relevant attributes that would be necessary to select one variety from the 92. Quite plausible. But not necessarily correct. To see why not, we go back to approximately 1960 and briefly review the history of the controversy as it is so elegantly traced in Brown (1976).

FUZZY CATEGORIES AND COMMUNICABILITY. Important work during this period was done by Lenneberg (1957) who presented color chips to his subjects and asked them simply to name each color. Some chips were universally named, for example, one of the chips was called *blue* by everybody. Other chips were variously categorized; thus, one chip was sometimes called *blue,* sometimes *green,* and sometimes *aqua.* From these results Lenneberg concluded that colors (and probably most concepts) are not proper sets. Category membership is not an all-or-none matter but rather one of degree. To use the terminology of Zadeh (1965, 1971), colors are "fuzzy sets." Furthermore, as Lenneberg also found, fuzzy concepts are much more difficult to learn than proper ones.

At about the same time, Brown (1958) wrote his classic paper entitled "How Shall a Thing Be Called?" Here, Brown observed that although people often talk about *the* name for an object, most objects can be correctly named in many different ways. "The dime in my pocket is not only a *dime.* It is also *money,* a *metal object,* a *thing,* and, moving to subordinates, a *1952 dime,* in fact a *particular 1952 dime* with a unique pattern of scratches, discolorations, and smooth places" (p. 14). The term *dime,* however, is somehow the name that fits the object, the basic name. In most contexts, *dime* is at the level of abstraction with the greatest utility. To call a dime merely *money* would fail to distinguish it from pennies, quarters, and dollar bills. To call it a *1952 dime* and distinguish it from 1960 or 1965 dimes would generally serve no purpose. (The level of usual utility can change as a person grows up; thus, for a very young child a dime might well be called money, in that like all money it should not be put in the mouth and should not be thrown away. Later, money will give way to dime, quarter, and so on.)

Just as every object has a basic name, so do colors, according to the work of Berlin and Kay (1969). These investigators found that every language takes its basic color terms from a list of only eleven color names (black, white, red, yellow, green, blue, brown, purple, pink, orange, and gray). Some languages use only two terms, while others use all eleven. In languages with two terms, one term means black and the other white. In languages with three terms, the terms are always equivalent to black, white, and red. The complete hierarchy is shown in Figure 5-3.

Another important step was the realization that codability, or naming agreement, is not necessarily as important as communicability, or communication accuracy. That is, sometimes the name *green,* which is a good name for describing certain colors, is not as informative as *green like the color of grass,* which is longer but might communicate more, especially when the set of greens is especially large. Following upon earlier work, Lanz and Stefflre (1964) discovered that communicability was more highly related to recognition ability than were the original codability scores. Thus it became a general principle that for a given language community, how well information about an object could be communicated from one person to another was highly correlated with the memorability of that same object.

COLOR NAMES AND COLOR MEMORY.   With this background behind us, let us now examine some tests of the Whorfian hypothesis. Recall the Brown–Lenneberg contention that the *recognition* scores of two cultures that slice up the color continuum very differently would correspond in large measure to their *codability* scores.

Heider and Olivier (1972) found two cultures to study, the American and the Dani, a Stone Age agricultural people of Indonesian New Guinea.

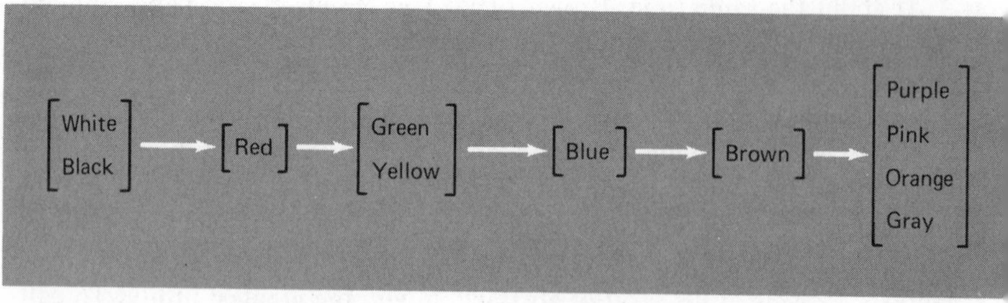

$$\begin{bmatrix} \text{White} \\ \text{Black} \end{bmatrix} \longrightarrow \begin{bmatrix} \text{Red} \end{bmatrix} \longrightarrow \begin{bmatrix} \text{Green} \\ \text{Yellow} \end{bmatrix} \longrightarrow \begin{bmatrix} \text{Blue} \end{bmatrix} \longrightarrow \begin{bmatrix} \text{Brown} \end{bmatrix} \longrightarrow \begin{bmatrix} \text{Purple} \\ \text{Pink} \\ \text{Orange} \\ \text{Gray} \end{bmatrix}$$

FIGURE 5–3.   Languages with four terms include white, black, red, and either green or yellow. Those with more terms add whichever of these terms on the third level has not evolved and continue first with blue, then brown. Next comes a set of four which occur arbitrarily. Berlin and Kay believed this ordered sequence to be a universal one.

The Dani have just two terms for color: *mili* for dark and cold hues and *mola* for bright and warm hues. (The Dani could designate other colors with long strings of words just as we can say "a soft, pale pink," but only *mili* and *mola* were used by all speakers.) Each subject (both Dani and American) first had to name each of 40 color chips (codability test). Later a recognition test was administered, in which a chip was shown for 5 seconds, then, after 30 seconds, the subject picked out the one he had seen from the array of 40. The important finding of this work is that the differences in naming structure for the two cultures were *not* related to different cognition structures. In another study, Heider (1972) showed that highly codable (in English), "focal" colors were remembered better than "nonfocal" colors, even for the Dani, a culture for whom all colors were the same with respect to codability. Thus, the hypothesis of differential "codability" which had been invoked to explain the original recognition memory results was discredited by the fact that the Dani also exhibited better recognition of focal than nonfocal colors.

Linguistic Relativity Versus Linguistic Universals

Current emphasis has shifted from how various linguistic structures "produce" differences in their speakers' thought processes to what is *common* among speakers of different languages. Focal colors are one example of what has been termed a linguistic universal. Certain colors, for example, a good red, have been found to be more memorable, easier to recognize, than other colors, whether the subjects speak a language having a name for the focal color or not. Thus, even though the number of basic color terms varies from two, as among the Dani, to eleven, for human beings the world over, the total domain of recognizable colors consists of 11 small focal areas in which are found the best instances of the color categories named in any particular language. This discovery of universals represents, according to Brown (1976), a fundamental breakthrough in behavioral science that we owe to this long controversy.

LANGUAGE AND COGNITIVE BEHAVIOR

One result of the work with colors is the principle that the communicability or codability of an object is closely related to the memorability of that object. Experiments have revealed an interesting relationship between the naming of an object and its configuration in our memory. The classic experiment of Carmichael, Hogan, and Walter (1932), later replicated by Herman, Lawless, and Marshall (1951) provides an example of this powerful relationship. Ambiguous figures such as that shown in Figure 5-4*A* were presented to subjects, who were told that they would later have to reproduce them as accurately as possible. Before each figure was presented,

A. Stimulus figure

B. Reproduction for "curtains in a window"

C. Reproduction for "diamond in a rectangle"

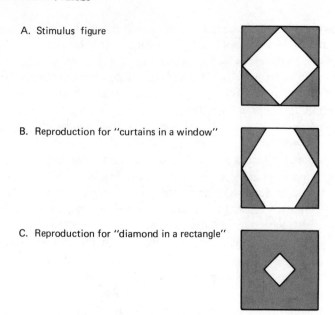

FIGURE 5–4. Verbal labels affect the reproduction of stimulus figures.

the experimenter said, "The next figure resembles a ———," filling in a name that resembled the figure. For Figure 5-4*A*, one group was given the label "curtains in a window," another group, the label "diamond in a rectangle." When the subjects later attempted to recall the figures by drawing them, the drawings conformed to the label they were given. The example figure was often reproduced as in Figure 5-4*B* by those told it was "curtains in a window" and as in Figure 5-4*C* by those told it was a "diamond in a rectangle." The 12 shapes used in the experiment, along with the two labels used for each shape, are shown in Figure 5-5. For all of these shapes, the labels influenced the reproduction. Subjects who heard the label *eyeglasses* for the fifth figure might put a bend in the shaft between the two circles and those who heard the label *dumbbells* might put a double shaft between the two circles. The results suggest that the label was encoded concurrently with the shape. At the time of recall, the subjects apparently recalled the labels and used them in their reproductions of the figures. Again, this is an instance in which the name applied to a figure influenced the nonverbal behavior (in this case, the drawing of that figure), providing further support for the powerful role of language on nonlinguistic behavior.

In a more recent investigation employing a more realistic situation, Loftus and Palmer (1974) showed subjects a film of a traffic accident and then asked them several questions about the accident. The critical question had to do with the speed at which the cars were travelling. Some subjects were asked "About how fast were the cars going when they hit each other?" whereas others were asked "About how fast were the cars going

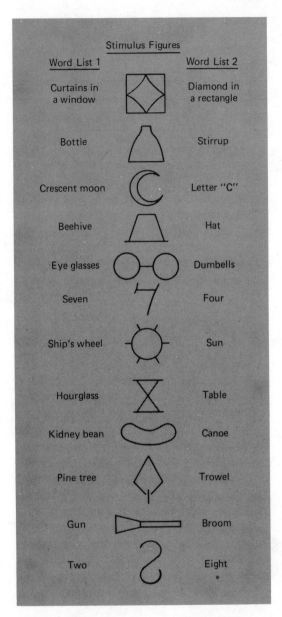

FIGURE 5–5. Stimulus figures and verbal labels. (From Carmichael, Hogan, & Walter, 1932. Reprinted by permission of the author and American Psychological Association.)

when they smashed into each other?" The latter question elicited a much higher estimate of speed.

One week later, the subjects returned to the laboratory and, without viewing the film again, they answered a new series of questions about it.

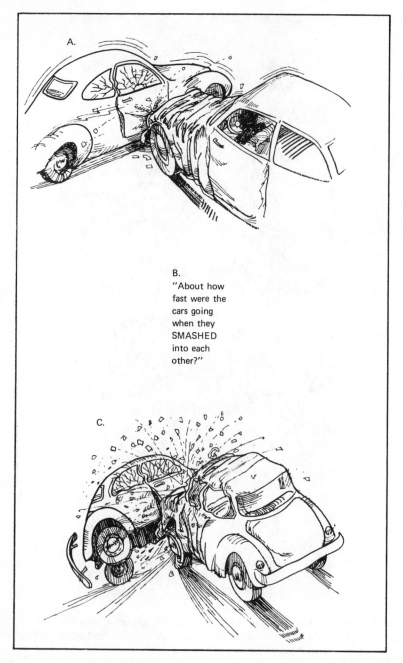

FIGURE 5–6. Original information (*A*); is transformed through external information (*B*); into a resultant "memory" (*C*). (From Loftus & Loftus, 1976, p. 161. Courtesy of Lawrence Erlbaum Associates, Inc.)

This time, the critical question asked whether the subject had seen any broken glass. There had been no broken glass in the film. Over twice as many subjects interrogated with the word *smashed* the week before reported seeing the nonexistent glass as those who were questioned with *hit*. This is what is to be expected if the verb *smashed* influenced the subjects to remember the accident as being more severe than it had actually been; they would be likely to recall details that were not shown but were consistent with an accident that was severe and had occurred at high speed.

This result points toward the view that a memory can undergo a transformation as a result of information provided subsequently. The phrasing of the question in this case provided additional information that, when integrated into the information already extant in long-term memory, brought about the transformation. The basic idea has been schematized in Figure 5-6.

There is clearly some connection between the Loftus–Palmer study and the work of Carmichael et al. on the influence of verbal labels on memory for visually presented stimuli. Carmichael's early study and the more recent work of Daniel (1972), who established that *recognition* memory was similarly affected by verbal labels, both lead to the conclusion that verbal labeling actually effects a shift in the memory strength toward those forms which are better representatives of the label. In the Loftus–Palmer study, the verb *smashed* is thought to act as a verbal label which causes a shift toward greater severity in a subject's memory representation. Both types of studies provide nice illustrations of the complex interaction between language and memory, a topic we will treat again toward the end of this chapter.

Having indicated some of the ways in which language affects our behavior, we now turn to a discussion of what we know about language itself.

STRUCTURE OF LANGUAGE

Language, it is said, is a uniquely human accomplishment (although some believe in the possibility of animal languages as well). Students of the psychology of language, called *psycholinguists,* have as a primary goal to understand how sounds and symbols are translated into meaning. For this, a thorough knowledge of the basic units and structure of language is a prerequisite.

UNITS OF LANGUAGE

The basic units of sound of every known language are called *phonemes.* English has 46 phonemes, other languages may have as few as 15 or as many as 85. In English the phonemes correspond to vowel and consonant sounds, as well as combinations of letters such as the *sh* and *th* sounds. Although English has only 46, these phonemes can be combined, according to the rules of our language, to produce a much larger variety of basic sounds.

Sounds combined in certain ways produce *morphemes,* which are the smallest units of meaning in a given language. Morphemes include both words (*house, telephone, hobble*) and meaningful prefixes (*anti, pre*) and suffixes (*ing, ed*). Of course, a word such as *learned* would consist of two units of meaning, *learn,* which designates a particular action, and *ed,* which indicates that this action took place in the past. The 46 English phonemes that we began with can be combined to produce over 100,000 morphemes. The study of the ordering of sounds to produce morphemes, called *morphology,* consists of a fairly well defined set of rules. For example, in English a morpheme can never begin with more than three consonant sounds; /spl/ is acceptable, but no additional consonants could be added. In Russian, on the other hand, it is possible to have combinations which use more than three consonant sounds; /stch/ would thus be acceptable.

Morphemes can be combined together to produce coherent phrases or sentences, and the rules for this process are known as *syntax.* Again the rules are well defined. "Mary chased Oscar" conforms to our rules, but "Mary Oscar chased" does not. Both morphology and syntax are concerned with the problem of sequencing of units, the former with the sequencing of sounds to make morphemes, and the latter with the sequencing of morphemes to make sentences. Together these constitute *grammar,* which is simply the study of the sequencing of units to produce acceptable utterances.

CONSTITUENT STRUCTURE

A sentence, then, is a collection of morphemes. But some collections produce acceptable, or grammatical, sentences while others do not. There are several linguistic theories which attempt to set forth formulae for generating only grammatically correct sentences. Before we consider these theories, let us examine the process of dividing a sentence.

Take the sentence "The scrawny astronaut ate the greasy pizza." We observe immediately that the sentence consists of an ordered string of seven words, but, in addition, the words fall into groups. If asked to divide this sentence into two parts in a way that seems most natural, most people would divide the string into:

The scrawny astronaut   ate the greasy pizza.

We can make this division easily, something we would not be able to do if the string had consisted of the following list of apparently unrelated words:

pizza the scrawny greasy ate astronaut the

The difference between the sentence string and the nonsense string is that the former has a structure. It consists of natural units, clusters that naturally go together.

"The scrawny astronaut ate the greasy pizza" can be divided even further, as we observe in the diagram shown in Figure 5-7*A*. Diagrams such as these have been called *tree diagrams,* since they resemble upside-down trees. Continuing our division of the sentence, we eventually arrive at a diagram that looks like the one shown in Figure 5-7*B*. The sentence itself, as well as all the clusters or groupings into which it is divided, are termed *constituents.* Carrying our tree diagram to its ultimate conclusion, we thus arrive at 13 constituents for the sentence, "The scrawny astronaut ate the greasy pizza."

Having analyzed the *constituent structure* of our sentence, we are now in a position to compare it with another sentence to determine whether they have identical constituent structures.

Consider this sentence:

The depressed psychologist analyzed the noisy data.

As can be seen from Figure 5-8 this sentence has the same constituent structure as "The scrawny astronaut ate the greasy pizza." As Dale (1972) has noted, this similarity of structure suggests that what makes a string of words a grammatical sentence is whether or not that string has a correct English constituent structure. Any linguistic theory must still, of course, explain what it means for a sentence to have a correct constituent structure.

As it turns out, we need to know the constituent structure of a sentence not only to determine whether it is grammatical, but also to comprehend its

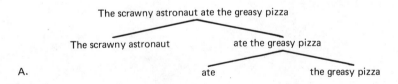

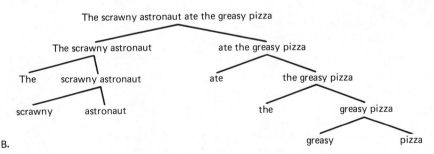

FIGURE 5-7. Tree diagrams for the sentence, "The scrawny astronaut ate the greasy pizza."

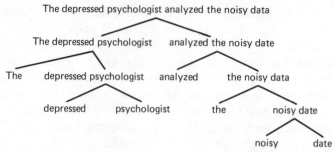

FIGURE 5–8. Tree diagram for the sentence, "The depressed psychologist analyzed the noisy data."

meaning. When we listen to a sentence, we have many tasks to perform: We must of course perceive the words in the sentence, but at the same time we must determine its constituent structure. As an example, consider the sentence, "They are flying planes." This is an ambiguous sentence that can be interpreted to be either about planes or about people. The constituent structures that correspond to these two meanings are shown in Figure 5-9. It should now be obvious that the ambiguity arises because there are two equally plausible constituent structures. Knowing the speaker's intended constituent structure would clarify this sentence and similar ones such as "They are frying chickens" which might mean "They fry chickens" or "They are chickens for frying."

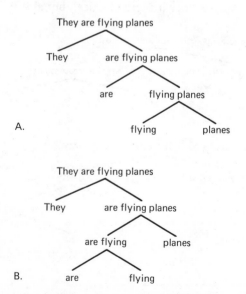

FIGURE 5–9. Two constituent structures for "They are flying planes."

What knowledge must speakers of English have in order to create and understand the unlimited number of sentences that occur in our language? What knowledge allows us to distinguish grammatical sentences from nongrammatical ones? The approach that a phrase structure analysis takes is similar to the process of parsing a sentence that we learn in grade school. Phrase structure grammars attempt to give detailed descriptions of the structures of sentences in order to determine the relations between the constituent parts of the sentences.

Take the sentence whose constituent structure we already analyzed, "The scrawny astronaut ate the greasy pizza." Our linguistic intuition told us that "The scrawny astronaut" constituted a unit, but that "astronaut ate the" did not. Another way to express this is to note that "The scrawny astronaut" could be replaced by "he," whereas the latter string of words could not.

What we have not yet done, but will do now is to name or label the different kinds of constituents that we observe. For example, the first word in our example sentence "The" is an article (T), and the second word, "scrawny" is an adjective (A), and the third word is a noun (N). Together they form a noun phrase (NP). "The greasy pizza" is also a noun phrase. The verb, "ate" combines with this second noun phrase to form a verb phrase (VP). At the most complete level, the first noun phrase "The scrawny astronaut" is combined with the verb phrase "ate the greasy pizza" to form a grammatical sentence (S). When we introduce the names of the constituents into our tree diagram, we get the result shown in Figure 5-10.

Phrase structure grammar actually consists of a series of *rewrite rules*, or

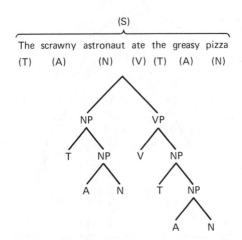

FIGURE 5–10. Labeled constituents for "The scrawny astronaut ate the greasy pizza."

rules for transforming one symbol into another. If we have a rule of the form X → Y (which is read *X can be rewritten as Y*) it means that when X occurs we can substitute Y for it. In phrase structure grammar, we begin with the sort of symbols that we've already seen: T, N, V, NP, and so on. The top portion of Figure 5-11 gives us the rewrite rules we would use to create our sample sentence. Starting with the basic sentence, S, and following rewrite rules 1 through 7, we arrive at the grammatical construction, "The scrawny astronaut ate the greasy pizza." Rules 1 through 3 bring us to the bottom of the tree diagram in Figure 5-10. Following the remainder of the rules allows us to rewrite the symbols into their *terminal elements*. T becomes *The*, A becomes *scrawny*, N becomes *astronaut*, V becomes *ate*, A becomes *greasy*, and N becomes *pizza*. These are terminal

Rewrite rules in a simple phrase structure grammar

1. S ⟶ Noun phrase (NP) + Verb phrase (VP)
2. NP⟶ Adjective (A) + Noun (N)
       Article (T) + Noun phrase (NP)
3. VP⟶ Verb (V) + Noun phrase (NP)
4. T ⟶ the
5. N ⟶ astronaut, pizza
6. V ⟶ ate
7. A ⟶ scrawny, greasy

Sample derivation

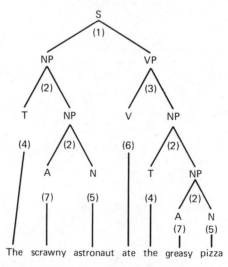

FIGURE 5–11.   A simple phrase structure grammar.

elements since there are no rules for rewriting them. We've gone as far as possible. When all of the elements are terminal, we have formed a complete sentence.

Click Migration

Some evidence for the psychological importance of constituent structure comes from experiments using the click migration technique. The basic procedure has been used in numerous experiments (for example, Bever, 1971; Fodor & Bever, 1965; Garrett, Bever & Fodor, 1966; Garrett & Fodor, 1968). The subject, wearing earphones, listens to sentences played in one ear, while click sounds are played into the other ear at the same time. The subject has to write down each sentence after it is played and indicate the point in the sentence where the click occurred. Typically, there is a marked tendency for the subjects to displace the click from its actual point of occurrence toward a major phrase boundary or major constituent break. For example, when "The scrawny astronaut ate the greasy pizza" is broken into its two major constituents, there is a constituent break between *astronaut* and *ate*. The perceptual displacement of the clicks toward the constituent break is called click migration.

The study by Garrett, Bever, and Fodor (1966) is typical. Pairs of sentences were constructed in such a way as partially to overlap in content. Here are two:

1. (As a direct result of their new invention's influence) (the company was given an award.)
2. (The retiring chairman whose methods still greatly influence the company) (was given an award.)

As the parentheses indicate, for the first sentence the deepest constituent break occurs between *influence* and *the;* for the second it occurs between *company* and *was*. The common portion for both sentences is "influence the company was given an award."

The question of interest was how often subjects would displace the click so that it would occur at the constituent break for a given sentence. Garrett and his co-workers found that there was a direct relationship between click displacement and constituent break, even though the sentence fragment was identical in both members of a sentence pair. On the average, 24 percent of the clicks move in the direction of the constituent break, whereas only 5 percent move in the other direction. In our sample pair of sentences, when a click occurred during *company* in the first sentence, it was often perceived as occurring closer to *influence*. When it occurred in the same place in the second sentence, it did not migrate toward *influence*.

These results suggest that subjects are in a sense analyzing the constituent structure while they are listening to the sentences. Basic psychological units such as phrases are resistant to extraneous stimuli like clicks. As a consequence the clicks are perceived as occurring outside these units. Another way of stating this is that once a subject begins to process a phrase, he does not process extraneous stimuli until he reaches a constituent break. Reber (1973) has termed this explanation for the click migration phenomenon the "linguistic hypothesis."

Language or Nonlanguage

The click migration results seemed, at first glance, to provide compelling support for the psychological reality of grammatical phrases until a study by Reber and Anderson (1970) appeared. They argued that if click migration could be observed with nonlanguage materials as well as language materials, then the phenomenon probably had nothing to do with phrases or syntactic structure at all. In their words:

> . . . the analysis of any linguistic input must involve a complex set of operations. As a beginning we feel that it is essential to distinguish between the linguistic and the nonlinguistic operations. By linguistic we refer to operations based on such factors as intonation, syntax, and semantics. By nonlinguistic we refer to operations based on such factors as memory and attention. (p. 81)

In one of many experiments, one group of subjects heard a list of six word sentences of the form "(Disturbed mental patients) (consult noted doctors)." A click occurred at some location, and the subjects indicated where by placing a slash mark where they thought they heard it. A second group of subjects were exposed to the identical procedure, except that instead of sentences, they heard six noise bursts. A click occurred at some point, and the subjects indicated its location. Remarkably, the responses of the "noise" subjects were almost identical to the responses of the "sentence" subjects leading Reber and Anderson to conclude that "an interpretation of click migration phenomenon must be based . . . upon nonlinguistic factors" (p. 87). Furthermore, in another experiment with sentences, even when no click occurred at all, people tended to report it as having occurred during the major constituent break. This suggests that people have some sort of bias for thinking a click occurred at the major break, even when they have heard nothing. Reber (1973) has challenged the linguistic hypothesis, proposing instead an "attentional hypothesis," which claims that click migration depends largely on how the subject attends to the material and what biases he brings with him. When an item is important, or has priority, it will be perceived as occurring sooner than in fact it does. If the click has priority it is perceived as occurring sooner. Similarly, if the sentence has priority, the click is perceived as occurring later. In sum, the literature on click displacements is somewhat ambiguous.

Some of the click displacement effect can apparently be attributed to response bias—people tend to respond with clicks at the boundaries even when no clicks are presented. But this does not seem to explain the whole effect. The work is still taken to indicate that people identify constituent breaks, and that these breaks are useful.

To summarize, phrase structure grammars which rely on constituent structure analysis assign a structural description to every sentence, making possible (1) detailed comparisons of the similarities between sentences, (2) analyses of the relationships among various constituents within a single sentence, and (3) explanations of sentence ambiguity. Aside from these advantages, phrase structure grammars are consistent with psychological data on sentence perception, although a full explanation of those data (click migration) has yet to be offered. In the next section, however, we will see that a phrase structure grammar cannot account for everything we know about English; it leaves certain obvious problems unaccounted for. The inadequacies of phrase structure grammar motivated the invention of *transformational grammar.*

TRANSFORMATIONAL GRAMMAR

It was Noam Chomsky (1957), noted linguist, who erected the theory of transformational grammar, motivated by his observation that phrase structure grammar failed to describe language adequately. In order to appreciate fully the necessity for this other linguistic position, we must consider the distinction between surface and deep structure which Chomsky realized very early on.

Surface Structure Versus Deep Structure

To put it simply, the surface structure of a sentence consists of the words and their organization, whereas the deep structure refers to the abstract, underlying representation (or, roughly, "meaning") of the sentence. The deep structure exists as a set of abstract concepts and rules, all of which are stored in long-term memory. Surface structure is derived from the deep structure by rules called *transformations.*

Consider this sentence, which we have encountered in our discussion of constituent structures: "They are flying planes." The two meanings of the sentence actually correspond to two different surface structures, for which we could construct two different tree diagrams. In shorthand form, using parentheses, the two versions are:

(They)/ (are) (flying planes)/

and

(They) / (are flying) (planes)/

Ordinarily the context will cue us as to the intended meaning. In any event, in this instance there are two surface structures corresponding to two different deep structures.

Now consider this sentence: "Visiting relatives can be a nuisance." It also has two meanings, one corresponding roughly to "Relatives who visit can be a nuisance," the other to "It can be a nuisance to visit relatives." But, in this case, the surface structure is identical for the two different meanings. For both versions, the surface structure is:

(Visiting relatives) / (can be) (a nuisance) /

In other words, the surface structure in this example does not admit of two distinct meanings. The ambiguity in the sentence thus arises because there are two deep structures corresponding to a single surface structure. Here we begin to see where phrase structure grammar fails.

Consider two more sentences.

1. I have no money.
2. I don't have any money.

These two sentences have different surface structures but they mean very nearly the same thing. In a phrase structure grammar, sentence 2 would be more similar to some totally unrelated sentence that happened to have the same surface structure than it would be to sentence 1—to which it is synonymous in meaning. Again, we begin to understand the necessity for something more than a phrase structure grammar, which fails to clarify the relationship between sentences of different form.

Transformations

Simply put, the theory of transformational grammar claims that every sentence has both a surface and a deep structure; the two are related by rules of transformation. Actually both transformational and phrase structure rules are rewrite rules, but the former rewrite entire strings of symbols (whole sentences), while the latter rewrite only single symbols.

To illustrate transformational rules, consider the set of sentences presented in Table 5-1. Clearly these sentences are related to each other in a very definite way, but a way which is not revealed by phrase structure descriptions. Transformational grammar suggests that the sentences are related because they represent the results of applying various transformational rules to a single underlying string, known as the *kernel string*. A kernel sentence is roughly parallel to a simple, affirmative, declarative, active sentence, such as "The mechanic fixed my car." The passive transformation (P) is a rule that rewrites the kernel string so that it becomes "My car was fixed by the mechanic." Two other transformations, the nega-

TABLE 5–1. P, N, Q SENTENCE FAMILY.

Sentence	Transformations Applied
The mechanic fixed my car.	Kernel
My car was fixed by the mechanic.	Passive (P)
The mechanic did not fix my car.	Negative (N)
Did the mechanic fix my car?	Question (Q)
My car was not fixed by the mechanic.	P + N
Was my car fixed by the mechanic?	P + Q
Didn't the mechanic fix my car?	N + Q
Wasn't my car fixed by the mechanic?	P + N + Q

tive (N) and the question (Q), are also illustrated in Table 5-1. The entire set of eight sentences has been called a P,N,Q sentence family (Clifton & Odom, 1966), since it consists of all three transformations. Further, because each of these three transformations rewrites a single string as another single string, they are all known as singular transformations. In contrast, generalized transformations rewrite two or more strings as a single string: *"The mechanic fixed my car," "My car is blue,"* and *"The mechanic is old"* can be rewritten as *"The old mechanic fixed my blue car."*

With a good introduction to the idea of transformations under our belt, let's look at how a transformational grammar handles active and passive sentences a bit more fully. Consider these sentences:

1. Astronauts like pizza.
2. Pizza is liked by astronauts.

In transformational grammar, both the active sentence 1 and the passive sentence 2 have essentially the same deep structure that has been diagrammed in Figure 5-12. When the active sentence is converted into the passive, "Pizza is liked by astronauts," the position of the two nouns *astronaut* and *pizza* is inverted, the form of the verb changes from *likes* to *is liked,* and the *by* is added as a function word. A transformational grammar "knows" that sentences 1 and 2 mean the same thing because their deep structure is the same, and, according to the theory, it is the deep structure that is related to the meaning of a sentence. Many people try to simplify the definition of deep structure by saying it is the same thing as meaning. It is not. It is an abstract representation that corresponds to meaning. Unfortunately no really good definition beyond this exists.

With this framework, many other aspects of English can be understood. For example, the sentence "The children are ready to eat, Mr. Jones" might mean that the children will eat something, or that Mr. Jones will eat the children. There is only one constituent structure for this sentence although

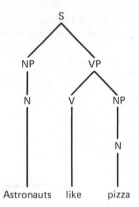

FIGURE 5–12.   Structure for "Astronauts like pizza." When the passive transformation is applied, this becomes "Pizza is liked by astronauts."

it has two possible meanings. Transformational grammar resolves the ambiguity by proposing that there are two underlying deep structural representations corresponding to each of the interpretations. Different transformations have been applied to the two deep structures, and these coincidentally resulted in identical surface structures.

An immense amount of work has been done to refine the details of transformational grammar. For example, two collections of papers, Bach and Harms (1968) and Jacobs and Rosenbaum (1970) deal exclusively with these modifications. Chomsky himself (1965) has made revisions in his initial thinking. Initially he proposed that some transformational rules were optional (in contrast to phrase structure rules which had to be applied whenever possible). In the more recent versions of the theory, Chomsky questioned the idea of some transformational rules being optional.

Transformational Grammar: A Final Note

It is appropriate to conclude this section with a quote from Chomsky, who believed that transformational grammar was universal, applicable to all human languages.

The grammar as a whole can thus be regarded, ultimately, as a device for pairing phonetically represented signals with semantic interpretations, this pairing being mediated through a system of abstract structures generated by the syntactic component. Thus the syntactic component must provide for each sentence (actually, for each interpretation of each sentence) a semantically interpretable deep *structure and a phonetically interpretable* surface *structure, and, in the event that these are distinct, a statement of the relation between these two structures. . . .*

Roughly speaking, it seems that this much structure is common to all theories of generative grammar, or is at least compatible with them. Beyond this loose and minimal specification, however, important differences emerge (1964, p. 52).

SEMANTICS

It would not be fitting to write a chapter about language without discussing meaning. Meaning is what language is for. A person who knows how to pronounce all the words of a language and knows every rule for generating grammatical sentences would be at a loss if he did not know what the words and sentences meant. Semantics, the study of meaning, is perhaps the most important component of language.

Psychologists seem to understand semantics less well than other aspects of language. Nonetheless, psychological theories have abounded. Skinner (1957), Osgood (1952, 1957), and Deese (1965) have proposed association theories of semantics, whereas Katz and Fodor (1963) have proposed a semantic marker theory. To give the flavor of association-type theories, consider some of the reasoning of Deese (1965).

Rather than looking at words in isolation, which had been quite a common practice, Deese interested himself in entire networks of associated words. He advanced the notion of "associative meaning," which referred to the range of single words that were elicited by a given stimulus word. He suggested that two words have the same meaning if they have identical distributions of associative responses and similar in meaning to the extent that their distributions overlapped.

To be more specific, take two words, *moth* and *butterfly*. What responses do these two words elicit? Deese assumed that any word always elicits itself first, as a "representational response" and then elicits other words. Table 5-2, then, shows the frequency with which each word in the left-hand

TABLE 5-2. ASSOCIATIVE OVERLAP BETWEEN MOTH AND BUTTERFLY.

Response words	Stimulus words		Associative Overlap
	Moth	*Butterfly*	
Moth	50	7	7
Butterfly	1	50	1
Insect	1	6	1
Wings	2	5	2
Fly	10	4	4
			15

column was given as a response, either to *moth* or to *butterfly,* for 50 subjects. Thus, *moth* elicited *butterfly* once, and *butterfly* elicited *moth* seven times. The table lists only response words which the two stimulus words had in common. In the last column of the table, a measure of "associative overlap" is given.

What is nice about Deese's procedure is that it allows us to calculate the similarity of two words, which by his definition is simply the degree of associative overlap between the two words. Although the calculations become much more complicated for a whole set of words, it is possible, using basically the same procedure, to calculate the degree of associative overlap. To reiterate, the meaning of a word is given in terms of the associative overlap of its responses with the associative overlap of the responses of other words.

The Katz-Fodor semantic marker model provides an alternative to the association-type theories exemplified by Deese's model. To best appreciate this viewpoint, we begin by asking what a person needs to know in order to understand the meaning of a sentence. Obviously he must know the meanings of the individual words in the sentence. Thus, he must have a "dictionary in his mind," or, to borrow Miller's (1969) term, he must have a *subjective lexicon.* In addition, the person must have some notion of how the various words in the sentence relate to one another, because meaning is often dependent on context. The word *bank* provides a nice example. "He deposited his money in a bank" and "He sailed close to the river bank" both act to select a particular meaning of bank. ("It was a beautiful bank" does not.)

How are we able to use the other words in a sentence to understand the meaning of a given, otherwise ambiguous word? Katz and Fodor postulate two parts to the meaning of a word. The first is a set of markers, or semantic features. Each marker specifies a single part of the meaning of the word. The word *bachelor,* for example, is (human), (male), and (unmarried). These are three of its features. The word *wife,* on the other hand, has one feature in common with bachelor, (human), but two that are different, (female) and (married).

Besides the markers for individual words, there are also restrictions on possible combinations of words, and these are called selection restrictions. The phrase "married bachelor" violates these restrictions, because *bachelor* includes the feature (unmarried). (How can you be a married unmarried?) Similarly "bachelor's wife" won't work either, because a wife is (married) and a bachelor is (unmarried). Further, one of the semantic features for the "money" interpretation of *bank* corresponds to the selection restrictions of money, but violates the selection restrictions for "river bank." In this way meaning is clarified. When a feature appears in more than one word, the two words can be said to have something in common. A bachelor and a wife are both (human).

Semantics: A Final Note

The major purpose of linguistic theorizing, and the empirical research that both sparks it and follows it, is to uncover the psychological structure of our semantic spaces. Exploration of that space has been slow in progress. As one recent survey of the psychology of language put it:

> *it is hardly surprising that psychology has thus far failed to produce theories of any importance in the area of semantics. We cannot ask pertinent or insightful (to say nothing of experimentally resolvable) questions about how the semantic system of the speaker–hearer is used, or about how it is learned, until something substantial is known about the properties of that system. The part of theory construction which consists in conceptual analysis is, in this sense, methodologically prior to the part which considers questions about application or assimilation of concepts. It is highly probable, although doubtless depressing, that specifically psychological work on semantics will continue to be largely impertinent until a great deal more theoretical insight has been gained about the structure of formal semantic theory than is currently available. (Fodor, Bever & Garrett, 1974, p. 220)*

Of course, this statement was made two years before the publication of *Language and Perception* (Miller & Johnson-Laird, 1976) which promises to be an important contribution to the study of meaning.

The work on language leaves no doubt that language is extremely complex. The description of language provided by linguistics makes language learning appear to be a monumental achievement. We are used to dealing in words, and sentences, and ideas; we are not used to thinking about phonemes, morphemes, noun phrases, verb phrases, and transformations. Even though they are in some sense one step removed from what we actually experience, we have mastered them.

The emphasis on phrase structure grammars supplemented with transformational constructs is central to today's thinking about our language. Phrase structure grammar concerns the units that make up a sentence, whereas transformational grammar deals with the relations between sets of sentences that are members of the same "family." This entire field of inquiry has been, to borrow a phrase from Miller and Johnson-Laird (1976), something of an intellectual battleground. While significant research has been conducted in this area, it is likely to continue to be a major focus of new development in linguistics right into the 1980s. The study of meaning, or semantics, will go on simultaneously.

Art Buchwald is always very funny. One of his columns began as follows:

(Seattle Times, August, 1976),
There is something going on in the clothing industry of which you may not be aware. Designers and manufacturers are putting labels on the outside of the clothes instead of the inside.

It started a few years ago when Pierre Cardin, Courreges, Christian Dior, Gucci and others discovered that since women had paid so much for their outfits, they wanted everyone to know where they bought them.

The practice soon spread, and the saying, "You are what you eat," has been replaced by, "You are what you wear."

I was at a party the other evening and I noticed a lady with a large, "CD" on the back of her fur coat. "What a beautiful Christian Dior coat," I said.

"How did you know it was a Dior?" she said in amazement.

"I just guessed from the cut of it," I replied. I helped her off with the coat, and she gave me her silk scarf. It had "Givenchy" printed all over it.

"What a beautiful Givenchy scarf," I said.

"Oh, is that what it is? I just grabbed one out of a drawer."

The conversation continues in this vein to the point where the woman is told that it is obvious that she is wearing an Oleg Cassini slip since his name can be read on the lace through her Pucci blouse.

The day after reading this column one of the authors asked a colleague if he had seen the column, to which the colleague replied, "No, what was it about?" or words to that effect. The author said, "It was about wearing designer clothes with the label on the outside." The colleague asked for a copy.

Note that the author did not deliver to the colleague a verbatim repetition of the column, rather "the gist" was given. Almost never do we have to remember things word for word (except perhaps if we are acting in a play); usually we remember a part of what we have read or heard and that is all we relay. In the next section we will consider some of the psychological literature that deals specifically with what a person remembers after hearing a sentence, a paragraph, or a passage of verbal material.

FORM VERSUS MEANING

In 1966, Fillenbaum showed us that people remember *closed* as *not open* or *dead* as *not alive*. Let's examine his experiment in some detail. Subjects heard sentences of the form "The door was not closed" and later had a recognition memory test on these sentences. A test for this sentence might be as follows:

a. The door was not open
b. The door was not closed
c. The door was closed
d. The door was open

Of course the correct alternative is b. But considering only the subjects who choose incorrectly, which alternative do they tend to choose? Alternative c is dissimilar in both meaning and form, so we would tend to eliminate it. Reasoning further, if a subject remembered form at the expense of meaning, he would choose alternative a. However, as it turned out, if the subject failed to choose the correct alternative, b, he was much more likely to choose alternative d, which was similar in meaning, than to choose alternative a, which was similar in form. This result indicates that people tend to remember paraphrases of sentences, even when the paraphrases involve a change in the actual words or, alternatively, that they remember the meaning but not the surface structure.

An even more dramatic demonstration of this same phenomenon can be observed in the experiment of Bransford and Franks (1971). Instead of presenting their subjects with individual, unrelated sentences, Bransford and Franks presented sentences that were elements of a very short story. In fact the story could be expressed by a single sentence such as "The rock that rolled down the mountain crushed the tiny hut at the river." This story combines four simple elements:

1. The rock rolled down the mountain.
2. The rock crushed the hut.
3. The hut is at the river.
4. The hut is tiny.

In the first phase of the experiment, subjects saw a series of sentences containing one, two, or three elements. We've already seen the single-element sentences that might have been presented. Some two element sentences might be:

1. The tiny hut is at the river.
2. The rock crushed the tiny hut.

Finally, "The rock crushed the tiny hut at the river" is an example of a three-element sentence.

The design was such that the sentences that a subject heard from this story were randomly intermixed with one-, two- and three-element sentences from other stories. So, a subject might see "The hut is at the river," then see a few sentences that were unrelated to the story, then another sentence from the story, and so on.

The subject's task was to answer a brief question about each sentence. So the question for "The hut is at the river," might be "What is?"

It was a surprise to the subjects when, after all the sentences had been presented, an unexpected recognition test occurred. Old sentences that the subject had actually seen before were presented along with new sentences consisting of novel combinations of the elements of the story. The subjects judged, for each sentence, if it was identical to one they had heard before or not. They also rated the degree of confidence they had in their answer.

The results of this experiment are shown in Figure 5-13. The more elements of the story a test sentence contained, the more confident a subject was that he had heard the sentence before, a finding which has been termed the *linear effect*. Thus a subject was more confident that he had heard "The tiny hut is at the river (a two-element sentence) than "The hut is at the river" (a one-element sentence). Of interest is the fact that subjects were most confident that they had heard the sentence containing four elements, which happened to be a sentence that had never been presented to them.

The Bransford-Franks result indicates that when subjects hear the initial sentences, they integrate them into a holistic story and store the entire story in memory. They do not store information about the form of the original sentences. The reason that the complete four-element sentence looks so familiar to them is that it most closely matches their representation of the complete story.

Because the original results have been replicated in so many other lab-

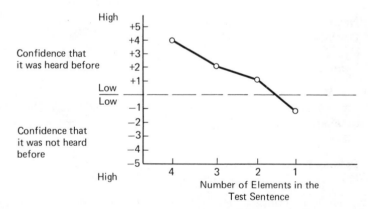

FIGURE 5–13.   Confidence that a test sentence had been heard before, for various types of sentences. The more elements of the whole story that a sentence contained, the more confident the subject was that he heard it before. Subjects were most confident about the four-element sentence, which had never even been presented. (Adapted from Bransford & Franks, 1971. Courtesy of Academic Press, Inc.)

oratories (for example, Cofer, 1973; Flagg, Potts, & Reynolds, 1975; Singer, 1973), the field has generally been impressed by the findings and appears to have accepted the underlying assumptions proposed by Bransford and Franks. There have been a few exceptions, however. For example, Katz (1973; Katz, Atkeson, & Lee, 1974) argued that the findings might be due to an artifact of the procedure used, or that they might be due to a guessing strategy that the subjects adopted. Reitman and Bower (1973), who observed the linear‚effect using nonsemantic alphanumeric characters instead of sentences, do not believe the linear effect is semantic in nature. Although many of these objections have yet to be dealt with in a satisfactory fashion, the impact of the original study has been powerful.

Advance Warning

One possible problem with generalizing from experiments such as those of Fillenbaum or Bransford and Franks is that in those cases the subjects did not know they would be tested for wording. The question thus arises whether people treat differently material whose wording they know they will be tested on.

Sachs (1967) performed a study relevant to this question. In her experiment, subjects listened to stories that contained a single critical sentence. That sentence was either in the active or the passive voice. An example follows.

There is an interesting story about the telescope. In Holland, a man named Lippershey was an eye-glass maker. One day his children were playing with some lenses. They discovered that things seemed very close if two lenses were held about a foot apart. Lippershey began experimenting and his "spyglass" attracted much attention. He sent a letter about it to Galileo, the great Italian scientist. Galileo at once realized the importance of the discovery and set about to build an instrument of his own. He used an old organ pipe with one lense curved out and the other in. On the first clear night he pointed the glass towards the sky. He was amazed to find the empty dark spaces filled with brightly gleaming stars. . . . (p. 438)

At this point, the subjects were given a recognition test. The following three sentences might have been presented and the subject's task was to choose the one he had read in the story.

1. He sent a letter about it to Galileo, the great Italian scientist.
2. Galileo, the great Italian scientist, sent him a letter about it.
3. A letter about it was sent to Galileo, the great Italian scientist.

If sentence 1 was your choice, then you correctly recognized the original sentence in the story. Comparing sentence 2 to sentence 1, we see that the meaning has been altered. Sentence 3, on the other hand, preserves the essential meaning, but changes the form of the original sentence from the active to the passive voice. The subjects were given the recognition test either immediately after the critical sentence occurred, or after a delay corresponding to either 80 or 160 syllables.

Sachs' results are clear-cut. The subjects were very likely to detect any change in the sentence when the test followed immediately; recognition scores were over 90 percent. However, when tested after a delay of 80 or 160 syllables, subjects were only about 60 percent accurate (where chance performance is 50 percent) in detecting a change in the *form* of the sentence. In contrast to this poor recognition memory for sentence wording, subjects maintained almost 80 percent accuracy in detecting changes in the meaning of the original sentence. This ability was particularly remarkable considering that some of the meaning changes were extremely subtle. For example, after 80 syllables, nearly all of the subjects recognized the difference between these two sentences:

1. There he met an archaeologist, Howard Carter, who urged him to join in the search for the tomb of King Tut.
2. There he met an archaeologist, Howard Carter, and urged him to join in the search for the tomb of King Tut.

This result is important in suggesting that even when people know they will have to remember the wording of a sentence, they still cannot do it very well. The meaning, the gist, however, is retained. The superiority of semantic recognition scores over those for recognition of form has been reaffirmed in later investigations both by Sachs (1974) and by others (for example, Soli & Balch, 1976).

Isolated Sentences Versus Sentences in Context

In the Sachs experiment, the critical sentence occurred as part of a meaningful, rather lengthy paragraph. The form of the sentence was not retained after a delay. But perhaps it is the paragraph context that encourages the subject to retain only the gist of the sentence. It is entirely possible that the wording of the sentence in isolation could be remembered if the subject put his mind to it.

These notions are given empirical teeth by the results of a study by Anderson and Bower (1973). The subjects in their study were shown a series of active and passive sentences, that either made up a story (in one experiment) or appeared randomly as a list of unrelated sentences. When, after a delay of two minutes, the subjects had to tell whether a critical sentence had been presented in the active or passive form, subjects in the "story experiment" were correct 56 percent of the time, not doing much better than a chance score of 50 percent. So far, these results replicate those of Sachs. However, subjects who had been presented with a list of unrelated sentences performed much better than chance; they were correct in telling whether a critical sentence had been active or passive over 74 percent of the time. Anderson and Bower reached the conclusion that "subjects can represent passive (or active) relations in long-term memory if the task emphasizes verbatim memory for surface features of the sentences" (p. 226). Later, they speculate that subjects might "have control (conscious or not) over whether they (a) represent and encode all inputs as 'active' sentences in the logical deep-structure, thus converting passives to actives, or (b) represent and encode the input in accordance with the active or passive relation asserted in the sentence. The 'natural' processing of sentences in the meaningful context of discourse, dialogue and text is to adopt option (a) and convert sentences to the active deep-structures. However, when necessary or advantageous, the subject will adopt encoding strategy (b). . . ." (pp. 227–228)

A Reiteration: Form and Meaning

The evidence we have reviewed here lends support to the notion that when we are given some meaningful material to learn, we remember the meaning, or at least the gist of it, much better than we remember the exact form in which the sentence occurred. If we put effort into the task of remembering wording, and particularly if the material consists of isolated sentences out of natural context, we may retain some information about form. It is clear that what we do depends in large measure on what the demands of our task involve.

CONTEXT AND MEMORY

Suppose we told you that last week we walked into a restaurant owned by our friend Sally only to discover that the floor was dirty because Sally had used the mop. Furthermore, Sally's husband's shirt looked terrible because Sally had ironed it. You might think to yourself, "That's strange. Mops usually make floors clean. I guess the mop must have been dirty. It's also strange that the shirt looked terrible because shirts usually look better when they have been ironed. I guess Sally must be terrible at ironing." In other words, you would be making a few special assumptions in order to understand or comprehend the information you had been given. In fact comprehension may be nothing more than supplying the necessary special assumptions, or context, that make a bit of material understandable.

Bransford and Johnson (1973) performed a relevant experiment that supported just this hypothesis. In their experiment subjects saw sentences like these:

1. The floor was dirty so Sally used the mop.
2. The floor was dirty because Sally used the mop.

The first sentence is easy to understand from our knowledge of the world without any special assumptions. The second sentence only makes sense if we make the assumption that the mop was dirty. In a recognition test given later on, the subjects falsely recognized (thought they saw before) the sentence "Sally used a dirty mop" only after having heard sentence 2, but not after having heard sentence 1. Bransford and Johnson's result indicates that subjects do spontaneously make special assumptions, and furthermore, that these special assumptions are stored in memory. More important, results like this indicate that we have to go a bit further than asking whether the surface structure or the meaning of a sentence is stored. Clearly, something else is involved in our recall of ordinary language materials, and that is our general knowledge of the world.

A more recent example of this phenomenon can be seen in the work of Schweller, Brewer, and Dahl (1976) on *illocutionary forces*. In the early 1960s, Austin (1962) proposed that sentences not only have content but they also have a function. When a person utters a sentence such as "Boy, it's cold in here," in the appropriate context that sentence not only conveys information but also has an illocutionary force that roughly corresponds to the intent of the speaker. In this case, his intention might be to ask someone to do something (such as close the window). The work of Schweller et al. showed that when a person hears sentences containing reported utterances, he has a tendency to confuse these original sentences with new sentences that contain illocutionary forces consistent with the original sentences. For example, subjects who heard the sentence, "The cute little girl told her mother she wanted a drink," thought they had heard "The cute little girl asked her mother for a drink," which has the same illocutionary force. Hearing "The cute little girl told her mother she wanted to be a plumber" did not have the same sort of effect. The results provide another bit of evidence that when a person hears a sentence he elaborates it and stores the elaboration. Elaborations, like special assumptions, are then confused in memory with the material originally presented.

Carrying this one step further, if we cannot elaborate, or if we do not know what the special assumptions are, or if we cannot generate the appropriate context, almost nothing will get into memory. Subjects who heard an apparently nonsensical (but perfectly grammatical) sentence like "The haystack was important because the cloth ripped" had a hard time remembering it. But, supply the context "parachutist" and it suddenly becomes easy to remember (Bransford & Johnson, 1973). Thus, we can completely understand all of the words in a sentence, and the sentence can be perfectly grammatical, but if we don't have a way to fit it into our knowledge structure, these advantages are nearly useless.

Here is another example. Read the following passage once and try to remember as much of it as you can.

The procedure is actually quite simple. First you arrange things into different groups. Of course, one pile may be sufficient depending on how much there is to do. If you have to go somewhere else due to lack of facilities that is the next step, otherwise you are pretty well set. It is important not to overdo things. That is, it is better to do too few things at once than too many. In the short run this may not seem important but complications can easily arise. A mistake can be expensive as well. At first the whole procedure will seem complicated. Soon, however, it will become just another facet of life. It is difficult to foresee any end to the necessity for this task in the immediate future, but then one never can tell. After the procedure is completed one arranges the materials into different groups again. Then they can be put into their appropriate places. Eventually they will be used once more and the whole cycle will then have to be repeated. However, that is part of life.

What do you remember from the passage? What was it all about? Did it make any sense at all? If you are like most people, you remember very little. It just doesn't make sense. But, if the verbal label "washing clothes" is supplied for you, the picture changes dramatically. Now do you remember anything? Reread the passage with that label in mind. If you're like most people, it is much easier to comprehend, and much easier to remember (Bransford & Johnson, 1972). But why? How can supplying two ordinary words make such a difference? It is because whenever we are presented with new material which we must comprehend or later recall, we try to integrate it with existing information. We understand new information in terms of old. In this case, the verbal label "washing clothes" refers to a whole body of "old" knowledge concerning this common activity, and the passage is understood in light of that knowledge.

Just as we can supply a phrase to make some material more comprehensible and memorable, so we can provide a picture. This should come as no surprise, since a picture, as we know, can sometimes be worth many words. Bransford and Johnson (1972) provided the demonstration. They presented the following passage to their subjects:

If the balloons popped the sound wouldn't be able to carry since everything would be too far away from the correct floor. A closed window would also prevent the sound from carrying, since most buildings tend to be well insulated. Since the whole operation depends on the steady flow of electricity, a break in the middle of the wire would also cause problems. Of course, the fellow could shout, but the human voice is not loud enough to carry that far. An additional problem is that the string could break on the instrument. Then there would be no accompaniment to the message. It is clear that the best situation would involve less distance. Then there would be fewer potential problems. With face to face contact, the least number of things could go wrong.

In the "no context" condition, subjects listened to the passage and tried to remember it. They found it very difficult to remember any of the ideas in the passage. However, if they had been provided with some "context" in the form of a picture (see Figure 5-14), they found the passage to be much more comprehensible and they remembered nearly twice as many ideas from it.

It is evident that we must rely on context or previous knowledge to un-

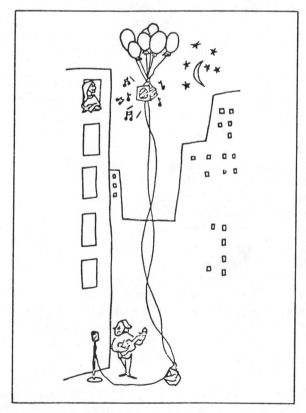

FIGURE 5–14.　This picture helped subjects remember the material in a difficult passage in the Bransford and Johnson experiment (1972). (After Bransford & Johnson, 1972. Courtesy of Academic Press, Inc.)

derstand new material. The way this works has been discussed quite elegantly by Haviland and Clark (1975). Imagine that you are at a picnic, waiting for your friends to arrive with the beer. An old Chevrolet pulls up, the driver gets out, goes to the trunk, lifts some beer out and says, "The beer is warm." Naturally, this sentence is easy to understand because the context lets you know exactly what is meant by "the beer." In a laboratory situation, the context can also be provided, this time by a relevant sentence preceding the one to be comprehended. Thus, subjects in an experiment were faster to comprehend "The beer is warm" when it was preceded by "We got some beer out of the trunk" than when it was preceded by "We checked the picnic supplies." Merely identifying the word "beer" is not enough; in order to comprehend its meaning in the sentence, a person must know what concept the word is referring to. Put another way, to understand the meaning of a language item, we must take context into account, which is where our general knowledge, or long-term memories, comes into play. Haviland and Clark (1975) have proposed that all sentences contain old (given) information and new information. We use this old information as an address to the relevant parts of memory, and then connect the new information in the sentence with what is already known. This is called the "given–new strategy" of comprehension.

COMPREHENSION AND INFERENCES

The "elaborations" we discussed in the previous section are actually one special type of *inference* that people make. When some material is presented to us, we listen to it and try to figure out what it means. While the actual words presented convey some meaning, much of the "meaning" is created by us in response to the material presented. In other words we add, we infer, we create. All this is a necessary part of the comprehension of natural language.

It is important to ask whether we do this "creating" at the time the material is presented to us—that is, during comprehension—or whether it occurs later, when we are tested about the material to which we have been exposed. A series of studies by Keenan and Kintsch (1974) and McKoon and Keenan (1974) addresses this issue. Subjects read a short paragraph, varying in length from 17 to 160 words. The paragraphs were designed so that one version expressed a particular proposition explicitly while the other expressed it implicitly. Table 5-3 gives an example of one of the paragraphs, expressed in both forms. After reading either the explicit or implicit version, subjects had to verify a test sentence, in this case, "The gas caused an explosion." Note that the test sentence is not explicitly stated in the second version of the paragraph; however, it must be inferred by the reader in order for the paragraph to make sense. The test sentence was

TABLE 5–3. EXPLICIT AND IMPLICIT PARAGRAPHS FROM THE EXPERIMENT OF KEENAN AND KINTSCH (1974).

Explicit

A gas leak developed in the heating system of a house on 5th Street. The gas caused an explosion which destroyed the house and started a fire that threatened several neighboring structures.

Implicit

A gas leak developed in the heating system of a house on 5th Street. An explosion destroyed the house and started a fire that threatened several neighboring structures.

presented either immediately after the paragraph or after a delay of 20 minutes, and the subject had to indicate whether the sentence was true with respect to the paragraph. Figure 5-15 presents the results.

The interesting result is that after a delay there is no difference in the time to verify an explicit versus an implicit test sentence. This implies that the inference was made during the reading or comprehension of the paragraphs, not later when the subjects were asked questions about the paragraphs. If subjects had made the inferences at the time of the test, reaction times would have been longer for implicit paragraphs. But, you may be asking, the reaction times were shorter for the explicit sentences on the immediate test. Why? We know from previous work described in this chapter that immediately after a sentence is presented there is a bit of verbatim memory for that sentence. Thus, for a short time, subjects can use this verbatim memory, the memory for surface structure, to facilitate recall.

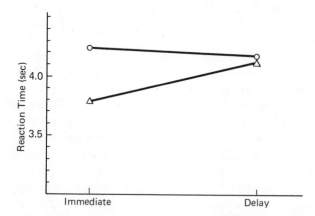

FIGURE 5–15. Reaction times for verification of explicitly stated sentences (triangles) and implicitly stated sentences (circles). (After Keenan & Kintsch, 1974. Courtesy of Lawrence Erlbaum Associates, Inc.)

After a 20-minute delay, particularly one filled with interfering material, the surface memory is lost.

Another type of inference that people make when they comprehend a new sentence has to do with the "presuppositions" of that sentence. A presupposition of a sentence is simply a condition which must hold in order for the sentence to be contextually appropriate. So, for example, the sentence "It is the girl that is riding the bicycle" presupposes that the bicycle is being ridden by someone. The sentence asserts that it is the girl who is doing the riding. Put another way, whenever a speaker utters a sentence he assumes that certain facts are already known to the person being addressed. These already known facts are the presuppositions of the sentence. How do we know what the presuppositions are? We can determine them quite easily, for they always remain true even if the sentence itself is negated. Thus, "It is the girl that is riding the bicycle" and "It is not the girl that is riding the bicycle" both imply that the bicycle is being ridden by someone. "Jane ignored her nagging husband" and "Jane did not ignore her nagging husband" both imply that the husband was being a bit obnoxious. One last example: The word "again" carries a presupposition, namely that whatever is being talked about has happened before. "This New Year's Eve, George got smashed again" and "This New Year's Eve, George did not get smashed again" both imply that George got smashed on some previous New Year's Eve.

Research with sentences that contain presuppositions has shown that the presuppositions are "figured out" during the process of comprehending a sentence, and that they are encoded in memory (Haviland & Clark, 1975). In other words, the presence of a presupposition causes a listener to infer the information and to encode it into memory.

This can be very important, of course, if it occurs in the course of courtroom testimony. Witnesses who testify during a court trial are liable for perjury when they make false assertions, but not when they make false presuppositions. If jurors encode the false presuppositions and remember them while they are deliberating, this could have a serious outcome on the eventual verdict. Harris, Teske, and Ginns (1975) gave subjects a mock trial testimony containing either direct assertions or false presuppositions. After hearing the testimony, the jurors were given a test on the facts that had been presented during the testimony. The subject-jurors had a tendency to remember the false presuppositions as if they were actually direct assertions. This occurred even when subjects received detailed instructions about distinguishing facts from inferences. This is very discouraging, of course, because in the courtroom trial it is exceedingly important that jurors accurately remember the information they have been exposed to. The fact that they can so easily be misled can create real problems for the administration of justice. We will return to this subject in a later chapter when we take up the practical applications of research in cognitive psychology.

SUMMARY

We began by noting that our knowledge of language is part of our long-term memories, perhaps one of the most important things we "know" about. Whether we speak English or French, Russian or Arabic, it is with language that we both speak and comprehend messages and ideas that we wish to communicate. All languages seem to have something in common with each other. They contain phenomes and morphemes; they all have a grammar. More importantly, the language we speak seems to have an influence on our nonlanguage behaviors in interesting ways. There is ample evidence that speakers of different languages have very similar perceptual experiences, but also good evidence that within a language community, the particular words that are used can affect the way we remember a given perceptual experience. Language affects how we remember both verbal and pictorial material to which we have been exposed. Language affects the ease with which we can solve problems ,and how we reconstruct our past experiences. In these ways, language affects thought.

chapter six

CONCEPT FORMATION

outline

WE HAVE TALKED A GREAT DEAL in the preceding chapters about the concepts people have, how concepts are embedded in memory, and how concepts are retrieved and used when required by the situation at hand. We discussed these processes as if everyone knew what concepts are, but we said nothing about how concepts are learned or formed in the first place. Concepts come from somewhere; they are not just there, in your mind, when you happen to need them. Concept formation has been an active area of research in psychology for some time. This chapter is an effort to review the facts and theories about concept formation that psychologists have developed in recent years.

Sometimes we learn concepts by being given a list of exemplars along with the functions the item can serve. Consider the following.

(1) A corplum *may be used for support.*
(2) Corplums *may be used to close off an open place.*
(3) A corplum *may be long or short, thick or thin, strong or weak.*
(4) A wet corplum *does not burn.*
(5) You can make a corplum *smooth with sandpaper.*
(6) The painter used a corplum *to mix his paints.*

(Werner & Kaplan, 1950, p. 251)

Did you learn anything from these sentences? Do you have any idea now what a *corplum* is? What is your best guess? Most people conclude that a *corplum* is a stick or a piece of wood. If you drew a similar conclusion, then we would say that you learned a new (though probably not particularly useful) concept, the concept of *corplums,* which, in our artificial language, covers what we would otherwise call pieces of wood.

Consider a different example. Suppose I tell you that within a set of geometrical designs, some are DAXs and others are not. Then I proceed with the following statements.

1. A DAX can be large, bright, red, and triangular.
2. A large, dull red square is a DAX.
3. A DAX can be small, dull, red, and triangular.
4. A small, bright green triangle is not a DAX.
5. A DAX cannot be large, bright, green, and triangular.
6. A small, dull red square is a DAX.

From these statements, can you tell me what a DAX is? If you conclude that DAXs are red geometrical figures, you are entirely consistent with the information that has been given. Furthermore, you have learned a new concept, which is identified by the nonsense word DAX and which allows you to categorize into DAXs and non-DAXs the members of a population of geometrical designs.

Let's try one final example, about a more useful concept, which will come up in later theoretical discussions in this chapter. The following statements pertain to the concept of an H.

1. An H guides a person's behavior.
2. A person usually can express his H verbally.
3. Hs commonly occur in problem solving.
4. An H is a possible problem solution.
5. A person may consider several Hs before he solves a problem.
6. In any problem, only one H is correct.

H is a shorthand designation for hypothesis. At the present time in this field, hypothesis theory is probably the most widely accepted account of how people solve concept problems or acquire new concepts. The theory is based on the idea that people are never at a loss for responses in a problem-solving situation. Their behavior, that is, their attempts at solution, is always guided by one or more hypotheses about what the correct answer is. Finding the solution to the problem is primarily a matter of finding out which of many hypotheses is correct.

As the foregoing examples would suggest, most concepts are categories and are identified primarily by the nouns of our natural language. Our knowledge of the world is composed largely of concepts and relationships among concepts. Somehow, the concepts that we learn throughout a lifetime become encoded and represented in semantic memory and, discounting forgetting, are available for retrieval and use in later interactions with the world. While we have spoken before of concepts and their representation in semantic memory, we have said relatively little about how concepts come into being or about the complex rule structures upon which they are based. That is the primary purpose of the present chapter.

THE REPRESENTATION OF CONCEPTS

As we have seen, one type of theory characterizes a concept in semantic memory in terms of its features. Objects, processes, events, and states of affairs in the world are categorized and encoded conceptually in memory through the extraction of their common features. Thus, in general, we do not treat each encounter as new but classify it in terms of others in our experience with which it shares features. The classification process is performed by matching up the features of the present encounter with those of various concepts represented in semantic memory.

In this theory, a concept is defined in terms of some relationship among its relevant features. To be formal,

$$C = R(x, y \ . \ . \ .)$$

where C is a concept, x, y, . . . are the relevant or defining features of that concept, and R is the rule that integrates those features (Bourne, 1974). For example, the concept of a canary can be defined in terms of a collection of features such as "is yellow" *and* "can sing" *and* "is a common pet" *and* . . . . The concept of a strike in baseball, is "a pitched ball passing through a prescribed but imaginary rectangle over home plate" *and/or* "a pitched ball which the batter swings at and misses." Both examples have been somewhat simplified, but you can see how a feature of a given situation enters into the definition of an applicable concept. Notice that the rule or the relationship among features is not the same in the two examples. In the first case, the relationship requires that all attributes be present before a given instance can be classified as canary. For the strike, an instance need not have both characteristics in order to qualify. The rule for integrating defining features in the two cases is different, and this is a matter we will need to consider when we discuss the structure of concepts in detail.

CONCEPTUAL PROCESSES

These considerations lead us directly to the distinction between feature or attribute learning and rule learning. To form a concept requires that an individual both learn, or identify, the critical features of instances of that concept and also how those features interrelate. To say that a person has acquired concept X implies that he has learned or identified (most of) the defining features of concept X and, further, that he has learned the specific relationship among those features. To some extent, feature learning and rule learning may be different processes, despite the fact that they proceed simultaneously or in parallel. If they are different processes, then their course may be affected by different variables. It becomes important to be able to observe, experimentally, each process independently of the other. This is a characteristic of recent research on concept formation.

The study of feature learning can be observed essentially in isolation if the learner is provided with preliminary information specifying the rule to be used. If the learner knows the rule at the outset, the only task that remains is to identify the defining features. If the learner knows the defining features at the outset, the task that remains is to learn their relationship. These two situations provide the essentials for studying feature learning and rule learning independently.

The basic format of concept learning tasks used in most experiments is inductive. The learner or the subject of the experiment is given certain information, such as the rule or the defining features, at the outset. He is then presented, as in the examples that began this chapter, with a series of stimuli some of which illustrate and others of which do not illustrate the concept. Typically, the subject will be asked to categorize each stimulus as it appears. Subsequently, the subject receives informative feedback regarding the correctness of his response. Each trial of the problem provides the subject with a new instance and some new information about the unknown component of the concept. If the concept is not too difficult, the subject eventually discovers the missing component and begins to assign stimuli to response categories without error. At that point, we can say that the subject understands the concept in question.

A variety of kinds of concepts, stimulus materials, and rules have been used in experimental studies of concept formation. In Figure 6–1 we present some illustrative stimulus materials. Almost any stimuli will work, though dimensionalized geometric designs are very common. Rules also differ from study to study, but we will leave our discussion of that fairly complicated issue until the next chapter. Finally, there have been many variations on the general task format. Commonly, stimuli are presented to the subject one at a time. In some circumstances, however, two stimuli occur in a single trial, and the subject's task is to identify the positive one. In still other circumstances, all stimuli are laid out at once, with individual ones designated either by the experimenter or the subject for test on a given trial. Typically, the subject is asked to make a category response to each stimulus. It is also common to have the subject hypothesize periodically, indicating his best guess of the solution at the time. More rarely, the subject might be asked to give some confidence estimate for his response. Which variation on the procedural theme is employed depends, as always, on the purpose of the study. We will make note of important procedural characteristics of various experiments as we examine them throughout the chapter.

HOW ARE CONCEPTS FORMED?

A variety of ideas has been expressed about how people form concepts for representation in semantic memory. These ideas fall into three classes, which we will discuss and illustrate in the following sections. We should note at the outset, however, that all of the theories are based on the process of attribute or feature identification. In other words, the emphasis has been on those characteristics of the stimulus that allow a person to decide whether it does or does not illustrate the concept. In contrast, there has been relatively little said about the acquisition and use of rules or relationships among attributes.

A: Geometrical Designs*
A population with three dimensions, each with four levels

red

| ○ | ○ ○ | ○ ○
○ ○ | ○ ○
○ ○ | + | + + | +
+ + | + +
+ + | △ | △ △ | △
△ △ | △ △
△ △ | ✳ | ✳ ✳ | ✳
✳ ✳ | ✳ ✳
✳ ✳ |

yellow

| ○ | ○ ○ | ○ ○
○ ○ | ○ ○
○ ○ | + | + + | +
+ + | + +
+ + | △ | △ △ | △
△ △ | △ △
△ △ | ✳ | ✳ ✳ | ✳
✳ ✳ | ✳ ✳
✳ ✳ |

green

| ○ | ○ ○ | ○ ○
○ ○ | ○ ○
○ ○ | + | + + | +
+ + | + +
+ + | △ | △ △ | △
△ △ | △ △
△ △ | ✳ | ✳ ✳ | ✳
✳ ✳ | ✳ ✳
✳ ✳ |

blue

| ○ | ○ ○ | ○ ○
○ ○ | ○ ○
○ ○ | + | + + | +
+ + | + +
+ + | △ | △ △ | △
△ △ | △ △
△ △ | ✳ | ✳ ✳ | ✳
✳ ✳ | ✳ ✳
✳ ✳ |

*Dimensions (and values) are: Color (red, yellow, green, and blue); Shape (circle, cross, triangle, and star); and Number of figures (one, two, three, and four).

B: Faces**
A population with three dimensions, each with three levels

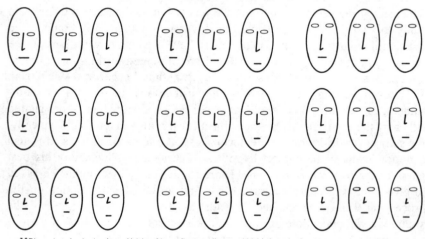

**Dimensions (and values) are: Height of brow (low, medium, and high); Length of nose (long, medium, and short); and Strength of chin (strong, medium, and weak).

C: Words***
A population with three dimensions, each with two levels

+++	++−	+−+	+−−
college	bird	bridge	beauty
progress	child	metal	evening
−++	−+−	−−+	−−−
force	burn	black	poor
tax	worry	rock	sorrow

(*** see footnote page 167)

FIGURE 6–1. Several Illustrative Populations of Stimulus Patterns Used in Concept Learning Experiments.

One of the very earliest definitions of a concept was in terms of those elements or stimulus features which members of the class held in common. Although we are unsure when or with whom this idea originated, its first strong advocate in the psychological literature was Clark L. Hull (1920). Hull described concept formation as the abstraction of elements identical to a class of stimuli and the attachment of a single response to those elements. New stimuli sharing those elements would elicit the same response, leading to a phenomenon called *stimulus generalization*. Hull went on to demonstrate the feasibility of his theory for concept learning in the following experiment. Adult subjects were taught to respond with a unique nonsense name to each of 12 different Chinese characters. Each character had its own unique radical (element) imbedded within it. Altogether, six different lists of 12 different characters were used, each of which contained one of the basic 12 radicals. Six of these radicals and character sets are shown in Figure 6–2. The six sets were learned as paired-associate lists by each subject with the same nonsense name response assigned to a given radical in each list. Learning improved from list to list and the subject's ability to give the correct nonsense response to each character on its first presentation increased from less than 30 percent correct on the first trial of the second list to approximately 60 percent correct on the first trial of the sixth list. To Hull, this signified that the subjects were abstracting the element, that is, the radical, common to a given class of characters and responding primarily to that radical. Hull also concluded the learning process must be relatively unconscious, for most subjects were unable to verbalize in any coherent way the basis for their reaction to new characters.

The idea of common elements as a theoretical description for concepts and concept formation persisted in popularity through the 1950s. The most recent formulation of this idea was the mathematical theory developed by Bourne and Restle (1959). Their argument, basically, was that any stimulus encountered by the subject gives rise to a multiplicity of cues, some of which are common to a given category and therefore relevant to that category and others of which are not common or are irrelevant. Bourne and Restle argued that the response which identifies the category becomes conditioned to the common elements. Thus, whenever a significant number of those common elements is present in a new stimulus, the category response will

---

*** Dimensions (and values) are: Evaluation (good, +; bad, −), Activity (fast, +; slow, −), and Potency (strong, +; weak, +). Plus-minus designations in the examples above refer to the values on the dimensions in the order listed. Two examples for each combination of values are given. Examples are taken from a normative study of semantic dimensions reported by Heise (1965). Note that the attributes of this population are defined more abstractly, by use or by function, than those of populations A and B which are concrete, physical stimulus features. (From D. D. Heise, Semantic differential profiles for 1000 most frequent English words. *Psychological Monographs*, 1965, 79, No. 8. Copyright 1965 by the American Psychological Association and reprinted by permission.)

Name	Radical (concept)	List 1	List 2	List 3	List 4	List 5	List 6

FIGURE 6–2. Some of the stimulus materials used by Hull (1920). Each of the six different radicals is embedded in a unique character in each list. Each radical is associated with a nonsense name, which is the response to be given to that radical regardless of the character in which it occurs. (Reprinted by permission of American Psychological Association.)

occur. Irrelevant elements, because of their inconsistent association with the category response, are adapted out—that is, the subject learns to ignore them. Thus, when a concept has been formed, the subject is said to base his conceptual response on a perceptual analysis of each new stimulus designed to determine whether it contains a sufficient number of category-relevant elements.

While identical elements are undoubtedly involved in the definition of some concepts, this idea seems much too simplistic to account for all we know about concept formation. For one thing, the description is too mechanical. It states that concepts are formed more or less through the automatic function of feedback one receives about his responses. Furthermore, it relies too heavily on the formation of associations in a gradual fashion across a series of encounters with different stimuli. Associations, not any thought process, determine our response to new stimuli. This type of characterization is sometimes referred to as stimulus–response (S–R) associationistic and as noncognitive in nature.

Psychological research on human concept formation did not begin in earnest until the 1950s. Prior to that time the empirical evidence was fragmentary and scattered throughout the literature. In the 1950s under the leadership of Carl Hovland and Jerome Bruner, experimental psychologists began an intensive analysis of the variables affecting and processes underlying concept learning. It was largely because of Bruner's work that the associationistic view of concept learning fell into disfavor. Bruner and his co-workers (Bruner, Goodnow, & Austin, 1956) discovered that people tend to use systematic strategies in their effort to discover some unknown concept. These strategies were difficult to describe in terms of elemental stimulus–response associations. These researchers felt that concepts, rather than being formed passively through the repeated occurrence of common elements in concept exemplars, were formed via an active, strategic, hypothesis-testing process.

Strategies for Feature Identification

The following experiment illustrates the approach of Bruner, Goodnow, and Austin. An array of stimulus materials such as those depicted in Figure 6–1 is laid out before the subject. Suppose the stimuli have four dimensions—Number, Size, Color, and Form—each with three values. Some one stimulus within the array, say, *one large red triangle,* is designated as a positive instance of an unknown concept, to be discovered by the subject. On the basis of this single example, the subject is asked to formulate his best guess, that is, his hypothesis, about the unknown concept. Subsequently, the subject is allowed to select any other instance from the array and ask the experimenter whether it is a positive or negative instance of the concept. The experimenter responds truthfully and then asks the subject for his current best guess. This procedure repeats itself until the subject is confident about being able to name the concept.

The manner in which subjects go about formulating hypotheses and selecting subsequent stimuli for testing is not erratic or unsystematic. Many subjects perform as follows. After the first positive stimulus has been identified by the experimenter, the subject proceeds to formulate a hypothesis which contains within it all features of that stimulus. This is a global hypothesis. It says, in effect, "In the light of the information presently available, *one, large, red,* and *triangle* are all potentially relevant features of the unknown concept. I have no basis for ruling out any of them. I can, however, rule out two and three, small and medium, green and blue, and circle and square as possibilities." The subject then proceeds to select a new instance which differs in one and only one attribute from the first. He might select, for example, *two large red triangles.* Such a selection is guaranteed to pay off in new information. If the selection is positive, the subject can immediately determine that the Number attribute is not important to the concept. If both single and double patterns are members of the concept, then Number does not distinguish members from nonmembers. Thus, the subject can now formulate a revised hypothesis, "large red triangles are positive." If, on the other hand, the newly selected instance is negative, the subject has a different kind of information. Such an outcome tells him that Number *is* an important attribute and that positive instances must be singular. Therefore, the subject should state, as his hypothesis, the same features as contained in his first hypothesis. The third, and all subsequent stimulus selections vary one other attribute from the initial positive instance, for example, *one small red triangle*. Once again, depending upon the outcome of selection, the subject can determine whether the changed attribute, in this case, Size, is relevant to the concept.

This procedure is called the *conservative focusing strategy*. In Bruner's experiments, a sizable number of subjects adopted such a strategy. It is perhaps the easiest strategy to use in problems of this type. Its main advantage is the relief it provides for the subject's memory. Rather than having to remember each stimulus selected and its category, positive or negative, the subject merely needs to remember the current hypothesis, for the current hypothesis contains within it all features which are still possibly relevant. The subject cycles systematically through all variable attributes of the stimuli, identifying them as positive or negative, and, when he completes the cycle, he has enough information to state the correct concept. An illus-

TABLE 6–1. EXAMPLES OF FOCUSING STRATEGIES.

	Stimulus Patterns	Category	Hypothesis
A: Conservative focusing			
Focal stimulus	1LR△	+	"1LR△"
Subject's selections			
1.	2LR△	+	"LR△"
2.	1SR△	−	"LR△"
3.	1LG△	+	"L△"
4.	1LR□	−	"L△"
	Concept: L△		
B: Focus gambling			
Focal stimulus	1LR△	+	"1LR△"
Subject's selections			
1.	2LG△	+	"L△"
2.	1LR□	−	"L△"
3.	1SG△	−	"L△"
	Concept: L△		

trative sequence of stimulus selections and hypothesis statements under the conservative focusing strategy is given in Table 6–1.

Of course, not all subjects follow the exact same strategy. Bruner identified three other possibilities within the same experimental problem. One is essentially a variation on the conservative focusing strategy, called *focus gambling* (see Table 6–1). The strategy begins in the same way as conservative focusing. The first positive instance provides the basis for a global hypothesis. In one or more of his stimulus selections, however, the subject varies more than one attribute of the stimulus. Say, for example, on Trial 2 the subject selects *two large green triangles* and determines its status. The subject is, in effect, gambling that the stimulus will be positive. If it is positive, the subject can immediately rule out Number and Color as relevant attributes. Changing both makes no difference in category; the stimulus is still positive. The solution must have something to do with Size and Form. There is some risk, however. Suppose the second stimulus is negative. This implies that either Number or Color or both are relevant and the subject will have to make some additional selections to determine which is the case. Thus the name focus gambling—the subject gambles and there is both potential payoff and potential risk. If the subject's gamble is correct, he accomplishes in one trial what would otherwise require two or more. If his gamble fails, he runs the risk of getting no information at all from his stimulus selection. This is not a particularly popular strategy, although its frequency of occurrence increases when the subject is put under time pressure to solve the problem or where significant rewards are contingent upon rapid solution.

The remaining strategies are fundamentally different from focusing. Rather than formulating a composite hypothesis based on the first positive instance, subjects in these cases formulate one or more hypotheses involving only certain features of the first positive instance. There are many such hypotheses. Some subjects appear to formulate and test these hypotheses one at a time, checking the possibility, for example, that all triangles are positive and, if that fails, moving on to the possibility that all large figures or all large triangles are positive. Each stimulus selection pertains to the single hypothesis under test on any given trial. Because there are many such individual hypotheses, such an approach could lead to very slow problem solving. A related alternative is for the subject to try to test several hypotheses at once. Trying to remember each of several hypotheses and whether or not the feedback information is confirmatory produces a considerable strain on the subject's ability to remember and to process information. Thus, there are serious cognitive problems with each of these individual hypothesis-testing strategies. Nonetheless, they were observed to occur with some frequency in Bruner's experiments and, as a consequence, were adopted as possibilities in later theoretical work. These strategies are referred to as *scanning* strategies. When the subject tests one hypothesis at a time, it is called *successive scanning*. When he tests more than one, it's called *simultaneous scanning*.

Bruner's research initiated an entirely new line of theories about concept formation. Clearly, the subject is an active participant in solving conceptual or, for that matter, any other kind of problems. The fundamental theoretical construct is a mental or cognitive unit called a hypothesis, which the subject formulates, remembers, tests, and revises in the light of incoming information. Bruner's work was primarily descriptive, concerned with verifying the existence of hypothesis behavior and describing some of its characteristics. Following Bruner's work came some fundamental changes in concept formation theory. This work was primarily the effort of Restle (1962) and Bower and Trabasso (1964). While there are some differences in how these theorists thought about concept formation, the similarities among them allow us to treat their ideas as a single theory.

The simplest version of the theory is as follows. For any concept problem, the subject will think of a number of possible solutions. This set of ideas is called a hypothesis pool. Prior to his response to any stimulus, including the first, a person will sample one or more hypotheses from the pool and respond accordingly. Assume for the moment that he samples only one. Whatever the hypothesis, it will give the problem solver a way to respond to the stimulus presented. In a problem like the one described by Bruner, for example, the subject might select the hypothesis that "all single figures are examples of the concept and to be responded to positively, while all non-singular figures are negative." If the first stimulus is *one large red triangle,* the person responds positively in accord with his hypothesis. If the stimulus is *two medium green circles,* he responds negatively. The subject follows a "win–stay, lose–shift" strategy. That is, if the experimenter calls the subject's category response correct, the subject uses the same hypothesis on the next trial (win–stay); if the experimenter calls the subject's response wrong, the subject returns his hypothesis to the hypothesis pool and resamples (lose–shift). Notice that, in this theory, the subject returns his hypothesis to the pool before he samples again. This is called *sampling with replacement* and it allows for some probability that the subject will pick a rejected hypothesis on the very next or some later trial. The sequence of events continues until the subject samples a correct hypothesis. When he has the correct hypothesis, he will no longer make any errors, will not resample from the hypothesis pool, and will have solved the problem.

Several aspects of this theory deserve special attention. First of all, it assumes that a person solves concept problems in an all-or-none, insightful fashion. Problem solving occurs when and only when the subject samples the correct hypothesis. Prior to that time, while the subject is dealing in incorrect hypotheses, he flounders and his performance (probability of assigning stimuli to the proper category) remains at a chance level. When he samples the correct hypothesis, performance moves from a chance level to a perfect level. Thus, in contrast to S–R associative theories of concept formation, which assert that the concept is learned gradually over a series of encounters with positive instances, this theory says that problem solving is instantaneous and occurs on the trial when the subject samples the correct hypothesis.

Second, the theory claims that learning occurs only on error trials. An error is the only occasion on which the subject changes hypotheses. Correct responses can be made for the wrong reason. Suppose, for example, the subject is testing the hypothesis that large stimuli are positive, where the actual solution is that triangles are positive. If he runs into a series of stimuli which are both large and triangular, for example, *one large red triangle, two large green triangles, three large blue triangles,* he will respond correctly to all of them. His category response is correct only because each of the stimuli is a triangle. The subject, however, thinks that he is correct because the stimuli are large. He has no basis for changing his mind or changing his hypothesis until he encounters some large non-triangular stimulus or some small or medium triangular stimulus. On that occasion, his hypothesis will lead him to make an incorrect category response which in turn will be the occasion for him to change his hypothesis. The subject, in a sense, learns nothing when he is correct. He merely sticks with what he has been doing all along.

Third, the theory has been called a "no memory theory." This is because the subject is said to sample with replacement. Such an assumption implies that a rejected hypothesis has the same probability of being sampled on subsequent trials as any other hypothesis, including hypotheses which have not been tested. Thus, the theory attributes to the subject no (episodic) memory record for previously tested and rejected hypotheses.

Finally, the theory takes a simplistic view of a person's information-processing capacity. It asserts that the subject considers only one hypothesis at a time. We already know from Bruner's work that this is a relatively rare approach, which can be quite time-consuming if there are many hypotheses to consider. While each response may be evaluated solely in the light of one predominant hypothesis, it seems unlikely that the subject limits his overall consideration of the information fed back to him in terms of that hypothesis alone.

These are the major characteristics of early hypothesis theories. We turn our attention now to some of the empirical evidence that has been generated and how that evidence helps to shape subsequent theoretical developments.

ALL-OR-NONE VERSUS INCREMENTAL LEARNING.   While the issue seems clear conceptually, it is difficult in practice to determine whether learning is incremental or an all-or-none phenomenon. The all-or-none assumption asserts that a person's probability of making a correct response to any given stimulus is at chance (.5 where two equally probable responses are available to the subject) until he samples the correct hypothesis. But on any given trial, a subject either responds correctly or he does not. There is no way to determine what his "probability" of a correct response is. If one combines subjects and determines an average probability of correct response beginning on Trial 1 of the problem and working through to the trial in which the last subject solves, the result will appear to be incremental. But that result is not definitive, for it might merely reflect the fact that individual subjects within a group achieve solution on different trials. An example of such an outcome is shown in Table 6–2*A*.

TABLE 6–2. HYPOTHETICAL RESPONSE PROTOCOLS OF TEN SUBJECTS.

A. Forward learning curve

Subject	Trial									
	1	2	3	4	5	6	7	8	9	10
A	E	C	C	E	E	C	E*	C	C	C
B	E	E	C	E	E	E*	C	C	C	C
C	C	E	E	C	E*	C	C	C	C	C
D	C	C	E	E*	C	C	C	C	C	C
E	C	C	E*	C	C	C	C	C	C	C
F	E	E*	C	C	C	C	C	C	C	C
G	E*	C	C	C	C	C	C	C	C	C
H	C	E	E*	C	C	C	C	C	C	C
I	E	E	C	C	E*	C	C	C	C	C
J	C	C	C	E	C	E*	C	C	C	C
Probability of a correct response	.5	.5	.6	.6	.6	.8	.9	1.0	1.0	1.0

B. Backward learning curve

Subject	Trial						
	−5	−4	−3	−2	−1	TLE	+1
A	C	C	E	E	C	E	C
B	E	E	C	E	E	E	C
C	—	C	E	E	C	E	C
D	—	—	C	C	E	E	C
E	—	—	—	C	C	E	C
F	—	—	—	—	E	E	C
G	—	—	—	—	—	E	C
H	—	—	—	C	E	E	C
I	—	E	E	C	C	E	C
J	C	C	C	E	C	E	C
Probability of a correct response	.67	.60	.50	.50	.56	.00	1.0

Note: Asterisk designates trial of last error (TLE).

Bower and Trabasso (1964) suggested a technique to get us out of this difficulty. The technique is to compute what is called a backward learning curve. The first step is to align all subjects in a group at each subject's trial of last error. Instead of computing means successively from Trial 1 on, the first mean that is computed is the mean probability of a correct response on the trial just before the last error trial. Because subjects solve in different trials, this trial number will differ from subject to subject. On the last error trial, of course, the probability of a correct response will be zero, by definition, for all subjects make an error on this trial. Moreover, on the trial just after the last error trial, the probability of a correct response will be 1.0, for equally obvious reasons. But what about the trial just before the last error trial? If hypothesis-testing theory is correct, subjects have not learned at this point—they learn the solution on the last error trial, when they finally sample the correct hypothesis. Therefore, the probability of a correct response averaged over the group should be near chance, that is, .5. It should indeed be at chance level over all presolution trials. A "learning" curve which shows no improvement over trials is called *stationary*. According to a theory which assumes gradual learning, the probability of a correct response should be high, and certainly significantly different from chance, on trials immediately before the last error trial; that is, the learning curve should be nonstationary. This is because the subject has been learning something from preceding trials, even though he does not yet know the solution. The two alternative possibilities are portrayed graphically in Figure 6–3.

When data from backward learning curves are analyzed, the results seem entirely consistent with expectations based on hypothesis theory (see Figure 6–4). Moreover, this pattern holds over a wide class of problems, although we should note that departures from stationarity in the learning curve do occur when problems are more complex than the type we have examined. Certainly, however, the all-or-none assumption of hypothesis theory seems reasonable for at least this class of concept problems.

LEARNING ON ERROR TRIALS. It is conceivable that a subject will, on some occasions, possibly by chance, change his mind, resample, and come up with the correct hypothesis after he has made a correct response on a given trial. Early hypothesis theories took a strong stand on this issue, however, and asserted that hypotheses are changed only when a subject makes an error. Therefore, problem solving can occur only after an error trial. Bower and Trabasso (1963) offer the following kind of empirical evidence in support of that assumption.

The performance of two groups of subjects is compared. One group of subjects solves a standard concept problem. The stimuli are multidimensional. Only one feature, however, distinguishes positive from negative instances. For example, all stimuli that are red are called positive and all

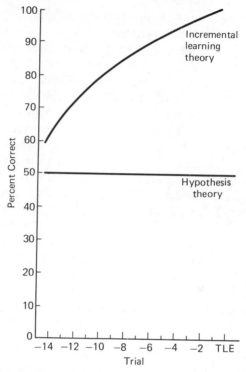

FIGURE 6–3. Idealized backward learning curves for two theories of concept learning.

stimuli that are green are called negative. The form of the stimulus, its size, its position on a viewing screen, and so on make no difference. The second group of subjects solves a problem which, however, involves multiple shifts in the solution—that is, every other time the subject makes an erroneous response, the solution is shifted without his knowledge. Several kinds of shifts are possible, but let's consider a shift which reverses the initial solution. The problem to begin with is to place red figures in the positive category, green ones in the negative category. When the subject makes his second error, the solution changes to green–positive, red–negative and the subject's response is called correct. The problem continues until the subject makes another two errors. On the second of these two errors, the response is called correct and the solution is shifted once again to the original solution. This routine repeats itself until the subject stops making errors, if he ever does. The protocol from a sample problem is shown in Table 6–3.

On the surface, a problem in which the solution shifts periodically ought to be very difficult. In fact, if one holds to a theory which says that a subject learns only gradually over a series of consistent reinforcements for his behavior, it might be impossible for the subject to learn at all under these conditions. As the subject begins to build up response tendencies in accord

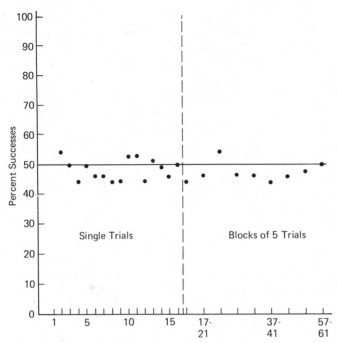

FIGURE 6–4. Backward learning curve: Percentage of successes plotted over trials preceding the last error (Data available in Bower & Trabasso, 1964.)

with his first solution, he encounters his second error and those response tendencies become inappropriate to the task. He must then drop those response tendencies and build up new ones. When the solution flip-flops back and forth, there does not appear to be enough consistency in the reinforcement for the subject ever to reach solution.

On the other hand, if one adheres to an all-or-none learning theory,

TABLE 6–3. SCHEMATIC OUTLINE FOR REPEATED REVERSAL EXPERIMENT.

		Trials														
Stimulus	*Category*	*1*	*2*	*3*	*4*	*5*	*6*	*7*	*8*	*9*	*10*	*11*	*12*	*13*	*14*	...
Red	A	C	E	C	Ⓔ			C	E	Ⓔ			C	E		...
Blue	B															
Blue	A				C	C	E	C	Ⓔ		C	E	C	Ⓔ		
Red	B															

Note: This is an illustrative subject-protocol in a repeated reversal experiment. The solution, always involving color, is reversed on every other error trial. Circled errors represent trials on which the solution is shifted, the subject being told "correct" on these occasions.

where the learning takes place only on error trials, the multiple-solution shift problem should be no more difficult than the standard problem. The rationale is as follows. The subject begins the problem with a certain hypothesis. The fact that he makes his first error signifies that his hypothesis is incorrect. He returns the hypothesis to the hypothesis pool and samples a new hypothesis. The fact that he makes a second error signifies that his new hypothesis is wrong. If the new hypothesis is wrong, then the subject does not have the solution. We can change the solution to the opposite of what it was without affecting his behavior and start giving feedback consistent with the changed solution. If we happen, by chance, to shift into the subject's hypothesis, then he will no longer make any errors and solve the problem. If, however, the subject's current hypothesis involves a different dimension, he will, eventually, make an error. At that point he returns to the hypothesis pool and selects a new hypothesis. If he selects the correct one, he will make no further errors. If he selects an incorrect one, he will make a second error at which point we can shift back to the original solution. None of these solution shifts will have any effect at all on the subject's overall performance or eventual selection of the correct hypothesis. Clearly, the number of trials to the last error will increase because of our shifts back and forth and our failure to give an error signal on certain trials. On the other hand, the total number of errors the subject makes and is informed of, and, therefore, the total number of times the subject returns to the hypothesis pool and samples a new hypothesis should, on the average, be no different from the performance levels in the standard problem.

Over a variety of different types of solution shifts, Bower and Trabasso have shown that for college students performing on relatively simple concept problems of the type we've described, there is no difference in number of informed errors between standard and multiple-shift problems. This evidence is consistent with both the all-or-none assumption and with the assumption that learning occurs only on error trials (Trabasso & Bower, 1968).

A SIGNIFICANT LIMITATION.   The evidence from this multiple-solution shift experiment seems powerfully to favor the principle of all-or-none learning on error trials. But there are significant exceptions to this finding, one of which we will discuss briefly. Douglass and Bourne (1971) reported a study of performance on multiple-solution shift problems by individuals of differing ages, from first-grade through college. The idea was that hypothesis-testing behavior may be a sophisticated kind of performance which rests on the significant accumulation of prior problem-solving experience. Thus, while a relatively bright college student might have no more difficulty with a solution shift problem than with the standard problem because of his overall intellectual level and accumulated knowledge, a younger child might find the multiple-shift problem very difficult. In line with this expectation, it was observed that grade school children had considerably more difficulty with problems in which solutions changed periodically (see Figure 6–5.) An examination of the learning curves at these ages shows distinct non-stationarity. Apparently, at the middle-most ages used in the study, problem solving does not occur in an all-or-none fashion on error trials. Rather, there seems to be the need to accumulate information over a series of trials before solution is achieved. Thus, if the solution shifts periodically, eventual attainment of solutions will be delayed.

Interestingly, there appeared to be only a small difference in performance between standard and multiple-solution shift problems at the first-grade level. Douglass and Bourne argued that solution to either type of problem at that age level was largely a matter of chance. Some children at that age failed to reach the criterion of problem solving at all. Those who did seemed more or less to happen upon the correct way of doing it without really understanding the basis of performance.

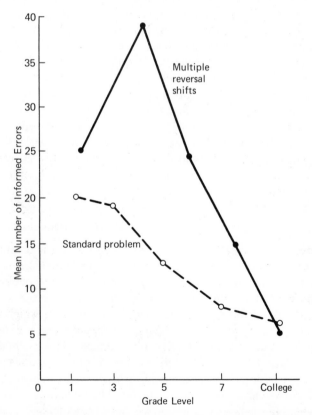

FIGURE 6–5. Trends with age in performance on a standard attribute identification problem and one with reversal shifts in solution on every other error trial. (Adapted from Douglass & Bourne, 1971.)

These results extend the basic observation of Bower and Trabasso. For sophisticated subjects, performance in simple feature identification problems may indeed be an all-or-none affair, happening on some error trial. The underlying process of problem solving may be hypothesis testing. But this kind of performance is reserved for those individuals who have achieved what Piaget (1950) has called the stage of formal reasoning in intellectual development. For younger children, in the concrete operational or pre-operational stages, the ability to work with hypotheses at an abstract level may not yet have developed. Their performance may be mediated by the establishment of at least some associations between stimulus patterns and response categories. Whatever the mechanism, the evidence for hypothesis-testing behavior seems to be limited to a fairly simple type of problem and sophisticated problem solvers.

OTHER CONSIDERATIONS.   There are two remaining characteristics of early hypothesis-testing theory: (1) that the subject samples hypotheses with replacement, and (2) that he tests only a single hypothesis at a time. These characteristics will be considered in detail in the next section, which examines more recent developments and the current status of hypothesis-testing theory. It should be sufficient to note at this point that neither of these assumptions has stood up well in the face of empirical examination. As we will see, the subject does appear to use some form of memory for previously tested hypotheses, reducing the probability that he will respond in accord with a rejected hypothesis, at least for some number of trials. Furthermore, the subject can derive information from each trial with respect to hypotheses other than the one which currently governs his behavior. The evidence on these matters leads to a basically different and more elaborate version of hypothesis theory.

LEVINE'S HYPOTHESIS-TESTING THEORY

Hypothesis theory reached its apex of sophistication and refinement in the work of Marvin Levine (1975). The development of Levine's theory is a classical illustration of the interplay in science of methodological, empirical, and conceptual considerations. At the outset, Levine (1966) was primarily concerned with the development of a procedure which would externalize and directly measure the subject's hypotheses and hypothesis-testing behaviors in a feature identification problem. This methodology led to interesting new kinds of data and insights into the processes underlying feature identification. These insights, in turn, allowed for clearer, more explicit, and more exact theoretical statements. The theory, as it evolved, suggested changes in methodology and new ways of examining concept formation empirically. Thus, over a period of approximately ten years, through the continual interplay of method, results, and theoretical ideas, Levine produced what is perhaps the most dominant theoretical position on conceptual behavior in the field today.

METHODOLOGY.   As noted, Levine wanted a way to measure directly whether or not people used hypotheses in feature identification, and if so, which hypothesis was being used at any given time. After examining a variety of possibilities, Levine adopted what he called a Blank Trials Procedure. In its simplest form, the Blank Trials Procedure requires the learner to respond to a series of stimuli in the absence of any corrective feedback. If the subject responds systematically to those stimuli, it is possible to determine a unique basis for his response. This unique basis is then said to be a subject's hypothesis.

Let us be more specific. In the typical Levine experiment, the subject responds to somewhat abstract stimuli, usually the alphabetical letters X and T. The stimuli differ on four attributes: First, they are two different letters; then either letter can be large or small, black or white, and, in a given pair of stimuli, either appear on the left or right. Thus, the dimensions are Letter, Letter Size, Letter Color, and Letter Position, each dimension with two values. Stimuli are presented to the subject in pairs, and the two letters in each pair differ on all four characteristics. Thus, if the stimulus on the left is a large, white T, the figure on the right is a small, black X. The subject is instructed that one of the figures is positive, that is, an example of the unknown concept, while the other figure is negative. Only one attribute, for example, black versus white, determines the positive–negative distinction. The subject is asked to pick the stimulus that he believes to be positive.

In this stimulus population, there are eight possible single value hypotheses. The positive stimuli could be the large ones, the small ones, the ones on the left, or on the right, the black, the white, the Xs, or the Ts. One and only one feature determines which are the positive and which are the negative stimuli. Levine assumes that one such hypothesis governs the subject's response selection on any trial. Suppose that, in the example given, the subject chooses the left-hand stimulus, that is, the large, white T. This indicates that the subject's governing hypothesis is one of the following: "left," "large," "white," or "T." It would not be clear at this point, however, which one of these hypotheses really did govern the subject's response selection. Suppose the subject is told that his response is correct. In Levine's theory, as in other hypothesis-testing theories, this should confirm whatever hypothesis the subject holds and gives him no basis for changing that hypothesis. The uniqueness of Levine's methodology derives from the next step. The subject is presented with a series of four trials, each constructed more or less like the trial described above, on which he makes a selection between two stimuli. On these trials, however, the subject is given no feedback on his responses—these are the so-called "blank trials." Levine's assumption is that, because the subject is given no feedback, he has no basis for changing his hypothesis over this series of trials.

A hypothetical sequence for a blank trial is shown in Figure 6–6. The four pairs of stimuli presented to the subject during such a sequence are chosen in a particular way. To be specific, in a blank trial sequence, each possible hypothesis, "black," "white," "X," and so on yields a unique sequence of four responses. The response pattern corresponding to each of the eight possible hypotheses is shown by the positions of the dots in the columns of Figure 6–6. For example, if the subject chose the left member of Stimulus 1, the right member of Stimulus 2, the left member of Stimulus 3, and the right member of Stimulus 4, we would know that his hypothesis was "Black." It is possible to inspect any sequence of responses made by a subject over a series of four blank trials, and making all the necessary assumptions, determine the hypothesis, if any, the subject is using. Notice that the response sequences listed in Figure 6–6 are not the only ones possible. These sequences correspond to the eight possible systematic hypotheses. In contrast to these sequences, a subject might, for example, pick the left-hand stimulus on the first three pairs and then switch to the right-hand stimulus. Such a pattern corresponds to no single-valued hypothesis. In all, there are eight possible response sequences which do *not* correspond to *any* particular hypothesis. Thus, there are eight hypothesis sequences and eight non-hypothesis sequences. If a subject does not follow or test hypotheses, we would expect 50 percent of each type to occur in the course of a feature identification problem. If a subject does test hypotheses, we expect, of course, a predominance of hypothesis sequences. Incidentally, it

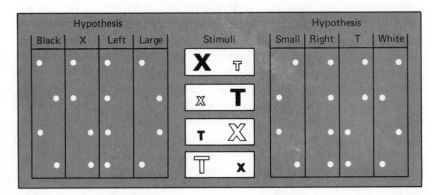

FIGURE 6–6.   Eight patterns of responses corresponding to each of the eight hypotheses which a subject might test in one of Levine's experiments. (Reprinted by permission of the author and American Psychological Association.)

is possible to spot hypothesis from non-hypothesis sequences rather easily. All hypothesis sequences have a 2–2 (two rights and two lefts) or a 4–0 (all rights or all lefts) structure to them. Non-hypothesis sequences have a 3–1 ratio of rights and lefts.

Characteristically, in Levine's experiments, a subject is presented with several blocks of five trials. The first of any block is an outcome or feedback trial and the remaining four are blank trials. The basic arrangement is shown in Figure 6–7. While we shall not work out the details here, Levine arranges each problem so that a subject has sufficient information to identify the critical feature after he has been given feedback on three trials. The first feedback trial eliminates four of the eight possibilities, leaving four in contention. The second feedback trial eliminates two of the remaining four. The third feedback trial eliminates one of the remaining two, leaving the subject with the correct hypothesis, if he has processed all the given information optimally. The problems are simple in structure. Subjects learn to solve them rather quickly, although optimal information processing is not characteristic of all subjects. Because each problem can be solved in a relatively short period of time, it is possible for Levine to give many problems to each subject and to collect a substantial amount of data, adding to the reliability of his findings in any experiment.

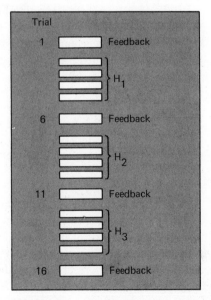

FIGURE 6–7. A representation of the 16 trials of a Levine-type problem. The subject is provided with feedback for his responses on Trials 1, 6, 11, and 16. The intervening blank trals are used to detect his hypotheses (H_1, H_2, and H_3). (Reprinted by permission of the author and American Psychological Association.)

THEORY.   According to Levine, hypothesis formulation and testing proceeds in the following fashion. The subject's hypothesis pool or domain consists of all eight (or whatever the number) single-valued hypotheses. He is instructed and pretrained to consider solutions only within this domain. When the first pair of stimuli is presented to the subject, he picks one, possibly randomly, calls it positive, and verbally encodes its feature set. The stimuli are then removed and the subject is given feedback. If the subject has chosen correctly, the feature set he has encoded becomes the hypothesis pool for the forthcoming series of blank trials. The subject picks one hypothesis from that pool as his focal or working hypothesis and responds on the blank trials accordingly. He tries to monitor the remaining three hypotheses, however, for use on the next feedback trial. If feedback to the subject indicates that he chose incorrectly, the subject must alter his verbally encoded hypothesis set. Because the two stimuli on any given trial differ in all their features, this alteration involves mainly taking the complement of the encoded features. However, because this process must be done mentally, in the absence of the two stimuli, it will take some time and it opens up the possibility for mistakes. In any case, the recoded set now becomes the hypothesis pool for the second blank trial series. Again the subject selects one hypothesis to work with and monitors the remainder of what he remembers.

The same set of principles applies to all remaining blocks of five trials, one feedback plus four blank trials. The major sources of difficulty for the subject are (1) monitoring hypotheses which are still viable but not currently in use, and (2) taking the complement of an encoded hypothesis set, when an error trial dictates. If we assume that the subject can do both of these mental tasks perfectly, then a certain set of expectations about performance follows, including the fact that the subject should solve every problem after exactly three feedback trials. We can compare actual performance against this theoretically perfect model, and determine where, if at all, the subject deviates and what sorts of difficulty he has with a problem.

There are a number of ways in which Levine's theory differs from earlier hypothesis theories. For one thing, according to Levine, a subject learns something about the solution on all trials, regardless of whether he is correct or incorrect in his stimulus selection. For example, at the outset, the subject has eight hypotheses to consider. He chooses one of the two stimuli presented and, whether he is correct or incorrect, can, on the basis of the feedback given, narrow the hypothesis pool from eight to four possibilities. In fact, in Levine's theory, it is harder to learn on error trials than it is on correct response trials because of the necessity for recoding after an error signal has been received. Second, in contrast to other theories which assume hypothesis sampling with replacement, Levine's theory allows for perfect hypothesis processing. That is, the optimal subject will consider all possible hypotheses at once. Further, he will partition the hypothesis pool into "potentially correct" versus "known to be incorrect" ones and proceed to sample from the "potentially correct" set. Levine attributes considerable memory capacity to the subject, allowing the data to determine just how much the subject does remember. The one point of agreement among theorists is that the subject's probability of making a correct selection between the two stimuli on any given trial will remain stationary prior to the trial on which he finally isolates the correct hypothesis.

EMPIRICAL RESULTS. Let us look briefly at the results of some experiments which use Levine's methodology and bear upon his theory (Levine, 1975). First of all, it has repeatedly and consistently been found that subjects use (approximately 98 percent of the time) a single-valued hypothesis on blank trial sequences. The percentage of 3–1 response sequences is small enough that it might be attributed simply to inattentiveness on the part of the subject. As Levine's theory implies, subjects typically exhibit a "win–stay, lose–shift" strategy with regard to their hypothesis. That is, if the hypothesis used by a subject on a given series of blank trials is confirmed on the succeeding feedback trial, in 95 percent of the cases he employs the same hypothesis on the next blank trial sequence. If the hypothesis is disconfirmed on the feedback trial, 98 percent of the time the subject switches to a different hypothesis. It should be noted that, once disconfirmed, the probability of a hypothesis being repeated is far below what would be expected if the subject were sampling with replacement. Because there are eight possible hypotheses, if the subject were sampling with replacement, he would have a probability of 1/8, or .125, of repeating a disconfirmed hypothesis on the subsequent blank trial sequence. The observed probability (.02) is well below that figure, indicating that subjects do not sample with replacement in these problems.

When an hypothesis is disconfirmed by feedback, the new hypothesis, used on the succeeding blank trial series, tends to be chosen from the hypothesis set currently being monitored by the subject. In other words, the subject's new hypothesis is consistent, with a probability of .9, with previously given information. This observation suggests that subjects actually do narrow down the original hypothesis pool as information on the relevancy of certain hypotheses is accumulated.

Another kind of evidence also implies the narrowing down process. Response latencies in a feature identification task decrease, on the average, over trials, especially as the subject approaches solution. Since, in theory, there are fewer and fewer hypotheses to consider on each successive solution trial, this latency reduction is to be expected. It is interesting to note that latencies also decrease over trials after the subject commits his last error,

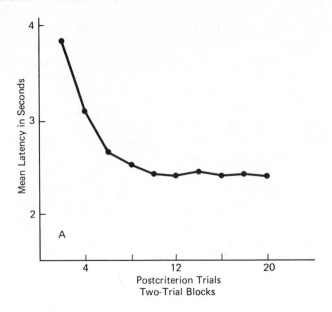

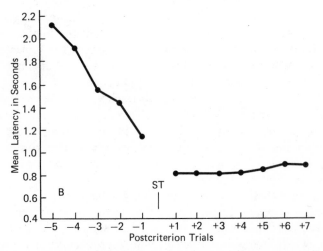

FIGURE 6–8. Mean response latency on trials following the last error. *A*. Continuously decreasing latency function reported by Erickson, Zaikowski, and Ehmann (1966). (Adapted from Erickson, Zaijowski, & Ehmann, 1966. Reprinted by permission of the author and American Psychological Association.) *B*. Mean latencies at successive trials before and after the solution trial (ST) (*not* the trial of last error), as reported by Levine (1966). (Reprinted by permission of the author and American Psychological Association.)

that is during the "criterion run," as can be seen in Figure 6–8*A* (Erickson, 1968; Erickson, Zajkowski, & Ehmann, 1966). If one were to imagine that the subject finally adopts the correct hypothesis and only the correct hypothesis after the trial of his last error, such a latency decrease would not be expected. Levine's theory can accommodate this result, however, in the following way. The subject enters the criterion run monitoring more than just a single hypothesis. He may, in fact, be using the correct hypothesis as his focus, but there is a distinct possibility that he monitors several other still untested possibilities. As successive feedback trials occur, the subject responds correctly because he uses the solution hypothesis as a basis for his responses. These trials will provide the subject with information necessary to reject the other alternatives he is monitoring. As he rejects more and more of the incorrect hypotheses, his response latency should decrease and become stable only at the point that all possibilities except the correct one have been rejected.

To verify this interpretation, Levine (1966) asked subjects to indicate, by ringing a bell, the exact trial on which they thought they had determined the solution to the problem. Typically, the solution trial indicated by the subject occurred well after the trial of last error, that is, during the criterion run. When response latencies were plotted over trials before and after the indicated solution trial, it was observed, as Levine theorized, that the decrease occurs only prior to and not after the solution trial (see Figure 6–8*B*).

There are direct, but complicated ways of computing and plotting the actual size of the hypothesis pool from which a subject samples over a series of trials. We have already noted that the pool decreases systematically, by one-half, if the subject is able optimally to process the information provided by the experimenter. If there are problems in the hypothesis-monitoring process or in the recoding process following an error, then the subject will deviate from the optimal function. If the subject were just sampling with replacement, then there would be no change whatsoever in the hypothesis pool over trials. Actual performance falls somewhere in between—but closer to perfect processing, called *global focusing* by Levine, than to sampling with replacement. A curve constructed by Levine is shown in Figure 6–9. Under the circumstances of this particular experiment, subjects could decrease the size of the pool at the level of proficiency close to that of optimal processing.

Global focusing requires not only optimal information processing, but also complete memory either for rejected hypotheses or for hypotheses still viable as solutions. Subjects often approach global focusing in Levine's studies because he gives them extensive training over a series of practice problems designed to facilitate the appropriate information-processing routines. Dyer and Meyer (1976) have shown that performance on the

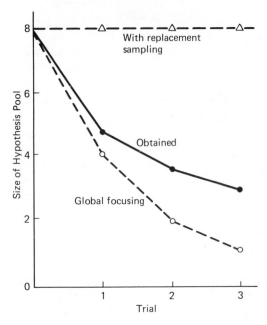

FIGURE 6–9. The estimated size of the hypothesis pool from which the subject samples immediately following a wrong response. (Data from Levine, 1966. Reprinted by permission of the author and American Psychological Association.)

part of untrained subjects can similarly be improved by providing instruction in the use of visual imagery as a mnemonic device for remembering positive instances. The effects of using an imagery mnemonic were especially noticeable in a task which required the subject to solve two concept problems concurrently, thus placing heavy demands on both processing and memory capacities.

Whether or not imagery can be used to assist memory in a concept task depends on the "imageability" of the stimulus material. Dyer and Meyer used pictorial stimuli which are, by definition, imageable. But what if the stimulus material is verbal? As we know, some words are concrete and readily suggest a visual (or other) image; however, others are abstract and provoke little or no imagery. Katz and Paivio (1975) found that names of concepts vary widely in their imagery-arousing capacity. Further, they observed that concepts rated easy-to-image were attained or identified more readily in a problem-solving task than concepts which were difficult to image. Finally, these experimenters demonstrated that only the attainment of easy-to-image concepts is facilitated by instructing the subject to use imagery as a means of remembering concept instances.

Let's consider one final result. According to Levine, more cognitive effort and more complicated information processing is required after an error trial than after a correct response. This implies that, given the opportunity to pace himself, the subject should take more time after an error trial than after a correct response trial. As it turns out, subjects do, in fact, take longer to advance to the next stimulus pair when allowed to self-determine the intertrial interval. On the other hand, if the experimenter determines the interval, the outcome is less clear. In one study (Bourne, Dodd, Guy, & Justesen, 1968) the experimenter provided, for different groups of subjects, (I) a 10-second interval on all trials; (II) a 10-second interval on error trials, and a 1-second interval on correct response trials; (III) a 1-second interval on error trials and a 10-second interval on correct response trials; and (IV) a 1-second interval on all trials. From Levine's theory, we might expect groups I and II to be near equivalent, for both have a longer interval to mull over the information after an error trial, and for both of them to perform better than Groups III and IV. As it turned out, however, Group I performed better than either II or III, which were equivalent, and both II and III performed better than Group IV. Such an outcome suggests that the subject can use the intertrial interval for processing information with much the same advantage on correct and incorrect response trials.

A later study by White (1972) helps to clarify the discrepancy in results between experimenter-determined and subject-determined response intervals. White argued that the group of totally naive subjects used in the Bourne et al. experiment might be comprised of two subgroups—those individuals who attempt to solve the problem via hypothesis testing and those who employ more associative, rote learning processes. He therefore pretrained two groups of subjects, one in hypothesis-testing techniques and the other in an associative method for solving these problems. Where subjects had been pretrained to be hypothesis testers, the result favored Levine's interpretation, that is, $I = II > III = IV$. Longer experimenter-determined intertrial intervals following error were facilitative relative to longer intervals following a correct response. For associatively trained subjects, the response pattern was very much like that obtained in the Bourne et al. experiment. A summary of White's data appears in Figure 6–10. Taken together, the results of these studies do appear to be consistent with Levine's assumption about the necessity for greater cognitive work following an error in a feature identification task.

DEVELOPMENTAL CHANGES.   Levine's theory and methodology imply high-level, sophisticated performance on the part of subjects. While such a level can be achieved by the adult college students with whom Levine has done most of his experiments, there is some question about the capability of younger or less intelligent individuals (Douglass & Bourne, 1971). Accordingly, Levine and collaborators (Gholson, Levine, & Phillips, 1972) undertook a series of developmental studies with children ranging in age from approximately seven years through adulthood. Their main interest

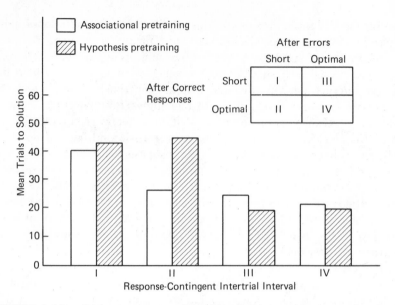

FIGURE 6–10.   Performance on attribute identification problems as a function of the type of pretraining and the contingency between length of intertrial interval and the correctness of the subject's response. (Data from White, 1972.)

was to determine to what degree theoretical assumptions must be modified for less well-prepared subjects; to observe whether hypothesis behavior was characteristic of young people; and, finally, if so, to determine how hypothesis behavior changes developmentally.

One of the first and most basic findings of Levine's study was that all probabilities pertaining to correct hypothesis behavior observed for adults changed in the downward direction for younger children. For example, the probability of staying with a hypothesis that was confirmed on the preceding feedback trial was .93 for adults but only .88 for second graders, .89 for fourth graders, and .92 for sixth graders. Thus, children are less systematic in performance on a Levine-type task, as indexed by overall measures of this sort.

Levine investigated a variety of possibilities before deciding that there were two major capacity limitations on the behavior of young children. He found evidence for his basic assumption that children as well as adults are hypothesis testers. However, young children, especially kindergartners, often sample from the wrong domain of hypotheses. In addition to whatever they understand about single-valued hypotheses of the sort that are required by the problem, young children frequently exhibit three strategies: (1) position perseveration, for example, always choose the right-hand stimulus, no matter what; (2) position alternation tendencies, for example, choose right and then left, then right again, and so on; and finally (3) stimulus preferences, for example, invariably pick the large stimulus no matter what feedback is provided. All of these "hypotheses" come from a different and inappropriate domain. None of them, except by chance, will solve the problem. A second problem identified by Levine is that young subjects, even if they sample in the correct domain, are unable to use as sophisticated a strategy for hypothesis testing as global focusing.

Both the domain and the strategy limitations are readily apparent in Levine's data. Kindergartners, the youngest subjects tested by Levine, showed predominantly nonsolution response tendencies. Indeed their preferred mode of response was position alternation. Less than 10 percent adopted even the most rudimentary strategy for testing single-valued hypotheses. By the time children reach the second grade, almost all evidence of sampling in the wrong domain disappears. There is some evidence of stimulus preference, however, even up through sixth graders. Second graders and older children do seem to be capable of narrowing their hypothesis choices to the correct domain and adopting a strategy for evaluating hypotheses, although not necessarily the most efficient strategy.

Levine was able to identify three distinct methods of evaluation. The first, termed *hypothesis checking*, is a rather unsophisticated strategy which, like Bruner's successive scanning, considers one hypothesis at a time. Having formulated a hypothesis domain consisting of eight single-valued hypotheses, the subject proceeds to check these, one at a time, against feedback, without monitoring the implications of feedback for any of the hypotheses than the one under consideration. A more sophisticated strategy is *dimension checking*. The subject who uses this strategy considers one dimension at a time. This, in effect, is to consider two hypotheses (two values per dimension) at once. Finally, there is the *global focusing strategy* which most college adults approximate, as we have seen in earlier work.

There appears to be an evolution toward these strategies as children grow older. In Levine's data, hypothesis checking is the most common strategy among second graders, dimension checking the most common among fourth graders, and focusing the most common among adults. In other words, as subjects mature, they become able to (1) entertain hypotheses of the sort required to solve this type of task, (2) sample within that domain rather than in some other initially preferred domain, and (3) adopt and maintain a more sophisticated strategy for testing hypotheses. While there is no way to identify in these data any distinct stage-wise changes in the qualitative aspects of a subject's performance, nonetheless, results of this research program tend to strongly support any theory that attributes developmental changes in the efficiency of problem solving to ontological changes in the cognitive skills available to subjects for use in the task.

Incidentally, the error of sampling from an inappropriate hypothesis domain is not limited to children. Lane, McDaniel, Bleichfeld, and Rabinowitz (1976) have shown that college-aged adults can be induced to test hypotheses of a particular type, either single attribute or double attribute conjunction, via experience with solving a series of problems of that type. Subjects so trained have inordinate difficulty with a later problem the solution to which lies in a different domain.

AN ALTERNATIVE MEASURE OF HYPOTHESIS BEHAVIOR. One serious problem with Levine's measure of hypothesis behavior is that it is cumbersome. In order to get a fix on the subject's current hypothesis, the experimenter must give four blank trials between every learning (feedback) trial of the problem. Fortunately, the problems are simple, so that the interpolated blank trial sequences do not unduly prolong an experimental session. However, the very simplicity of the problems may limit the generality of observed results. Other techniques for eliciting hypotheses have been tried with some success, including merely having the subject verbalize his best guess between trials. These techniques, in general, constitute viable alternatives to the blank trial procedure in many cases.

One technique which deserves special mention has been developed by Millward and Spoehr (1973). It is sometimes called the "pick-a-view" procedure, for reasons that will become obvious. As in the typical feature identification task, the subject is required to learn how to classify multidimensional stimuli. The basis of classification is a single unknown feature chosen from one of the stimulus dimensions. The domain of hypotheses at the outset consists of all features of the stimuli. On any given trial, a multivalued stimulus is prepared for presentation to the subject. The stimulus as a whole is not automatically presented to the subject on each trial, although the subject could ask to see it. The subject is allowed to control the stimulus in the sense that he may ask to see any or all of the features of the stimulus that has been prepared. The number of features chosen is, according to Millward and Spoehr, an index of the hypotheses the subject still considers potentially relevant, that is, the current hypothesis domain. The hypothesis domain will be limited, as we have seen, by the subject's strategy, but also by the subject's capacity to deal with several possibilities at a given time. In other words, if the initial hypothesis universe is very large, the subject might attempt to limit it in order to keep memory problems under control.

The subjects in the Millward and Spoehr experiment were given a total of 28 problems to solve. The number of errors to solution for "pick-a-view" and control conditions, in which the complete stimulus is shown to the subject on each trial, were virtually identical over the range of problems given. The conclusion from this is that, even when the entire stimulus is available for inspection, subjects may limit their consideration to certain features thought at the time to be potentially relevant. Considering only the "pick-a-view" subjects, the following results were obtained. The average number of features sampled on any trial within a problem decreased as the subject approached solution. It was not uncommon, however, for a subject to consider more than one feature beyond the trial of last error. In other words, there was some decrease in sample size and further refinement of one's hypothesis during the criterion run.

Subjects' hypothesis-testing routines appear to increase in efficiency and sophistication with successive problems. This is in part revealed by the trend in number of errors to solution, which decreases from an average of 20 on early problems in the series to an average of 7 on later problems. It is also reflected in the fact that the number of features selected for examination on the early trials of a problem *increases* with successive problems. In other words, on early problems, the subject may consider fewer than the actual number of viable features as possible solutions to the problem. If the subject samples unfortunately, this can delay problem solution. On later problems, the subject tends to consider all features as potentially relevant until proved otherwise. As we have seen in other contexts, subjects move in the direction of conservative or global focusing as they become more sophisticated with the problem-solving task.

The "pick-a-view" procedure also provides some more incisive measures of performance. One area of interest concerns the subject's use of a win-stay, lose–shift strategy. If the subject is an efficient information processor, he should not resample previously rejected attributes, at least not on the very next trial after their rejection. Furthermore, he should continue to sample an attribute which is consistent with the feedback of a preceding trial. What a subject actually does changes with experience. On early problems, the subject keeps consistent attributes in his focus with probability better than .9, but his probability of eliminating inconsistent ones is roughly at chance (.5). The picture improves with successive problems. At the end of the problem series, subjects have a probability of near 1.0 of keeping consistent attributes and better than .9 of eliminating inconsistent ones. Again, the evidence is that subjects move in the direction of optimal information processing as they become more familiar with the task. One can push this question further. What about the probability of the subject's reselecting an inconsistent and previously eliminated attribute within a certain number of trials, say, 5, after it has been disproved? This probability, which is slightly above chance on early problems of the series, decreases to about .25 in successive problems.

The following conclusions appear to be justified by the Millward–Spoehr research. First of all, overt sampling does not bias a subject's performance in a feature identification process and is a fair reflection of what are assumed to be the covert hypothesis-testing processes underlying performance. The size of the subject's hypothesis sample varies, tending to decrease in size over trials, including trials following the last error, and to increase in size over successive problems. A subject progresses in the direction of a win–stay, lose–shift strategy with successive problems. The results are by and large consistent with those which one would derive from Levine's analysis and theory. The "pick-a-view" procedure offers a promising and more efficient alternative to the blank trial approach as a means of revealing in more detail the processes underlying feature identification.

SUMMARY

A concept is an abstraction in the sense that it refers to no particular object, process, state of affairs, or event but rather to a collection of such concrete entities. Concepts have two fundamental components, a set of defining features and a relationship among them. Concepts are learned through experience with real entities. When a person learns a concept, he learns both the defining features and their relationship. Most empirical and theoretical work has dealt with how features are learned or identified. The best available description of the learning process characterizes it as a matter of hypothesis testing, guided by some overall strategy. Bruner, Goodnow, and Austin were able to isolate several different strategies (such as conservative focusing) for hypothesis testing in conceptual problems. Based on this early empirical work, Restle, Trabasso, and Bower formulated mathematical versions of hypothesis-testing theory. Their assumptions were (1) that hypotheses control overt responses, (2) that hypotheses are sampled from a domain or pool, (3) that learning takes place on the trial on which the subject first samples the correct hypothesis, (4) that error signals are the occasion for resampling from the hypothesis pool, and (5) that the subject has little or no memory for hypotheses previously tested. The most elaborate and complete version of hypothesis-testing theory has been formulated by Levine. His theory includes an assumption that subjects monitor more than one hypothesis at once and that learning or problem solving can take place both on correct response and on error response trials. The weight of recent empirical evidence supports Levine's theory, although its application may be limited to fairly simple conceptual problems. Among other things, Levine has been able to show that the nature of the subject's strategy for hypothesis testing changes developmentally. Millward and Spoehr have recently developed a new technique for studying hypothesis behavior in which the subject is allowed to select as many features of the stimulus as he wishes to examine on each trial.

chapter seven

THE STRUCTURE
OF CONCEPTS

outline

IN THE LAST CHAPTER, we were concerned primarily with a description of the cognitive processes of a person attempting to form or identify some unknown concept. Over the years, a number of theories have been proposed, the most generally accepted of which at the present time is, as we have seen, the hypothesis-testing model. For the most part, laboratory research which has tested these processing theories has used artificial concepts, often involving a single relevant stimulus feature and based on a simple logical operation. This research has recently been severely criticized by Rosch (1973) and others for its lack of concern with the structure of concepts, especially natural concepts.

The stimuli to which laboratory concepts have been applied are typically based on only two, or at most a few, discrete values on some small number of completely independent stimulus dimensions. Concepts are defined by a single arbitrary value or some artificial combination of a few values. The concepts are completely deterministic in the sense that the stimulus either is or is not a member of the concept; any one instance is as good as any other instance. If, for example, the concept is *red square,* then any stimulus which has both of those features is a positive instance and is as representative of the concept as any other positive instance.

This state of affairs is not typical of concepts we encounter in the everyday world. Natural concepts, such as the category *table* or *bird,* are not easily described as arbitrary combinations of discrete values taken from some number of independent stimulus dimensions. Neither are all tables or all birds equally good examples of their respective categories. Most people would probably agree that a robin is a "better" exemplar of *bird* than a penguin or an ostrich. The dimensions of natural concepts are often hard to specify and may themselves be made up of subtle combinations of underlying dimensions. The dimensions typically are continuous rather than discrete, and they may not be entirely independent of one another. While one might perform a dimensional or feature analysis on the instances of any natural concept, this is not characteristically the way we treat the concept in everyday life. Rather, as some of the semantic memory data of Chapter 4 suggested, we view the concept in terms of some global overall organization of good and bad examples. It might further be noted that some natural concepts are not readily amenable to categorization. Markman and Seibert (1976) have called attention to the *collection,* for example, *pile, family, bunch,* which differs in a variety of structural and pragmatic ways from classes or categories. While little is known at this time about the formation and use of collective concepts, they seem integral and more holistic than other forms of concepts and resist description in terms of feature lists.

Rosch's points are well taken. There is good reason to be concerned about the arbitrariness of simple laboratory concepts used in the study of problem-solving operations. There is more to the structure of concepts than processing research has taken into account. In this chapter we shall concern ourselves primarily with research whose focus has been to define the structure of concepts. This line of research provides an important parallel to the processing research covered in the last chapter and helps to round out our general understanding of the way in which concepts are formed and used and of the relationship between concept formation and memory.

CONCEPTS AND PROTOTYPES

Implicit in the work on processing models for concept learning is the idea that concepts are best defined in terms of a listing of their relevant features. This idea is consistent with a theory that says that the memory representation of any concept takes the form of a set of defining features, and that any stimulus brings to mind (consciousness) a particular concept or category to the extent that the features of the stimulus overlap the features of the memory representation of that concept (Rips, Shoben, & Smith, 1973). As we have seen in earlier chapters, feature theory or the set-theoretic model of memory is certainly not the only viable one. Among the other possibilities is a Gestalt or holistic interpretation in which concepts are represented memorially in part by their best examples or prototypes (Rosch, 1975). In other words, a major aspect of our understanding of any concept is in terms of examples which best illustrate it. When one thinks of the concept *bird,* a robin (or a sparrow) is more likely to come to mind than a penguin.

But, of course, penguins are classifiable as birds. Thus one's understanding of a concept must include not only the prototype but also a dimension which Rosch refers to as degree of category membership. Categories or concepts are, in Rosch's view, fuzzy. Some stimuli are clearly classifiable as belonging to a particular concept. Others that one may encounter at the borders are typically unusual, bizarre, abnormal, or distorted cases, which are not clearly either instances or non-instances. For example, is a tomato a fruit; is a whale a fish?

PERCEPTUAL CONCEPTS

Rosch claims that this structure—prototype plus degree of category membership—characterizes all natural concepts, including the simplest and most primitive concepts that we use. Even the dimensions of color and form are structured into nonarbitrary categories centering around perceptually salient natural prototypes (Rosch, 1973). Contrary to Whorf's hypothesis (see Chapter 5), these categories do not vary with variation in linguistic practice. Within our culture, particular categories of color, for example, red, include some wavelengths which do seem best or purest examples. Relative to other, even nearby wavelengths, these wavelengths tend to attract the viewer's attention. They are, in a sense, easier to "see" and, according to Rosch, they serve as the foci for organizing the range of different values that we ordinarily classify together as, say, red. As we discussed in Chapter 5, this is a view that many former adherents of linguistic determinism have come to accept (Brown, 1976).

In the case of basic dimensions like color, Rosch hypothesized that prototypicality might be determined by fundamental neurophysiological processes. That is to say, the best red may be best because, among all red wavelengths, the human visual system is most sensitive to that one. If this is the case, then it seems likely that peoples of different cultures would pick up the same focal points or prototypes for the color dimension.

Rosch had a chance to examine this possibility during an anthropological excursion to New Guinea to study a Stone Age people known as the Dani. In the Dani culture, there exist only two color terms, and these apply to the brightness rather than the hue dimension. In other words, people in this culture exhibit no vocabulary or verbal semantics for natural color categories. Nonetheless, Rosch theorized that, because they have the same

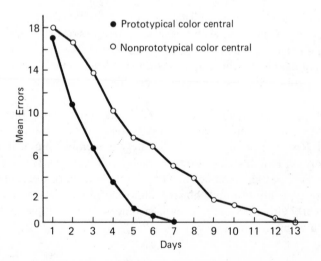

FIGURE 7–1. Mean errors per test per day by Dani subects in a learning experiment when the focal or prototypical color is central or when a nonprotypical color is central to the category to be learned. (Data from Rosch, 1973. Courtesy of Academic Press, Inc.)

nervous system, these people ought to be sensitive to the same prototypical values as people of Western culture. The reason for their lack of color categories may simply be a matter of the lack of utility of color discriminations in everyday affairs. In any case, Rosch did a number of studies reflecting on her hypotheses about the existence of prototypes. To summarize them briefly, in both short-term and long-term memory experiments, Dani subjects attended to and remembered color values which were typical of Western color categories better than they did nontypical values. In a learning experiment, natural prototypes were learned more quickly and classifications in which the prototype is central were learned faster than any other arrangement. Whether central or not, however, the natural prototype was the first stimulus attended to and learned. Some of the results are summarized in Figure 7–1. Much the same outcome was observed in parallel experiments on basic form categories such as square and triangle. The results tend to confirm the idea that natural concepts have an intricate internal structure, with certain allowable variations among instances and with the prototypical stimulus playing a central role as the basis of their organization. This appears to be true along even the simplest, most basic perceptual dimensions.

ILL-DEFINED CATEGORIES

The idea that prototypes represent categories is not a particularly new one. Long before experimental psychologists found their vocation, philosophers debated the process of abstraction and what type of "ideal" forms it would yield. Some argued that abstraction leads to an analog-like representation of a category of things. The representation has all the basic features of the category, though it may be different from any particular instance which a person has encountered. Others have found it impossible to imagine what such a composite might be. Where, even in your wildest imagination, can you find the abstraction of a triangle which is neither equilateral, isosceles, scalene, or any other, yet equally representative of all of them.

The idea of abstract analogical representations of concepts may have made its biggest impact in modern psychology through the work of Bartlett (1932) on memory schemata. In Chapter 5, we discussed how this work leads to the conclusion that textual materials leave in memory not a word-for-word replica but rather a basic set of facts which capture the essence or gist of what has been read. In the area of concept learning, the first significant studies on schematic representations for categories appears in the work of Attneave (1957), Evans and Edmonds (1966), and Posner (Posner, Goldsmith, & Welton, 1967; Posner & Keele, 1968). Consider Posner's studies; the stimuli used were rather unnatural, though the concepts were familiar enough. Posner constructed prototypical forms, such as a triangle or a block letter of the alphabet, from patterns of dots placed on a 30″ ×

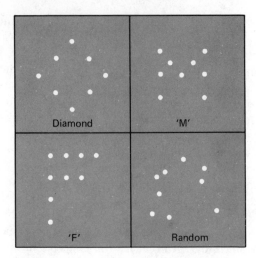

FIGURE 7–2. Basic dot patterns defining four categories. (From Posner, Gold-smith & Welton, 1967. Reprinted by permission of the author and American Psychological Assocation.)

30″ grid. Each form was comprised of nine dots, as shown in Figure 7–2. Four of these original nine-dot patterns served as prototypes, each for a separate category. The experimenters then proceeded to construct distortions of each prototype by moving any or all of its nine dots away from their original positions. Examples of distortions of a base pattern are shown in Figure 7–3. In one study, six distortions were constructed in each of three different degrees—slight, moderate, and high— from each of four original prototypes (Posner & Keele, 1968). Distortions of the prototypes (but never the prototype itself) were presented to the subject one at a time and the subject was required to learn which of four unlabeled and unmarked categories the stimulus belonged to. Unknown to the subject at the outset, each category contained distortions of a *single prototype*. A feedback light indicated the correct answer after the subject had responded to each stimulus. Different groups of subjects saw distortions of low or moderate degree. After subjects had learned to classify the distortions consistently into their appropriate categories, a transfer test was given. In the transfer test, new distortions and old distortions of all three degrees and *all four prototypes* were presented for the subject to classify.

As might be expected, it took longer to learn to classify moderate-level than low-level distortions correctly. The distortions which the subject had learned to classify during training were more easily classified on the transfer test than were new distortions at the same level, indicating some specific memory for acquisition stimuli. One remarkable feature of the experiment is that the prototype, which the subject had never seen during the original

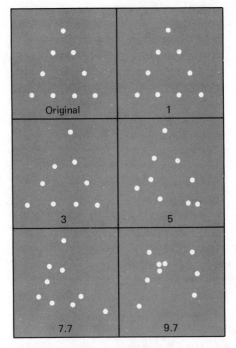

FIGURE 7-3. Original and five levels of distortion, increasing according to the numbers indicated, for a basic triangular dot pattern. (From Posner, Goldsmith, & Welton, 1967. Reprinted by permission of the author and American Psychological Association.)

learning, was classified into the correct category just as readily as the originally learned distortions. Transfer to all three levels of new distortions was better when training was on moderately distorted stimuli. This result suggests that, during learning, the subject acquires information not only about the prototypical stimulus but also about the variability among instances of a given class. Indeed, if a subject had learned only the prototype, then learning on the basis of the least distorted stimuli should have produced better transfer, because it is easier to define the prototype from less variable patterns. The results were in the opposite direction, indicating that subjects learn some information about individual patterns which they use in later transfer tests.

It is not at all clear from these data exactly what kind of mental representation of a category a subject forms. Perhaps performance on the transfer test is controlled by some verbal encoding of the stimuli, or perhaps a mental image of the individual instances or of the abstracted central tendency—or some combination of the two—or something more abstract. What is clear, however, is that subjects do know the best instance of the

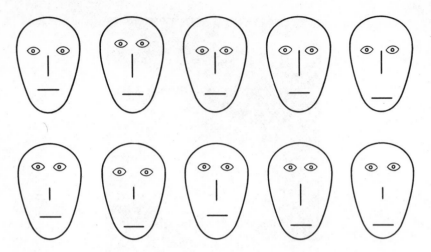

FIGURE 7–4.   Schematic faces used by Reed (1972). The upper faces represent Category 1 and the lower faces represent Category 2 in Reed's experiment. (Courtesy of Academic Press.)

category, plus something about the allowable variability or distance among admissible stimuli.

Reed (1972) reported a series of experiments similar to those of Posner but with more "naturalistic" stimuli, namely, schematic faces in which dimensions like eye placement, length of nose, height of forehead, and placement of nose were the variables. Examples of these faces appear in Figure 7–4. In one experiment, Reed presented ten faces simultaneously, five of which belong to one category and five of which belong to another (see Figure 7–4). Subsequently, subjects were asked to classify other schematic faces into Category 1 or Category 2 in accord with their knowledge of the two categories. On the basis of his data, Reed concluded that people use the acquisition stimuli to define the central tendency (or mean) and the variability of a category, and to identify the features which discriminate between categories. The mean is like a prototype or best example and may be represented mentally as an image. New faces are thus assigned to the category whose mean features are most like the exemplar. This experiment, like others we have reviewed, leads to the conclusion that items are represented in conceptual or semantic memory not in terms of the specific properties of their exemplars but rather in terms of some schema, or underlying similarity dimension, which captures the gross characteristics of the set of exemplars.

PROTOTYPE PLUS TRANSFORMATIONS

In Posner's studies, prototype or central tendency of a set of instances was a familiar entity, for example, a triangle or a block letter (F or M). Distortions from the prototype were arranged arbitrarily by a statistical rule for moving each dot from its "prototypical" position. Like Reed, Posner argues that distortions differ from the prototype according to some distance measure on a similarity dimension. The greater the distortion, the less the similarity. Two questions arise from this research. First, how important is it that the category to be learned be developed around a prototype which is already meaningful to the subject? It may be that a subject can derive a prototype and a category from a succession of dot patterns only if he is already familiar with the category. This could certainly account for why subjects correctly classify the prototype in the transfer test even though it has never been presented in the training instances. Subsequently, it has been shown (Peterson, Meagher, Chait, & Gillie, 1973) that a meaningful prototype or category is *not* necessary for learning and transfer in these tasks. Meaningful prototypes are generally more easily identified than meaningless ones, but both can be abstracted as the "central tendency" of a set of stimuli.[1]

A second issue pertains to the rules for variation within a category. Posner used arbitrary statistical distortion rules, which are likely to be difficult for a subject to identify. This almost forces the subject to rely on some intuitive judgment of similarity. Under different circumstances, it might be possible for a person actually to learn something more precise about the allowable variations within a category. This possibility was addressed by Franks and Bransford (1971) in a series of studies which led them to formulate a theory of category representation in terms of *prototype plus transformation*. They used the following procedure to investigate their theory. First of all, they selected a prototypical stimulus configuration consisting of a particular arrangement of four discrete, discriminable visual attributes. They then defined a set of formal but arbitrary transformational rules and produced distortions by varying the prototypical pattern in accord with various combinations of these rules. An example of the kind of materials used is presented in Figure 7–5. To begin with, subjects are exposed to an acquisition set of stimuli, that is, cards showing various types of transformation, with all variations represented equally often. Any particular stimulus in the acquisition set might be the result of one transformation, a combination of two, or a combination of three of the allowable transformations. The prototypical pattern might consist, for example, of a small red triangle on the left bottom, a large blue square on the left top, a large yellow diamond on the right bottom, and a large green heart on the right top of the stimulus card. The acquisition set consists entirely of distortions of the prototype. The allowable transformations are to (1) switch the right-left position of pairs of figures, (2) exchange the up-down positions within a

---

[1] It should be noted that one of the categories used by Posner and Keele (1968) was a random array of dots. Subjects need not have learned this "random prototype," however. If the three meaningful categories were learned, patterns which did not belong to any of them might have been assigned correctly but by default to the random category.

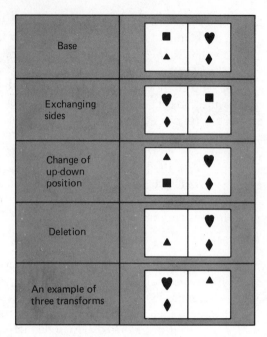

FIGURE 7–5. Examples of a base pattern and transformations on it used by Franks and Bransford (1971). (Reprinted by permission of the author and American Psychological Association.)

pair, (3) delete a figure, or (4) substitute a new figure for an old one, such as a hexagon for the square.

Following exposure to the acquisition set, subjects were shown a series of recognition stimuli and asked to decide whether they had seen each pattern in the acquisition set and to rate their confidence on a five-point scale. The results indicated that the prototype (which, remember, was not included in the acquisition set) received the highest positive (recognized) rating, followed by patterns in order of increasing transformational distance. Interestingly, patterns that could not be produced by the formal allowable transformational rules tended to receive negative (not recognized) ratings. The results of this experiment are portrayed in Figure 7–6. Franks and Bransford concluded that subjects abstract out of a welter of stimuli belonging to a category, the single best example. The category is represented in memory as a schema, consisting of two components. One component anchors the acquisition set in the best possible or middle-most example. The second component is a set of allowable rules which one can perform on the best example and still remain within the category. During acquisition, subjects apparently learned something more than simply the ability to reproduce the particular configurations that had been presented. They apparently acquired general information about the whole set of events. This

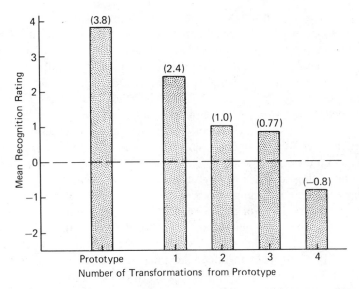

FIGURE 7–6. Recognition performance of subjects on stimulus patterns at varying transformational distances from a prototype. (Data from Experiment II, Franks & Bransford, 1971.)

information allowed them to recognize novel configurations and to order these configurations in terms of their transformational distance from the abstracted prototype. The exact nature of the acquisition processes for abstracting the prototype is, at this time, not specified in the Franks–Bransford theory.

SEMANTIC CONCEPTS

The research we have discussed thus far may be criticized on much the same grounds that Rosch criticizes traditional laboratory work. The stimulus material on which conceptual problems have been structured is relatively simple, highly dimensionalized, and artificial. There is a real need to move beyond this kind of material and into the domain of natural concepts.

The individual who has pioneered this extension of laboratory work is Eleanor Rosch. We have already seen how her theory can be applied to clarify simple color concepts in her work with the Dani. But her characterization extends beyond these simple concepts. Rosch's fundamental hypothesis is that natural categories have an internal structure—that is, categories are composed of a core meaning (prototype or best example) and a distance dimension defined by the decreasing similarity of other instances to the prototype. The idea is that our perception of stimuli tends to be organized around certain natural foci which become prototypes for learned categories.

DEGREE OF CATEGORY MEMBERSHIP.   Rosch's research on semantic categories began with the development of a method for identifying which items, if any, are natural prototypes. Unlike color and form, semantic categories have no obvious perceptual basis; most of them are culturally determined. To find out whether there are any sensible prototypes for semantic categories, Rosch (1975) employed the direct approach of merely asking people. Subjects rated members of a given category in terms of how well they exemplified that category. The outcome of this study is entirely consistent with Rosch's hypothesis. Prototypes and "gradients" of category membership do exist in semantic categories, in the sense that subjects consider this rating task a meaningful one. Further, there is high agreement among subjects concerning which is the best example of a given category and about the rankings of other exemplars. We show in Table 7–1 some of the norms for category membership that Rosch collected.

In subsequent experiments, Rosch (1975) reasoned that degree of category membership ought to affect the time needed for a subject to judge whether that stimulus belongs to a given category. Subjects were presented with statements of the form "an x is a y", when x was a good example (say, *robin*) of y (*bird*) or not a very good example of y (say, *penguin*). As a control, subjects responded to sentences in which x was a good or not good example of some inappropriate category. The results showed that it took longer for subjects to respond *true* to the true statement of category membership when x was a relatively poor member than when x was a central member of y. No differences occurred for false statements, which suggests that poor members are not in and of themselves difficult to comprehend or respond to. Furthermore, the differences were considerably more extreme for 10-year-olds than for adults, which suggests that children probably learn category membership of the prototypical members earlier than that of other, more peripheral members.

THE MEMORY CODE.   When you hear a category name, for example, *bird,* what sort of mental representation, if any, occurs to you? Is it a list of defining features of that category, a code for the category prototype, an image, or what? A task that offers promise in the investigation of such questions is a "matching" paradigm in which subjects are required to decide as rapidly as possible whether two simultaneous names are the same or different. *Same* can be defined as physical identity, for example, *robin–robin* or as the same category, for example, *robin–sparrow*. Suppose the subject is primed with the category name *bird* prior to the presentation of these stimuli. This manipulation may help us to determine the precise nature of the subject's mental code for a category. If the code generated by priming is like a list of defining features, *same* responses to pairs of items of any degree of category membership should be facilitated since, to be members at all, the items must possess the defining features. If, on the other

TABLE 7–1. Norms for Goodness-of-Example Rating for Four Semantic Categories. (From Rosch, 1975.)

Member	Goodness of example Rank	Member	Goodness of example Rank
Furniture		*Vehicle*	
Chair	1.5	Automobile	1
Sofa	1.5	Station wagon	2
Couch	3.5	Truck	3
Table	3.5	Car	4
Easy chair	5	Bus	5.5
Dresser	6.5	Taxi	5.5
Rocking chair	6.5	Jeep	7
Coffee table	8	Ambulance	8
Rocker	9	Motorcycle	9
Love seat	10	Streetcar	10
Chest of drawers	11	Van	11
Desk	12	Honda	12
Bed	13	Cable car	13
Fruit		*Weapon*	
Orange	1	Gun	1
Apple	2	Pistol	2
Banana	3	Revolver	3
Peach	4	Machine gun	4
Pear	5	Rifle	5
Apricot	6.5	Switchblade	6
Tangerine	6.5	Knife	7
Plum	8	Dagger	8
Grapes	9	Shotgun	9
Nectarine	10	Sword	10
Strawberry	11	Bomb	11.5
Grapefruit	12	Hand grenade	11.5
Berry	13	A-bomb	13.5
		Bayonet	13.5

hand, the code activated by priming is more like a category prototype, responses to pairs closer to the prototype should be more strongly facilitated. In one study, Rosch chose items from nine categories to represent high, medium, and low degrees of category membership. For example, in the fruit category, apple is high, grapefruit is medium, and watermelon is low in membership. For birds, robin, owl, and penguin are high, medium and low, respectively. Items were presented in pairs which were either physically identical (*robin–robin*), belonging to the same category (*robin–sparrow*), or belonging to different categories (*robin–apple*). There was an overall facilitative effect of priming on *same* responses but not on *different* responses. The effect was observed for both identity matches and category matches, occurring more consistently, however, for good examples of the category. This finding seems to indicate that what a subject generates when he hears a category name is not a list of features shared by all members of the category but rather a representation of the best category member. Rosch argues that because the priming effect occurred for physical *and* category matches, the mental representation must be a general image of the prototype.

BASIC-LEVEL OBJECTS IN NATURAL CATEGORIES

There has been a tendency in psychology to treat the world as essentially unorganized—"a blooming, buzzing confusion" upon which each human being learns to impose an idiosyncratic or culturally determined structure. The world per se does not contain intrinsically meaningful things. Rather, the child learns to apply to the world a kind of semantic matrix which serves to distinguish a large number of separate categories, each with its own label. Contrary to this viewpoint, Rosch argues that the world *does* contain intrinsically separate things. It does so partly because the attributes of things in the world do not occur independently of one another. Creatures with feathers, for example, are more likely to have wings and fly than are creatures with fur. Objects with the visual features of tables are more likely to have functional put-on-able-ness than objects with the appearance of birds. Rosch carries her argument one step further: Of the many possible levels of abstraction on which an object can be classified—for example, it might be said to be a chair, an article of furniture, a household object, an inanimate thing—there is one level which is psychologically the most basic. The basic level is one at which the organism can obtain the most information with the least cognitive effort. Rosch assumes that categorization occurs to reduce the infinite differences among stimuli to manageable proportions. If so, it is to the organism's advantage both to have each classification as rich in information as possible and simultaneously to have as few classifications as possible. The basic level of classification is a compromise between these two principles. It is the most general and inclusive level at which categories are able to correspond to real-world stimulus structures.

The basic level of abstraction means more, however, than simply the most inclusive level at which things have features in common. Human beings also interact with objects, employing typical and repetitive forms of movement. In short, human beings have consistent motor programs which they use with respect to objects. Rosch, Mervis, Gray, Johnson, and Boyes-Braem (1976) hypothesize that the basic-level categories are the most inclusive categories at which identical (or similar) motor programs are employed for all objects of a class.

A final criterion for basic level has to do with the appearance of objects, since this remains an essential part of the identification process. Rosch hypothesizes that the basic level of objects is the most inclusive level at which a large increase in objective similarities in shapes occurs and at which an *average shape* of two objects is recognizable as that kind of object. Thus, the basic level may be the most inclusive level at which it is possible to form an image of the "average" member of the class and the most abstract level at which it is possible to have a relatively concrete image as the prototype.

SUPERORDINATE, BASIC, AND SUBORDINATE CATEGORIES. Studies designed to confirm these hypotheses have the following characteristics. Within a given group of related concepts, three levels of abstraction are chosen, superordinate, basic level, and subordinate. For example, the superordinate category, furniture, has as two basic-level categories, *chair* and *lamp*. Subordinate to the basic level are kitchen chair and dining room chair, desk lamp and floor lamp. For her experiments, Rosch chose nine superordinate categories such as furniture, clothing, vehicle, fruit, and so on. Each was subdivided into several hypothesized basic-level objects, each of which was further subdivided into several hypothesized subordinate level objects.

In one experiment (Rosch et al., 1976), subjects were asked to list all the features which they could think of for items at each of the three levels, superordinate, basic level, and subordinate. Relatively few features were listed for superordinate category names. A much greater number was listed for the basic level, but subordinate objects did not receive significantly more features than those at the basic level. If we take number of features as a measure of the information conveyed by a name, then it is clear that basic-level objects are informationally richer than the superordinate category to which they belong and that little additional information is supplied by moving to a subordinate of the basic level.

In a subsequent experiment, the same words were presented to a subject with the instruction to describe, in as much detail as possible, the sequence of muscle movement he or she would make when using or interacting with the object. How does one interact, for example, with a living room chair, with an automobile, with a tree? Subjects' responses were analyzed first by noting any general activity, such as sitting down on a chair, that was part of the description. Each major activity was then classified according to part of the body used and further into the specific movements made by that body part. The results were that virtually no movements occurred in common for superordinates. There were, in contrast, a large number of movements common to basic-level objects. Few additional movement patterns were elicited by subordinates when compared to the basic-level objects. To illustrate, there are few motor programs that we carry out on all items of furniture. What common responses are there to chair, table, and lamp? On the other hand, several specific motor programs are carried out in regard to all chairs, namely, sitting. Moreover, we sit on kitchen and living room chairs using essentially the same motor program. The commonality of interaction is thus maximal at the level of basic-level objects.

For purposes of their next experiment, Rosch and her co-workers tried to develop an objective measure of the extent to which objects look alike. Four superordinate categories were chosen for which it was possible to obtain a very large sample of pictures. Four pictures of four different basic-level objects in each category were chosen such that each object was roughly the same size and orientation. Similarity in shape was measured by the amount of overlap of any two outlines when juxtaposed. The results indicated that the ratio of overlapping to non-overlapping area when two objects from the same basic-level category, for example, two chairs, were compared was far greater than when two objects from the same superordinate category, for example, a chair and a bed, were compared. While some gain in ratio of overlap to non-overlap also occurred for subordinate category objects, for example, two kitchen chairs, it was significantly less than the gain between the superordinate and the basic-level objects. The point of this exercise is to demonstrate that objects in a basic-level category are at the highest level at which a generalizable image can be formed. Another bit of evidence on the same point was obtained when the same objects used in the preceding experiment were used to draw an "average" outline of the overlapped figures. These averages were like a composite photograph of the individual objects of a given category. Subjects were then asked to identify both the superordinate category and the specific object depicted. The results showed that the basic level of objects is the most general level at which the object depicted could be identified. Furthermore, overlaps of subordinate objects were no more easily identifiable than objects at the basic level.

A MATCHING STUDY. If it is possible to form an image of an average member of a basic-level category, then, as we have seen, advance information concerning the category should facilitate responses to stimuli which are near the average. In a follow-up to their earlier work with the matching paradigm (see pp. 206–8), Rosch et al. (1976) tested the priming effect for two types of category names. When the superordinate category is used as a cue to compare the sameness of two stimuli, there is no significant priming effect; however, the basic-level name is clearly facilitative of the correct response. Thus, once again, the evidence indicates that representations of categories in prototype format occur at the basic level but not higher.

CATEGORY DEVELOPMENT. Rosch's theory and her experiments on the convergence of properties of basic-level objects have certain developmental implications. The developmental literature in psychology indicates that children, unlike adults, do not put things together because they are the same sort of thing but rather because of associations, occurrences within stories, and other such criteria (Rosch et al., 1976). In these studies, however, the categories to be used by children were invariably at a superordinate level, which clearly has implications for writers of children's literature. In this same work, Rosch cites a study in which subjects aged three years through adulthood were given the opportunity to sort sets of colored pictures of common objects into groups at either the basic level or the superordinate level. The results were simple and consistent. At all age levels groupings of superordinate objects occurred far less frequently than groupings of basic levels of objects and even the youngest children experienced no difficulty with sorts at the basic level. These and other data are used by Rosch to support the argument that the basic level is the first learned classification (regardless of language), the most used in language, and the most vital level to be coded in everyday commerce with the environment.

THE BASIS OF INTERNAL CATEGORY STRUCTURE

The evidence that natural categories are represented in memory in a manner which reflects their analog structure is impressive. As yet, however, we have not considered the problem of how the internal structure of concepts arises in the first place. That is, what principles govern the formation of category prototypes and gradients of category membership?

Rosch and Mervis (1975) examined the hypothesis that members of a category come to be viewed as typical to the extent they bear a family resemblance to other members of the same category. Family resemblance was defined as the possession of attributes which overlap the attributes of other members. The converse of this hypothesis implies that items which are viewed as most typical of one category will be those with least family resemblance to members of other categories. This hypothesis is closely related to an older idea of cue validity (Bourne & Restle, 1959). Mathematically, cue validity can be defined as a conditional probability, namely, the frequency with which a cue is associated with the category in question divided by the total frequency of that cue over all categories. Rosch and Mervis used the term *family resemblance,* borrowed from the philosopher, Wittgenstein, rather than cue validity primarily to emphasize that they were dealing with a description of structure and not with process models, which commonly refer to cue validity.

Rosch and Mervis conducted several experiments to test the family resemblance hypothesis. One of these experiments examined the structure of superordinate semantic categories, such as furniture and vehicle. These categories are of particular interest because they are relatively abstract and have few, if any, attributes common to all members. Thus, such categories may consist almost entirely of items related to each other by means of family resemblance.

In the first of their experiments, Rosch and Mervis attempted to discover the distribution of attributes of members of a number of superordinate natural categories and to tease out any relation between number of shared attributes in a category member and its rated typicality. The specific hypothesis was this: Degree of family resemblance of items to other members of the same category is significantly correlated with typicality ratings of these items. Subjects were given the name of a common object and were asked to write down all of the attributes of that object they could think of in 90 seconds. Each subject responded to six items, representing six superordinate categories. Over the entire group of subjects, a total of 120 items, 20 from each category, were rated. For each category, all attributes mentioned by subjects were listed. Then, each attribute was given a score ranging from 1 to 20, representing the number of items in the category which had been credited with that attribute.

Figure 7–7 shows the mean frequency distribution for the number of attributes applied to each number of items within a category. As had previously been reported for superordinate categories, few attributes were given which were true of all 20 members of a category. Only a few items

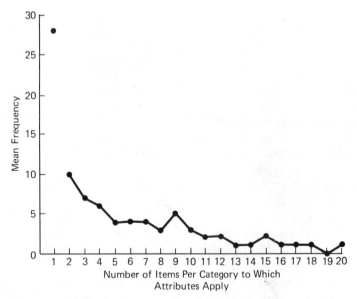

FIGURE 7–7. Frequency distribution showing the number of attributes which were applied by subjects to various numbers of items within a given category. (Data from Rosch & Mervis, 1975. Courtesy of Academic Press, Inc.)

shared any substantial number of attributes. Thus, the salient attribute structure of these categories tended to reside not in defining features common to all members of the category, but in a large number of attributes true of some but not all category members. The major hypothesis of the experiment was that family resemblance structure and typicality would be significantly correlated. The measure of typicality was the mean rating on a 7-point scale of the extent to which items fit the subject's idea of the meaning of the category names. The measure of family resemblance for an item was the number of attributes of that item which it shared with other items in the same category. The correlations ranged from .84 for the vegetable category to .94 for the weapon category.[2] Thus, the results strongly confirm the hypothesis that the more an item has attributes in common with other members of a given category, the more it will be considered a representative member of the category. Further, it was observed that while category members as a whole may not share attributes, the five most typical items of each category tended to have many more attributes in common than any five less typical members. Thus, if a subject thinks of the best examples of the category when hearing the category name, the illusion of common elements is likely to arise and persist. According to Rosch and Mervis, it is this illusion which makes the definition of categories in terms of defining features appear so reasonable.

Basic-level categories are the categories for which the cue validity of attributes within categories should be maximal. Superordinate categories have lower cue validity than basic because, as has been demonstrated, there are fewer common attributes within the category. Subordinate categories have lower cue validity than basic because they share attributes with contrasting subordinate categories (for example, *kitchen chair* shares most of its attributes with *living room chair*). Thus, one would expect the most typical members of a subordinate category to be those which are most distinct from members of related categories. Rosch and Mervis conducted essentially the same experiment as described above with basic-level objects and found, once again, that the more typical items are those which have most attributes in common with other members of the category. In a final experiment, with subordinate categories, they obtained evidence in support of the corollary of their major hypothesis. The more typical of a subordinate category a picture is rated, the fewer attributes it shares with categories in direct contrast with it. Thus, the most typical kitchen chair is the one having fewest attributes in common with contrasting categories such as dining room chair or camp chair.

The conclusion from this work is that members of a category come to be viewed as typical of the category as a whole in proportion to their family resemblance to other members of the category. Conversely, items viewed as

[2] The highest possible positive correlation is 1.00.

most typical of one category will be those with least family resemblance to or membership in other categories.

PROTOTYPE OR FEATURE LIST?

The view against which Rosch has sought to provide counterevidence is that concepts or categories are represented and processed mentally in terms of a list of common features, critical for category membership. She has sought to disprove that natural language category names mean or designate just those defining features. In her view such a representation implies that all members of a category are equivalent in their degree of membership in the category, since all must possess the necessary and sufficient criteria for membership. Her alternative hypothesis, as we have seen, is that natural categories are represented and processed in terms of a prototype and allowable distances from the prototype.

It may be that Rosch has taken too simplistic a view of the feature list theory of concepts. While it is true that, in many laboratory situations, critical features are perfect predictors of category membership, that is not necessarily the case nor is it strictly implied by feature list theory. Indeed, the notion of cue validity has been a part of feature list theories for many years (for example, Bourne & Restle, 1959) and there have been related laboratory experiments with arbitrary concepts based on less than perfect validity for all cues (among others, Haygood & Bourne, 1960). The outcome of those experiments, which we will not review here, has in general been compatible with the broader assumptions of feature list theories.

The work just reviewed, by Rosch and Mervis, is consistent with the notion that features (of differing validity) are important in the definition of any concept. These data, and some others that we shall examine, suggest that the prototype and feature list theories are not nearly so far apart as Rosch's discussion of them would imply. To show that prototype and category membership phenomena can be derived from feature list considerations, consider some recent work by Neumann (1974, 1975). Neumann's research began with a reanalysis of the data of Franks and Bransford (1971) which we considered earlier. Franks and Bransford propose that concepts might be defined generally in terms of a prototypical stimulus pattern plus an allowable set of transformations. The nature of the experimental paradigm used by Franks and Bransford suggests that their results are equally amenable to predictions from a feature frequency model which associates each stimulus with a set of frequency counts, one for each of its discriminable features. Frequency counts are compiled from the acquisition stimuli shown to the subject. The number of appearances of each feature of each dimension is counted and represented in memory. For example, if stimuli vary on the dimensions size and color, the number of times each size and color occurs in the acquisition set is registered. Neumann's model makes no formal assumptions as to the processes by which frequency information is coded, stored, retrieved, or evaluated.

After the acquisition set, stimuli are presented to a subject for recognition. If a stimulus incorporates one or more features or feature combinations that did not occur in the acquisition pattern, the stimulus will be judged as new or as not having occurred in the acquisition set. The role of differential feature frequencies is in determining the confidence of a subject's recognition and rating of degree of category membership for a stimulus. High frequencies produce high confidence ratings and low frequencies produce low confidence ratings. The order of final ratings of a set of recognition stimuli is predicted, from highest to lowest, by the order of the sums of the frequencies for each of those recognition patterns. By means of such an analysis, Neumann (1974) showed an even more accurate accounting of the Franks and Bransford data than the authors themselves provided.

In feature list theories, a concept is defined in terms of some relation among a set of relevant features. Not all members of the category need to have all relevant features. Indeed, features do occur with differing probabilities among members of natural categories. Some features are highly likely, having a probability approaching 1.0. Others are relatively unlikely. Each dimension of some unknown concept can be represented by an underlying probability distribution, built up as the person learns about the concept. Some one or more values on each dimension will have maximal or modal probability over all instances and will become the "relevant features." The stimuli belonging to any particular category may vary on many dimensions not considered critical. These are dimensions having a flat (or rectangular) probability distribution. No particular feature or value on those dimensions stands out as being associated with the concept in question.

From this point of view, the concept is fully defined by a set of features, their probability values, and the relationship among the features. The prototype would be predicted to be that stimulus which contains all (or the maximal number of) modal features. Other stimuli rank order themselves with respect to the prototype in terms of degree of category membership on the basis of how many modal features they have, which ones, or how similar the features are to the modal ones. In such a theory, the prototype has no special status. It does not serve as the focus for organizing the category. Neither does degree of category membership become a special characteristic of categories. Rather, these phenomena are derived from some more basic process, namely the emergence of probability distributions associated with stimulus dimensions.

There is no way of knowing at the present time whether a prototype or a feature list theory will serve the science of cognitive psychology better. Both are presently being used to guide research. Eventual answers will be found in the outcome of that research. For the present time, both seem viable and we may discover, as has so often been the case in the past, that these two seemingly antagonistic theories actually reduce to very much the same results when we know how to look at them in proper perspective.

CONCEPTUAL RULES

This is a chapter about the structure of concepts. Thus far, our discussion has centered upon the role that stimulus features play in determining structure. Likewise, in the previous chapter, we were almost exclusively concerned about the relevance of stimulus features and how a subject identifies them. But at the very outset of our discussion we made it plain that more than stimulus features are involved in the definition of a concept. We must know in addition something about the relationship of features. A feature relationship is like the predicate of a proposition (see Chapter 5). Arguments alone do not define a proposition. One must know how they relate to each other, as specified by the predicate. Likewise, features alone don't define a concept. One must know how the features go together.

To give a simple example, take a category defined deterministically by the two features *red–triangle*. The category *red and triangle* is quite different from the category *red and/or triangular*. In the first case, the stimulus must have both relevant features in order to be included. In the second case, it need have only one. The difference between these categories is a matter of which rule is applied to the two relevant features.

There has been far less research and theorizing on the acquisition and use of conceptual rules than on feature identification. What research has been done is limited to logical concepts based on rules taken from simple systems such as set theory or the calculus of propositions. But the role of rules or relationships among features is clearly not limited to simple logical concepts. While one might need to employ a more powerful theoretical system to describe them properly, rules or relationships are no doubt involved in natural semantic concepts as well. We view the work of Kintsch (1974) and others, which is primarily designed toward a propositional analysis of English textual materials and their representation in memory, as a demonstration of the importance of feature relationships in natural semantic concepts.

SOME PRELIMINARY CONSIDERATIONS

By the early 1960s, it had become abundantly clear that concepts of different logical types (rules) varied in difficulty and in the kind of process required for their acquisition or discovery. Bruner, Goodnow, and Austin (1956) were among the first to report a difference, in their case a difference between the conjunctive (*and*) type concept and the disjunctive (*and/or*) type. Bruner et al. reported that disjunctive concepts were more difficult

TABLE 7–2. Sixteen Unique Partitions of a Stimulus Population.

Stimuli	Partition															
	A	B	C	D	E	F	G	H	I	J	K	L	M	N	O	P
Both features present	+	+	+	+	−	+	+	+	−	−	−	+	−	−	−	−
First present, second absent	+	+	+	−	+	+	−	−	−	+	+	−	+	−	−	−
First absent, second present	+	+	−	+	+	−	+	−	+	+	−	−	−	+	−	−
Both absent	+	−	+	+	+	−	−	+	+	−	+	−	−	−	+	−

and speculated that the difference might be attributable to the differing strategy requirements of the two concept types. Subsequently, Hunt and Hovland (1960) reported a similar difference and offered an interpretation based on the differing amounts of information contained in examples of conjunctive and disjunctive concepts. Conant and Trabasso (1964) suggested that people have a tendency to focus upon positive instances of concepts and therefore find that negative instances, which are often more informative than positive instances in the disjunctive case, are difficult to work with.

The most complete of the early studies on conceptual rules was reported by Neisser and Weene (1962). These authors noted that conjunction and disjunction are only two of several possible logical relationships that can hold between two stimulus features. In all there are 16 possible ways of assigning a set of stimulus patterns to positive and negative response categories based on the presence or absence of (at most) two critical features. These 16 different rules are presented in Table 7–2. A careful examination of the rules of Table 7–2 reveals that they can be grouped into four levels in terms of the three primitive operations. Two of the rules, A and P in Table 7–2, are trivial because they assign all stimulus patterns either to the positive or to the negative category. We shall refer to these as Level 0 rules. Four other rules, F, G, I, and K, have assignments which are based only on the presence or absence of a single feature. We refer to these as Level I. The remaining rules depend upon the presence or absence of both defining features. At Level II are rules B, C, D, E, L, M, N, and O. Each of these arrangements can be described as a conjunctive or a disjunctive combination of the presence or absence of the two critical attributes. Finally, at Level III are rules H and J which, according to Neisser and Weene, require both conjunction and disjunction for a complete description. Examples of the descriptions which apply at Levels I, II, and III are shown in Table 7–3.

Neisser and Weene theorized that adult subjects are, at best, limited to the use of three primitive logical operations, namely, negation, conjunction, and disjunction. Therefore, a subject's comprehension of any relationship among features of logical concepts must be reduced to some combination of these operations. Neisser and Weene's theory says that the difficulty of any particular concept will be a function of how many primitive logical

TABLE 7–3. CONCEPTUAL RULES AT EACH OF THREE LEVELS DEFINED BY NEISSER AND WEENE (1962).

Name and Symbolic Designation	Description of Positive Instance	Example
Level I		
Presence (A)	A must be present	Vertebrate: must have a backbone
Absence ($\overline{A}$)	A must not be present	Invertebrate: must not have a backbone
Level II		
Conjunction (A ∩ B)	Both A and B must be present	Good quality: both material and workmanship must be first class
Inclusive Disjunction (A ∪ B)	Either A or B or both must be present	Allergenic: a food which contains either tomatoes or strawberries (for example)
Exclusion (A ∩ $\overline{B}$)	A must be present and B not present	Eligible for driver's license: must have passed test and not have committed felony
Alternative Denial ($\overline{A}$ ∪ $\overline{B}$)	Either A or B, or both, must be absent	Poor quality: either material or workmanship is not first class
Joint Denial ($\overline{A}$ ∩ $\overline{B}$)	A and B must both be absent	Nonallergenic: a food which contains neither tomatoes nor strawberries (for example)
Conditional ($\overline{A}$ ∪ B)	A may be absent, but if A is present then B must be also; thus $\overline{A}$ implies B	Ineligible for Driver's license; must either have not passed test or have committed felony
Level III		
Biconditional (A ∩ $\overline{B}$) ∪ ($\overline{A}$ ∩ B)	Either A or B must be present, but not both together	Negative product: either factor negative, but not both
Exclusive Disjunction (A ∩ B) ∪ ($\overline{A}$ ∩ $\overline{B}$)	Both A and B must be present, unless neither is	Positive product: both factors may be negative, or neither, but not just one

operations it requires. In other words, concepts at Levels 0 through III should increase in difficulty. Note that this prediction neglects the already well-established difference in difficulty between conjunctive and disjunctive concepts. According to the Neisser and Weene analysis, there should be no difference. Nonetheless, these authors reported an extensive experiment in which all but the trivial Level 0 types were included. The results in general conform to their logical analysis. There was, however, a significant difference, as had previously been found, between conjunctive and disjunctive concepts. Furthermore, a rule designated as D (which we shall call the conditional rule) in Table 7–2 was considerably more difficult than expected, falling closer to Level III concepts than to the Level II group to which it theoretically belonged. Overall, however, the Neisser and Weene analysis did demonstrate that (a) rules differ in difficulty and (b) differences among them are related to structural considerations such as the number of logical operations one must employ to describe the concept.

FEATURES AND RULES

The results of Neisser and Weene's study are somewhat ambiguous. The problems they presented to subjects contained two unknowns. When the subject began any problem, he knew neither the relevant features nor the rule of the concept. As a consequence, rule difficulty might be attributed to a difference in the feature identification process required by different rules or, alternatively, might be intrinsically associated with the rules themselves. In order to determine which of these two factors contributes to rule difficulty, one must find an experimental paradigm in which the two processes can be examined separately.

Such a paradigm was developed by Haygood and Bourne (1965). In their experiment, these authors studied separately the performance of subjects on problems wherein the rule or the relevant features, but not both, were the unknowns to be discovered. The feature problem essentially resembled the type used in previous research. To study feature identification, the experimenter must be sure that the subject understands, at the outset, the general form of solution required by the task. This information is usually imparted through preliminary instructions and examples of the rule to be used and may be accompanied by actual practice in using the rule. If the subject thoroughly understands the rule, his only task is to find the unknown feature or features. By contrast, in a rule problem, the subject is provided, at the outset, with the name or names of the features which are relevant. The task that remains, then, is to discover how these features are combined in the construction or definition of the unknown concept. Suppose the concept to be learned is *red and/or triangle*. In a feature problem, the subject would be told that the concept is disjunctive, that there are two attributes of the concept, namely, x and y, and that they are combined by the *and/or* rule. The subject's task is thus to determine the unknown features x and y according to the concept "x and/or y." In a rule problem, the subject would be told that the two relevant features are *red–triangle*. He would be instructed that redness and triangularity are somehow combined

TABLE 7-4. CONCEPTUAL RULES DESCRIBING PARTITIONS OF A POPULATION WITH TWO FOCAL ATTRIBUTES (BOURNE, 1970).

Parti-tion	Name	Basic rule Symbolic description*	Verbal description	Parti-tion	Name	Complementary rule Symbolic description*	Verbal description
E	Affirmation	R	All red patterns are examples of the concept.	H	Negation	$\overline{R}$	All patterns which are *not* red are examples of the concept.
K	Conjunction	$R \cap S$	All red *and* square patterns are examples.	D	Alternative Denial	$R \mid S$ $[\overline{R} \cup \overline{S}]$	All patterns which are *either not* red *or not* square are examples.
A	Inclusive Disjunction	$R \cup S$	All patterns which are red *or* square *or both* are examples.	N	Joint Denial	$R \downarrow S$ $[\overline{R} \cap \overline{S}]$	All patterns which are *neither* red *nor* square are examples.
C	Conditional	$R \rightarrow S$ $[\overline{R} \cup S]$	*If* a pattern is red *then* it must be square to be an example.	L	Exclusion	$R \cap \overline{S}$	All patterns which are red *and not* square are examples.
F	Biconditional	$R \rightleftarrows S$ $[(R \cap S) \cup (\overline{R} \cap \overline{S})]$	Red patterns are examples *if and only if* they are square.	J	Exclusive Disjunction	$R \overline{\cup} S$ $[(R \cap \overline{S}) \cup (\overline{R} \cap S)]$	All patterns which are red *or* square *but not both* are examples.

by a rule to form the concept. The concept is red $\underline{\ ?\ }$ triangle and the subject's task is to find the rule that connects the two known relevant features.

Haygood and Bourne (1965) used a slightly different scheme for classifying logical rules than did Neisser and Weene (1962). They agree on the triviality of Level 0 rules and on the fact that rules based on the presence or absence of a single relevant attribute (Level I) ought to be easier than those based on both features. The remaining rules, Levels II and III from Neisser and Weene, are shown by Haygood and Bourne to reduce to four different pairs, each with a basic rule and its mirror image. All rules involving two critical attributes belong to one of these four pairings. The basic rules are labeled conjunctive, disjunctive, conditional, and biconditional. The relationship of the Haygood–Bourne analysis to that of Neisser and Weene is shown in Table 7–4. Most of the research of Bourne and his colleagues has focused upon the relative difficulty of the four primary bidimensional rules.

To establish the difficulty level of various rules, subjects were asked to solve a problem in which the relevant features were named and some one of the four primary bidimensional rules was an unknown. The subject was instructed to learn as quickly as he could the initially unknown relationship between two given relevant features of a concept. The stimuli were presented to the subject one at a time and the subject responded to each by classifying it either as a positive or a negative instance. Immediate corrective feedback was provided and the series of instances continued until the subject could either state the rule or make a certain number of correct category responses in a row. Using this procedure, Bourne and his associates (for example, Haygood & Bourne, 1965) have established that logical rules in themselves represent various levels of difficulty. The order of rule difficulty typically observed is conjunctive, disjunctive, conditional, and biconditional from easiest to most difficult for the naive or inexperienced subject.

Rule difficulty changes with practice. In a number of rule learning experiments, it has been shown that initial differences in difficulty disappear if practice is extended long enough. Typically in these experiments, each of a group of subjects solves a series of problems based on the same conceptual rule. The difference from one problem to the next is merely in terms of the particular pair of features designated to be relevant. The results of one such experiment (Bourne, 1970) are portrayed in Figure 7–8. As you can see, after about six problems, all subjects were essentially perfect on the rule to which they were assigned—that is, they made no errors. The subject knows the pair of relevant features from preliminary instruction—he comes to know the rule through practice. Therefore, in later problems, he can sort the stimuli with no errors whatsoever. Prior to attaining this level of performance, the order of rule difficulty remains the same, al-

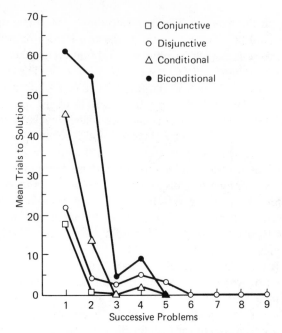

FIGURE 7–8. Mean trials to solution of nine successive rule learning problems based on the four primary bidimensional rules. (From Bourne, 1970. Reprinted by permission by the author and American Psychological Association.)

though later experiments have shown the difference in rule acquisition to be somewhat attenuated (Bourne, 1974).

Any particular concept has both abstract and concrete components. The concrete components are the specific perceptible stimulus features which are relevant to the concept. The abstract component is a rule. There is no concrete or physical realization of a rule. Rather it is defined as a relationship between or among concrete entities. The acquisition of a rule, then, as distinct from identifying relevant stimulus features or learning any particular concept, is an abstract process. It is an essentially different level of performance from that required by feature identification or the acquisition of any particular concrete concept.

HIERARCHY OF LOGICAL CONCEPTS

Most of what we have studied so far pertains to the acquisition and use of a single concept or category. In the last section, however, we discussed the acquisition of a general rule covering an indefinite number of individual concepts. For example, disjunctive relationship can be used as a connective for any pair of features to form a unique category. Thus, the disjunctive rule subsumes a large number of subsidiary categories. Bourne (1970) and

Hiew (1973) observed the emergence of another, even more abstract level in the hierarchy of logical concepts. The general aim of these studies was to assess the degree of transfer between one rule and others within the group of primary bidimensional rules. These experiments were arranged such that each subject solved three successive problems based on each of the four primary bidimensional rules, a total of 12 problems of training. The order in which problems were administered was counterbalanced across subjects. Then, in one study (Bourne, 1970), the subject was given a final rule identification problem to solve. The instructions to the subject were that this final problem was based on one of the four previously practiced rules. In a second study (Hiew, 1973), subjects were given essentially the same training routine but, for their final problem, were asked to find a solution based on an unfamiliar rule from the same rule system.

The outcome of these experiments was roughly as follows. Within any set of three problems based on the same rule, interrule transfer (or rule learning) of essentially the same magnitude as had been reported earlier (Bourne, 1967) was observed. As might be expected, when the rule changed from one block of three problems to the next, performance got worse. On the whole, however, there was significant positive transfer from training on one rule to performance on another. The results are portrayed in Figure 7–9.

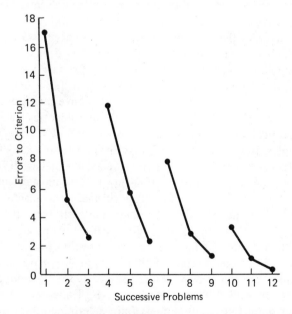

FIGURE 7–9. Mean errors to solution of 12 successive rule-learning problems. Problems were blocked into sets of three, each block being based on one of the four primary bidimensional rules. (From Bourne, 1970. Reprinted by permission of the author and American Psychological Association.)

At the end of 12 problems, most subjects approached the level of perfect performance, even though they were given only three practice problems on any particular rule.

Now consider the final rule identification problem. The subject is instructed that the solution to this problem is based on one of the four "known" rules, and he has to determine which one. As a theoretical minimum, the subject will need to see four stimuli: one representing the subset of stimuli that contain both relevant attributes, one representing the subset containing neither relevant attribute, and one representing each of the two subsets containing one but not the other relevant attribute. As is evident from Table 7–2, once the assignment of a stimulus from each class has been determined, the remaining stimuli can be assigned by the subject without error. Eighty-three percent of the subjects in this experiment solved the problem (that is, did not make any further errors) after one example of each of the four stimulus subsets (Bourne, 1970). Performance was not quite as good when the final problem was based on an unfamiliar rule. Nonetheless, 58 percent of the subjects met the criterion of perfect performance (Hiew, 1973).

What these results suggest is that after sufficient practice with some of the rules within a given system, the subject comes to know or to understand the system as a whole. He is able to perform at a high level on any other rule within the system, whether he has had practice with it or not. The subject's familiarity with the structure of the rule system allows him to induce new rules which are consistent with that system based on his prior experience. Reasonable familiarity with the four basic primary rules seems to be sufficient for complete transfer to the entire system for a majority of subjects. We are tempted to say that these subjects have mastered the system as a whole. The system, in this case the set of categories defined by the calculus of propositions, subsumes a variety (a total of 16, see Table 7–2) of different rules. It is thus, in a sense, superordinate to the rules themselves. The subject's acquisition of the system reveals the highest level of comprehension of concepts and their relationships that we have discussed.

The basis for transfer within the propositional system actually reduces to a quite simple strategy, called the truth table strategy, because of its obvious relationship to the logical bidimensional truth table of formal logic. The four subsets of stimuli described above correspond to the logician's TT, TF, FT, and FF combinations, where T is true and F is false for any premise. The translation required is merely to allow the presence of an attribute to be called T and its absence F. Knowing the truth value (category) of these four combinations fully determines the truth function for any combination of arguments in logic or the response assignments of stimulus patterns in a bidimensional rule learning task. In a sense, then, subjects in the foregoing experiments may, on some intuitive level, have induced the truth table, an algorithm recognized to have considerable power within formal logic.

PROCESSES IN RULE LEARNING

What accounts for initial differences in rule difficulty? A variety of theories has been offered. We have already discussed the Neisser–Weene theory, which places an emphasis on the complexity of a rule when reduced to primitive operations. But that theory can be rejected out of hand for its failure to account for the difference between conjunctive and disjunctive operations. Other theories have assigned rule difficulty to the difference in appropriateness of a positive focusing strategy for the various rules or to the differing amounts of information conveyed by positive (or negative) instances of each concept. Suffice it to say that none of these theories has been particularly successful in accounting for the empirical order of rule difficulty.

The theory that offers the most satisfactory account at the present time is structured in terms of the subject's response biases when he enters a rule problem (Bourne, 1974). The theory goes briefly as follows. The subject has certain pre-established tendencies at the outset of any rule problem. One of these tendencies is to place stimuli with both relevant features (TTs) in the positive category. Another is the tendency to place stimuli with neither relevant feature (FFs) in the negative category. Somewhat weaker is the subject's tendency to place stimuli with one but not both relevant features (TFs and FTs) into the negative category. These tendencies will change over time in the light of disconfirming feedback from the experimenter but, while the tendencies are in force, the subject will make errors. It can be shown that rule difficulty aligns rather well with the number of changes in these initial tendencies that is required by any rule. We think of these tendencies as operations or procedures in a person's semantic memory or knowledge of the world.

Knowledge of procedures is not fixed or rigid. It changes in at least two ways as a consequence of experience with rule-learning problems. Within the context of a single problem, operations of the sort "FF instances are negative" can be changed to the complement "FF instances are positive," as required by a given rule. Some number of disconfirmations of an inappropriate operation are required before the change is effected, however. Over a series of problems based on a variety of different rules, there is another kind of change in the subject's set. As the subject learns, through experience with a variety of different problems and different rules, that for some rules TTs are positive and for others TTs are negative, procedures probably become more abstract. Rather than entering a problem with a particular bias with respect to each stimulus, the subject learns to adopt a neutral set, observing the placement of an instance belonging to a particular class before determining the proper assignment of all instances within that class. It is at this point, of course, that the subject has adopted the truth table strategy.

The truth table strategy is deceptively difficult. Its use depends upon a variety of cognitive operations. To employ it, the subject must attend only to those dimensions of the stimuli that have been confirmed as relevant and ignore all others. Further, he must be able to focus upon the relevant values or features within those dimensions. Beyond attending selectively, the subject must form all possible combinations of relevant features—both features present, one but not the other present, neither present. In addition, the subject must understand what it means to negate or take the complement of an attribute, because some of the stimulus subsets he deals with are defined in terms of characteristics which the stimulus *does not have*. Finally, the subject must be able to deal simultaneously with four unique coded classes or subsets of the stimuli.

All of these skills are present, obviously, in the performance of a well-trained adult subject. In the experiments we have reported, a majority of subjects do attain the truth table level of performance. Had training been carried further in these experiments, there is every reason to believe that nearly all subjects would reach this level of proficiency. However, for the naive adult subject, this is not a natural way to organize and perform such a task. Achieving facility within the system of rules is something that takes considerable time, effort, and ability.

FACTORS AFFECTING THE EFFICIENCY OF RULE LEARNING

TRUTH TABLE PRE-TRAINING. If subjects do acquire knowledge of the truth table as a consequence of experience with a variety of logical rule problems, and if a working understanding of the truth table is the process underlying efficient performance on these problems, then it follows that pre-training directly on the truth table should facilitate subsequent rule learning performance. That issue was investigated by Dodd, Kinsman, Klipp, and Bourne (1971) with positive results. Different groups of subjects were given 0, 1, 3, or 5 problems which involved learning to sort stimuli into the four categories of a truth table based on two given relevant features. Subsequently, subjects were tested for their ability to solve a rule-learning problem based on a previously unpracticed rule, namely, the biconditional. Figure 7–10 shows that performance on a rule-learning problem improves steadily with amount of truth table pre-training, directly documenting the importance of truth table knowledge for rule learning performance.

DEVELOPMENTAL CHANGES. As we have noted, knowledge and use of truth table strategy depends on the prior existence of a number of component skills, such as the ability to recode a stimulus population into a

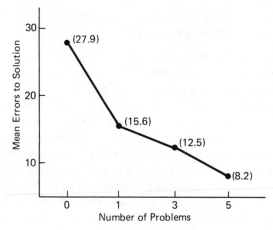

FIGURE 7–10. Performance on a rule-learning problem after practice on various numbers of truth table pretraining problems. (Data from Dodd, Kinsman, Klipp, & Bourne, 1971.)

smaller number of classes. Because these skills are cognitive in nature and likely to evolve developmentally with experience, we might anticipate less evidence of rule learning in younger children than in adults. Bourne and O'Banion (1971) explored this issue in the following way. Subjects at six different age levels, grades 1, 3, 5, 7, 9, and college, attempted to solve three successive rule-learning problems all based on the same rule. As one might expect, overall performance was better for older subjects, although seventh and ninth graders did not perform significantly worse than adults. The means are shown in Table 7–5. The major empirical question of interest concerns the degree of improvement or transfer across the three successive problems. Whereas adult subjects showed approximately a 75 percent reduction in number of trials to solution between the first and third problem, younger children showed a minimal change, with first graders evidencing only a 15 percent improvement. These results suggest that, while even the youngest children could solve any of the problems administered, the degree to which subsequent performance profits from prior experience is developmentally related. Young children do not show much interrule transfer, or rule learning, which may be a consequence of any number of factors,

TABLE 7–5. Mean Trials To Last Error, Averaged Over Four Different Rules and Three Problems Per Subject. (Data from Bourne & O'Banion, 1971.)

		Grade Level			
1	*3*	*5*	*7*	*9*	*College*
49.4	33.4	23.2	20.7	20.2	15.4

for example, their inability to recode the stimuli or to use the mental operation of negation, as required by truth table strategy.

STIMULUS FACTORS IN RULE LEARNING. There is another issue in need of further examination. We have treated rule learning as an abstract process related to the acquisition of a general principle which applies in any context and to any stimulus object. Recent evidence by Reznick and Richman (1976) raises some question about this treatment. In particular, these experimenters observed that, contrary to the usual result, a disjunctive rule problem is easier for the naive subject to solve than a conjunctive problem when certain pairs of stimulus features are involved. Evidence to this effect also appears in an earlier report by Dominowski and Wetherick (1976). If this research is valid, it implies of course that rule difficulty—and, in all probability, rule learning—is not independent of the particular stimulus context in which it occurs. Some pairs of features may coalesce or unitize naturally, corresponding to Garner's (1974) notion of integral dimensions. Such features lead naturally (or perceptually) to a conjunctive organization of the stimulus population, because the positive instances of the concept are by definition a conjunction based on the joint presence of the two critical features. Logical operations are acquired only if the features must be artificially separated in order to sort the stimuli according to some other rule. Other pairs of features may be naturally disparate, corresponding to Garner's notion of separable dimensions. The perceptual nature of these features leads directly to a disjunctive sort, based on the independent appearance of either feature in a stimulus. In this case, the conjunction, which requires a joint treatment of features, necessitates additional mental activity for solution and is therefore more difficult.

Evidence such as the foregoing strongly suggests that one cannot completely divorce rule learning from the stimulus context in which it occurs. There will, no doubt, be any number of studies on this problem in the next several years.

FINAL COMMENT

Throughout the latter part of this chapter, we have talked about the calculus of propositions as a system of logical rules for forming or describing concepts. This system of rules is interesting to examine for research purposes but is at best limited in its generality and power. All concepts, including alogical, natural concepts can probably be represented by some relationship among critical features. This is clearly the working hypothesis of those theorists who use propositions—that is, statements consisting of relations and arguments—to describe the gist of a text and its representation in semantic memory. On the other hand, the relationships required may be something other than the ones contained in the calculus of propositions. It will probably take a more general and a more powerful system of rules to encompass all of the conceptual or categorical possibilities that the human being deals with. Such an extension of rule learning research is needed not just to represent reasonably the range of concepts with which human beings deal, but also to make the link between concepts and their memory representations clear and investigable. This kind of theoretical work remains largely a challenge for future research efforts.

SUMMARY

Laboratory studies of concept formation have traditionally used arbitrary tasks in which the concepts bear little resemblance to ordinary natural concepts. This approach has been criticized for its failure to tell us much about how natural concepts are acquired or about their memorial structure once they are known. Research on natural concepts suggests that their representation may take the form of a prototype or best instance and that members of a natural category can be evaluated in terms of their goodness of category membership. This structure seems characteristic of a wide variety of concepts all the way from simple perceptual ones, like *colors,* through complex semantic ones, like *animals.* There has been some discussion of the basis of category membership. In some cases, the basis may be physiological; in others, where the categories are ill-defined, it may be a similarity judgment; in still other cases, the basis seems to be a matter of transformations on the prototype.

Natural concepts align themselves hierarchically. In the hierarchy, there is a basic level with certain characteristics that make it unique. Categorization occurs to reduce the infinity of differences among stimuli to manageable proportions. The base level of classifications preserves a great deal of information about the item, while at the same time reducing real-world variation to as few classifications as possible. Further, it is the highest level in the classification hierarchy at which a person can interact with exemplars using consistent movement patterns. Finally, the base level is the highest at which a recognizable "average" object can be identified by shape. The basis for forming categories, particularly base-level categories, seems to be shared attributes in some sort of a family resemblance relationship.

The definition of a concept involves both features and a rule or relationship among those features. Differences among rules is a factor to consider when one is measuring concept formation. Research has shown that rules taken from the calculus of propositions vary in difficulty. While a number of explanations has been offered for this difference, the most successful at the present time is couched in terms of a subject's initial response tendencies. Difficulty of a given concept is a function of how many of his initial tendencies are appropriate and how many have to be changed. In any case, rules are learnable components of concepts. Over series of problems based on different concepts, all of which have the same rule, performance approaches a level of optimal efficiency. Furthermore, when the rules in question are all chosen from the same system, for example, the calculus of propositions, there is interrule transfer. Experience with some subset of rules is sufficient for complete transfer to all rules within the system. Under these circumstances, the subject has learned more than a concept or a rule; he has learned the system as a whole.

There are many factors affecting rule learning, not the least of which is the developmental level achieved by the subject. Because rule learning is a relatively abstract learning process, it requires considerable experience and intellectual maturation before it can be achieved. To date, research on rule learning has involved only simple deterministic rules. In future research, we expect to see an extension of this line of experimentation to more complex and more natural relationships.

chapter eight

PROBLEM SOLVING

outline

PROBLEMS COME IN ALL SHAPES AND SIZES but generally share the characteristic that the individual must discover what to do in order to achieve a goal. Whether looking for the screwdriver that isn't where it's supposed to be, searching for a friend's house in an unfamiliar neighborhood, trying to figure out why the car won't start, or working on a mathematics exam in school, a person faces a situation in which the correct response is somewhat uncertain. In addition to the problems presented by everyday living or the demands of occupations, people often seek out problems to solve. An enormous amount of time is spent by people working on crossword and jigsaw puzzles or playing games such as bridge, checkers, and chess. During their lifetimes, people face many problems varying tremendously in difficulty and importance.

In order to gain understanding of how people try to solve problems and to identify the factors which make problems hard or easy, researchers need to have a good idea of what problem a person is working on. For this reason, researchers have tended to use fairly well-defined problems with clear beginnings and ends (solutions). Some tasks are borrowed from everyday life or slightly modified, while others have been constructed to have special properties which can help illuminate some aspect of problem solving. Some examples of tasks which are used in studying human problem solving are shown in Figure 8-1. Study these examples closely because we will refer to them throughout the chapter.

Whether we consider just the examples in Figure 8-1 or the larger domain of "all possible problems," it is clear that, even though all the tasks fit nicely the notion of a problem, there are obvious differences among them. Indeed, the differences may be more important than the similarities because there are sound reasons for assuming that the details of a problem-solving process are largely determined by the nature of the particular problem being solved. For example, the details of what a person would do in trying to solve the chess problem in Figure 8-1A are really quite different from the details of solving a scrambled word problem like those in section B. Although the process of solving any specific problem might have many unique aspects, there are also features of the process which are seen in solving other problems as well. In this chapter we will concentrate on the more general characteristics of problem solving, using a variety of problems as illustrations.

Black: 4 pieces

White: 6 pieces

A. White to move and mate in two moves regardless of Black's response.

B. ANAGRAMS: Rearrange the letters in each set to make an English word:

EFCTA
IAENV
BODUT
LIVAN
IKCTH

C. MATCHING PROBLEM: Sitting at a bar, from left to right, are George, Bill, Tom, and Jack. Based on the information below, figure out who owns the Cadillac.
1. George has a blue shirt.
2. The man with a red shirt owns a VW.
3. Jack owns a Buick.
4. Tom is next to the man with a green shirt.
5. Bill is next to the man who owns a Cadillac.
6. The man with a white shirt is next to the Buick owner.
7. The Ford owner is furthest away from the Buick owner.

D. HOBBITS AND ORCS:

Three hobbits and three orcs stand on one side of a river. On their side of the river is a boat which will hold up to two creatures. The problem is to transport all six creatures to the other side of the river. However, if orcs ever outnumber hobbits, orcs will eat the hobbits. How should they get across?

E. TWO-STRING PROBLEM:

Two strings hang from the ceiling in a large, bare room. The strings are too far apart to allow a person to hold one and walk to the other. On the floor are a book of matches, a small screwdriver, and a few pieces of cotton. How could the strings be tied together?

F. PYRAMID PUZZLE: Place a piece of paper on a table and draw three circles on it, labeling them A, B, and C. On circle A stack four coins—from top to bottom, dime, penny, nickel, quarter. The task: Moving only one coin at a time, moving only the top coin in any stack, and moving a coin only from one circle to another, get the coins stacked in exactly the same way on circle C. Important restriction: A coin may never be stacked on top of a smaller coin (e.g., the nickel cannot be placed on top of the dime, etc.)

Note. See Table 8-5 for the solutions.

FIGURE 8–1.

What happens when a person works on a problem? If we look beyond measures of efficiency such as whether or not the person solved the problem or how much time was needed, what activities will we find occurring in the course of work on a problem? Over the years, different answers have been given to these questions, and psychologists' views of problem solving have changed dramatically in recent years.

TRADITIONAL APPROACHES. Some theorists attempted to explain problem solving in terms of principles of associative learning derived from studies of classical and instrumental conditioning (for example, Maltzman, 1955). According to this view, an individual enters a problem situation with an existing complex of stimulus-response associations as a result of prior experience. The problem is more likely to elicit some of these associations than others, with the clear implication that problem difficulty will depend on the strength of the correct associations relative to the strength of other, incorrect associations. In the course of problem solving, the associative complex gets rearranged as some tendencies are weakened through extinction (failure) and others strengthened through reinforcement (success). Very briefly, this viewpoint stresses the transfer of prior learning to the problem situation and to the learning which takes place during problem solving.

A different view of problem solving was proposed by the Gestalt psychologists. These theorists emphasized the importance of the structure of the problem situation and the formation of new combinations of "old" ideas. Maier (1940), for example, distinguished between solving problems on the basis of direct transfer of prior learning (reproductive thinking) and solving problems by integrating previous experiences in a novel fashion (productive thinking). Maier argued that forming new combinations is guided by *directions* stemming from the problem situation itself (conversely, that analyzing past experience is not sufficient for understanding such problem solving).

Both the associative and Gestalt views of problem solving have led to considerable research; some predictions have been confirmed while others have not been supported. Neither approach has proved sufficiently comprehensive to serve as a framework for understanding problem solving in its various manifestations. The major aspects of associative and Gestalt views have been incorporated into a general information-processing approach to problem solving in which the individual is considered as an active processor of information who has certain processing limitations and who employs both general and specific processing routines.

INFORMATION PROCESSING AND COMPUTER SIMULATION. During the 1950s, computers were sufficiently well developed that scientists began attempting to program computers to perform tasks of greater and greater complexity. In the ensuing years, computers have been programmed to play checkers and chess, to prove theorems in symbolic logic, to learn word lists, and to understand language, to cite a few examples. Trying to make a computer perform a complex task is basically an attempt to produce *artificial intelligence*. Strictly speaking, work on artificial intelligence does not have any necessary connection with human psychology because a computer might be programmed to perform a task in a manner quite different from that used by people. However, a number of researchers have tried to program computers to perform tasks in ways which resemble human behavior. Such *computer simulation* research has had a profound influence on the psychology of human cognitive processes. In essence, the method consists of programming a computer to work in a specified manner and comparing its performance to that of human subjects given the same task. Similarities between computer and human performance suggest that people are using processes like those which have been programmed into the computer, while discrepancies indicate differences between computer and human processes.

Both the computer programming itself and the comparison of computer and human performance are quite complicated and difficult to summarize. If you desire further information, you might wish to consult Newell and Simon's (1972) detailed account of computer simulation research or Raphael's (1976) description of work on artificial intelligence. Researchers employing computer simulation have made major contributions to the development of an information-processing view of problem solving. In this chapter we will make use of the insights they have provided in discussing human problem solving.

A problem requires a person not only to register information from the environment but also to operate on, modify, or transform that information in some way in order to reach a solution. Solving a problem also requires the retrieval of both factual and procedural knowledge from long-term memory. Especially for longer problems, reaching a solution might involve repeated storage and retrieval of information generated early in the problem for use in later stages. Even this brief listing clearly indicates that problem solving is not a single cognitive process but rather involves a number of activities which need to be properly executed and organized to be successful. Some problems highlight certain processes while other processes seem essential for other problems. For this reason, we will discuss simple and complex problem solving separately after presenting a general overview.

In Chapters 2 through 4, we discussed some basic features of the human information-processing system. Problem solving, like any other human activity, is constrained by the nature of the system. Drawing from several sources (Hunt, 1971; Newell & Simon, 1972; Norman & Bobrow, 1975), let us outline the major features which affect problem solving:

1. Attention to environmental information is limited and selective.
2. Performance on a task is a joint function of the quality of data available and the allocation of processing resources. Both immediately available environmental information and content held in short-term memory (STM) constitute data. There is some limit to the processing resources available; when task demands exceed this limit, performance is likely to decline gradually, although performance may show abrupt failure under some circumstances.
3. Processing resources are required to maintain content in STM. Maintaining content in STM and operating on that content compete for the limited resources available.
4. Information is both entered into and retrieved from long-term memory (LTM), which has unlimited capacity. Entering information into LTM requires processing resources, and, while some information in LTM is retrieved with minimal processing demand, retrieval may fail.
5. The major processing steps in problem solving occur in an essentially serial (rather than parallel) fashion.

These features place clear constraints on the manner in which people will attempt to solve problems and suggest various ways in which difficulties can be encountered. If the problem situation is information-rich, the person might be unable to take in the necessary information or might select poor information on which to base problem-solving efforts. If solving a problem requires retrieval of information from LTM, failure can occur simply because retrieval is not effective. The fact that a person can know something but fail to retrieve that information in a given situation is nicely illustrated by the "tip-of-the-tongue" phenomenon (Chapter 4). Although some mental operations seem to function in parallel fashion (see Chapter 2) and thus operate simultaneously without mutual interference, many information-processing activities involve a central processor of limited capacity working in serial fashion. If we consider what appears as *conscious* work, our own intuition suggests that we tend to work on one thing at a time (serial processing) with clear limits on how much we can do.

Problem solving is a real-time activity involving information held in STM, the limitations of which constrain problem solving. It is important to recognize that problem solving requires active memories (those in STM). For example, a person may know (have stored in LTM the information) that $7 + 9 = 16$, but nothing will be done with that knowledge until it is activated (brought into STM). The limited capacity of STM was discussed in Chapter 2; in the context of a memory task, the focus is on the amount of content which can be held in STM. Problem solving imposes further requirements because the person must not only hold information in STM but also operate on it. Posner and his colleagues (Posner & Konick, 1966) have demonstrated that mental operations interfere with holding content in STM; for example, people who are shown a trigram such as XLT have difficulty remembering it over very short intervals if they must, during the interval, decide if 85 is an odd or even number greater than or less than 63. In general, problem solving involves such competition because the problem solver must both hold content in STM and perform operations on that content to solve the problem.

Consider the following problem: $19542 + 68471 + 85263 = ?$. If a person tries to solve this problem "in the head" (without paper and pencil), the problem proves difficult even though it is easy if paper and pencil are used. The problem is difficult "in the head" because attending to the numbers, adding them together (a step at a time), and remembering the outcomes of previous additions are all competing for limited processing resources. If you find multiplying somewhat harder than adding (which is not unusual), you might be able to "sense" the differences between problems (a) and (b) below:

(a) $11 + 8 + 13 = ?$
(b) $11 \times 8 \times 13 = ?$

We might expect to find some slight differences in difficulty between the problems if paper and pencil were used but a larger difference if the problems were done "in the head," because multiplying requires more processing resources or, alternatively, more content must be held in STM. The limitations on human information-processing capacity suggest four statements about problem solving worth remembering:

1. A problem might be easily solved by a solution strategy which human beings will be unable to use because of their limited processing capacity.
2. People will encounter a variety of difficulties in problem solving because of limited capacity—that is, failing to use all pertinent information, forgetting earlier solution attempts, and so forth.
3. People with greater experience and knowledge can find certain problems easier because their expertise allows them to work on the problem with a reduced load on processing capacity.
4. Problem solving should be quite different depending on whether or not a person has a memory aid available.

Limited processing capacity can also have a slightly different, indirect effect on problem solving. Bruner, Goodnow, and Austin (1956) proposed that a person faced with a mental task can have a conflict of goals. One goal is to complete the task as efficiently as possible, but this can conflict with minimizing *cognitive strain* (mental effort or stress on processing capacity). An ideal solution strategy is one which both leads to an efficient solution and minimizes cognitive strain. However, a person might elect to use a less efficient approach in order to keep cognitive strain within acceptable bounds.

STAGES IN PROBLEM SOLVING

Solving a problem involves a great many component processes; in fact, any number of processes might be identified, depending on how detailed one wishes to be in specifying a "process." At a fairly general level, problem solving may be said to consist of preparation, production, and judgment (or evaluation). Some of the activities included within each of these stages are shown in Table 8-1. Logically, it would seem that preparation is the first step, production the second, and judgment the third. However, complex problem solving generally involves considerable recycling through

TABLE 8–1. STAGES IN PROBLEM SOLVING.

Preparation: Understanding the Problem
Included Activities
Identifying the givens or the initial state of the problem
Identifying the solution criteria
Determining the constraints imposed on solution attempts
Comparing the problem with those previously experienced (in LTM)
Outcome: Construction of a representation of the problem
 Options:
 Dividing the total problem into parts or subproblems
 Constructing a simpler problem by ignoring some information

Production: Generating Possible Solutions
Included Activities
Retrieving facts and procedures from LTM
Scanning information available in the environment
Operating on the content of STM
Maintaining outcomes of prior operations in STM
Storing information in LTM for possible later use
Outcome: A potential solution

Judgment: Evaluating the Solutions Generated
Included Activities
Comparing the generated solution with solution criteria
Choosing a decision rule for deciding that a sufficient match exists
Outcome: Decision that the problem is solved or that more work is needed

---

these stages. For example, a person trying out one idea after another is cycling repeatedly through production and judgment. When evaluation leads to the decision that production is proving fruitless, a person might well reenter the preparation stage to try developing a different interpretation of the problem. Also, if there is a great amount of problem information to be assimilated, a person might forget some of it and return for this reason to the preparation stage. Johnson and Jennings (1963) employed special techniques in order to measure the time spent in different stages, but a clear separation of the stages is the exception rather than the rule. With this qualification in mind, let us consider what happens in these problem-solving stages.

PREPARATION. The amount of time and effort spent in preparation varies greatly over problems and among people given the same problem. For example, the chess problem shown in Figure 8-1 consists of (1) the existing positions of the pieces on the board, (2) the goal of ending the game in two moves (by white, with one move by black in between), and (3) the constraint that only moves consistent with the rules of the game may be made in finding a solution. An experienced chess player will assimilate this information rather quickly and is likely to concentrate on part (1) and to spend little time on part (3) since information concerning legal moves has been well learned and is readily (perhaps automatically) retrievable from LTM. A true novice, in contrast, might spend considerable time in preparation asking questions like "What moves can I make with this piece?"

The outcome of preparation is an interpretation of the problem, a representation of the problem as seen by the person who must try to solve it The nature of a person's interpretation is an important determinant of how readily the problem will be solved. Since the person's interpretation is strongly influenced by the structure of the problem itself (as viewed objectively), it is possible to present the "same" problem in different ways, some of which lead to easier solutions than others (we will review such findings later in the chapter). In addition, individuals differ in the kinds of representations they construct, with definite effects on their chances for success. We can illustrate this finding with the matching problem shown in Figure 8-1.

The information in a matching problem is usually presented in sentences, as in Figure 8-1. However, problem solvers, using pencil and paper, have been found to represent that information to themselves in various ways. Figure 8-2 shows three different ways in which the information in sentences 1 through 3 may be represented. The list format is essentially a shorthand version of the sentences themselves, while the network format includes all relevant items with connecting lines showing matches. The matrix format allows the representation of both matches and impossible

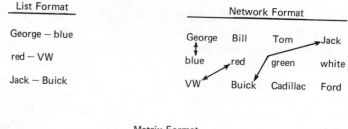

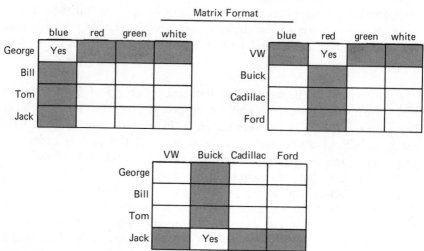

FIGURE 8–2. Representations Used for Matching Problems.

relations (if George has the blue shirt, then he doesn't have a different color shirt and nobody else has the blue shirt). These representations have quite different properties, which affect their usefulness. Both the network and matrix formats, by including all the items, provide some idea of what matches need to be found, while the list format does not. Only the matrix format provides a ready representation of impossible relations, which is an advantage. A person using the matrix format, upon reading sentences 4 through 6, can mark the following as impossible relations: Tom–green shirt, Bill–Cadillac, white shirt–Buick. Research has shown that people who use the matrix representation are much more successful at solving matching problems (Schwartz, 1971). Studies using other problems have led to the conclusion that a major characteristic of good problem representations is that they minimize the load on STM, which is consistent with the results from studies of matching problems.

PRODUCTION.   Finding a solution to a problem can involve many different activities, as suggested in Table 8-1. Solving a simple problem might depend primarily on retrieving the right information from LTM, whereas more complex problems such as matching problems, chess, and hobbits/ orcs require extended solution strategies. It is convenient to distinguish between two general classes of solution methods, algorithms and heuristics. *Algorithms* are solution methods which, if followed, guarantee a solution. For example, an algorithm for solving the anagram EFCTA would be a systematic method for generating all possible orders of the five letters (thus EFCTA, EFCAT, EFTCA, EFTAC, EFACT, EFATC, ECFTA, ECTFA, ...), offering each order as a possible solution, until eventually the correct order (FACET) is produced and the problem solved. Algorithms may be efficient or rather cumbersome (as in the above example); later in the chapter we will discuss research on using algorithms. An important point is that algorithms do not exist for many problems (for example, the two-string problem); in addition, an algorithm might be so cumbersome and time-consuming that it might as well not exist since it will not be used. Newell and Simon (1972) have argued that human problem solving is typically not algorithmic but heuristic in nature.

Heuristics are "rules of thumb" which might lead to very quick solutions or to no solution at all. Heuristics are selective or restricted solution methods which usually reduce cognitive strain. For example, a person faced with the chess problem in Table 8-1 might use the heuristic of "trying only moves which place the opponent's king in check," thereby reducing the number of moves which need to be considered. Heuristics differ in the scope of their possible application; there are different special-purpose heuristics for anagrams and for chess, for example. However, Newell and Simon have identified several general heuristics which frequently characterize human problem solving, and we now consider them, noting that these heuristics overlap the stages of preparation and production.

A *planning process* refers to the creation of a simplified, more abstract problem space resulting from the problem solver's ignoring some of the problem information. A planning process produces a simpler problem for which finding a solution is likely to be easier; the solution to the simplified problem might then be applied intact to the entire problem or used as a guide to finding the complete solution. Some examples of possible planning processes for problems in Table 8-1 are: (1) Trying to solve the chess problem while ignoring possible moves by the opponent's pawns; (2) trying to solve the matching problem by working on relations between names and shirt colors, ignoring relations involving cars; (3) trying to solve the anagram BODUT by thinking of words containing B, O, D (ignoring U, T). The usefulness of a planning process depends on the extent to which the solution to the simplified problem will be helpful when the complete problem is considered.

If we think of a problem in terms of an initial state and a desired (solution) state, the problem exists because of one or more differences between these two states. The general heuristic of *means-end analysis* refers to the process of testing for a difference between what currently exists and what is desired, subsequently performing some operation on the existing state in an attempt to reduce the difference. The use of this heuristic leads the problem solver to choose moves which reduce differences between the existing and desired states and to avoid moves which increase such differences. For example, since having the opponent's king in check is part of the solution state for the chess problem in Figure 8-1, means-end analysis leads to a preference for initial moves which place the king in check. Since the goal in the pyramid puzzle is to have the coins stacked on circle C, means-end analysis would lead a person to move a coin from A to C rather than to B, and to avoid moving coins back to circle A. Application of means-end analysis to the hobbits-and-orcs problem leads to choices of moves which transport the maximum number of creatures across the river in the forward direction and moves which transport the minimum number of creatures across the river in the backward direction when the boat is being returned to the starting side. In effect, means-end analysis involves persistent efforts to make identifiable progress toward the solution. This approach is generally useful because eliminating differences between the initial and desired states is logically required for solution of the problem. However, problems sometimes require indirect solutions; that is, at some point the best move might *not* be the one which minimizes the differences between the current state and the desired solution. For example, solving a pyramid puzzle frequently requires moving a coin from circle A to circle B (the "extra" circle) rather than to the target circle (C). In such circumstances, rigid application of means-end analysis can lead to inefficient solutions or to no solution at all.

Means-end analysis is a one-step-at-a-time, forward-looking solution method. A third general heuristic is its complement, *working backward* from the desired state toward the existing state. For example, a person working on the chess problem, rather than examining the current situation and determining which moves seem promising (forward-looking), might notice that the problem would be solved if a particular arrangement were attained, that achieving that arrangement would be easy if the pieces were located as follows, that the one-step-away arrangement could be readily produced if preceded by another particular arrangement, and so on. People working on mathematical proofs often employ a working-backward approach. Of course, working backward might not be helpful since the person might never make his way back to the existing situation. Generally, some mixture of working forward (means-end analysis) and working backward will be most efficient because the combination of strategies will maximize the chances of pursuing fruitful directions.

JUDGMENT. Whenever a potential solution has been generated, its adequacy must be evaluated. For many problems, this step is rather easy. For example, a person working on the anagram *trawe* who produces the arrangement *water* will have little difficulty in deciding that it is an English word. There are two general circumstances in which judgment is more complicated. When the solution criteria are somewhat vague ("write a *good* title for this story"), the problem solver must, in some sense, redefine the stated criteria. In this case, different people can arrive at different meanings of the criteria, which will result in their offering various kinds of ideas as solutions or solutions varying in quality (when viewed by a third party such as an experimenter, the boss, or society). In addition, judgment can be complex and uncertain in the earlier stages of a fairly well-defined problem. For example, a person is unlikely to have any difficulty determining that the coins are in fact stacked on Circle C at the point of completing the pyramid puzzle, but deciding "which move is best" earlier in the problem is much more uncertain. Judging the adequacy of alternative moves in a game of chess is quite complicated, and one characteristic which distinguishes better from worse players is the completeness of their evaluations and the decision rules used for selecting moves. It should be clear that, for many problems, a person may fail to solve a problem, take a long time in so doing, or even arrive at a poor quality solution not because of inadequate production of ideas but because of inadequate evaluation of those ideas.

INCUBATION. Preparation, production, and judgment are logically necessary parts of problem solving. A fourth stage of incubation has often been proposed as an optional but potentially important addition. Incubation refers to a period during which a person does *not* actively (consciously) work on a problem which has been started but not yet solved. The idea that incubation can help solve problems is attractive to many people. In Chapter 1, we described the experience of Professor Kekulé, who arrived at the structure of the benzene molecule after dozing in front of his fireplace and dreaming of a snake seizing its own tail. Other eminent thinkers have reported having the solution to a problem come to them "out of the blue" or easily finding the solution to an unsolved problem after a period of inactivity. Such reports have led researchers to study the question of whether taking time off from an unsolved problem is better than continuing to work on it.

Several theorists have proposed plausible reasons for expected positive incubation effects (time off better than continuous work). When a person has worked on a problem for some time without success, it is reasonable that some mental fatigue has set in; furthermore, since the problem has

COGNITIVE PROCESSES

not been solved, it is likely that the problem solver is pursuing an inappropriate direction. Taking time off might allow recovery from fatigue or allow the inappropriate set to dissipate such that the person takes a fresh look at the problem upon returning to work. Many inventors seem to believe that positive incubation effects are due to unconscious work on the problem during the rest interval. Another possibility is that failing to solve the problem produces frustration which leads to competing responses—that is, the person responds to his frustration rather than working on the problem. During the rest interval, frustration probably dissipates, thus allowing the person to resume work with less interference.

To study incubation effects, researchers employ an experimental design like that in Table 8-2. Both an incubation group and a control group are exposed to an initial period of work (A), but the problem is not solved during this period. Before resuming work during period (B), the incubation group gets a "rest period" while the control group does not (for the control group, period (B) follows immediately after period (A) without interruption). The "rest period" is usually filled with some activity to keep incubation subjects from working on the problem. The question is "Who does better during period (B)?" If the incubation group does better during period (B), a positive incubation effect is demonstrated. An examination of actual research results reveals that positive incubation effects sometimes do and sometimes do not occur (for example, Dominowski & Jenrick, 1972; Murray & Denny, 1969). There is clearly a need for further research because incubation effects might well depend on the kind of problem used, the length of the rest interval, and the nature of the activities filling the rest interval—many combinations have not yet been tried. At the present time, the idea that a person will profit by taking time off from an unsolved problem remains an appealing notion which has received only partial support.

SOLVING SIMPLE PROBLEMS

Some problems are relatively well defined, easy (compared to the total domain of problems), and do not involve extensive creation of subproblems or very elaborate solution strategies. Basically, the person is given informa-

TABLE 8–2. EXPERIMENTAL DESIGN FOR STUDYING INCUBATION.

Incubation group:	Work Period A—Rest Period—Work Period B
Control group:	Work Period A— No Rest —Work Period B

Note: The problem is not solved during Period A; groups are compared during Period B.

tion which describes the problem rather clearly and "need only" find the solution. Solving such problems might require several steps, but the steps are not complicated and are usually few in number. Examples of this type of problem include anagrams, object-use tasks like the two-string problem, and simple search tasks of various sorts (jigsaw puzzles, guessing tasks, and troubleshooting tasks involving uncomplicated "machines"). Research on simple problems has led to the identification of factors which reliably affect problem difficulty. We will consider these factors in the following sections.

The very first step in problem solving is the interpretation of the information initially presented. Research on a variety of problems has shown that the way in which the problem is initially presented affects the difficulty a person will have in reaching a solution. The idea is that initial solution attempts are based on minimal changes in the problem as presented. The problem solver tries to find and use clues present in the initial problem structure, and the clues might be helpful or misleading.

Let's consider some examples. Suppose a person is given the task of finding the word *bacon* when given the five letters in some scrambled order. The letters in anagram form can be ordered in many different ways, and some orders are much easier to work from than others. People are likely to find the solution *bacon* faster if given the anagram *aconb* than if presented with *nobca;* the anagram *bocan* is also likely to yield faster solutions than *nobca.* Notice that *aconb* contains a very useful clue, the letter sequence *acon* which is also part of the solution; *bocan* has three of the five letters in the same positions they occupy in the solution word *bacon.* In contrast, *nobca* has no useful clues and might contain misleading clues (if, say, people try to think of words having *ca* in them), which makes finding the solution more difficult (LeMay, 1972).

Figure 8-3 provides another example. For the "candle problem," the person sits at a table on which there are tacks, a box, matches, and candles, and is asked to attach a candle to a "wall" (a piece of cork or cardboard placed vertically at the side of the table) in such a way that the candle will not drip wax on the table or floor when it is lit. What is important is how the tacks and box are arranged when the materials are presented. The problem is quite easy when the box is empty and the tacks lie on the table, but it is much more difficult when the tacks are in the box (Glucksberg & Weisberg, 1966). When the box holds the tacks, people think of the box as a container or don't really notice the box as a separate object, thus they are less likely to think of using the box as a platform for the candle.

Other research has shown that the quality of organization of the initial problem presentation is also important. The idea, originally proposed by

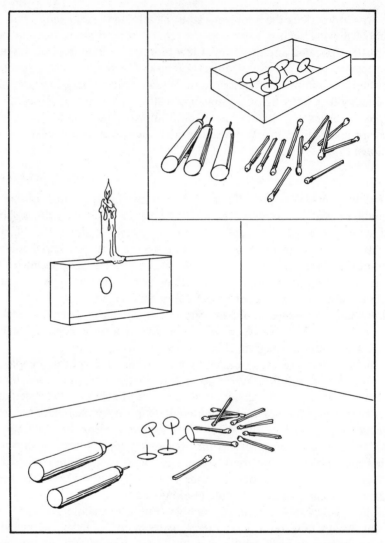

FIGURE 8–3. The candle problem. The upper panel shows the equipment available for mounting a candle on a wall. The lower panel shows the solution. (From Bourne, Ekstrand, & Dominowski, 1971.)

the Gestalt psychologists, is that, since the initial problem state must in some way be changed to solve the problem, the better organized it is, the harder it will be to reorganize. For example, anagrams which are easier to pronounce are harder to solve. Try pronouncing *rlfuo, lrufo, lurof, flour; rlfuo* does not conform well to the structural rules for English words and is hard to pronounce, but *lurof,* while not a word, has good structure and is fairly easy to pronounce. Both *lurof* and *rlfuo* could be used as anagrams to be solved for *flour,* and research shows that easily pronounced anagrams tend to be harder to solve than those which are hard to pronounce. Furthermore, having people practice pronouncing anagrams makes the anagrams both easier to pronounce and harder to solve (Dominowski, 1969).

These findings as well as others demonstrate that a person's interpretation of a problem is strongly influenced by the way in which the problem is initially presented. When given a well-organized but incorrectly structured initial problem state, people tend to keep that organization and thus have difficulty changing their representations and reaching a solution. People look for possible clues in the problem as presented, for better or worse depending on whether the clues are appropriate or misleading. Consequently, the "same" problem can be presented in various ways that are more or less difficult.

HINTS. Giving a hint to a person working on a problem is equivalent to changing the problem situation by introducing a new element. Usually, hints are given with the intention of helping the problem solver, although a hint might have no effect or even be misleading. It is important to distinguish between the hint giver's perception of the problem and that of the person trying to solve the problem. Very simply, the hint giver knows the solution but the problem solver does not. Consequently, the connection between a hint and the solution might be clear to the hint giver, but the clarity of this relation might be lost to the problem solver. Hints can be ignored, be interpreted as consistent with the problem solver's current direction, lead to a different, incorrect solution attempt, or yield a solution (Burke, Maier, & Hoffman, 1966). The essential question is, "How will the problem solver use the hint?" It should not be surprising (nor is it very informative) if subjects given a hint do not solve more efficiently than those left alone.

We will use the "hatrack problem" to illustrate what can happen when a hint is given (see Figure 8-4). For this problem, the person is brought into a rather bare room in which there are two fairly strong sticks about five feet long and a C-clamp. The task is to construct a hatrack stable enough to hold a winter coat (sometimes a coat is provided for testing a construction). The best (or only) way to solve this problem is to wedge the sticks between the floor and the ceiling, joining them in the middle with the C-clamp which also serves as a coat hook. People given this problem frequently try other solutions such as "base" solutions (an "L" or inverted "T" structure with the clamp joining the sticks at the floor level) or "balance" solutions (leaning the sticks against each other in an "X", "T", or inverted "V" structure with the clamp joining them above the floor level). These structures are unstable and thus incorrect.

One hint which has been used with this problem is the "clamp hint," which consists of the statement that the clamp serves as the coathook in the solution. Notice that the clamp hint is consistent with both the correct floor-ceiling structure and the incorrect balance structures; it is inconsistent with base structures. Giving this hint to a person already trying a balance solution is unlikely to have any effect, since the hint is consistent with what the person is already doing. People trying base solutions are likely to switch when the clamp hint is given; however, research shows that they are most likely to switch to balance structures, which are also incorrect (Burke et al., 1966). Research suggests that the effectiveness of a hint depends on the number of incorrect solution attempts it eliminates (Burke, 1969).

The Gestalt view of problem solving holds that a problem solver follows some direction in trying to find a solution, with the direction serving as a force which must be overcome before a different type of attempt will be made. Based on this view, a plausible prediction is that a hint will be less effective when given while a person is working on problem, compared to giving the hint at the outset of the problem or when a person returns to a problem after a rest period. The idea is that the person actively working on the problem has already adopted a particular direction which, if inconsistent with the hint, will lessen the hint's effect. Plausible though this idea might be, there is no clear evidence that the timing of a hint makes any difference in how a hint affects problem solving (Dominowski & Jenrick, 1972; Maier & Burke, 1967). Since there has been little research on this question, it would be best to keep an open mind regarding the importance of the timing of a hint.

SOLUTION FAMILIARITY

We have been emphasizing the influence of features of the problem situation; now let us look at the other side of problem solving—namely, the solution. Solving simple problems often depends on thinking of a particular idea, which makes problem solving much like cued retrieval of information in semantic memory (see Chapter 4). Research on problem solving has concentrated on the importance of the familiarity of the item which is needed for solution. As a general rule, problems are easier when their solutions require the production of more familiar ideas.

Familiarity effects have most often been studied with simple verbal problems such as anagrams or word-guessing tasks such as "think of a word starting with W that is the name of a tree." Researchers have a great deal of information about the frequency of occurrence of words in general language

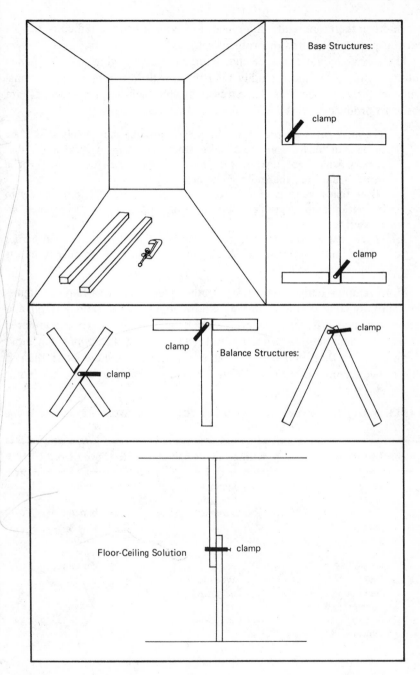

FIGURE 8–4.   The Hatrack Problem.

use and can therefore relate differences in frequency to the difficulty people have in producing words in problem settings.

There is abundant evidence that word problems having high-frequency solutions are solved more readily than those with low-frequency solutions. Duncan (1973) identified three reasons why high-frequency words are easier to produce:

1. The more often a word occurs in general use, the more likely it is to be in an individual's knowledge store (there are many words in the dictionary which are unknown to many people, and the odds favor a person's knowing the more common words).
2. Given that a word is in a person's knowledge store, it is more likely to be retrieved in a problem setting as its frequency of occurrence increases.
3. Given that a word is retrieved, it is more likely to be retrieved earlier as its familiarity increases. A diagram of these three frequency effects is shown in Table 8–3.

More familiar items have retrieval advantages over less familiar items. Furthermore, one of the things we know about words (and letters, and letter sequences) is, in a general way, how often we have encountered them. For example, you probably find it easy to tell that *apple* is a more common word than *ampersand,* that *e* is a more common letter than *x,* that *th* occurs more often than *sw.* It is thus reasonable to state that famil-

TABLE 8–3. ILLUSTRATION OF FREQUENCY EFFECTS ON WORD RETRIEVAL, USING THE EXAMPLE *Fruits.*

In the Language	Known to Person X	Retrieved from LTM *
apple	apple	apple
orange	orange	orange
banana	banana	banana
pear	peach	cherry
peach	cherry	lemon
cherry	lemon	avocado
grape	grape	cantaloupe
lemon	avocado	
cantaloupe	nectarine	
pomegranate	fig	
mango	cantaloupe	
avocado		
fig		
coconut		
nectarine		
kumquat		

* In order—that is, apple first, orange second, and so on.

iarity, or frequency of occurrence, is one of the attributes of memories in LTM. However, it does not appear that a familiarity attribute is itself the basis of the retrieval advantage which more familiar items have (Underwood, 1969). Rather, more familiar items are easier to recall because they share more relations with other items in LTM. Frequency itself can be used to make discriminations among items (as in comparing *apple* with *ampersand*), but it is a poor basis for finding a word in LTM. In other words, a person trying to solve an anagram or other word problem tries to retrieve the solution from LTM on the basis of other cues (for example, the letters of the anagram), and it happens that more familiar items are easier to recall because they are more strongly related to these cues.

If frequency itself were a useful basis for retrieval, then telling a person the appropriate frequency level should result in memory search being limited to that level. However, this does not happen. Stratton and Wathen (1972) gave people tasks such as "think of an uncommon word having the following structure: s _ _ _ e." Their subjects did *not* think of just uncommon words when given such instructions. Rather, they thought of a succession of words, based on the cues provided, and used frequency information to evaluate the words they thought of to determine if they met the stated criterion ("uncommon"). For example, a person given the above problem might think of *smile, store, stole, spare, share,* before thinking of and reporting *shale.* What these results indicate is that, while the frequency of occurrence of an item can be used to predict the difficulty a person will have in producing that item as the solution to a problem, the process by which the solution is produced involves much more than a simple search of LTM based on a frequency attribute.

Duncan's third reason states that people tend to produce items in *order* of familiarity. This relation between familiarity and order of responding also occurs when all people must do is select items from a set which is provided for them (eliminating the need for retrieval from LTM). For example, a person who is asked to guess the "correct" item among *er, et, eu, ew, ek* is most likely to guess *er* (the most common item) first and to continue guessing in order of frequency until told that the correct item has been selected. Because of this tendency, selection problems with infrequent items designated as "correct" are harder (require more guesses). However, the tendency to guess in order of frequency occurs only when people have no idea of the frequency level of the correct item. When information about the correct frequency level is available, people tend to select items at that level. Under these conditions, problem difficulty depends on the difficulty of discriminating the frequency levels of the items provided, and problems for which either the most familiar or the least familiar item is correct are easier than those for which items having intermediate frequency are the solutions.

Thus far we have considered familiarity as the result of long-term experience. Several researchers have manipulated familiarity by presenting items one or more times just prior to problem solving. Solving anagrams is much easier when a list of the solution words has been previously presented in the experimental situation. The effect of prior exposure can be quite striking; for example, anagrams which are ordinarily solved in about one-half minute are solved in two seconds if a list of the solutions has been presented before the first problem is given (Dominowski & Ekstrand, 1967). The effect of prior exposure cannot be interpreted as due to an increment in the frequency attribute associated with a word's representation in LTM (one presentation makes little difference in the frequency attribute of a common word but greatly helps producing that word as a solution). Nor can the effect be due to the person's holding the list of solutions in STM (eliminating the need to search LTM for a solution) because the list is too long to be held in STM, especially in view of the length of time between presentation and problem solving and the processing required to solve the problems. What prior exposure does accomplish is the attachment of the solution words to that situation, thus facilitating retrieval (from LTM) *in that situation*. The effect of prior exposure involves episodic memory more than changes in semantic memory, and we would expect the effect to diminish as the person's memory of that episode fades.

PROBLEM SIZE

A problem by definition allows two or more alternative courses of action, and it is perhaps not surprising that problem difficulty increases as more alternatives are available (provided that only one alternative will yield a solution). Researchers have tried to determine the precise form of the relation between difficulty and the number of alternatives; while all studies show an increasing relation, the precise form varies with the type of task. For problems such as finding the piece of jigsaw puzzle which fits a target piece or selecting the correct word from a list provided, difficulty is linearly related to the number of available alternatives (Dominowski, 1972). In such tasks each alternative must be separately considered to determine if it is the solution. If a problem solver can eliminate multiple alternatives simultaneously, difficulty then shows a negatively accelerated relation to the number of alternatives (Neimark & Wagner, 1964).

The difference between the two kinds of strategies and the difference in relations which results can be illustrated as follows. Suppose you are trying to find out which of 8 squares has been designated as correct (see Figure 8-5). If you must guess one square at a time, finding the correct square will take about 4 guesses on the average. With 16 squares, an average of 8 guesses will be needed, and with 32 squares, an average of 16 guesses will be required. With this one-at-a-time strategy, difficulty (number of required guesses) will have a linear relation with the number of alternatives. If, however, you use the more efficient "half-split" strategy, the 8-square problem will require 3 guesses, the 16-square problem 4 guesses, and the 32-square problem 5 guesses, thus producing a negatively accelerated relation between difficulty and the number of alternatives.

The statement that problem difficulty increases with the number of alternatives must be qualified in two ways. First, if a problem is already very large, further increases in size will probably have no impact on difficulty. The idea is that problem solvers lack the time or processing capacity to explore very large problem spaces; if the problem is already "too large" to explore fully, further increases in size will not matter. Second, increasing the number of alternatives is usually more detrimental to finding an unfamiliar solution, compared to finding a familiar solution (Dominowski, 1972). If people are asked to guess the "correct" item in a word list, they tend to guess familiar words first if no frequency cues are given. Because of this response tendency, adding less familiar words to the list as distractors will make little difference in problem difficulty. However, selecting an unfamiliar word will require more guesses if words of greater frequency are added to the list (see Figure 8-6).

Considerations of problem size are not limited to tasks in which a person chooses among alternatives provided in some obvious way. A number of findings can be interpreted as reflecting changes in effective problem size. For example, a better hint eliminates more incorrect ideas, which is equivalent to reducing the number of alternatives to a greater extent. Anagram solving is easier when the anagram letters enter into fewer combinations in the language (Ronning, 1965). For example, *hckit* is a fairly easy anagram because many of the possible letter combinations (*hc, tk, kt, kh,* etc.) don't occur in five-letter English words and can thus be ignored, reducing the number of alternatives to be considered. Telling a person that the solution to an anagram belongs to a particular category (animal names) reduces the number of possible solutions and thus decreases problem difficulty (Safren, 1962). These findings indicate that, whether the alternatives are physically present or exist only "in the head," the number of alternatives plays an important role in determining problem difficulty.

SOLVING MULTI-STEP PROBLEMS

Playing chess, working through a mathematical proof, or solving a problem like hobbits and orcs or the pyramid puzzle usually involves much more than selecting the right item or retrieving the right idea from LTM. Solving such problems requires an extended sequence of moves or steps; in effect,

The Problem: "Find the correct square"

| a | b | c | d |
| e | f | g | h |

"One-at-a-time" Strategy

Is it a?   (no)
Is it f?   (no)
Is it d?   (no)
and so on until
get a "yes"

Average guesses needed = 4

"Half-split" Strategy

Is it in the top row?   (no)
Is it e or f?   (no)
Is it g?   (yes or no, the
                square is found)

Guesses required = 3

The Problem: "Find the correct square"

a	b	c	d
e	f	g	h
i	j	k	l
m	n	o	p

"One-at-a-time" Strategy

Is it a?   (no)
Is it k?   (no)
and so on until
"yes"

Average guesses needed = 8

"Half-split" Strategy

Is it in the top two rows?   (no)
Is it in the bottom row?   (yes)
Is it m or n?   (no)
Is it p?   (yes or no, the square
                is found)

Guesses required = 4

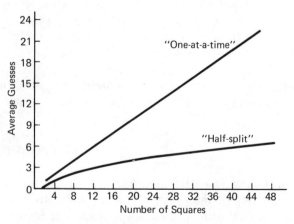

FIGURE 8-5. Two Strategies for Solving a Guessing Problem.

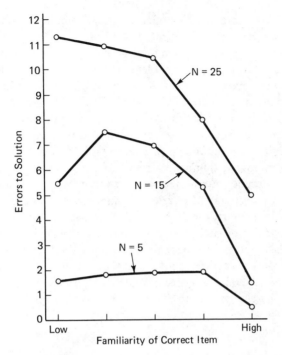

FIGURE 8–6.   Effects of increasing the number of alternatives on difficulty of selecting items of different familiarity. (Data from Dominowski, 1972. Reprinted by permission of American Psychological Association.)

the person faces a series of (sub)problems in proceeding from the beginning to the end of the problem. Choosing moves at each point in the problem and keeping track of what has been done are important aspects of the solution process. Considerable research has been done on this type of problem solving, including the construction of computer programs to simulate human problem solving. As mentioned earlier, detailed models are task-specific; we will emphasize the more general features of multi-step problem solving, using illustrative examples.

PROBLEM SIZE

The issue of problem size is more complex for multi-step problems than for the simpler problems discussed earlier. One can "count the number of alternatives" such as the number of pieces in a chess problem or the number of coins in a pyramid puzzle. However, it is often true that a person *must* take more steps to solve the problem when there are more items (additional items must be used rather than simply serving as distractors). Consequently, increasing problem size for a multi-step problem would be expected to have more complex effects. A larger multi-step problem might present the problem solver with more blind alleys at the start of the problem and might include longer blind alleys. A problem representation that is mildly inefficient for a small problem might be totally inadequate for a larger problem. Since the parts of the problem are typically interrelated, the difficulty encountered by choosing a blind alley or using a poor representation is likely to be magnified because of the person's limited capacity for processing data and keeping track of previous outcomes.

The difficulty of a multi-step problem tends to have a positively accelerated relation to the number of required solution steps. Successive increases in the number of required steps produce larger and larger increases in difficulty. For a pyramid puzzle, the number of necessary moves for a solution increases sharply with the number of coins to be moved; problems having 3, 4, and 5 coins necessarily require 7, 15, and 31 moves respectively. People usually make more than the minimum number of moves, and the number of *unnecessary* moves increases with the number of coins (Gagne & Smith, 1962). The size of a matching problem can be varied over a wide range by changing both the number of attributes (for example, cars,

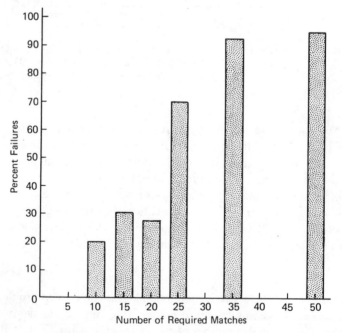

FIGURE 8–7. Likelihood of failing a matching problem as a function of the number of matches required. (Adapted with permission from Polich & Schwartz. The effect of problem size on representation in deductive problem solving. *Memory and Cognition*, 1974, 2, 683–686).

pets, jobs, hobbies) and the number of values per attribute (information might be given about 2, 3, 4, or more pets, cars, or what have you). As the number of required matches increases, difficulty increases ever more rapidly (Polich & Schwartz, 1974). Increasing the number of matches which must be worked out from 9 to 21 produces a slight increase in difficulty, but increasing the number from 21 to 35 results in a dramatic increase in difficulty (Figure 8-7).

People working on multi-step problems employ a variety of strategies. Earlier in the chapter, we described means-end analysis as a heuristic method applicable to many problems. We will now take a closer look at this strategy as it applies to the hobbits-and-orcs problem, comparing it with another strategy which people also use on this problem. A "3/3" hobbits-and-orcs problem begins with three hobbits and three orcs on the left side of a river (State A in Figure 8-8); the task is to get them all across the river (State O) using a boat which holds up to two creatures and never allowing orcs to outnumber hobbits at any location.

Means-end analysis is essentially a difference-reducing strategy. The problem solver, having identified one or more differences between the current state and the desired (goal) state, selects moves which reduce the differences. Applied to hobbits-and-orcs, means-end analysis leads to preferences for moves which take the maximum number of creatures from left to right and for moves which take the minimum number of creatures from right to left (backward) when the boat must be returned to the initial (left) side. This strategy can be contrasted with a balance strategy which leads to preferences for moves which equalize the numbers of hobbits and orcs on either side of the river. The difference between strategies is illustrated by a comparison of move preferences between states in the problem (see Figure 8-8).

A pure balance strategy leads to preferences like the following: AC > AD, CA > CE, EC > EJ, LM > LK, and NO > NL. States A, C, H, I, M, and O are balanced (equal numbers of hobbits and orcs on each side of the river), and a person strictly following a balance strategy will try to reach these states. A pure means-end strategy leads to preferences like: AC > AB, CE > CA, EF > EC, FG > FE, and MO > ML. When the boat is on the left side, a person using this strategy will try to move the maximum number of creatures across to the right; when the boat is on the right, this strategy leads to moves which transport the minimum number of creatures back to the starting side. Considering just these legal moves, it is apparent that the balance strategy leads to many preferences for backward moves, such as EC > EF, while the means-end strategy keeps the problem solver generally moving toward the goal. Figure 8-8 contains only

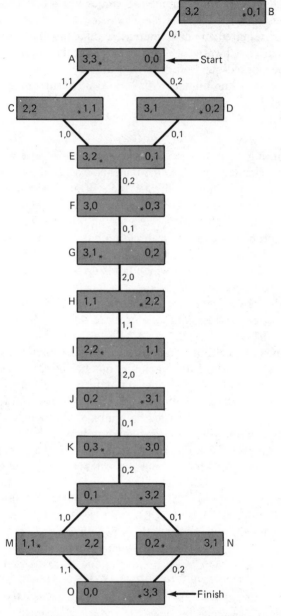

FIGURE 8–8. The space of legal moves for a hobbits-orcs problem. State A is the initial state and State O is the desired (solution) state. The asterisk indicates the position of the boat. In number pairs, the left number is for hobbits, the right for orcs. For example, in State G, three hobbits, one orc, and the boat are on the left side of the river; zero hobbits and two orcs are on the right.

legal moves; it is possible for people to propose illegal moves, and they sometimes do so. Notice that strict use of a means-end strategy at State H could lead to proposing the illegal move of one hobbit or orc back across the river (orcs would eat hobbits on one side or the other).

These pure strategies provide only a partial account of human performance. For example, a pure balance strategy would lead to endless cycling between States A and C, and no human subject does this. To describe human performance adequately, it is necessary to include an anti-loop test in the overall strategy, that is, a tendency to avoid states previously encountered. In addition, there is the question of what a person will do when a pure strategy leads to no move preference. For example, a person using a balance strategy would make move AC to start, then make move CE (rejecting move CA on the basis of an anti-loop test), reaching State E. If move EC is ruled out by anti-loop test, the balance strategy leads to no preference between moves ED and EF because States D and F are both unbalanced. Will the person choose randomly, choose the means-end move EF, or choose the move leading to the "less unbalanced state" (ED)? If it seems obvious to you that a person should choose move EF and rather odd that researchers might propose that a different choice will be made, keep in mind that the problem solver never sees the convenient solution graph in Figure 8-8 and does occasionally propose illegal moves. People seldom follow pure strategies in solving problems, with the possible exception of individuals with extensive experience who have learned and can execute the "ideal" strategy.

People tend to follow a balance strategy because of the constraint included in the instructions that orc will eat hobbits if they outnumber them. The balance strategy is "safe" but, as we have seen, does not produce much progress. How efficiently people will solve the hobbits-and-orcs problem depends on the speed with which they abandon the balance strategy in favor of the means-end strategy. Notice that solving the problem requires reaching state K, with three orcs on the left side and three hobbits on the right (distinctly unbalanced). Telling subjects that such an unbalanced state must be reached to solve the problem helps them solve it because this information pushes them away from a balance strategy and toward a means-end strategy (Simon & Reed, 1976).

As described, the means-end and balance strategies are local strategies dealing with the choice of a move at any particular state in the problem. There is other evidence indicating that people deal with the problem in terms of multiple-move units. For example, a person starting the problem might decide to "get the orcs across first," a subgoal encompassing a number of state-to-state moves. In other words, the problem solver, in addition to finding a way to choose moves from state to state, also tries to get a more general idea of the structure of the problem. Notice that telling subjects that state K must be reached to solve the problem, might, in addition to encouraging them to abandon a balance strategy for choosing moves, also provide them with a helpful, distant subgoal which improves their general understanding of the problem.

When people who have solved a hobbits-and-orcs problem are asked to do the problem a second time, their performance improves. A reasonable question is, "What does a person learn from solving the problem which makes it easier the second time?" There are several possibilities. Perhaps the most obvious (and least interesting) notion is that a person simply remembers and repeats the moves which worked. However, the evidence indicates that this is not what happens. In one study, some subjects first worked the second half of the problem (starting at State H) before they tried the whole problem (start at State A). These subjects did no better on the second half of the whole problem than people who did not have such prior experience, which indicates both that people do not concentrate on individual moves and that the person's understanding of the overall structure of the problem is important (Thomas, 1974). Other research indicates that people solve more efficiently when the problem is repeated primarily because, in solving the problem for the first time, they acquire better strategies for choosing moves and better understanding of the overall structure of the problem (Reed, Ernst, & Banerji, 1974).

MEMORY, KNOWLEDGE, AND PROBLEM SOLVING

Solving a complex problem involves both retrieval of information from LTM as well as processing and maintenance of current information in STM. Both kinds of memory affect problem solving in important ways. We have already discussed some ways in which STM limitations are involved and will consider others in this section. We will also address the question of how problem solving is affected by what a person knows (has stored in LTM).

STM AND SOLUTION STRATEGIES. At any point in a multi-step problem, a person must choose among several "next steps." Two components of this overall decision process can be distinguished, *scanning* among the various alternatives and *searching* down the path leading from any alternative. The immediate goal is to choose the best move, and both searching and scanning should be extensive enough to provide the person with proper information for making a choice. For example, consider the person contemplating a move in a game of chess. Any of a number of pieces might be moved, and considering many different moves (scanning) is quite sensible. In determining the consequences of a particular move, it would be better to see what might happen one, two, or three moves later (searching) rather than relying solely on the immediate effects. The major difficulty in completing an adequate search–scan scheme lies in the person's limited capacity for processing current information and maintaining the outcomes of that processing. To reduce the load on STM, people sometimes choose moves on the basis of local considerations, minimizing search and tending not to plan ahead. In searching down a particular path, people tend not to remember all the intermediate steps taken; rather they tend to return to some "initial or early state" if the path proves unproductive. Since choosing the best move might require more processing and remembering than can easily be accomplished, the problem solver might engage in *satisficing,* which is choosing the first move which seems "good enough" (Newell & Simon, 1972). In various ways, people adopt strategies which minimize the load on STM, typically with the result that problem solving is less efficient.

USING ALGORITHMS.   For understanding problem solving in relation to the contents of memory (LTM), it is useful to distinguish between propositional knowledge and algorithmic knowledge (Greeno, 1973), both components of semantic memory. Propositional knowledge refers to what people know about things; for example, a person might know *that* chairs are often made of wood, Buicks and Fords are cars, Nevada is part of the United States. Algorithmic knowledge refers to rules or procedures for doing things; a person might know *how to* fix a leaky faucet or use a formula to achieve the answer to a problem. With respect to problem solving, an *algorithm* is a procedure which if executed will yield a solution. For example, the problem "How much interest will be earned if a sum of $1000 is left for six months in an account earning 6% per year?" can be solved by applying the formula $I = P \times R \times T$ (interest = principal times rate times time); the formula represents an algorithm for solving the problem. Even very large multi-step problems can be readily solved if one can apply the proper algorithm. A pyramid puzzle of any size can be solved by using the following algorithm: Move the smallest coin on odd-numbered moves, and move the next-smallest coin that is exposed on even-numbered moves. If the total number of coins is odd, the smallest coin is moved from the start circle to the target circle to the extra circle (repeatedly), while the smallest coin is moved from start to extra to target circles if the total number of coins is even (Simon, 1975). Executing this algorithm requires that the problem solver keep track of only the type of move (odd or even) and the direction in which the smallest coin is moved.

If an algorithm exists for a problem and is not too complicated, it is the easiest way to solve the problem because the algorithm guarantees a solution and usually places a minimal load on STM capacity. Notice that it is one thing to know an algorithm (have it stored in LTM) and another matter to recognize that it applies to the problem confronted. Solving "word problems" for which a formula serves as the algorithm requires that proper

TABLE 8–4. WATER JAR PROBLEM.

General Format: A person goes to the river with three jars having the capacities listed. How should the person go about measuring the desired amount of water? Examples:

	Jar Capacities			
	A	B	C	Desired Amount
(1)	17	7	4	2
(2)	22	9	3	7
(3)	30	19	3	5
(4)	20	7	5	3
(5)	28	7	5	11
(6)	17	7	3	4

connections be found between the person's propositional knowledge and algorithmic knowledge (Greeno, 1973). Longer algorithms may consist of combinations of shorter algorithms. Knowing the part-algorithms will lead to a solution of a complex problem only if the person knows and uses a "higher-order rule" for combining them into a complete solution method (Scandura, 1974).

Acquisition of an algorithm has been studied with water jar problems like those in Table 8-4. Each of these problems can be solved by filling the largest jar (A), then pouring water from it into the medium-size jar (B) once and the smallest jar (C) twice. In other words, an algorithm for solving these problems is A −B − 2C. Research has shown that people acquire the algorithm over a series of problems like that in Table 8-4. Solutions for problem 5 are faster than solutions for problem 1, and people tend to use the algorithm for problem 6 even though a simpler solution (B − C) will work (Gardner & Runquist, 1958).

STRUCTURE OF KNOWLEDGE.   A person enters a problem situation with a store of knowledge, and the nature of that knowledge influences problem solving. We have already discussed some of the advantages and disadvantages of knowing a solution algorithm, but it will be useful to contrast algorithmic knowledge with propositional knowledge. These two kinds of knowledge have been compared in regard to performance on mathematical problems, such as those which can be solved by using the formula: $p(X = r/N) = \left(\dfrac{N}{r}\right)P^r(1 - P)^{N-r}$. This formula (the details need not concern us) can be used to solve problems such as "If a fair coin is tossed eleven times, what is the probability of getting exactly nine heads?" Two kinds of instruction have been compared. In *formula training* emphasis is on using the formula to compute answers (algorithmic knowledge), while in *general training* emphasis is on relating the terms in the formula to concepts already known to the subjects (propositional knowledge). Formula training begins with presentation of the formula and continues with step-by-step instruction in computation; general training does not include formula presentation until the very end, as a summary of the various concepts which have been discussed. After instruction, various kinds of test problems can be given.

For problems requiring straightforward use of the formula or simple algebraic manipulation of the formula, people receiving formula training perform better. Those receiving general training are better at recognizing unanswerable problems or answering questions about the formula (Mayer & Greeno, 1972). Problems requiring computation can be presented either in terms of the formula ($N = 4$, $r = 3$, $P = .2$, what is $p(X = r/N)$?) or as word problems (A person is in Las Vegas playing a game for which the chances of winning are one in three. If the person plays the game seven times, what is the probability of winning four times?). People who have received formula training find word problems much harder than those phrased in terms of the formula, while people with general training do about equally well on the two kinds of problems (Mayer, Stiehl, & Greeno, 1975). Notice that one cannot say that one or the other kind of knowledge is "better" to have, since the better form of knowledge depends on what the person is required to do. To be very efficient across a broad variety of problems, both kinds of knowledge are needed.

A related question is whether it is better for a person to discover a solution rule rather than having the rule directly taught. The idea is that people who are taught the rule will know the rule but little else, while people who must discover the rule will know the rule plus more general information about the problems, the combination being more useful for subsequent problem solving. Studies of discovery learning indicate that this idea has merit, but that the problem with discovery learning is that the person might not discover the solution rule. If people succeed in finding the rule during discovery training, they will do better in later problem solving than those who are directly taught the rule, but, if discovery training leads to little success in discovery, it is better to have been taught the rule (Anthony, 1973). For this reason, people with relatively low aptitudes for the kinds of problems encountered do better when they receive direct instruction (Mayer et al., 1975).

A person with increased knowledge can have multiple advantages in problem solving. The more knowledgeable person might know a better way to represent the problem information, might know a solution algorithm or useful heuristics, or have available a complex of information which helps in identifying critical problem features and in constructing solution plans. Increased knowledge leads to more organized solution attempts, one consequence of which is a reduced load on STM during problem solving. In addition to the examples we have already presented, there are other ways in which greater knowledge can reduce STM load and aid problem solving.

Knowledge of facts can greatly reduce problem difficulty. Consider the problem of multiplying 27 × 39. For most people, this problem might be nearly impossible to do "in the head" and modestly difficult if paper and pencil are used. For the person who knows that 27 × 39 = 1053 the problem can be trivial—that person merely needs to "read the answer" out of LTM, a process which is very rapid and interferes very little with other information-processing activities. In Chapter 1, we described the amazing mental calculations performed by Professor Aitken. One of the reasons why Professor Aitken could accomplish such feats is that he had a tremendous store of number facts. Without calculating, he could recognize that $1961 = 37 \times 53 = 44^2 + 5^2 = 40^2 + 19^2$ (Hunter, 1968). In effect, relevant factual knowledge can change a task from one requiring an extended sequence of operations to one which can be solved simply by retrieving the answer from LTM.

Studies of chess players of varying ability levels have shown how striking the effect of increased knowledge can be. In one experiment, after viewing the arrangement of 25 pieces in a game for only five seconds, a master player was able to reproduce the correct positions of 16 to 21 pieces while a novice was successful for only 4 to 8 pieces. This dramatic difference in accuracy is *not* due to the master's having a "generally better memory," because both master and novice did equally poorly when the pieces were randomly arranged on the board, getting only 2 or 3 correct (Chase & Simon, 1973). The master has an advantage only when the task is structured such that he can use his knowledge to perceive relations among the pieces (which the novice does not see) and thus use chunks containing more pieces.

CREATIVE PROBLEM SOLVING

For some tasks it is not possible to specify a particular correct answer or set of correct answers. The solution criteria are so broad or vague that they might be met by an unknown (and perhaps unknowable) number of responses. For example, one cannot specify ahead of time how many good titles there are for a particular story (someone might think of another good one tomorrow!). In such situations, attention has been given to the production of original and creative ideas. Original ideas are statistically infrequent—an idea offered by 50 people is less original than one given by 7 people, with maximum originality identified with the unique idea—offered by only one person. Creative ideas are usually defined as being both original and practical (or relevant to the situation). Both originality and practicality exist in degrees—ideas are more or less original and more or less practical. To simplify discussion, researchers usually select minimum levels of originality and practicality as criteria such that an original idea meets the criterion set for originality (uncommonness) and a creative idea meets the criteria set for both originality and practicality. Extremely creative ideas which receive social acclaim (such as the discovery of the theory of relativity) don't occur very often and are difficult to study. Therefore, researchers have studied more ordinary forms of creative thinking, asking for ideas such as titles for stories or uses for objects.

GENERATING IDEAS. When people are asked to produce ideas like "uses for an object" they tend to think of familiar uses first, with more unusual uses occurring later. The familiar ideas are produced fairly rapidly while the more original ideas occur more slowly. It is easy to eliminate the production of very common ideas simply by asking people to produce only "original ideas." In any situation, there are only a few familiar or common ideas but a great many unusual ideas possible, and, as a rule, people give more original responses as they continue to work at the task. Therefore, there is a tendency for the number of original ideas to be strongly related to the total number of ideas produced (Christensen, Guilford, & Wilson, 1957). Since creative ideas must be original (as one of the criteria), one might expect that more creative ideas will be produced with continued responding, but this is only partly correct. When people are asked to give creative responses, there is no systematic relation between order of output and the quality or goodness of ideas (Johnson, Parrott, & Stratton, 1968). Continued effort results in the production of ideas of all levels of quality; as more ideas are generated there will be an increase in the number of good (creative) ideas but also an increase in the number of poor ideas. The *average* quality of ideas decreases as more ideas are generated (Johnson et al., 1968).

The difference between generating original ideas and producing creative (original + practical) ideas was nicely demonstrated in a study by Manske and Davis (1968). People were asked to give uses for an object under different instructional conditions: Neutral ("give uses"), "Be practical," "Be original," "Be original and practical," and "Use your wildest imagination." Some of the results are shown in Figure 8-9. Changing the instructions resulted in large differences in the number of ideas produced, but the number of creative (original + practical) ideas was quite small and constant across conditions. These results and others imply that, while generating original ideas is fairly easy, producing creative ideas is a process that is both difficult and hard to influence. Simply put, most original ideas are not practical and thus fail to meet the dual criteria of creativity.

JUDGMENT. Given the production of some minimum number of ideas (of all levels of quality), success in creative problem solving might depend

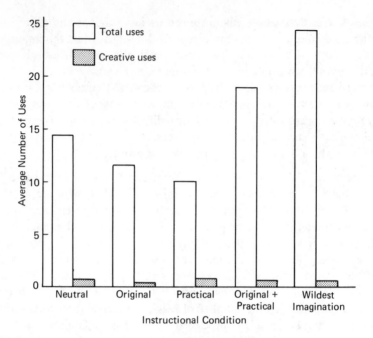

FIGURE 8–9.   Effects of different instructions on production of uses for an object. (From data by Manske & Davis, 1968.) (Effects of simple instructional biases upon performance in the Unusual Uses Test. Journal of General Psychology, 79, 25–33.)

on a person's success in selecting the best idea. Research on subjects' ability to judge the quality of their ideas has yielded some rather surprising findings. If people are asked to produce many ideas and then to select the best one, they are only mildly successful in making the choice. Differences in quality between preferred and nonpreferred ideas are either nonexistent or only slightly favor the ideas preferred by the people who produced them (Johnson et al., 1968). Providing people with simple statements of the criteria of a good idea such as "A clever title is an imaginative, creative, or unusual title for the plot" can help them in selecting one of their better ideas even though such statements seem vague and rather obvious. It seems that a person attempting creative problem solving produces ideas of all levels of quality (with relatively few of high quality) and has difficulty making valid distinctions among them.

Additional research has been directed toward two questions: Is it possible to improve a person's ability to judge solution quality? Does such training help the person produce and judge ideas when given another task? The answer in both cases appears to be *yes*. Judgment training consisted of presenting people with ideas of different levels of quality, explanations of the quality differences, and practice in judging ideas, with feedback. Introducing such training between the production of ideas and choosing one's best idea resulted in a larger difference in quality between subjects' preferred and nonpreferred ideas (Johnson et al., 1968). In addition, people who received training, when given a new task, produced fewer ideas but ideas of higher average quality, compared to untrained subjects. Creative problem solving is difficult because of the inverse relation between originality and practicality. It is fairly easy to think of unusual ideas in any given situation, but most of these will be impractical. Judgment training might help in part because the person's improved understanding of the criteria for creative ideas keeps production of original ideas "within bounds."

SUMMARY

In solving problems, a person engages in preparation, production, and judgment roughly in that order but with considerable recycling through the stages in many problem situations. These stages involve the extraction of information from the environment, maintenance of information in STM, operating on information in STM, and retrieval of information from LTM. A critical aspect of the human information-processing system is its limited capacity for processing current information. Because of this limitation, an individual can encounter many different obstacles during problem solving—important environmental information might be missed or forgotten, required processing might exceed capacity, or needed information might not be retrieved from LTM.

The process of solving simple problems emphasizes initial preparation and production of potential solutions. The nature of the problem as presented influences the person's interpretation of the problem and thus the problem's difficulty. Because people tend to look for clues in the problem as it is given to them, presentation can either help or hinder problem solving. Another factor that increases difficulty is an increase in the number of incorrect alternatives which are present and must be eliminated. Familiar ideas are more likely to be retrieved from LTM in a problem situation and are recalled earlier than less familiar ideas. Consequently, problems with familiar solutions are easier to solve and are less affected by increasing the number of distracting alternatives.

Multi-step problems can be very difficult for human problem solvers. Difficulty tends to increase more and more rapidly as the number of required steps increases. Efficient problem solving requires the use of solution strategies which keep the person moving toward the goal and problem representations which both suggest useful directions and provide good records of what has been done. Novice problem solvers seldom use such techniques. Choosing the best next-step involves scanning among alternatives and searching down possible solution paths; obtaining enough information before making a choice is difficult because of limitations on STM capacity. Knowing a solution algorithm can greatly reduce problem difficulty, although emphasizing the use of algorithms can lead to difficulty when novel problems are encountered. Relating a problem to a person's more general knowledge makes the person better able to deal with substantially modified problems. A person with greater knowledge can have multiple advantages in solving problems: Knowing the solution as a fact rather than having to work it out, having a solution algorithm available, or having greater understanding of the structure of the problem which allows better heuristics to be used and which reduces STM-load because larger chunks of information can be organized.

Creative problem solving involves the generation of ideas which are simultaneously unusual and relevant to some practical goal. Given sufficient time, people will produce many unusual ideas. However, most unusual ideas are impractical, thus creative ideas occur infrequently. People also sometimes err in evaluating the quality of the ideas they produce, and training in judgment aids in evaluation and in producing ideas of higher quality.

TABLE 8–5. SOLUTIONS TO PROBLEMS IN FIGURE 8–1.

A White's first move: N to QN3;
  if Black: K x N, then White: Q to R2.
  if Black: K to N4, then White: N to Q6.
  if Black: K to Q4, then White: Q to B5.
  if Black: K to Q6, then White: Q to R6.

B Anagrams: Answers are facet, naive, doubt, anvil, thick.

C Matching problem: Tom owns the Cadillac.

Person	*Shirt Color*	*Car*
George	Blue	Ford
Bill	Red	VW
Tom	White	Cadillac
Jack	Green	Buick

D Hobbits and orcs: See Figure 8–8 for solution.

E Two-string problem: Tie the screwdriver to the end of one string and set it swinging. Walk to the other string, grasp it, and wait for the swinging string to come over. The two strings may then be tied together.

F Pyramid puzzle: (In the answer, 10-A means move the dime to circle A, etc.)
  10-B, 1-C, 10-C, 5-B, 10-A, 1-B, 10-B, 25-C, 10-C, 1-A, 10-A, 5-C, 10-B, 1-C, 10-C.

chapter nine

REASONING

outline

REASONING CONCERNS DRAWING INFERENCES or conclusions from known or assumed facts; determining "what follows from what" roughly characterizes what reasoning is all about. Reasoning occurs in a wide variety of circumstances and with varying degrees of formality and attention. Consider the following, highly stereotyped situation (perhaps from a 1940s B-movie): Mary kisses John. John wonders, "Does that mean she loves me?" John concludes, "She loves me." Modern-day cynics might question such reasoning, but reasoning it is, faulty or not. We can cast John's reasoning into a formal structure called a *syllogism* (without implying that John did so):

PREMISE 1: A person who loves another person kisses that person (assumed to be true.)
PREMISE 2: Mary kissed me (apparent fact.)
CONCLUSION: Mary loves me.

Several questions can be asked about this reasoning: Is premise 1 true? Is premise 2 true? If premises 1 and 2 are true, does the conclusion necessarily follow from them? This analysis shows that John could reach the wrong conclusion for more than one reason; one or both of the premises might be false, or the conclusion might not follow even if both premises are true. In this particular case, we can suggest that, even though the two premises can be accepted as true, the conclusion still does not follow. Briefly, the problem lies in the meaning of premise 1, which is (presumably) correct but incompletely stated, for we could add "and sometimes a person who doesn't love another person kisses that person."

Suppose John recognizes the ambiguity of premise 1 and realizes that the connection between loving and kissing is not clear. Therefore, he tentatively formulates the hypothesis that kissing indicates loving and decides to collect some evidence. Fortunately, John is a photographer and frequently works at weddings (everyone knows, and we shall accept, that people getting married love each other). At eight consecutive weddings, John observes the bride and groom kissing. Noticing that his hypothesis that kissing means loving has received eight confirmations (since in each case the people kissing did love each other), John now concludes that his hypothesis is in fact correct. The critical question here is how one should go about collecting evidence to test a hypothesis in order to determine if it is correct or incorrect. John has poor evidence for deciding that his hypothesis is correct, and we may note that he is concentrating on how often it's been right, without making any attempt to see if it's wrong.

Let us now give John considerable expertise. He realizes that one can't reach yes-or-no decisions about such matters; rather, the question is, what are the chances that Mary loves him? John takes note of certain (statistical) facts. He notes that there are probabilities or odds to be determined for a number of relevant circumstances: The odds that if someone kisses you, she loves you; if someone invites you home for dinner, she loves you; if someone loves you, she'll be two hours late for a date, and so on. After estimating all the particular odds, John arrives at the conclusion that "the odds are three to one that she loves me." All we will say at this point is that the evidence suggests that John is probably wrong in figuring the odds that Mary loves him.

We have used this example to illustrate three kinds of reasoning which are important and which have been extensively studied. Syllogistic reasoning is concerned with the task of relating premises to conclusions; the internal consistency of an argument is the point at issue. Proposition testing involves relating evidence to the truth or falsity of a statement (proposition)—what kinds of evidence prove or falsify a proposition, and how should we go about gathering evidence? Both syllogistic reasoning and proposition testing usually are related to absolute standards of truth or falsehood. In contrast, statistical reasoning deals with uncertain information. How should, and how does a person interpret uncertain information in reaching conclusions about how likely it is that some statement is correct? Analyzing the internal consistency of arguments, testing propositions, and processing information known to be uncertain are the three kinds of reasoning we will discuss.

Reasoning plays a part in many other cognitive activities. For example, the conservative focusing strategy described in Chapter 6 is a special form of a reasoning strategy: "Given that a large, red square is an example of an unknown conjunctive concept, and given that a large, blue square is not an example, does it follow that color is an irrelevant attribute?" Testing hypotheses about a concept is a special case of testing propositions. The ill-defined categories discussed in Chapter 7 present a person with uncertain information which must be used to make decisions about category membership. In forming and using concepts, a person makes a great many decisions or repeatedly engages in reasoning. In Chapters 6 and 7, our focus was on the nature of concepts and concept formation, and decision processes represent only a part of that topic. In this chapter, we will concentrate on the ways in which people reach conclusions in a variety of circumstances. At several points in the chapter, we will make comparisons between reasoning as it occurs in concept formation and reasoning in other situations.

LOGIC AND HUMAN PERFORMANCE

Logic is a formal discipline which concerns systematic methods for reaching accurate conclusions. Prior to the beginning of psychology as a separate discipline, logic was frequently discussed as "the way in which the human mind works." Once observations were systematically made of human performance on logical tasks, however, it became clear that people are often "illogical." Specifically, people do not always reach conclusions in the manner dictated by logical systems. Indeed, some have argued that logic has little to do with the way in which people ordinarily think. As mentioned in Chapter 1, logic has held varying positions in relation to conceptions of human thinking: As descriptive of it, as irrelevant to it, or as a standard to which human performance can be compared. Rather than trying to choose one of these relations as the "correct" one, it makes more sense to realize that all three relations can exist.

Logical systems are the products of human thinking, and people do learn to reason in accord with such systems. Consequently, it is obvious that logic is descriptive of at least some human reasoning. It is also abundantly clear that at least some people on some occasions reach conclusions in ways which have no clear relation to formal systems of logic. A logical system provides a means of drawing conclusions in a coherent fashion; indeed, the correct or best response to a reasoning task is defined in terms of logic. In performing such a task, people may or may not conform to logical principles. The first step in studying human reasoning is to compare human performance to the standards derived from logic. As indicated above, research has shown many discrepancies between logical prescriptions and ordinary human reasoning. The second and more interesting step is to investigate, when people do not conform to the dictates of logic, how they do reach their conclusions and why they deviate from logic. It is important to keep in mind that people can and do learn to think logically; consequently, the question of interest is, "How do people who have not received formal training in logic perform on reasoning tasks?" The information-processing approach to cognition has proved helpful in understanding the relation between logic and human reasoning. Rather than viewing logic simply as the basis on which the correct response is defined, one can ask what a person must do in order to meet logical prescriptions. As we shall discuss shortly, performing logically can involve rather complicated processing, and some progress has been made in understanding which aspects of logical reasoning are and are not typical of untrained subjects.

A syllogism is an argument consisting of two or more premises and a conclusion. The premises are assumed to be true, and the question is whether or not, given the truth of the premises, a particular conclusion necessarily follows. Here is an example:

> PREMISE 1: All cats are animals.
> PREMISE 2: Some animals have tails.
> CONCLUSION: Some cats have tails.

The task of evaluating a syllogism consists of deciding whether or not the conclusion (some cats have tails) must be true if it is true that (1) all cats are animals and (2) some animals have tails. Notice what the person given a syllogism is *not* asked to do. The person is not asked to decide if Premise 1 or Premise 2 is in fact true; rather, the person is required to assume that they are true. Furthermore, the person is not asked to decide if the conclusion is factually accurate but only if it follows necessarily from the premises. To emphasize the internal orientation of a syllogistic reasoning task, consider the following example:

> PREMISE 1: All dogs are airplanes.
> PREMISE 2: Some airplanes have leaves.
> CONCLUSION: Some dogs have leaves.

Based on our general knowledge of the world, we would find the statements in the first example to be reasonable (cats are animals, etc.) while those in the second example wrong, strange, even bizarre. From the viewpoint of logic, the two examples are identical. With respect to analyzing the internal consistency of the argument, questions regarding whether dogs really are airplanes or airplanes really have leaves are irrelevant. The sole question is, If the premises are true, does the conclusion necessarily follow? Familiar, meaningful terms need not be used, as indicated by the following:

PREMISE 1: All X's are Z's.	PREMISE 1: All zeks are gac.
PREMISE 2: Some Z's have Y. or	PREMISE 2: Some gacs have mish.
CONCLUSION: Some X's have Y.	CONCLUSION: Some zeks have mish.

Whether one uses words, letters, or nonsense syllables in the statements of a syllogism is logically unimportant because the premises are assumed to be true for the purpose of determining if the conclusion follows from the premises. In describing syllogisms, letters are usually employed (A, B, C or X, Y, Z), a practice we will follow. Although the content of the statements in a syllogism (meaningful, abstract, or whatever) is logically irrelevant, content can be psychologically important, as we shall discuss later.

LOGICAL SPECIFICATIONS

We will deal with syllogisms consisting of two premises, one relating terms A and B and one relating terms B and C; conclusions will consist of statements relating A as the subject with C as the object in the sentence. Table 9-1 presents a sample of the syllogisms which can be constructed by varying the types of relations given in the premises; the logical conclusion for each sample syllogism is also indicated.

As illustrated in these examples, there are four kinds of statements that can be made (all, some, some not, no). With one exception, the statements are ambiguous in that they apply to more than one possible relation (considered more closely). A statement like "All A are B" tells us something about the relation between "the set of things called A" and "the set

TABLE 9-1.

Premises	Logical Conclusion	Premises	Logical Conclusion
(1) All A are B. All B are C.	All A are C.	(11) Some A are not B. All B are C.	Can't say.
(2) All A are B. Some B are C.	Can't say.*	(12) Some B are A. No B are C.	Some A are not C.
(3) No A are B. All C are B.	No A are C.	(13) All B are A. All B are C.	Some A are C.
(4) Some B are not A. All B are C.	Can't say.	(14) Some A are not B. Some B are not C.	Can't say.
(5) All A are B. No C are B.	No A are C.	(15) Some B are A. Some C are not B.	Can't say.
(6) No B are A. Some B are not C.	Can't say.	(16) All A are B. All C are B.	Can't say.
(7) Some A are B. All B are C.	Some A are C.	(17) No B are A. Some B are C.	Can't say.
(8) All B are A. All C are B.	Some A are C.	(18) Some B are not A. Some C are B.	Can't say.
(9) No A are B. No B are C.	Can't say.	(19) All B are A. No B are C.	Can't say.
(10) Some A are B. Some B are C.	Can't say.	(20) All A are B. No B are C.	No A are C.

* The conclusion "Can't say" means that no specific statement relating A to C necessarily follows from the premises.

of things called B," but it does not have a single meaning, as shown in Figure 9-1.

Figure 9-1 shows that the statement "All A are B" can refer to either of two relations between the sets A and B: The set A might be included in the larger set B, or sets A and B might be one and the same. The first relation (A inside of B) is called class inclusion, as in "All dogs are animals"; the second, coincident relation represents equivalence, best illustrated by definitions such as "All mothers are female parents." The essential point is that, in logic, the statement "All A are B" is consistent with two different set relations. The only unambiguous statement is "No A are B" which can only mean that there is no overlap between the sets A and B (there are no AB's). Statements involving "some" or "some/not" are highly ambiguous since each type can have several different meanings. Figure 9-1 also shows the unusual meaning of "some" in logic; notice that the last two meanings shown for "Some A are B" are the two possible meanings of "All A are B," and that the last meaning for "Some A are not B" is the meaning of "No A are B." In logic, "some" means "at least some and perhaps all," which makes the term "some" very ambiguous. In ordinary language we would not use "some" when we could say "all"; typically, if we say "some are" it also implies that "some are not," and vice versa. Consequently, the untrained subject may have difficulty dealing with statements including "some." In these instances failing to arrive at the logical conclusion provides uninteresting data. For this reason researchers usually explain the special, logical meaning of "some" to subjects when presenting syllogisms, although it is not clear that doing so makes any difference in the kinds of conclusions people reach. Notice that, even if we were to restrict the meanings of "some" and "some/not" to the first two, "natural" meanings, both statements are still ambiguous.

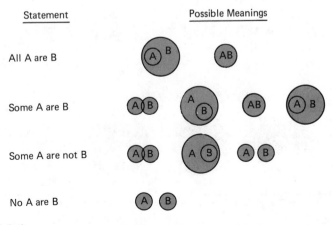

FIGURE 9–1.

In logic a conclusion follows only if it applies to all possible combinations of all possible meanings of the premises. "Being logical" thus requires considerable information processing. The person must consider all possible meanings of each premise, construct all possible combinations of the various meanings of the premises, and determine that a conclusion is consistent with all the combinations generated. A logical analysis of syllogism 8 in Table 9-1 is shown in Figure 9-2.

We can state the logical requirements in the opposite way as well: A conclusion does not follow if it is possible to construct one or more combinations of the premise meanings to which the conclusion does not apply. The many syllogisms in Table 9-1 for which "can't say" is the logical response do not allow any specific conclusion because no statement covers all the possible premise combinations. Consideration of the processing requirements for logical reasoning suggests several ways in which a person might fail to perform logically. The person might fail to consider all the possible meanings of a premise, fail to construct all the possible combinations of the premises, or fail to check a conclusion against all the combinations. Given what we know about the limits of human processing capacity, we should not be surprised if people fail to reach the logical answer, not because logic is irrelevant to their behavior but because they fail to complete all the processing required by logic. We would expect people to have particular difficulty in analyzing arguments when they have to do it "in their heads." In most research on reasoning, people are allowed to use pen-

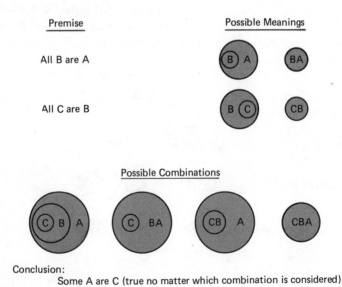

Premise | Possible Meanings

All B are A

All C are B

Possible Combinations

Conclusion:
Some A are C (true no matter which combination is considered)

FIGURE 9–2. Logical Analysis of a Syllogism.

cil and paper, which should make the task easier if they know how to make effective use of the memory aid. In contrast, evaluating the argument presented in, say, a political speech should be quite difficult because listening, comprehending, and evaluating the arguments all compete for the same limited capacity. It is quite possible that a person, in trying to determine if the speaker is presenting a logical argument, might forget parts of the argument in the course of analysis.

THEORIES OF REASONING

How might we account for the conclusions people reach when given syllogisms? Several, quite different explanations have been proposed. As we have already pointed out, at least some people perform a logical analysis of syllogisms, thus *logic* provides an account of their behavior. However, most people without training in logic deviate from the logical conclusion when given difficult syllogisms. To explain such "illogical" behavior, two different kinds of theories have been suggested. One implies that people are *alogical*—they reach conclusions in ways totally unrelated to logical precepts. The other view proposes that people are *partly logical*—they try to be logical but fail in one or more ways to complete the analysis.

ATMOSPHERE HYPOTHESIS. One view which has been quite popular for a long time is that people arrive at conclusions on the basis of the atmosphere or global impression established by the premises. For example, premises containing "some" are assumed to create an atmosphere for accepting conclusions containing "some." This view originally developed as a means of predicting the kinds of illogical conclusions people will accept *when they accept illogical conclusions*. Invalid syllogisms are those for which the only correct response is "can't say"—*no specific* conclusion follows from the premises. If a person accepts a specific conclusion for an invalid syllogism, that is an error in reasoning, and such errors frequently conform to predictions based on the atmosphere hypothesis.

Begg and Denny (1969) stated the atmosphere hypothesis in terms of two principles: (1) When one or more of the premises is negative, a negative conclusion will be (most frequently) accepted; (2) when one or more of the premises is particular (includes "some"), a particular conclusion will be (most frequently) accepted. When the premises do not include negative or particular statements, a universal (affirmative) conclusion will be chosen. The atmosphere hypothesis thus makes a prediction concerning the conclusion people should accept for any pair of premises, as illustrated in Table 9-2.

Subjects' errors in accepting conclusions for invalid syllogisms have been consistently found to agree rather well with atmosphere predictions. Some illustrative data are presented in Table 9-3. There are several points

TABLE 9–2. Conclusions Predicted by Atmosphere Hypothesis.

Premise Pairs	Predicted Conclusion
All, all	All
All, Some	Some
All, Some not	Some not
All, No	No
Some, Some	Some
Some, Some not	Some not
Some, No	Some not
Some not, Some not	Some not
Some not, No	Some not
No, No	No

to keep in mind when examining such data. First, the data stem from only invalid syllogisms, a point we will return to shortly. Second, the syllogisms included only abstract terms of the type, "All X's are Y's." Third, there is not complete agreement between atmosphere predictions and data, and the level of agreement varies across syllogisms—notice that responses to syllogisms including premises of the form "No A's are B's" tend to show less agreement with atmosphere predictions than other forms.

Findings such as those in Table 9-3 indicate that people who are untrained in logic very often accept invalid conclusions, which suggests that logic, often called the science of correct thinking, has little or nothing to do with ordinary reasoning. Notice that the atmosphere hypothesis im-

TABLE 9–3. Errors Made for Invalid Syllogisms.

| | Observed Frequency of Choices | | | |
Premise Pair	All	Some	No	Some Not
All, All	22*	3	1	1
All, Some	6	91*	2	19
All, Some Not	3	34	6	147*
Some, Some	2	89*	4	40
Some, No	3	15	34	72*
All, No	1	3	51*	4
Some Not, No	8	76	44	98*
No, No	15	15	47*	15

Note: Frequencies vary from row to row partly because different numbers of syllogisms of each type were used in the study. The choice marked with an asterisk is the atmosphere prediction. (Adapted from data by Begg & Denny, Empirical reconciliation of atmosphere and conversion interpretations of syllogistic reasoning errors. *Journal of Experimental Psychology,* 1969, 81, 351–354. Reprinted by permission of the author and American Psychological Association.)

plies that people do not even attempt analyses of syllogisms which faintly resemble logical analyses. Rather, the hypothesis implies that a person, encountering a premise including "no" or "some," simply accepts a similar conclusion. The atmosphere hypothesis, and the characterization of human reasoning which it implies, have received strong criticism, which we will now consider.

PREMISE CONVERSIONS.   Several researchers, reacting against the atmosphere hypothesis, have proposed that people do try to reason logically, albeit with some errors. One proposal is that people tend to misinterpret the premises, but, given such misinterpretations, people then combine them to reach mostly logical conclusions (Ceraso & Provitera, 1971; Chapman & Chapman, 1959). As we have already discussed, most premises are ambiguous—only statements of the form "No X's are Y's" have only one possible meaning. The proposal is that people fail to consider the multiple meanings of ambiguous premises; rather, people "convert" the premises such that they infer only one of the possible meanings. The proposed conversion errors are shown in Figure 9-3, in both verbal and set terminology.

The effects of premise conversion are illustrated in Figure 9-4, where it can be seen that a conversion error may or may not lead to an error (from a logical viewpoint). For some syllogisms, use of a limited interpretation of a premise will lead to the same, valid conclusion as a complete logical analysis. For other syllogisms, premise conversions will lead to the acceptance of an invalid conclusion; however, the point is that, given the premise conversion, the "incorrect" conclusion does follow logically from the misinterpreted premises. To summarize, the notion of premise conversion argues that people do combine (their interpretations of) premises logically, failing only to consider the multiple meanings of ambiguous premises.

Considerable evidence has accumulated which is inconsistent with the atmosphere hypothesis and favors the postulation of premise conversion errors. People perform more accurately on logically valid syllogisms than

Premise	Postulated Misinterpretation	
All A's are B's	All A's are B's and All B's are A's	AB
Some A's are B's	Some A's are B's and Some A's are not B's	A◯B
Some A's are not B's	Some A's are not B's and Some A's are B's	A◯B

FIGURE 9–3.   Proposed Misinterpretations of Premises.

A. Conversion leading to error

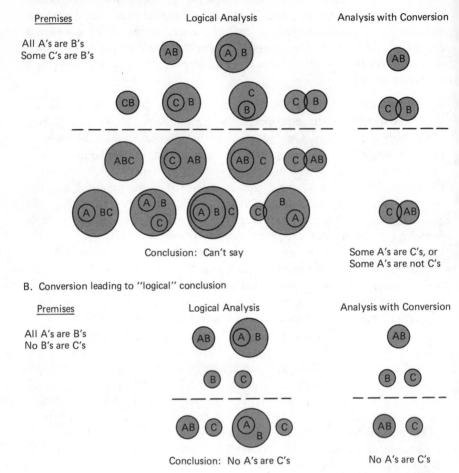

Premises   Logical Analysis   Analysis with Conversion

All A's are B's
Some C's are B's

Conclusion: Can't say   Some A's are C's, or
                                         Some A's are not C's

B. Conversion leading to "logical" conclusion

Premises   Logical Analysis   Analysis with Conversion

All A's are B's
No B's are C's

Conclusion: No A's are C's   No A's are C's

on invalid syllogisms (Ceraso & Provitera, 1971); according to a strict atmosphere hypothesis, the logical validity of a syllogism should make no difference because the person presumably does not make such a distinction. When premise conversions lead to the same conclusion as logical analyses, people perform better, compared to their accuracy when conversions lead to different, illogical conclusions (Revlis, 1973). If concrete premises which block conversions are used, performance improves (Revlis, 1973). For example, a person encountering the premise "All cats are animals" is very unlikely to interpret the statement as also meaning "All animals are cats." According to premise-conversion theory, but *not* according to the atmosphere hypothesis, such conversion-blocking premises should lead to more logical behavior, and they do.

PARTIAL COMBINATION. It is certainly not true that premise conversion is the only error people make in processing syllogisms. The most difficult syllogisms are those for which "can't say" is the proper response even if premise conversion is assumed. For example, no logical conclusion can be drawn from the premises "Some A's are B's" and "Some B's are C's" whether one considers all possible meanings of each premise or if the limited meanings (partial overlap) postulated by premise conversion are used. If A and B partly overlap and B and C partly overlap, there is no way to determine if A and C completely overlap, partly overlap, or do not overlap at all. In addition, premises of the form "No A's are B's" are unambiguous, thus "premise conversion" does not apply; nonetheless, people make many mistakes in dealing with such premises (see Table 9-3, especially for "No, No" premise pairs). Premise conversion itself is not a sufficient explanation for such results, and another factor must be proposed.

Logic requires that premise meanings be combined in all possible ways and that a conclusion be accepted only if it applies to all combinations. It is possible that people might accept conclusions which apply to most but not all combinations (Chapman & Chapman, 1959) or that people do not consider all possible combinations. Although both notions might be correct, we will devote attention to the latter, partial combination idea. The premise-conversion hypothesis implies that people fail to consider all the possible meanings of premises, and a reasonable extension of this idea is that people might also fail to consider all the possible combinations of the premises. Furthermore, responses to invalid syllogisms tend to be distributed over a number of choices, including "can't say," which is generally what would be expected if people were considering different, partial combinations of the premises. Partial combination is illustrated in Figure 9-5.

Ceraso and Provitera (1971) gave the pair of premises in Figure 9-5 to people with the instruction to select an answer from "All A's are C's," "Some A's are C's," "No A's are C's," and "Can't say." The percentages of subjects making each choice were: "All," 5 percent; "Some," 10 percent; "No," 35 percent; and "Can't say," 50 percent. Figure 9-5 illustrates that each of these conclusions could be reached in one or more ways; thus, perhaps the people who concluded "All A's are C's" considered just the possibility signified as combination 1, and so on. Erickson (1974) has shown that subjects' responses to valid and invalid syllogisms can be reasonably explained by assuming (1) that ambiguous premises tend to be misinterpreted (converted) and (2) that people tend to consider only some of the combinations of the premise meanings. Joining the idea of premise

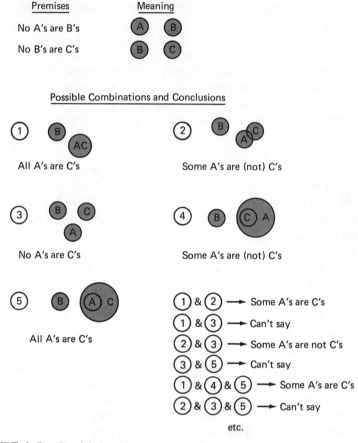

FIGURE 9–5. Partial Combinations of Premise Meanings.

conversion with that of partial combination leads to a characterization of human reasoning as "partly logical." Many of the details of this approach remain to be worked out; for example, why do people apparently sometimes consider just one combination, sometimes more than one, and why are some combinations apparently favored over others? We should expect to see further work on these questions in the near future.

A COMPOSITE DESCRIPTION. We have considered three different descriptions of human reasoning, as logical, alogical (the atmosphere hypothesis), and partly logical. Researchers have attempted to determine which view is "right," a task which is difficult because for some syllogisms, all three views lead to the same predicted response, while for others atmosphere and partly logical predictions are the same but differ from the logical prediction. Dominowski (1976) suggested that there is no need to choose one of these views as "necessarily correct"; rather, each might be a good description of some people's reasoning. He attempted to sort people into "types" by using various kinds of syllogisms, as illustrated in Table 9-4. Examination of subjects' responses to various syllogisms led to the following "best" descriptions: 12 percent logical, 7 percent "atmosphere," 67 percent partly logical, and 14 percent "other." The last category refers to those subjects who, when given syllogisms for which logical, partly logical, and atmosphere predictions all dictated the same answer, gave some other response. All that can be said in such cases is that the subject's behavior does not conform to any proposed view of reasoning. Overall, Dominowski's results agree with other findings: Most people untrained in logic can be described as partly logical. They try to analyze the syllogisms but tend to consider only some of the meanings of premises and only some of the combinations of premise meanings.

The findings we have discussed are based almost exclusively on the use of abstract premises such as "All X's are Y's." Many writers have suggested that such findings might give a misleading view of ordinary human reasoning, which typically involves meaningful statements. As we have already mentioned, concrete, meaningful statements tend to be unambiguous because of a person's knowledge of the world. For example, "All cats are animals" and "Some books are novels" do not have the ambiguity of "All X's are Y's" and "Some Y's are Z's." To the extent that meaningful statements are unambiguous, they should and do lead to more correct conclusions. However, it is *not* correct to state simply that people reason better with meaningful statements. A person's personal knowledge can lead him to

TABLE 9-4. Syllogisms That Can Be Used to Distinguish Logical, Partly Logical, and Atmosphere Responses.

---

(1) Logic = Partly logical = Atmosphere

               Premises: All A's are B's
                               All B's are C's
             Conclusion: All A's are C's

(2) Logic vs. Partly logical/Atmosphere

               Premises: All A's are B's
                               Some B's are C's
         Conclusions: Logic = Can't Say
   Partly logical/Atmosphere = Some A's are C's

(3) Partly logical vs. Atmosphere (vs. Logic)

               Premises: No A's are B's
                               No B's are C's
        Conclusions: Logic = Can't Say
                               Atmosphere: No A's are C's
   Partly logical = Any of "All, Some, No, Some not, Can't say"

judge conclusions on the basis of their empirical accuracy rather than deciding whether or not they follow from the stated premises (Henle, 1962). Conclusions which are empirically correct or which agree with a person's prejudices tend to be accepted (whether or not they follow from the premises), while people tend to deny logically valid conclusions which are empirically incorrect or inconsistent with their biases. The general point is that meaningful premises allow the person to evaluate conclusions, not on the basis of their logical validity, but in terms of their agreement with the person's knowledge or beliefs about the world. As Revlis has shown, from a logical standpoint, people given meaningful statements might perform better or worse than they do with abstract premises.

TESTING PROPOSITIONS

We have seen that one of the reasons people make logical errors in syllogistic reasoning is that they fail to consider all the possible combinations of premise meanings. Consideration of only some of the possibilities can lead a person to accept an invalid conclusion because the contradicting combination is not generated. Indeed it appears that generating counter-examples to contradict conclusions is a difficult task (Helsabeck, 1975). An interesting question is why people do not diligently search for potentially contradicting premise combinations. For meaningful syllogisms, a possible reason is that reaching a conclusion which is empirically accurate or consistent with a person's biases simply leads to acceptance of the conclusion and the end of processing. While such bias in favor of certain conclusions might be a factor, it cannot be a complete explanation because people make the same mistake, accepting invalid conclusions, when abstract premises are presented. It is difficult to imagine that people have a bias in favor of conclusions such as "Some A's are B's."

A broader explanation has been proposed, namely that people have a general tendency to confirm propositions rather than to falsify them. Applied to syllogistic reasoning, the idea is as follows. Given the premises "Some A's are B's" and "Some B's are C's" (which lead to no necessary conclusion), a person might arrive at the tentative conclusion "Some A's are C's." Logically, the person should attempt to determine if the premises can be combined in such a way that this conclusion would be false, which can be accomplished. However, the confirmation-seeking hypothesis holds that a person is less likely to do this than to check whether his conclusion is consistent with the premises (which it is). Having noted the consistency, the subject accepts the conclusion as valid. Such a tendency—to check only if a potential conclusion is consistent with the premises and to avoid trying to disprove it—would help explain why people have such difficulty with invalid syllogisms (for which "can't say" is the proper answer). There is no direct evidence from studies of syllogistic reasoning that people behave in this way, although recorded observations from other tasks strongly suggest that a confirmation-seeking tendency is frequently exhibited.

In several studies (for example, Wason, 1968), people have been given the task of discovering a rule which applied to three-digit series. To begin, the person is told that the series 2 4 6 conforms to the rule to be discovered, and the person is to propose additional series, with the experimenter indicating whether each does or does not conform to the unknown rule. In proceeding through the task, subjects formulate hypotheses, and, once the correct rule is given, the task is over. In fact, the rule to be discovered was "numbers in increasing order of magnitude." However, most subjects formulated more specific hypotheses as to the correct rule, and the manner in which they tested their hypotheses is what interests us here. A frequently observed behavior pattern was as follows. A subject, having been told that 2 4 6 conforms to the rule, might formulate the hypothesis that the rule is "numbers increasing by two." The subject might then test this hypothesis by proposing the series 4 6 8, 6 8 10, 20 22 24, and 11 13 15. Note that each series is consistent with the subject's hypothesis and also conforms to the rule (numbers in increasing order of magnitude); thus, the experimenter would indicate that each series does conform to the rule to be discovered. The typical result was that people became increasingly convinced that their limited (and incorrect) hypotheses were correct, even to the point that some became quite upset when they offered their hypotheses as the answer and were told that they were wrong.

Wason offers the following analysis of this problem. A person can test a hypothesis in one of two ways, by proposing a number series consistent with the hypothesis or by proposing a series inconsistent with it, for example, given the hypothesis "numbers increasing by two," proposing 4 7 8 and expecting the experimenter to say *no*. People clearly preferred to offer examples consistent with their hypotheses, which indicates a tendency to seek confirmations of their hypotheses (Wason, 1968). For this task, proposing consistent examples will never lead to a solution; rather, a specific, incorrect hypothesis like "numbers increasing by two" can be found to be incorrect only by proposing a counterexample (e.g., 4 7 8) and learning that it in fact conforms to the rule to be discovered (but not to the person's hypothesis). The tendency to seek confirmations might represent a fault in human reasoning, preventing people from discovering that their ideas are wrong and some other idea is correct.

Very striking evidence of a tendency to seek confirmation and an apparent lack of understanding of the value of falsifying evidence has been obtained using "selection tasks" like that illustrated in Figure 9-6. It will be worthwhile to try this task before reading further.

A Selection Task for Testing Propositions

"Assume that each of the boxes below represents a card lying on a table. Each card has a letter on one side and a number on the other side. Consequently, the card with "5" showing has some letter on the other side (which you cannot see) as does the card with "4" showing, while the card with "A" showing and that with "K" showing each has some number on the other side. Here is a rule which might apply to the cards: IF A CARD HAS A VOWEL ON ITS LETTER SIDE, THEN IT HAS AN EVEN NUMBER ON ITS NUMBER SIDE. Your task is to indicate which of the cards you need to turn over in order to find out whether the rule is true or false. Which card or cards would you select?"

FIGURE 9–6. A Selection Task for Testing Propositions.

When given such tasks, only about 10 percent of the subjects make the correct selections; for our example, the correct answer is to turn over the "A" and "5" cards. Rather than making this choice, nearly 50 percent of the subjects say they would turn over the "A" and "4" cards, about 35 percent that that only the "A" card need be examined, and the remainder make a variety of different choices. What is most striking is that very few subjects propose examining the "5" card, in any combination (Johnson-Laird & Wason, 1970).

To understand the answer to this problem, we must consider the meaning of the rule to be tested and the truth values it assigns to different possibilities. In shortened form, the rule is "If vowel, then even number," which is a particular example of the general form of conditional sentences or implications "If *p*, then *q*." The truth table for such propositions is shown in Table 9-5; truth values are based on propositional logic.

As shown in Table 9-5, an implication states that only one kind of instance is false (does not exist), $p\bar{q}$, or a card with a vowel and an odd number in our example. Notice what the rule does *not* state: It does not

TABLE 9–5. TRUTH TABLE FOR AN IMPLICATION.
General form of proposition: "If *p*, then *q*." Example: "If vowel, then even number."

Possibilities		Truth Value
General	*Example*	
pq	vowel, even number	TRUE
$p\bar{q}$	vowel, not even number (vowel, odd number)	FALSE
$\bar{p}q$	not vowel, even number (consonant, even number)	TRUE
$\bar{p}\bar{q}$	not vowel, not even number (consonant, odd number)	TRUE

specify anything for cards with consonants, nor does it specify that cards with even numbers must have vowels. It specifies only that cards with vowels must have even numbers. Let us now consider the four cards in Figure 9-6 with respect to the rule, from a logical viewpoint. The card with "A" showing must be examined; if it has an even number on the other side, this would confirm the rule, but, more important, if it has an odd number on the other side, this would disprove the rule. The card with "K" showing can provide no useful information; since the rule specifies nothing for consonant cards, it makes no difference whether an even or odd number is on the other side. Similarly, the card with "4" showing is not crucial; if it has a vowel on the other side, this would confirm the rule, but if it has a consonant on the other side the rule would still stand (since the rule does not require that even-number cards all have vowels). The card with "5" showing is crucial because it would falsify the rule if it has a vowel on the other side; should it have a consonant on the other side, the rule would still stand. In general terms, cards known to be q or $\bar{p}$ cannot provide crucial information, but cards known to be p or $\bar{q}$ must be examined because, should either prove to be a $p\bar{q}$ instance, the rule is falsified.

It should be clear that from a logical viewpoint greater importance is attached to falsifying evidence. No matter how many confirmations a proposition has received, it cannot be shown to be generally true, but *one* contradictory instance disproves the proposition. It seems equally clear that people do not approach the proposition-testing task with an eye toward falsification; rather, confirmation seeking is the more popular tendency.

The behavior which Wason observed in his proposition-testing tasks is by no means restricted to those situations. In concept-formation experiments, people exhibit a clear preference for direct tests of their hypotheses (Bruner, Goodnow, & Austin, 1956; Taplin, 1975). A person who has formulated a hypothesis about what the concept might be is much more likely to prefer receiving information about a stimulus which should be a positive example if the hypothesis is correct, rather than receiving information about a stimulus which should, according to the person's hypothesis, not belong to the concept. For example, if a person thinks that "small squares" is the correct concept, he is more likely to want category information about a "small blue square" than about a "large blue square." In concept-formation studies, people have been found to make unnecessary stimulus selections just to get direct tests, and this has led Bruner et al. (1956) to coin the descriptive phrase "thirst for confirming redundancy."

Although Wason's findings suggest that the major reason why people make errors in testing propositions results from a tendency to seek confirmations, another possibility is that some people misinterpret the meaning of the proposition. We will briefly examine this idea.

There are two ways in which subjects' interpretations of conditional sentences frequently vary from that shown in Table 9-5. Some people *mis*interpret conditional sentences as biconditional; that is, they interpret "If vowel, then even number" to also mean "If even number, then vowel." (Note the similarity to premise conversion in syllogistic reasoning.) However, even granting such misinterpretation, subjects' choices are not "logical." The biconditional meaning would specify that pq and $\bar{p}\bar{q}$ instances exist, that $p\bar{q}$ and $\bar{p}q$ do not exist; a proper test of this meaning of the rule would require examining all four cards, since any could be a $p\bar{q}$ or $\bar{p}q$ instance. Very few people make this choice, however. A second discrepancy is that many people consider $\bar{p}q$ and $\bar{p}\bar{q}$ instances, not as true under an implication but as irrelevant to the implication. In our example, cards with consonants would be considered simply as irrelevant to the truth or falsity of the rule. However, granting this alternative truth table for an implication (pq true, $p\bar{q}$ false, $\bar{p}q$ and $\bar{p}\bar{q}$ irrelevant), the proper test remains examining the p ("A") and $\bar{q}$ ("5") cards, an infrequent selection.

Johnson-Laird and Wason have proposed that people lacking insight into the importance of falsification will choose "A" and "4" (p and q) if they interpret the rule as biconditional, "A" (p) if they interpret the rule as conditional. These two patterns of choices are the most popular, implying that the vast majority of subjects seek confirmation and do not understand the importance of falsification. Subjects' performance in the selection task has proved rather resistant to attempts at improvement, although creating a conflict between subjects' selections and their subsequent evaluations of the cards has proved somewhat effective.

There are suggestions here, just as in syllogistic reasoning, that people perform better when testing concrete propositions (Wason & Johnson-Laird, 1972). Rather than presenting cards having letters and numbers, the concrete task is presented in relation to some realistic state of affairs. For example, the person might be told that the cards refer to a person's travel habits. Each card has a city name on one side and a method of transportation on the other, each card presumably referring to a different trip. Given cards showing "New York," "Los Angeles," "train," and "airplane," the person might be asked to test the rule "If I go to New York, I travel by train." With such concrete tasks, a somewhat greater percentage of subjects make the logical choice (New York and airplane). However, Gilhooly and Falconer's (1974) findings—that 9 percent of subjects made the logical choices with abstract material compared to 21 percent with concrete material—still indicate that most subjects made some form of improper test.

These findings consistently suggest that people have a tendency to seek confirmation. Does this represent some weakness in ordinary human reasoning? Since confirmation seeking leads to errors in the tasks we have cited, one can easily get the impression that some weakness does exist. However, this is not a universally accepted opinion. It is perhaps worth mentioning that logicians are still puzzling over the proper way to confirm or disprove hypotheses, an issue presently unsettled. Wetherick (1970) has argued that subjects' tendencies to seek confirmations and direct tests of hypotheses represent, not faulty reasoning, but transfer of generally appropriate and useful strategies. Roughly, his argument is as follows. First, the rule-discovery task (for number series) is quite unusual in that, given the nature of the "correct" rule, direct tests of specific hypotheses are useless. Under other circumstances, Wetherick argues that direct tests will work quite well. For example, in the environment of a standard concept-formation task, a subject who tests hypotheses by selecting instances which should be positive *will* find out whether or not a hypothesis is correct. More generally, identifying hypotheses or propositions *which work* is argued to be a proper goal for science and everyday living. Concentrating on identifying false statements would leave people knowing what is not true but wondering what is true! Potentially useful propositions must be *possibly* subject to falsification (otherwise they are useless) but need a history of confirmation to warrant attention. Most often, a proposition of the form "If p, then q" would be sensibly tested by finding instances which are p and checking to determine if they are q or $\bar{q}$—not by locating $\bar{q}$ instances to determine if they are p. For example, to test the (imaginary medical) proposition "If spots on the stomach, then stomach cancer," would it be more sensible to check people with stomach spots to determine whether or not they have cancer, or to check people without cancer to see if any has spots on the stomach? Wetherick clearly favors the former strategy. We need not adopt a firm position on this issue. Perhaps the tendency to seek confirmations in rule-discovery or proposition-testing tasks does represent transfer of generally useful strategies. However, we must point out that this same tendency, applied to syllogistic reasoning, would lead to the acceptance of invalid conclusions. In any case, confirmation seeking is a common observation. One final comment: Johnson-Laird and Wason's theoretical model of reasoning indicates that concentrating on falsification involves more information processing than confirmation seeking. Given the general view of human beings as limited information processors, it is not surprising that confirmation seeking should be more prevalent.

PROBABILISTIC INFERENCE

In syllogistic reasoning and proposition testing, people are required to deal with absolute states of truth or falsity. Such clear-cut differences between true and false statements do not characterize much of the information a person must process in everyday life. Instead, people are regularly faced with making decisions on the basis of uncertain information. A smiling face doesn't always indicate a friendly person, a positive result on a diagnostic test doesn't always mean that disease is present, and favorite recipes don't always lead to satisfied diners. Rather than dealing with information which is either true or false, people must process information which has some probability of being accurate. To reach proper decisions, a person must adequately understand the nature of probabilistic information and must combine such information correctly. Just as systems of logic specify rules for reaching decisions in syllogistic reasoning and proposition testing, probability theory and statistics provide formal models for dealing with probabilistic information. Clearly, people can and do learn to use these formal systems. However, research evidence indicates that, when people must intuitively process uncertain information, they deviate considerably from the dictates of formal models.

Probabilities are numbers ranging from zero to one; a probability of zero ($p = .00$) means that the event is impossible whereas a probability of one ($p = 1.00$) means that the event is certain to occur. Probabilities between these two extremes apply to things which are more or less likely to happen. Probabilities are related to odds; if the probability that a driver will stop for a red light is .95 while the probability that the driver will run the light is .05, the odds that the driver will stop are $.95/.05 = 19$ to 1. Two kinds of probabilities can be distinguished. Objective probabilities are based on the analysis of some well specified situation. For example, if a deck of 52 cards contains 13 spades, the probability of randomly selecting a spade from the deck is $13/52$ or .25; objective probabilities can be viewed as relative frequencies. In contrast, subjective probabilities exist only in a person's head; $p = 1.00$ means the person is certain about something, $p = .00$ means the person believes that something can't happen, and intermediate probabilities reflect various levels of confidence. John might believe that the odds are 4 to 1 that Mary loves him (p(Mary loves him) $=$

.80, p(Mary doesn't love him) = .20), but this "computation" is not based on the examination of some well specified situation or source—rather it is John's "guess" based in some way on his experiences (and perhaps his hopes).

Probability theory provides rules for combining probabilities. Consider the following situation which has been faced by subjects in many experiments:

You are sitting at a table facing a screen. Behind the screen are two boxes. The box on the left contains 70 red chips and 30 blue chips, while the box on the right contains 30 red chips and 70 blue chips. Behind the screen, the experimenter flips a coin to pick a box, reaches in and grabs some chips, which you are shown. The sample consists of 4 blue chips and 2 red chips. What do you think is the probability that the experimenter took the chips from the left box?

Before the sample of chips was shown, the probability that the left box had been chosen was .50 since there are two boxes each equally likely to be chosen by the coin flip. The question is, now that the sample of 4 blue chips and 2 red chips has been seen, how should that probability be adjusted. Does this sample make it more or less likely that the left box was chosen, and how much does the probability change? A typical answer in this situation is that, considering the composition of the sample of chips, the probability that the left box was chosen is somewhat less than .50, perhaps .40. In other words, most people conclude that the 4 blue/2 red chip sample makes it less likely that the left box was chosen. People's subjective probabilities can be compared to probabilities computed according to probability theory; such comparisons show that people are conservative —they don't adjust the probability as much as they should (Slovic & Lichtenstein, 1971). Application of the appropriate formula indicates that, given the sample of 4 blue/2 red chips, the probability that the left box was chosen is .14, much lower than most people's answers. The formula used to compute this probability is known as Bayes' theorem, which serves as the model for proper reasoning in such situations. The general sense of Bayes' theorem is that the probability that some hypothesis is correct *after* an observation has been made depends on (a) the probability that the hypothesis was correct *before* the observation was made, (b) the probability that the observation would be expected to occur if the hypothesis were correct, and (c) the probability that the observation would be expected to occur if any other hypothesis were correct. In the next section, we describe Bayes' theorem in some detail in order to show precisely how the formula is used to determine how probabilities change on the basis of evidence. If you really dislike mathematics, you might want to skip this brief section, but we do encourage you to devote some attention to it.

BAYES' THEOREM.   In one of its general forms, Bayes' theorem is the following:

$$p(H_1/D) = \frac{p(H_1)\, p(D/H_1)}{p(H_1)p(D/H_1) + p(H_2)p(D/H_2)}$$

In the formula, H_1 and H_2 refer to two different hypotheses, and D refers to the data which have been observed. Here are the verbal meanings of the terms: $p(H_1/D)$ is the probability that H_1 is correct given that the data have occurred; $p(H_1)$ is the probability that H_1 is correct *before* the data were observed; $p(D/H_1)$ is the probability that the data would occur given that H_1 is correct; $p(H_2)$ is the probability that H_2 is correct before the data are observed; and $p(D/H_2)$ is the probability that the data would occur if H_2 is correct. In the formula, placing two probabilities next to each other indicates that the probabilities should be multiplied—that is, $p(H_1)p(D/H_1)$ means multiply $p(H_1)$ times $p(D/H_1)$. This formula of course applies to hypotheses and data in general; however, to return to our original example, the initial probability that the left box was chosen is equal to the initial probability that the right box was chosen (both = .50) since the two boxes were equally likely to be picked by coin flip. By methods we will not present, it can be calculated that the probability of getting 4 blue chips and 2 red chips when drawing 6 chips from the left box is .0555, whereas the probability of 4 blue/2 red chips when drawing 6 chips from the right box is .3346. These probabilities show that getting 4 blue and 2 red chips is much more likely if the right box is chosen (recall that it has 70 percent blue chips) than if the left box is chosen (which has only 30 percent blue chips), and this is the critical factor. Substituting the values into the formula, we get:

$$p(\text{left/sample}) = \frac{(.50)(.0555)}{(.50)(.055) + (.50)(.3346)} = \frac{.02775}{.19505} = .14$$

ARE PEOPLE BAYESIAN?   Working through Bayes' theorem takes effort. If people are reasoning properly, they must in some intuitive fashion approximate the calculations based on Bayes' theorem. As we have mentioned, people seem to agree at least in positive/negative terms with the formula's predictions. When the evidence or data should lead to lowering a probability, subjects tend to lower it; when the data should lead to raising a probability, subjects tend to raise it. In general, however, people do not change probabilities as much as Bayes' theorem indicates they should—they are conservative. Such evidence has led some researchers to suggest that human probabilistic reasoning does generally resemble Bayesian reasoning, but with some error or slippage. Possible reasons for the slippage have been suggested. Perhaps people err in estimating the probability that particular data will occur if a given hypothesis is correct; perhaps they don't combine probabilities with sufficient accuracy. Based on research involving a variety of tasks, it has been suggested that probability theory and statistics provide a good initial model of "man as an intuitive statistician" (Peterson & Beach, 1967). However, recent evidence indicates that the way in which people *intuitively* process probabilistic information may have little or nothing to do with formal theory. Our intuitive understanding of probabilities appears to be quite different from "what it should be."

Kahneman and Tversky (1972, 1973; Tversky & Kahneman, 1971) have collected various kinds of evidence indicating that people are not "sloppy Bayesians" or "somewhat imperfect probability theorists." Rather, our intuitive understanding of probability, chance, and related concepts deviates systematically from probability theory. Furthermore, Kahneman and Tversky proposed that the process by which people reach decisions about uncertain events is unrelated to what one would do if one were using probability theory, however inaccurately. They propose that subjective probability judgments are governed by representativeness. People expect samples, even very small samples, to be representative of (to closely resemble) the population from which they come. People also expect random samples to "look random," that is, unsystematic, unpatterned. People judge more representative samples (in the two senses noted) to occur more frequently than less representative samples (contrary to probability theory). Let's consider some examples.

There are two programs in a high school. Boys are a majority (65%) in program A, and a minority (45%) in program B. There is an equal number of classes in each of the two programs. You enter a class at random and observe that 55% of the students are boys. What is your best guess—does the class belong to program A or to program B? (Kahneman & Tversky, 1972, p. 433)

Notice that, since there are equal numbers of classes in the two programs, a class you are about to enter is equally likely to belong to either program (before you check the percentage of boys in the class). In addition, the percentage of boys in the class you enter (55 percent) is exactly midway between the percentage of boys in program A (65 percent) and the percentage of boys in program B (45 percent). Nevertheless, the vast majority of people guess that the class belongs to program A, despite the fact that there is no sound reason for this choice! People apparently choose program A because the sample class is more "representative" of program A in a psychologically simple fashion—"there are more boys than girls in program A, and there are more boys in this class, so this class must belong to program A." This kind of reasoning, intuitively appealing as it might seem, just does not square with the facts.

Here is another example: A fair coin is being tossed a number of times. It has been tossed 7 times and has come up heads each time. What do you think are the odds that the next toss will yield tails?

Most people will say that the odds favor tails, that the probability of tails is greater than .50. However, the probability is in fact .50. This belief, that things will "balance out" in the short term, is well known as the gambler's fallacy. A fair coin *will* show heads and tails equally often *in the long run* (strictly, with an infinite number of tosses), but people expect it to also "balance out" in *short runs,* a belief probability theory very definitely debunks. In "personal terms," the coin does not know or care that it has shown heads 7 times in succession, and on the eighth toss it will just be itself, equally likely to show heads or tails. Casino owners have made a great deal of money because of the gambler's fallacy!

Let us return to the red chips/blue chips problem, in which a person must decide on the relative likelihood that a sample of chips has been taken from the "mostly red" box (70 red, 30 blue) or the "mostly blue" box (30 red, 70 blue). Probability theory indicates that the amount by which a person's confidence in one or the other hypothesis should change depends on the relative likelihood that a given sample could be obtained from either box. A sample with more red than blue chips should (according to probability theory) lead to increased confidence that the "mostly red" box is the source, while a sample with fewer red than blue chips should lower confidence in that hypothesis. An interesting case is a sample with equal numbers of red and blue chips; such a sample is equally likely to have come from either box and thus provides no diagnostic information—it doesn't favor either box. Application of Bayes' theorem indicates that such a sample *should* lead to absolutely no change in a person's confidence about the two hypotheses, yet people have been observed to change their confidence on the basis of such nondiagnostic information (Shanteau, 1975).

The "diagnosticity" of a sample depends on the difference in the numbers of red and blue chips in the sample. Assuming that the sample contains more red chips than blue chips, the greater the difference between the number of red chips and blue chips, the more likely it is that the sample came from the "mostly red" box and the more a person should (according to probability theory) adjust confidence in favor of the "mostly red" box. Here are some examples illustrating the relation between the composition of a sample and the relative amount by which a person's confidence ought to change in favor of the "mostly red" box: (number of red chips, number of blue chips in the sample) $4,4 < 5,4 = 4,3 < 4,2 < 5,1 = 8,4 = 16,12 < 10,5 < 20,10$.

In contrast to this ordering based on probability theory, people have greater confidence that the "mostly red" box was chosen if shown a sample of 5 red/1 blue chips (5,1) than when shown a sample of 20 red/10 blue chips (20,10), a clear-cut contradiction. People have greater confidence after seeing the (5,1) sample because this sample "looks more like the 'mostly red' box" (83 percent of the chips in the sample are red) than does the (20,10) sample (67 percent red). Their intuitions do not take into account the great importance of sample size for probabilistic outcomes. People do not seem intuitively able to appreciate the fact that smaller samples are *more variable in composition* than larger ones, which means that small samples are less diagnostic than larger samples. Instead, people expect small samples to be "just as representative" of the source as large samples, an intuition which is simply incorrect.

Examination of Bayes' theorem indicates that confidence *after-the-fact* should be related to confidence *before-the-fact*. A person should take into account how likely a hypothesis was before data were observed in deciding on its likelihood after the data are in. In contrast, people seem to ignore such prior likelihoods. Consider this example:

It is known that 5 percent of the population is afflicted with the disease rubadubitis. *A new diagnostic test has just been developed which is rather good. If a person has rubadubitis, the test gives a positive result 85 percent of the time. If a person does not have the disease, there is only a 10 percent chance of getting a positive result from the test. All in all, a pretty good test. Here's the situation: The test has just been given to John Doe and the test result is positive. What is the probability that John has rubadubitis?*

Most people indicate that there's about an 85 percent chance that John has the disease, assuming the odds to be about 6 to 1. However, application of Bayes' theorem indicates that the probability that John has the disease is only .31. Given the positive test result, the odds are about 2 to 1 that John does *not* have rubadubitis! The large errors people normally make result from ignoring the fact that the disease occurs very infrequently in the population (Hammerton, 1973). To make this point clear, let's suppose that the population consists of 10,000 people. Since 5 percent of the population has the disease, this means that 500 people have rubadubitis and 9500 do not. Of the 500 afflicted individuals, 85 percent or 425 will yield positive test results, while 10 percent or 950 of the 9500 *nondiseased* people will also have positive test results. Thus, of the 1375 positive test results, only 425 or 31 percent will come from people who actually have the disease.

Why do people reach such radically inaccurate conclusions in these situations? The psychological principle of representativeness provides an answer. The positive test result is psychologically very compelling; a person with a positive test result seems to "resemble" the diseased part of the population more than the nondiseased part, leading people to be quite sure that the disease is present. What people are ignoring is that the population contains a very small percentage of diseased individuals, that there will be many "false positives" (positive test results from nondiseased individuals). In other words, people are ignoring the fact that, *before* the test results are known, the odds are heavily *against* the person having the disease. Such reasoning errors are not limited to "ordinary" people given hypothetical problems like our example. Meehl and Rosen (1955) point out that erroneous conclusions have been made by professionals about the usefulness of diagnostic tests precisely because they have not considered information regarding the percentage of the population having the condition they are trying to diagnose.

PROBABILITY OR FREQUENCY?

The above findings indicate that intuitions about probabilities often do not correspond to probability theory, and that people ignore relevant information in making judgments about uncertain outcomes. Estes (1976) has obtained evidence that, in some circumstances, people base supposedly probabilistic judgments not on probabilities but on frequencies. The task which Estes gave his subjects had the following characteristics. People were told that they would receive information regarding the outcomes of a series of (imaginary) opinion polls. Each poll involved a comparison of two alternatives (two political candidates, two products, and so on); the results of each poll consisted of the number of choices of each alternative in the sample. A typical poll result would be: "8 people preferred product A, 3 preferred product B." The subjects in the experiments were shown such poll results, one at a time, after which they were asked to make predictions concerning future polls. The most interesting predictions concerned comparisons of alternatives which had not previously been compared and which had different histories of success in the poll results. For example, people might be asked to predict which product, A or D, will "win" when placed in contrast for a poll; product A might have appeared in 6 polls, winning 5 of them, while product D had appeared in 18 polls, winning 9 of them, but subjects had never seen the results of a poll comparing A and D. Consequently, subjects had to base their predictions on the impressions they had formed from viewing the poll results shown.

If people based their predictions on a comparison of the products' probabilities of winning, they would predict that product A will win since A has won 83 percent of the time in the past ($5/6 \times 100 = 83$ percent) while B has won only 50 percent in the past ($9/18 \times 100 = 50$ percent). However, subjects' dominant prediction was that product B would win! In general, Estes found that people based their predictions on the number of times an alternative had won and ignored information concerning the number of losses. The results led Estes to propose that human intuitions about probabilities will be accurate only if the alternatives have appeared in equal numbers of prior comparisons (assuming that people pay equal attention to all comparisons). In a sense, people will be right for the wrong reason when opportunities are equal among alternatives. For example, if product A and product D have both appeared in 20 comparisons, A winning 11 times and D winning 8 times (never against each other), product A will have both a greater probability of winning ($11/20 \times 100 = 55$ percent) and a greater frequency of winning (11) compared to product D's probability ($8/20 \times 100 = 40$ percent) and winning frequency (8). Thus a person would choose the alternative with the greater probability, but presumably the choice would be based on frequency. Estes considers an interesting implication of the finding that people use frequency rather than probability. General elections are often preceded by a large number of primary elections, and typically some candidates enter more primaries than others. Suppose that Candidate A has entered 15 primaries, winning 6 of them, while candidate B has entered and won 3 primaries; the two candidates have never run in the same primary. If people base their judgments on frequency of winning rather than probability, as Estes' findings suggest, then people will be more likely to consider Candidate A as a "potential winner" even though Candidate A has won only 40 percent of the time while Candidate B has won 100 percent of the time!

We have now discussed a number of examples indicating that human intuitions about probabilities are different from probability theory. The laws of probability are not intuitively obvious, and even people with considerable expertise in statistics and probability theory make intuitive errors for problems more complex than those we have presented (Tversky & Kahneman, 1971). These researchers suggest that one reason for using the heuristic of representativeness in making intuitive judgments about probabilities is that people use "mental effort" or "cognitive strain" to estimate probability. It takes more mental effort for people to imagine how some outcomes might occur rather than other outcomes, and "more mental effort" leads to "less likely." This relation between mental effort and subjective probability has been demonstrated in a different manner. Consider the following example:

Suppose you are going to open a book and select a word of three or more letters at random. Is it more likely that the word will start with a k *or that the word will have a* k *in the third position?*

Tversky and Kahneman (1973) found that the majority of people given such problems judged it more likely that the word would start with a *k*, compared to having a *k* in the third position. The process used to make this judgment was presumably to try to think of words starting with *k* and words having *k* in the third position. It is much easier to produce words starting with *k*, thus people judged such words to be more likely, even though in fact there are three times as many words with *k* in the third position.

Estes' finding that people base judgments on frequency rather than on probability (relative frequency) seems related to the tendency for people to seek confirmations. Earlier in the chapter we discussed evidence suggesting that people tend to confirm propositions and to avoid seeking falsifying evidence, and this tendency might explain why people accept invalid conclusions in syllogistic reasoning. The hypothesis "that Candidate A is a winner" is confirmed each time A wins a comparison and might be held with greater confidence as the number of confirmations increases, *if* contradictory evidence (losses) is ignored.

SUMMARY

Reasoning is the process of drawing conclusions from evidence of various sorts. The information which serves as the basis for conclusions may be known or assumed to be true, or it may be uncertain, having some probability of being correct. Logic and mathematics (probability theory and statistics) provide formal systems of reasoning which serve as the standard against which "ordinary" human reasoning is evaluated. Research has shown that people frequently and systematically deviate from the prescriptions of formal systems. Progress has been made in understanding how people solve reasoning problems when they are not strictly logical.

Syllogistic reasoning involves evaluating the consistency of an argument. From premises assumed to be true, the person must decide which conclusion, if any, follows from the premises. Logical analysis of syllogisms requires complete assessment of all the possible meanings of the premises and of all the possible combinations of premise meanings. Although people perform better when valid syllogisms are presented, they often accept logically invalid conclusions. The atmosphere hypothesis implies that people do not even attempt logical analysis, rather that they accept conclusions consistent with the "set" established by the premises, accepting particular conclusions if given particular premises ("some") and negative conclusions if given negative premises. Research indicates that the atmosphere hypothesis is unlikely to be an accurate description of most human reasoning. People make logical errors in part because they misinterpret the meanings of premises, although they combine the misinterpreted premises in a logical fashion. Errors also occur because people fail to consider all the possible combinations of premise meanings, which leads them to accept invalid conclusions. On the whole, most people untrained in formal logic seem to be "partly logical," reasoning in a way similar to logic but failing to conduct the complete analysis which logic requires.

Deciding on the truth or falsity of a proposition on the basis of empirical evidence is another reasoning task. Propositional logic dictates that attention be given to falsifying evidence since a proposition becomes only more likely on the basis of confirmations but must be false if a single contradiction occurs. Research on proposition testing indicates that people seek confirmations and typically do not appreciate the importance of potentially falsifying evidence, thus do not seek it. Whether the tendency to seek confirmations represents a flaw in human reasoning or a generally useful strategy is a matter of some debate.

In everyday life people confront a great deal of uncertain information. Probability theory and statistics provide rules for dealing with such information. Research shows that people often deviate from theoretical dictates. Intuitive understanding of probabilities is considerably different from probability theory. People often employ a heuristic of representativeness in making probabilistic judgments, expecting even very small samples to resemble the source population. In addition, information which is crucial for making accurate probability statements is sometimes ignored. Under some circumstances, people base decisions on frequency of "success," ignoring frequency of "failure" and thus probability of success. It has been suggested that people tend to use the amount of mental effort required to produce various alternatives to estimate probabilities, with alternatives requiring more effort being judged as less probable. In part, subjects' tendencies in making probabilistic inferences seems based on the tendency to give greater importance to confirmations or positive outcomes, which is also observed in syllogistic reasoning and proposition testing.

chapter ten

COGNITIVE DEVELOPMENT

outline

A NEWBORN PUPPY seems pretty much like an adult dog—smaller, cuter, and not as well coordinated, but not strikingly different in behavior. In contrast, the human infant lying in a crib provides few clues to the vast repetoire of information-processing skills which exist in adulthood. To dramatize the transition from infant to adult, an arbitrary selection of "developmental achievements" is given in Table 10-1. Clearly, there are remarkable changes from infancy through early and middle childhood to adolescence and adulthood.

In order not to underestimate developments during infancy, we must point out that infants are not lacking in cognitive processes. However, detecting such processes is difficult because of severe limitations on infants' activity. The problem is something like trying to find out what an adult is thinking who is conscious but completely paralyzed! Researchers studying infant cognition are often required to be very inventive. Assessment techniques include difficult procedures such as monitoring changes in sucking

TABLE 10–1. ILLUSTRATIVE EXAMPLES OF COGNITIVE DEVELOPMENT.

Approximate Age	Behavior Likely to be Observed
Birth	Reflexive sucking
3 months	Visual anticipation of future position of moving object
6 months	Prolonged repetition of actions (e.g., shaking a rattle)
8 months	Searching for hidden object if it has just been touched
8 months	Communicating with gestures
12 months	Laughing in anticipation of mother's playful kissing
15 months	Noticeable upset when parent leaves
20 months	Grouping objects on basis of function or color
2 years	Frequent production of two-word utterances
5 years	Understanding passive sentences
7 years	Understanding that amount of substance is unchanged when shape changes
8 years	Systematic construction of serial orders (e.g., sticks varying in length)
9 years	Understanding that weight of an object is unchanged when its shape is changed
14 years	Spontaneous use of proportional relations in problem solving
16 years	Generating all possibilities in a concrete "scientific experiment"

rate, heart rate, and eye movements. Even so, researchers have been able to demonstrate that there is a considerable amount of cognitive activity during infancy. At least in rudimentary form, infants exhibit such processes as attention, discrimination, and memory. For example, four-week-old infants smile brightly at the sound of their mothers' voices. After two months, infants prefer to look at novel pictures rather than familiar ones. Such behavior implies that some form of representation of familiar events exists (Pick, Frankel, & Hess, 1975; Sroufe & Waters, 1975). At about nine months, infants are likely to look for a toy that has disappeared under a cloth cover, implying that objects have permanence for them and suggesting that elementary hypothesis formation has begun (Kagan, 1972).

Although infancy is a cognitively active period, the infant's processes are quite different from those of the adult. In previous chapters, we have discussed a variety of cognitive processes, dealing almost exclusively with the behavior of adults. In this chapter we will illustrate some of the ways in which cognitive processes change as the individual develops, emphasizing memory, language, concept formation, and reasoning. Before considering these examples, we will first discuss some special issues related to cognitive development.

GENERAL ISSUES

When we contemplate a developmental process, cognitive or otherwise, we think of changes taking place as an individual grows older. Relating behavior to "age" (as in Table 10-1) is quite common and seems sensible. However, "age" is a tricky variable; it is useful to consider "age" as "time" (since birth or perhaps conception for some purposes). Put bluntly, the age of a person who behaves in a particular way explains nothing by itself. Rather, changes in behavior over time (with advancing age) are the basic observations of development, and the researcher's job is to find explanations for these changes (Wohlwill, 1970). The particular age at which some behavior occurs may be of little importance. A developmental theorist is more likely to be interested in the *order* in which various kinds of behavior emerge. That is, the crucial question can be whether behavior X precedes, follows, or emerges simultaneously with behavior Y; the particular ages at which X and Y are observed can be theoretically irrelevant. Indeed, comparisons of children of different ages are often used to study the ordinal relations between different behaviors. To summarize, age differences or age trends in behavior are useful observations which must be explained, and behavioral order may be much more important than age.

Developmental changes might occur for several reasons. In addition, the kinds of interpretations made of age trends tend to be different from those offered for, say, differences resulting from giving or not giving a hint in a study of problem solving. We will briefly consider these issues.

Any study of cognitive processes involves an assessment of what an individual *does* (performance). Developmental researchers often wish to infer what a person is capable of doing (competence) from performance. Inferring competence from performance is a tricky business. Competence is typically defined rather abstractly, in terms of certain forms of knowledge. For example, one aspect of "knowing a language" is understanding its phrase structure rules (see Chapter 5). A researcher interested in determining if an individual possesses such knowledge will try to devise a task which requires this knowledge. The desired situation is one in which competence can be inferred from success and incompetence from failure on the task. The difficulty arises because performance on any cognitive task involves a number of processes. It might be possible to achieve success on the task by some means not involving the competence in question, and failure might occur for reasons other than lack of competence. Klahr and Wallace (1970), after presenting a detailed information-processing analysis of tasks typically used for inferring various kinds of competence, suggested that it might be impossible to devise tasks which correspond to the desired relation (success = competence, failure = incompetence).

On cognitive tasks, children usually perform worse than adults, and younger children worse than older children. Those who fail are likely to be deemed as "lacking competence." This may be so, but it should be clear that such inferences about abstract competence must be treated cautiously. Researchers have found that children might fail to accomplish one version of a task but succeed when the task is slightly modified. Under such circumstances, deciding whether the child is or is not "competent" is quite difficult. We will present several examples of such research later in the chapter.

Is development a continuous process, or does an individual pass abruptly from one stage to another? Words such as *stage, period,* and *phase* are frequently used in talking about development, often quite loosely. For example, parents are quite often heard to describe their child as "being in the negative stage" when the child regularly answers *no* to every request. One might begin to wonder if the child who won't eat spinach is in the "Anti-leafy-green-vegetable stage!" Within the field of psychological research, theorizing about cognitive development has been dominated by the views of the Swiss psychologist-logician Jean Piaget, who has proposed many ideas in books and articles over a period of five decades. Other researchers may support or argue against Piaget's views, but in either case Piaget serves as the reference point—and Piaget argues for stages of development.

Piaget is interested in what he terms genetic epistemology, a study of both the formation and the meaning of knowledge (Piaget, 1970). Thus, he is interested in the forms of competence which underlie cognitive performance. Piaget divides development into several periods and stages; each major segment is characterized by a distinct structure of knowledge processes. According to Piaget, there are three broad developmental periods: The sensory-motor period, roughly from birth to 2 years, the period of concrete operations (2–11), and the period of formal operations (11–15, perhaps longer). Each period has subdivisions called stages, and occasionally there are also sub-stages. Children are assumed to pass from "stage to stage" (the ages are approximate), and different kinds of cognitive processes are postulated for different stages. A brief outline of Piaget's segmentation of development is presented in Table 10-2.

During the sensory-motor period, the infant moves from relatively undifferentiated, reflex-type behavior to a more systematic interaction with the immediate environment. The child deals with whole objects rather than analyzing features of objects or using symbolic representations. Sensory-motor schemes are developed; a *scheme* is whatever is repeatable and generalizable in an action. For example, the scheme of "pulling" applies to a

TABLE 10–2. OUTLINE OF PIAGET'S VIEW OF COGNITIVE DEVELOPMENT.

Segment	Approximate Ages	Characterization
Sensory-motor period	0– 2 years	Development of object permanence and sensory-motor schemes for dealing with objects in the immediate environment
Concrete-operations period	2–11 years	
Preoperational stage	2– 7 years	Gradual elaboration of mental process
Concrete-operational stage	7–11 years	Emergence of internalized, reversible operations for dealing with attributes of objects; formation of integrated groupings of operations
Formal-operations period	11–15 years	Emergence of abstract thought, hypothetical thinking; formation of completely integrated structure of mental operations

variety of specific action sequences. Piaget (1970) emphasizes that schemes have a kind of logical character. Schemes involve sub-schemes and thus exhibit the rudiments of hierarchical classification or inclusion (for example, using a stick to move an object involves relating the hand to the stick, the stick to the object, the object to its position in space). Extended action sequences involve ordered actions which Piaget views as the primitive basis of later linguistic and mathematical structures of order.

Many changes occur during this period. Much attention has been given to the emergence of *object permanence,* which refers to the understanding that an object continues to exist when it is no longer "in view." Infants' interactions with objects become increasingly sophisticated. Early on, an infant may cease attending to an object taken from its grasp; later, an infant might search for a hidden object only if it had just been held. Greatest sophistication is exhibited when, having seen an object hidden under a cup, the cup covered by a box and then withdrawn empty, the child searches for the object under the box (Harris, 1975). Kopp, Sigman, and Parmelee (1974) studied the development of several behaviors during the sensory-motor period, including reactions to hidden objects, use of tools to retrieve objects, and exploration of components of an object (would a child take apart and put back together a matchbox with a sliding-type mechanism?). A portion of their findings is shown in Figure 10-1.

During the concrete-operation period, the child learns to deal with at-

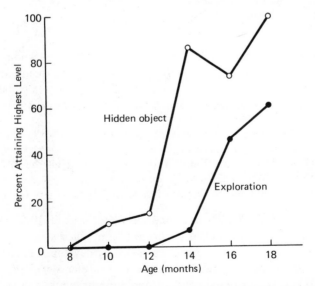

FIGURE 10–1. Development during the sensory-motor period. (Based on data from Table 1 in Kopp, Sigman, & Parmelee, 1974. Reprinted by permission of the author and American Psychological Association.)

tributes of objects in a more systematic fashion, to use symbolic representations, and to develop what Piaget considers truly intellectual operations—internalized operations which are reversible and systematically related to each other. In Piaget's view, to recognize that there is no gain or loss of clay when the clay is changed from the shape of a ball to that of a sausage requires an understanding that an operation can alter some attributes of an object while leaving others invariant. Conservation of concepts when objects are perceptually transformed has received a great deal of attention from researchers; we will describe this research later in the chapter. Other characteristics of developing concrete operations are the understanding of relations among classes and of relations among relations. With respect to relations among relations, it is considered important to determine if a child understands that the information "A > B" (A is greater than B) also means "B < A" (B is less than A), that, if A > B and B > C, it follows that A > C. One relation among classes which has been investigated is that of subordination–superordination, or class inclusion. Understanding of class inclusion has been assessed in several ways. One method concerns the child's use of terms like *all* and *some*. For example, the child might be shown a collection of objects consisting of five blue circles, two red squares, and two blue squares. A series of questions is asked:

1. Are all the circles blue?
2. Are all the blue ones circles?
3. Are all the squares red?
4. Are all the red ones square?

The likelihood of successfully answering all of these questions increases greatly during this period (see Figure 10-2). For a more quantitative test of class relations, the child might be given a box containing ten wooden beads, seven of which are red, three of which are yellow, and asked:

1. Are there more wooden beads or red beads in the box?
2. Shirley made a necklace of all the red beads. Then she put the beads back in the box, and Karen made a necklace of all the wooden beads in the box. Who made a longer necklace?
3. If you give me all the wooden beads, will there be any left in the box?

Success on this task also changes markedly (see Figure 10-2), suggesting that children's concepts of class inclusion become increasingly refined.

In Piaget's view, the child who possesses fully developed concrete operations has considerable intellectual skill, but further development is still possible. Whereas concrete operations apply to attributes of objects and are organized into separate groupings, formal operations apply to abstract entities such as propositions and constitute a single unified structure. The

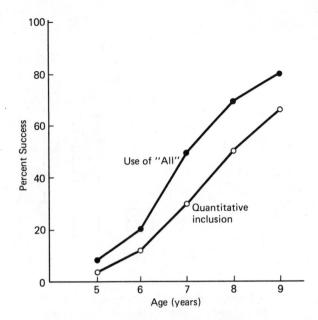

FIGURE 10–2. Development of class inclusion concepts. (From Tables 5 and 6 from Chapter 24, "Intellectual Operations and their Development", Jean Piaget and Barbel Inhelder, in *Experimental Psychology: Its Scope and Method,* edited by Paul Fraisse and Jean Piaget, VII Intelligence, by Pierre Oléron et al., translated by Thérèse Surridge, © 1963 Presses Universitaires de France; English translation © Routledge & Kegan Paul 1969, Basic Books, Inc., Publishers, New York.)

period of formal operations is characterized by truly hypothetical thinking, including formal logic and scientific reasoning. One feature of such thought is the use of a complete combinatorial system—the individual is able to "see all the possibilities." For example, the subject might be given five containers filled with colorless liquids, informed that some combination of the liquids will produce a colored liquid, and asked to produce the color. Interest lies in how the person goes about combining liquids. A concrete-operational child might try a small number of combinations, usually pairings such as 1 and 2, 2 and 3, and so forth. Only later do subjects begin systematically to test all possible combinations, two at a time, three at a time, four at a time, as well as all five mixed together (Figure 10-3). Dealing with propositions, generating all possible combinations, and considering what might be true are all involved in syllogistic reasoning and proposition testing, as discussed in Chapter 9. Considering the many errors made by adults on such tasks, Neimark (1975) suggested that many people might not complete the stage of formal operations as proposed by Piaget.

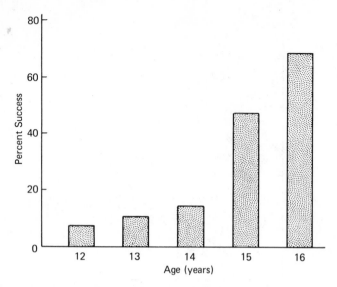

FIGURE 10–3. Development of an exhaustive system (with justification) for combining liquids. (From Tables 15 from Chapter 24, "Intellectual Operations and their Development", Jean Piaget and Barbel Inhelder, in *Experimental Psychology: Its Scope and Method,* edited by Paul Fraisse and Jean Piaget, VII Intelligence, by Pierre Oléron et al., translated by Thérèse Surridge, © 1963 Presses Universitaires de France; English translation © Routledge & Kegan Paul 1969, Basic Books, Inc., Publishers, New York.)

WHAT'S IN A STAGE? Obviously there are enormous changes in cognitive behavior from birth to adulthood. Furthermore, if we examine performance on cognitive tasks, we are likely to find a transition from complete failure through partial success to complete mastery as development proceeds. However, the term *stage* wouldn't mean much if restricted to a single task. For Piaget, a stage (or period) is characterized in terms of a particular kind of competence; qualitative changes in the structure and processes of thought are said to occur as the child moves from one stage to another. The competence associated with a stage is rather abstractly defined and can presumably be exhibited in a variety of different ways. We have already discussed the difficulties involved in attempting to infer competence from performance. There are also fundamental problems associated with the concepts of *stage* and *structure,* leading some to conclude that stage theories like Piaget's are not very useful (see, for example, Brainerd, 1975).

Flavell (1971) suggests that the concept of *stage* seems to imply an abrupt transition to an entirely novel cognitive structure which is evidenced in all possible relevant situations. Such neatness is seldom found in nature, and Flavell proposes that "stage" need not have these implications. His relatively positive conclusion is that stages like those proposed by Piaget do represent qualitatively different states, but that a stage might best be viewed as an end-point, preceded by gradual changes in the components used to characterize the stage. In short, the integrated cognitive structures associated with a stage might exist only at the completion of that stage.

DEVELOPMENTAL PROCESSES

How are we to account for the massive changes that occur as an individual develops? It is tempting to try choosing between "biology" and "experience" as explanations for development, but the matter is much more complex. An organism has a particular genetic endowment but also lives in a particular environment, and both are important. Theorists differ in the emphasis they give to one or the other of these general factors. Extreme examples illustrate the folly of trying to find *one* explanation: A kitten, a puppy, and a human infant exposed to the same environments will develop quite different cognitive processes, and a human infant who is locked in a bare room for life will not develop normal, adult-level functioning. Excepting extreme positions, there are interesting and intricate questions to consider.

Flavell (1976) argues that we must accept the tendency to develop as biologically given—it is part and parcel of "being human" to develop certain kinds of cognitive processes. Similarly, Lenneberg (1969) argues that every species is genetically predisposed to develop its own, species-specific cognitive processes. This does not mean that experience is unimportant, but it does mean that the fundamental "reason for developing" lies within the organism. Experience can alter the course of development, but experience is important only because the organism is predisposed to develop.

At the very least, the environment must provide the experience necessary for processes to come into existence. However, "necessary" experience might be a very broad concept—that is, no *particular* kind of experience may be necessary. Several writers have pointed out that, barring severe biological abnormality, children will develop certain cognitive processes in any of a wide variety of environments. The idea is that the kind of environment in which the child grows can influence the rate at which development proceeds, but that, sooner or later, certain processes will emerge. For example, the acquisition of language, sensory-motor schemes, and object permanence are often considered "developmental universals." A child growing up in an impoverished environment might take longer to develop sensory-motor schemes than one blessed with a stimulating environment, but in both cases, sensory-motor schemes will be acquired.

Flavell emphasizes the flexibility of the developing organism. There are alternate ways of developing any given cognitive skill, thus a wide variety of environments are developmentally interchangeable. The notion of flexibility can be viewed as having a "flip-side" as well. A number of writers have proposed that, since "language" (at some level) is universally acquired, human organisms must be endowed with a specific language-learning mechanism. However, this need not be so; Piaget (1970) argues against such a notion. The species-specific acquisition of language can be viewed as one aspect of the acquisition of species-specific cognitive processes. In simpler terms, if language is peculiar to human beings, so are other cognitive accomplishments, and language development does not proceed independently of general cognitive development. Rather than postulating genetically determined, specific mechanisms for particular cognitive accomplishments (when would the list end?), it seems more sensible to think of a broader, more flexible endowment which, during the course of development, leads to the acquisition of increasingly complex cognitive skills.

DEVELOPMENTAL RATE. We have stressed above the idea that a child is biologically predisposed to develop certain kinds of cognitive processes in any of a variety of environments. It is taking the biological emphasis a step further to propose that the rate of development is similarly "fixed." Explanations of development in terms of maturational processes tend to imply that cognitive skills will not be acquired until the brain has sufficiently matured. On the other hand, associating ages with particular accomplishments, for example, stating that concept conservation occurs at age 7, implies that one must "wait" until the child is seven to observe such behavior. Typically, such an implication leads learning-oriented researchers to try very hard to produce that behavior in younger children, thus emphasizing the importance of experience. Resolving such conflicts is extremely difficult because of methodological problems (what performance demonstrates competence?) and theoretical uncertainties.

It is well established that the brain changes during development, and it is easy to think of cognitive accomplishments as having to wait on the proper neural development. However, it is also true that different experiences affect the size, structure, and chemical composition of the brain (Rosenzweig, Bennett, & Diamond, 1972). Thus, there is a kind of basic uncertainty about the meaning of the fact that, say, five-year-olds have different brains and behave differently from one-year-olds. While it seems reasonable that neural growth places some limits on behavioral development, the nature of the brain–behavior relation is poorly understood.

The standard reaction of "environmentalists" to a maturational explanation is to provide children younger than the "critical age" with some form of special experience in an attempt to produce the desired behavior. As Kuhn (1974) has pointed out, such studies are beset by many difficulties, most noticeably a lack of agreement concerning the criteria for judging them successful. In addition, some experiments may begin with misguided premises. For example, is it reasonable to expect that an hour's special experience can take the place of a year or more of ordinary experience?

Cognitive processes operate in real time and take time to acquire, even for adults who are usually considered to have completed maturation. Complex skills are likely to have simpler skills as prerequisites, and providing the experience sufficient to acquire the highest level will have no effect unless the prerequisite skills already exist. For example, it makes little sense to try to teach advanced calculus to an adult who has no background in mathematics, and it might take that person several years to acquire the prerequisite knowledge and skills. The analogy to cognitive development should be clear. The time that children seem to require in order to develop certain cognitive processes might be due in part to neural maturation and in part to the time needed to acquire component skills, maturational considerations aside.

ASSIMILATION/ACCOMMODATION. In Piaget's account of cognitive development, great emphasis is given to the nature of the individual's interactions with the environment. Such interactions are necessarily two-sided affairs, affected by both the kind of information available in the environment and the nature of the individual's existing cognitive structures. In dealing with the environment, a person takes into account the nature of the information present in the environment but also interprets that information in the light of current knowledge. Piaget calls these two aspects of organism–environment interactions accommodation and assimilation, respectively.

Assimilation refers to interpreting objects and events in terms of one's current ways of thinking. *Accommodation* means taking into account the actual properties of the objects and events one encounters. These are not two separate cognitive processes but two intertwined aspects of organism–environment interactions. For example, suppose a rough, outline drawing looks like a bird to you. This outcome depends equally on your having some existing idea of what birds look like and on the drawing's having sufficient physical properties to enable you to identify it as a bird.

The process of assimilation/accommodation applies to all of an individual's interactions with the environment. The important point is that, as a child develops and repeatedly interacts with the environment, each new encounter leads to slight changes in his knowledge. For example, in the course of encountering a variety of birds, accommodating to their particular characteristics while assimilating them into a *bird* concept, the child leaves each encounter with a slightly modified understanding of the concept. As Flavell (1976) points out, the notion of assimilation/accommodation allows both for a gradual, step-wise development process and for drastic differences to evolve in cognitive processes when comparisons are made over longer intervals. This idea agrees nicely with Flavell's characterization of a stage as a qualitatively distinct state resulting from a succession of gradual changes. Each experience leaves the child only slightly different, but the cumulative effect of many encounters can be a radically different cognitive structure.

Adopting the model of assimilation/accommodation has important implications for understanding cognitive development. One must consider from the beginning of development both what assimilative capabilities the child has and what kinds of environmental information the child encounters. Cognitive growth requires proper experiences, but experiences will lead to growth only if they can be assimilated. Impoverished environments might lead to slower development, but (what appear to an adult to be) enriched environments might not result in faster development. Because a child is only slightly altered by each interaction, major changes in cognitive processes will require many interactions and thus rather long periods of time. On the whole, the assimilation/accommodation model implies that the course of development is neither biologically determined nor completely subject to environmental influences. Rather, cognitive growth results from organism–environment interactions in which both biological givens and environmental characteristics are important.

MEMORY

Adults and older children ordinarily "remember better" than younger children. Various tests of memory are regularly included in intelligence tests and show clear age trends. For example, a memory span test involves presenting the individual with a series of letters or numbers and asking the person to repeat the string immediately after presentation. The average score for 4-year-olds is about four items whereas 9-year-olds average about six items, adolescents and adults about seven items. As mentioned at the beginning of this chapter, infants give some evidence of memorial processes at an early age, such as responding differently to familiar and novel pictures, but it is not until nearly one year of age that other behaviors implying memory processes are observed (such as searching for a hidden object). Because of the difficulty of administering "formal" memory tasks to very young children, 2- and 3-year-olds have been the youngest subjects in the most innovative studies, while 5-year-olds are commonly the youngest group in many studies. It is generally true that, regardless of the age range included, older subjects remember better.

At this point, one cannot posit the existence of some fundamental memory capacity which increases as the individual develops. As we have indicated in earlier chapters, remembering is an active process involving a number of strategic components, and it is virtually impossible to separate what might be considered "pure memory capacity" from "functioning memory including use of mnemonic strategies." We will shortly consider recent work on memory development that emphasizes developmental differences in strategies used for remembering. First, however, it is worth noting that, before one can remember something, one must attend to the information in some fashion.

Controlled attention improves as an individual develops, and differences in attention are likely to affect performance on many different tasks. For example, attempts have been made to determine if there are fundamental differences in speed of information processing associated with different levels of development. To be sure, there are observed differences in processing speed; for example, "simple" reaction time might decrease from 400 milliseconds at age 4 to 160 milliseconds at age 16. However, these differences might well be due to differences in attentiveness to the stimuli or to other factors (Wickens, 1974). Memory tasks place greater demands on attention, and younger children might "remember worse" because they attended less well in the first place.

One way in which attentional differences on memory tasks have been demonstrated is by testing subjects on both *intentional* and *incidental* material. For example, subjects might be shown a series of pictures and asked to learn the location of each picture in the series (intentional material); each picture also happens to have a different-colored background, but nothing is said about this (incidental material). Research shows that older children regularly remember more of the intentional material than younger children, but there are no clear age differences in memory for incidental material (Pick, Frankel, & Hess, 1975). These findings suggest that older children are better able to direct their attention toward the material which the researcher wants them to remember (and will usually test for). In addition to differences in attentiveness, researchers have identified numerous strategy differences among children at different developmental levels.

REHEARSAL

It is well established that material will be forgotten quite rapidly, even over seconds, unless it is maintained in some way over the retention interval (see Chapter 2). This maintenance process, generally called rehearsal, assumes several different forms. There is now abundant evidence that younger children are less likely to rehearse and use less efficient rehearsal strategies when they do rehearse. Differences in rehearsal affect short-term remembering.

One way in which rehearsal effects have been studied is through examining serial position effects. If memory for items in different positions in a presentation series is examined, better memory for both early items (primacy effect) and for the last items (recency effect) are typically found (see Chapter 2). The primacy effect is of special interest because recall of early items is considered to depend on rehearsal. Consequently we would expect developmental differences to be more apparent in primacy effects than in recency effects, and this is the case. A study by Allik and Siegel (1976) provides illustrative data. In this experiment, the subject was shown a series of seven easily named pictures; the pictures were shown one at a time and then placed face-down in a row in front of the subject. After presentation, the subject was shown a duplicate of one of the pictures and asked to turn over the picture (in the row) which was just like it; by means of repeated trials, each subject was eventually tested on each serial position. The data, shown in Figure 10-4, show that developmental differences are most apparent on the first half of the series (primacy effect), an effect which is presumably due to differential use of rehearsal by younger and older subjects.

Rehearsal strategies have been studied by having subjects rehearse aloud. This technique was used by Kellas, McCauley, and McFarland (1975), who presented subjects with lists of nine words, one at a time, and tape-recorded their subjects' vocalizations to assess rehearsal. The data, shown in Figure 10-5, clearly indicate greater rehearsal by older subjects, espe-

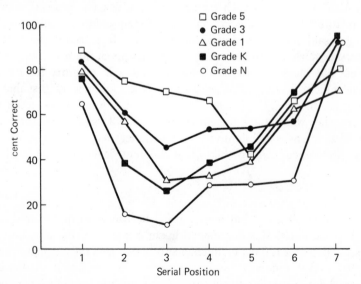

FIGURE 10-4. Percentage of correct responses at each serial position summed over one- and two-syllable items for children at each grade level. (From Figure 1 in Allik & Siegel, 1976. Courtesy of the author and Academic Press.)

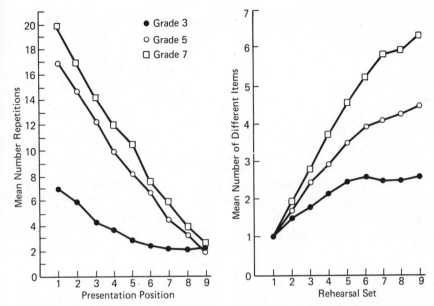

FIGURE 10–5. Mean repetitions and rehearsal set sizes for third, fifth, and seventh grades. (From Figure 1 in Kellas, McCauley, & McFarland, 1975. Courtesy of Academic Press.)

cially for items earlier in the list, where the largest differences in remembering are observed. Similar results were obtained by Ornstein, Naus, and Liberty (1975), who also found that the kind of rehearsal used by younger and older subjects was different. Younger subjects (third graders) tended to rehearse just the item most recently presented or minimal combinations, while older subjects (sixth and eighth graders) used a cumulative rehearsal strategy which results in integrated units. The difference can be illustrated as follows: If the series presented were *yard, cat, man, desk,* a typical rehearsal pattern for a younger subject after the presentation of *desk* would be *desk, desk, desk, desk.* For an older subject it would be *desk, man, yard, cat, man, desk, cat, yard.* Thus, the older child (and adult) is more likely to rehearse and to construct larger chunks by using a cumulative rehearsal strategy. It has been found that children as young as 5 years of age can be taught to rehearse, with a resulting improvement in memory. However, the children do not transfer the rehearsal strategy to subsequent tasks—they rehearse (and remember better) only on the task for which they have been directly taught to rehearse (Hagen, Jongeward, & Kail, 1975).

ORGANIZATION

When adults are asked to learn a list of words, they are very likely to seek out structural relations existing among the words in the list, trying to construct chunks containing several words each. Forming multiple-word chunks facilitates recall of the list because, in a sense, fewer "things" have to be remembered. For this reason, categorized lists in which words can be grouped into categories such as animal names, flower names, articles of furniture, result in more words being recalled, compared to uncategorized lists. In addition, adults tend to recall the words in categories, a phenomenon known as *clustering* (Bousfield, Cohen, & Whitmarsh, 1958), even when the words are presented in a mixed-up order (see Table 10-3). It would seem likely that clustering would show a developmental trend, and this appears to be true.

Although presenting categorized items (usually pictures) has been found to aid the recall of children as young as 2 years old, older children seem to benefit more from the presence of categories (Hagen et al., 1975). This trend is due in part to the older children's making greater use of categories in studying the material, as nicely illustrated in a study by Moely, Olson, Halwes, and Flavell (1969). Subjects at four developmental levels (kindergarten, first, third, and fifth grade) were asked to recall the names of pictures which they were shown. The pictures could be grouped into four categories—animals, furniture, vehicles, and clothing. During the study period, the subject was shown the pictures arranged in an irregular circle with no two same-category members next to each other. Subjects were given two minutes to study the pictures and were told that they could move the pictures around if they liked.

The investigators were interested in the extent to which subjects would group together pictures belonging to the same category. While most of the subjects moved the pictures around during study, the kindergartners hardly

TABLE 10–3. CLUSTERED RECALL OF A CATEGORIZED WORD LIST.

Presentation Order	Total Clustering	Partial Clustering
carrot	carrot	carrot
truck	peas	beans
gloves	corn	hat
bike	beans	gloves
peas	bike	truck
hat	truck	corn
wagon	wagon	car
beans	hat	
shirt	shirt	
corn	shoes	
shoes		
car		

Note: Clustering depends on the extent to which the words recalled are recalled in categories—the entire list need not be recalled. Clustered recall is typically higher than nonclustered recall.

ever grouped category members together; the first and third graders were only slightly better, while the fifth graders averaged about 60 percent grouping by categories during study. To see if the younger subjects could be induced to use a grouping strategy, other subjects from these same age groups were encouraged to group the pictures, label the categories, and count the number of pictures in each category during study. When given such special instruction, the younger subjects used a grouping strategy just as often as the older subjects had done spontaneously. Overall, the study showed that older children are much more likely to use a grouping strategy spontaneously, that younger children can be taught to use such a strategy, and that, at every age level, subjects who use a grouping strategy during study (whether spontaneously or through instruction) recall more items than those who do not. These results are quite similar to those obtained with respect to rehearsal; in both instances, younger children typically do not use helpful memorization strategies even though they are capable of using them, as shown by the success of teaching them the strategies.

METAMEMORY

The findings described above suggest that younger children often "do not know what to do" when they have to remember something. Many memory tasks are best accomplished by using some efficient strategy, and younger children seem to be unprepared in precisely this area. Recently, researchers have become interested in what children know about memory, termed *metamemory*. Kreutzer, Leonard, and Flavell (1975) conducted extensive interviews with children of different ages, asking the children to make choices related to remembering and to explain their answers; a small portion of their data is presented in Table 10-4.

The "savings" item assessed whether the subject knew that prior learning would aid subsequent relearning even if a person could no longer recall the material. The child was told that two boys had to learn the names of all the birds in their city, that one boy had learned them last year but forgotten them while the other had never learned them. The child was then asked which boy would find it easier to learn the birds' names now, and why. While the majority of subjects at all ages chose the relearner, older children were more likely to provide an adequate justification for their choice. The "immediate-delay" item was intended to determine if the children knew that forgetting can occur quite rapidly (loss from STM). The subject was asked whether it would make any difference if he phoned immediately or got a drink of water first when someone had just told him a phone number he wanted to call. Subjects were also asked what they do when they want to remember a phone number. The results suggest that older children are more aware that information can be lost from memory quite rapidly; in

TABLE 10–4. CHILDREN'S ANSWERS TO QUESTIONS ABOUT MEMORY. (ADAPTED, WITH PERMISSION FROM DATA BY KREUTZER, LEONARD, & FLAVELL, 1975.)

		Grade Level		
Questions	*K*	*1*	*3*	*5*
A. Savings				
Percent choosing relearner	55	55	60	65
Percent explaining choice	30	50	50	65
B. Immediate-delay				
Percent aware of loss	40	70	95	95
C. Remembering phone				
number				
Percent "write down"	55	55	80	45
Percent "rehearse"	0	10	10	45
Percent other/no answer	45	35	10	10
D. Story-list				
Percent "story easier"	50	75	100	85
Percent explaining choice	15	20	70	80
E. Opposition-arbitrary				
Percent "opposites easier"	30	50	80	100

addition, only the older subjects suggested rehearsal as a means of combatting forgetting.

Other items tested the subject's knowledge of the advantages of organizational constraints in remembering material. Subjects were asked whether it would be easier to remember a set of pictures if they were just presented ("list") or if a person were told a story about the pictures. Another item involved asking the child whether it would be easier to learn a pair of words which were opposites or a pair of unrelated words (examples were used in cases referring to types of materials). It can be seen that the older children were more likely to be aware of the memorial advantages which structural constraints provide.

Overall, the findings indicated that kindergartners generally know a fair amount about memory. They are aware of the fact that forgetting occurs, that a lot of material is harder to remember than a little material, that more study time is better than less study time, and that some things can be done to prevent forgetting/aid remembering. The investigators were especially impressed with the younger children's tendency to use external memory aids—writing things down, strings on fingers, and other people. Of course, there is a great deal the younger child does not seem to know, and there is a great deal of growth in metamemory during middle childhood, although the fifth graders were far from experts. The implications of this research are quite interesting. Performance on a memory task is affected by the kinds of strategies people use to remember, but strategy usage depends on what people know about memory. Therefore, differences in remembering might reflect differences in knowledge about memory.

LANGUAGE

It is often said that children "essentially master their native language" by the age of 5, although it is quite clear that considerable language acquisition occurs during middle childhood and beyond (Palermo & Molfese, 1972). Because of the complexity of language as formally described by linguists—and the general belief that "true language" is unique to human beings—it is tempting to concentrate on language processing and development as separate from other aspects of cognitive development. However, recent work has emphasized the view that functioning language (at whatever level) is an integrated whole which psycholinguists have broken down into various levels—phonology, morphology syntax, semantics—for purposes of formal analysis and that language development must be considered in the context of general cognitive development.

For example, MacNamara (1972) has pointed out that, while it seems logically necessary that identification of the phonemes present in linguistic input must precede analysis of the syntax (structure) of a sentence, it is also necessary to base the learning of phonology on knowledge of syntax. Similarly, while it would seem that syntactical analysis would precede semantic analysis (one must discern the structure of a sentence before one knows what it means), it is likewise necessary to base the learning of syntax on knowledge of meaning. These apparent contradictions can be resolved by understanding that functioning language is indeed a totality and that levels exist purely for the purpose of formal analysis. Thus, meaning, the highest level—and not phonemes, the lowest level— seems to dominate the linguistic behavior of young children. Early speech is commonly characterized as *holophrastic*—young children use single words to express entire "ideas." Thus a child might say "ball" to mean "the ball is rolling," "give me the ball," or "see the ball." Well-formed, adult sentences tend to be imitated in reduced form, that form representing the "core meaning"— "Mommy will get you the ball" might come back as "Mommy ball." Two-year-olds respond just as well to distorted sentences (for example, "Mommy clown to the show") as to well-formed sentences ("Show the clown to Mommy") (Ginsburg & Koslowski, 1976).

It might seem incredible that infants and their parents (or other adults) ever understand each other. However, it is important to keep in mind that speech is *about something* in everyday life (the child's acquisition environment); formal analyses of language tend to deal with language in isolation and may thus give a misleading impression. For very young children, comprehension probably involves recognizing a few familiar words and arriving at some meaning of an expression on the basis of those words and the objects and events surrounding them. Suppose you were abruptly deposited in the middle of a community whose inhabitants spoke a language you knew absolutely nothing about. In trying to figure out what people were saying, you would surely make use of many nonlinguistic cues such as gestures, facial expressions, objects, actions, and reactions. The young child is in similar circumstances and attempts to deal with language in a similar fashion.

Even if there exist concepts that apply solely to the acquisition and structure of language (Osheron & Wasow, 1976), most writers have stressed the relation of language development to general cognitive development. As Lenneberg (1969) has put it, it is not language itself which distinguishes human beings; rather, the human species has a species-specific form of cognitive functioning of which language is an integral part. Piaget (1970) argues that intellectual operations give rise to linguistic progress, and not vice versa. According to this view, language development is based on prior nonlinguistic development. For example, the subject-object distinction of language is preceded by and presumably based on the agent-action distinction contained in the sensory-motor schemes developed in the first year or so of life. Similarly, vocabulary development seems to depend on prior concept formation (see Moerk, 1975).

Nelson (1974) argues that learning the name of something is the last step in the development of core concepts. If so, children should engage in consistent classification before "learning the words." To test this hypothesis, Nelson (1973) placed various collections of objects in front of subjects aged 19 to 22 months; interest lay in whether or not the child would rearrange the objects into groups. (Although the experimenter said, "Here, you fix them up, put them the way they ought to go," after mixing the objects in front of the child, the categorizations were largely spontaneous since most children did not understand the instructions.) The basis of possible classification varied among collections; four large blue plastic planes and four small blue plastic planes were presented to determine if the child would sort on the basis of size, while four different small green plastic animals and four different small green plastic eating utensils were presented to see if function would be used, and so on for a number of dimensions. Nelson's young subjects had active vocabularies ranging from 15 to over 300 words so that, from one classification basis to another, the number of children who knew possibly relevant labels varied greatly.

Two major results were obtained: First, children formed groups for which they did not have labels, supporting the main thesis. Second, the children were much more likely to form groups on some bases rather than others. Overall, Nelson's results suggest that functional concepts dominate the thinking of preverbal children ("balls roll," "a hole is to dig"), which fits nicely with the idea that cognitive development through the sensory-motor period lays the foundation for language development.

As language development proceeds, children show increases in the size of their vocabularies as well as increases in the average length of the utterances they produce. Children's comprehension of language is typically greater than their production—they understand more than they say. All of these aspects of language development are illustrated in a study by Goldin-Meadow, Seligman, and Gelman (1976). These investigators studied vocabulary development in children between the ages of 14 and 26 months. The children were tested in their homes; in addition to recording the children's spontaneous speech, comprehension and production tests were given. The words used were nouns which could be represented by familiar toys and verbs which could be portrayed in action by a person or toy. During the testing sessions, approximately 70 different toys were spread out on the floor. Comprehension was assessed by asking the child to point to or to otherwise respond selectively to a named object (nouns) or by asking the child to perform the action indicated by a particular verb. Illustrative questions were "Where's the truck?" and "Make the doll lie down." Production was tested by having the experimenter select a toy and ask the child "What's this?" (nouns) and by having the experimenter perform an action, asking the child "What am I doing?" (verbs). On the production test, children who consistently used idiosyncratic words—for example, "nite-nite" for "pillow"—were considered to have a production word for the object. The major results are shown in Table 10-5.

The authors suggested that their subjects could be meaningfully divided into two groups. The first four children, with comprehension/production ratios of 2.7 or higher for nouns, were labeled the Receptive Group. These children understood many more nouns than they produced, produced no verbs at all although they understood a fair number, and produced few combinations in speaking—that is, quite short utterances. In contrast, the remaining children, with noun ratios of 1.5 or less, were labeled the Productive Group. These children said most of the nouns they understood, produced verbs, although not as many as they understood, and produced more and longer combinations in their spontaneous speech. The authors proposed that the Receptive and Productive patterns represent different phases of language development, with the receptive phase preceding the productive phase. To test this hypothesis, they continued to study three of the children (Lexie, Melissa, and Jenny) for several months, repeating the tests on a monthly basis. Several months later, each of these children ex-

TABLE 10–5.   Vocabulary Development in Young Children. (Adapted, with Permission from Tables 2 and 3 in Goldin-Meadow, Seligman, & Gelman, 1976. Courtesy of Elsevier Sequoia, S.A.)

Child	Age (mos.)	Nouns No. Compr./ No. Prod.	Verbs No. Compr./ No. Prod.	Utterances Avg. Length	Longest
Michael	26	46/6 = 7.7	22/0 =	2	2
Lexie	22	35/7 = 5.0	22/0 =	2.1	3
Melissa	21	22/5 = 4.4	14/0 =	—	1
Jenny	14	27/10 = 2.7	9/0 =	—	1
Ray	27	49/32 = 1.5	21/4 = 5.3	2.1	4
Sarah	23	41/31 = 1.3	20/4 = 5.0	2.7	4
Perry	24	49/38 = 1.3	28/10 = 2.8	2.5	4
Leah	26	56/43 = 1.3	27/10 = 2.7	2.9	6
Harry	25	56/45 = 1.2	23/8 = 2.9	3.2	8
Chris	26.5	54/45 = 1.2	23/7 = 3.3	2.3	4
Peter	23	49/43 = 1.1	26/15 = 1.7	4.5	7
Lee	26	54/52 = 1.0	28/16 = 1.8	4.2	7

hibited noun comprehension/production ratios of 1.6 or less and had begun producing verbs and longer utterances, thus supporting their hypothesis.

These findings indicate that early vocabulary development is characterized by a considerable discrepancy between a child's comprehension vocabulary and production vocabulary. Subsequently, the gap between comprehension and production is closed for nouns; the production vocabulary grows more rapidly than the comprehension vocabulary, and the child tends to use most of the nouns he understands. At about the same time, the child begins to produce verbs and increases the production of multiword utterances. The authors argue that the emergence of this "productive skill" cannot be explained on the basis of improved motor control (articulation); rather, production seems to depend on the development of some cognitive skill which remains to be identified.

CONSERVATION OF CONCEPTS

In general terms, conservation refers to the fact that the individual understands that something remains the same (is conserved) even though other things change. Conservation can be considered at several levels. *Qualitative identity conservation* is exemplified by the recognition that an object remains the same object although some aspects of its appearance are altered. At a primitive level, the infant who recognizes *mother* as *mother* even though she has changed her clothes is conserving the concept of mother.

Standard tests of qualitative identity conservation typically use ordinary objects such as balls of clay or water; if the clay is molded into a different shape or the water poured into a different sized container, this form of conservation is demonstrated by the child's understanding that "it is the same clay" or "it is the same water." *Quantitative identity conservation,* on the other hand, refers to the ability to recognize that the *amount* of clay or water has not changed when the shape of the material or its container is altered. *Quantitative equivalence conservation* involves two distinguishable objects, initially judged to be equal with respect to some attribute; the subject's task is to decide if that equivalence still holds when one object is transformed. For example, a child might be shown two objectively equal sized balls of clay and agree that they are equal in amount; then, one of the balls is flattened or rolled into a snake, and the child is asked whether the two forms are still equal in amount. Conservation consists of understanding that the initial equivalence remains despite the perceptual transformation of one of the objects.

Qualitative conservation (that an object is the same object although perceptually modified) represents the lowest level of conservation and is typically mastered during early childhood (roughly between the ages of 2 and 7). Because qualitative conservation is so obvious to adults, it might be worth emphasizing that, from the viewpoint of, say, a 3-year-old, some clay which is changed from a ball-shape to a sausage-shape isn't really the same clay it used to be! Quantitative conservation (identity or equivalence) is mastered later in development, during middle childhood (7 to 11 years). It appears that conservation of quantitative identity (single object) precedes conservation of quantitative equivalence (two objects) at least to some extent (Brainerd & Hooper, 1975). Illustrative age trends for the three kinds of conservation are shown in Figure 10-6.

Quantitative conservation (perhaps especially equivalence or "two-object" conservation) has received a great deal of attention because of the special place it holds in Piaget's view of cognitive development. Piaget considers quantitative conservation to be based on internalized, *reversible* operations that are characteristic of the stage of *concrete operations.* Two kinds of reversibility are distinguished, simple reversibility (the amount of clay is the same when changed from ball-shape to sausage-shape because it can be changed back to the ball-shape) and reciprocal reversibility (although the clay sausage is longer than the clay ball, it is also thinner, and longer × thinner = the same amount). Because of Piaget's association of conservation with theoretically postulated structures of thought, there has been much concern over what children must do to demonstrate that they are "conservers." For example, Piaget requires that a child both make the correct judgment (that the amount is the same after transformation) and give an adequate justification for the judgment (like those mentioned above) to be considered a conserver. In contrast, Brainerd (1973) has strongly argued that conservation should be assessed solely in terms of correct judgments. This debate is unlikely to be quickly resolved; we can note that children are likely to be deemed "conservers" earlier in development if a judgments-only criterion is used.

MEMORY FACTORS

In Piaget's view, quantitative conservation reflects the presence of concrete operations in the child's thought structures, and nonconservation indicates their absence. Thus Piaget wishes to use performance (conservation) to infer competence (presence or absence of particular thought structure). Several investigators have suggested that *non*conservation might have other explanations—a child's failure to pass a quantitative conservation task might not mean that the child is incapable of such conservation. To understand the nature of this approach, let us consider an outline of a typical conservation task, using liquids. There are three major steps (see Figure 10-7):

1. The child is shown two glasses of the same size and shape (A and B), both containing the same amount of water. The child is asked if there is the same amount of water in the two glasses, and the child agrees.

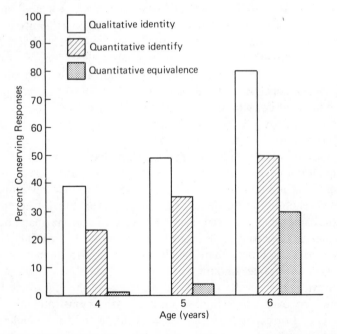

FIGURE 10–6. Age trends in conservation. (From data by Rybash, Roodin, & Sullivan, 1975. Courtesy of the author and Academic Press.)

2. In front of the child, the water in glass B is poured into a taller but thinner glass (C).
3. The child is asked if there is just as much water in glass C as in glass A. To be considered as conserving, the child must state that the amounts of the water are the same (and, for Piaget, give an adequate justification for the judgment).

To solve this problem, the child must both understand that the transformation (Step 2) did not change the amount of water (B = C) and remember the original equivalence (A = B). Thus one possible reason for failure may be that the child has forgotten the original equivalence. To test this hypothesis, Rybash, Roodin, and Sullivan (1975) provided some children with a memory aid, marking the water level in glass B before the transformation and reminding the children, after the transformation, that the water had come up to the marker when it had been in Glass B. With the memory aid, more children (ages 4 to 6) met criteria of equivalence

Step 1:

   Presentation:

Question: Same amount of water in the two glasses?
Child's response: Yes

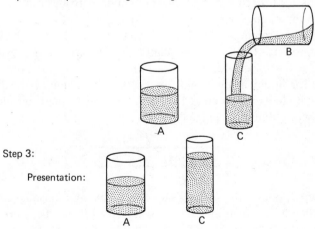

Step 2: Water poured from glass B to glass C (transformation)

Step 3:

   Presentation:

Question: Same amount of water in the two glasses?
Child's response: Conserver — Yes. Nonconserver — No (likely to say glass C has more)

FIGURE 10–7.   Testing Equivalence Conservation for Liquid Amount.

conservation (23 percent) compared to those without the memory aid (10 percent). These results suggest that, at least to a degree, failure to conserve quantitative equivalence can result from memory failure.

ATTENDING TO IRRELEVANT ATTRIBUTES

It has also been suggested that children may fail conservation tasks because they attend to and base their judgments on an *irrelevant* dimension of the stimulus. In the context of the liquid conservation task outlined above, suppose that the child's judgment of "same" in Step 1 is based on the equal *heights* of the columns of water rather than on equal amounts per se. In Step 3, after the height of one water column has been noticeably changed, the child will thus conclude that the original equivalence no longer exists. When shown stimuli varying in several ways (which is virtually always the case), young children generally tend to have their attention drawn to a single, salient dimension. Furthermore, stimulus attributes which change are more likely to attract attention than those which remain constant, for children and adults alike. Let us look again at the liquid conservation task. In everyday life, height is a rather good indicator of amount —tall glasses usually hold more than shorter glasses, bottles contain less to drink as the level goes down. Thus young children show a strong tendency to judge liquid amount in terms of height (Miller, 1973). In addition, during the transformation (Step 2), this salient attribute undergoes a clear change, encouraging attention to height. By this account, conservation failures might be due to attention problems.

Attempts have been made to "teach" children to discriminate relevant and irrelevant dimensions of stimuli and subsequently to determine the effects of such training on conservation. Gelman (1969) obtained very interesting results. First, several quantitative conservation pre-tests were given to five-year-old children in order to identify nonconservers; included were tests for liquid amount and for length. The standard test for length involves first showing the child two sticks of equal length which are perfectly aligned, obtaining a judgment of "same" (Step 1):

During Step 2, one of the sticks is moved, producing a misaligned arrangement for Step 3, at which the child is again asked if the sticks are the same length:

Conservers say *yes* while nonconservers say *no*. Having identified a number of nonconservers for liquid amount, length, and other quantities, Gelman then provided some of the 5-year-olds with oddity training for some of the dimensions. An oddity task involves presenting three stimuli, two of which are alike in some (experimenter-determined) dimension while the third differs; the "odd" stimulus might share irrelevant attributes with one of the "same" stimuli. For example, in oddity training for length, the child saw arrangements such as the following:

(a)   (b)   (c)

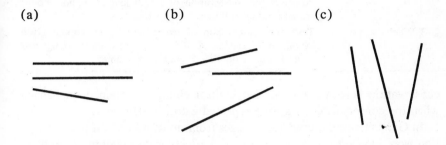

When asked to choose "two that are the same," the child had to select the two equal-length sticks to be told "correct," whereas two of unequal length had to be selected when asked to choose "two that are different"; incorrect choices received "wrong" feedback without explanation.

The children who received oddity training were given six trials (like those above) on each of sixteen problems, with the sizes, colors, and shapes of the sticks changing from problem to problem. It is important to note that oddity training was given for only some of the dimensions; For example, no child received oddity training for liquid amount. Conservation post-tests were given to trained and untrained (control) subjects on both trained and untrained dimensions. The basic logic of Gelman's design (but not the complete experiment) is outlined in Table 10-6.

The results of Gelman's study were quite striking. First, the children who received oddity training mastered the oddity tasks with relatively little difficulty. On conservation post-tests for trained dimensions, for example, length, the training group showed near perfect conservation (95 percent conserving responses) while the control children remained nonconservers (4 percent conserving responses). The oddity training also produced dramatic improvements on untrained dimensions such as liquid amount; while the control group showed no conservation, the training group averaged 60 percent conserving responses. In addition, the children who received oddity training were able to provide adequate justification for their conserving responses nearly all the time (between 78 and 97 percent of conserving responses were adequately justified). Finally, the differences in

TABLE 10–6. EXPERIMENTAL DESIGN: ODDITY TRAINING AND CONSERVATION.

Day 1:	Pre-tests given for conservation of length and liquid amount. Children who fail the tests are identified and continue in the experiment. Nonconserving (failing) children are randomly assigned to training and control conditions.
Day 2:	Children in the training condition receive oddity training for length. Children in the control condition are exposed to the materials used in oddity training but receive no training.
Day 3:	Post-tests for conservation of length and of liquid amount are given to all children.
2–3 Weeks Later:	Tests for conservation of length and liquid amount given again, to determine if differences between training and control groups on Day 3 persist over time.

conservation between training and control children remained unchanged when the conservation tests were repeated 2 to 3 weeks later.

In Gelman's study, dramatic changes from nonconservation to conservation were induced in 5-year-olds by a relatively small amount of training. As Gelman pointed out, it is extremely unlikely that the children "acquired the concept of quantitative invariance" during oddity training. Rather, the children already possessed some understanding of quantity and invariance but had to learn to respond consistently to quantity instead of being distracted by irrelevant cues. Stated conversely, these results strongly suggest that the children failed standard tests of quantitative conservation because of attention to irrelevant stimulus dimensions. In addition to these two explanations of conservation failures in terms of memory or attention, it has also been hypothesized that failure may result from differences in the child's understanding and use of language (questions and answers, descriptive terms such as *bigger*) vis-à-vis an adult's. While all of the findings have not been as impressive as those of Gelman's study, there is a general trend resulting from modifications of standard conservation tests. Providing memory aids, increasing attention to relevant stimulus dimensions, and using nonverbal assessment techniques (Miller, 1976) have all been found to increase the incidence of quantitative conservation.

From a Piagetian viewpoint, quantitative conservation/nonconservation is important because performance can be used to infer the presence/absence of specified intellectual structures and operations. However, as mentioned earlier, inferring a particular kind of competence from performance is always dangerous. Klahr and Wallace (1970) have carefully delineated the many different cognitive processes involved in tests of "concrete operations." Research on the effects of memory, attention, and language usage support their analysis. There is no necessary incompatibility between Piaget's logical analysis of children's thinking and information-processing analyses stressing other cognitive processes. However, the totality of results indicates that the connection between the "logic of thought" and performance on cognitive tasks is much less direct than might be suspected, and that many different cognitive processes are changing during middle childhood. Success on tests of quantitative conservation is affected by more than one of these developments.

REASONING

It is generally believed that children become more logical as they grow older. In Piaget's view, truly logical thinking is associated with the period of formal operations, the last proposed stage of cognitive development. In Chapter 9, we emphasized that "being logical" involves a number of different cognitive processes and that adults might fail in one aspect but otherwise reason systematically or logically. Similar analyses have been made in developmental studies of reasoning.

CAUSAL INFERENCES

Causal inferences refer to explanations for physical events—what causes the wind or rain, what makes a car go, what makes a light go on? During middle childhood, there is an increase in the frequency with which proper (adult) explanations are given. This sequence of development has often been compared with the set of explanations that has historically been advanced to account for physical events. Thus early (in development or history) explanations presumably center on "magic," personal agents, and authoritative assertions, these subsequently giving way to an articulated understanding of regularities which occur in nature. However, this analogy may completely miss the mark—perhaps younger children fail to give "proper" explanations to questions like "What causes rain?" simply because they lack relevant knowledge, not because their conception of "cause" is fundamentally different from that of adults. Siegler and Liebert (1974) proposed that children's causal reasoning is better studied by presenting them with a novel situation which embodies the presumably important features of "natural" events.

The apparatus used to study causal reasoning is illustrated in Figure 10-8. The event to be explained is the illumination of a light bulb which is connected to two possible "causal agents," a card programmer (left) and a "computer with flashing lights" (right). The insertion of a card into the card programmer represents a discrete source to which causality might be attributed, while the flashing lights (and associated clicking sounds) of the computer represent possible alternative causes (the rest of the world). In this situation there was no systematic relation between the computer's activity and the illumination of the light bulb, but there did exist a consistent relation between insertion of a card and lighting of the bulb. The central question is, What variables affect the likelihood that children will

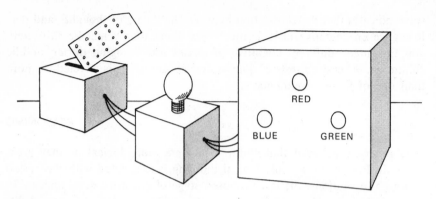

FIGURE 10–8. Apparatus used to study children's causal reasoning.

attribute causality to card insertion? Traditionally, a "cause" has a *regular* and *contiguous* relation to an "effect": If B always follows A, A is more likely to be a cause of B than if B only sometimes follows A; second, causality is more likely if B follows A closely in time rather than with some delay. Siegler and Liebert (1974) attempted to determine if variation in contiguity and regularity differentially affected younger and older children's inferences about causality.

The subjects were kindergartners (5 to 6 years old) and third graders (8 to 9 years old). Each child had a number of observational opportunities and was asked whether the card or the computer "made the light go on." For some children, the light always went on after a card was inserted, while the light went on only half the time after a card was inserted for others. Also varied was the temporal interval—the light flashed either immediately after or 5 seconds after the card was inserted. Overall, the older children were more likely to attribute causality to the card than were the younger children (who tended to choose the computer). Both age groups were more likely to infer causality when the light flashed immediately after card insertion (compared to the 5-second delay). Only the older children were influenced by regularity, inferring causality more often when the light flash always followed card insertion than when the light followed card insertion only half the time. This explains why the older children were more likely to attribute causality to the card insertion. The younger children, on the other hand, were less likely to view the card as "cause" and, while influenced by contiguity, were not influenced by the regularity of the card–light relation.

Siegler (1975) has pointed out that there are many possible reasons for such developmental differences. Four possibilities are that the two groups of children might differ in (1) detecting and remembering the systematic relation between card insertion and light flashing, (2) detecting and remembering the *unsystematic* relation between computer activities and light flashing, (3) comparing these two relations, or (4) deciding what criteria to use in defining a "causal relation." A series of experiments involving modifications of the basic situation indicated that, when there was a delay between card insertion and light flash, the younger children were less able to detect the regularity of the card–light relation due to the distraction resulting from the flashing, clicking computer. There was little evidence for a developmental difference in the "meaning of causality"; rather, the younger children, largely because of distractibility, are less successful in detecting regular relations existing over time.

CONDITIONAL REASONING

In logic, a proposition of the form "If p, then q" has a specific meaning (see Chapter 9). Such a conditional statement specifies that the event "p, not q" is false (does not exist) while other events, "p, q", "not p, q", and "not p, not q" are possible (true). The ability to understand logical systems is associated by Piaget with the period of formal operations, beginning roughly at age 11. In view of the difficulties which many adults have with syllogistic reasoning and proposition testing, Piaget's formal operations might best represent an ideal state which some adults attain (Neimark, 1975). However, from various viewpoints (including Piaget's) we might expect children to become "more logical" as they develop.

Rather than accepting the notion that children progress from being illogical to being logical (more or less), Taplin, Staudenmeyer, and Taddonio (1974) suggested that a closer look at "logical performance" was in order. They proposed that a distinction be made between the manner in which a person interprets a conditional ("if . . ., then . . .") statement and the consistency with which the interpretation is used. In a nutshell, a person who appears "illogical" might interpret propositions differently from what is dictated by formal logic but might deal logically (consistently) with that interpretation.[1] Thus, the question posed was, Do younger and older children interpret conditional statements differently?

The task required the subject to decide on the truth or falsity of one statement, given that two other statements were true. Two examples follow:

(a) Affirming the antecedent
Assume true:

1. If there is a D, then there is a K.
2. There is a D.

   True or False?
3. There is a K. (Correct = true)

(b) Affirming the consequent
Assume true:

1. If there is a D, then there is a K.
2. There is a K.

   True or false?
3. There is a D. (Correct = not necessarily so)

---

[1] Recall that in Chapter 9, a similar analysis of adults' syllogistic reasoning errors was proposed: People misinterpret premises but combine (their interpretations of) premises logically (consistently).

Remember that, according to propositional logic, a statement of the form "If *p*, then *q*" asserts only that *p* entails the existence of *q*. A conditional statement does *not* imply that *q* can occur only in the presence of *p* (not *p, q* events are possible). Taplin and his co-workers gave a variety of tests of this sort to children in grades three to eleven (age range 8 to 17). In terms of overall performance, there was a clear improvement with age (Figure 10-9). However, this "average trend" is somewhat misleading because, on some tests there was little or no improvement with age, while on other tests age trends were quite striking.

Subjects' responses were more closely analyzed to determine (1) how the individual interpreted the conditional statement and (2) whether the individual was consistent in dealing with that interpretation. Here the results were most interesting. Across ages, there was no clear increase in the number of consistent subjects—that is, there were just as many third graders who responded consistently as there were eleventh graders. The major difference was in the manner in which the "if . . ., then . . ." statement was interpreted. Only the oldest subjects tended to interpret such statements as conditional statements according to formal logic. The youngest subjects often interpreted such statements as conjunctive rather than conditional; that is, "if D, then K" meant that only "DK" could occur. The groups in the middle age ranges tended to adopt a biconditional interpreta-

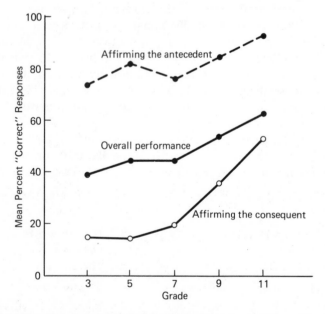

FIGURE 10–9.   Developmental trends in conditional reasoning. (From data by Taplin, Staudenmeyer, & Taddonio, 1974. Courtesy of the author and Academic Press.)

tion; in effect, "D implies K and K implies D", that is, "DK" and "not D, not K" are possible, but "D, not K" and "not D, K" are not possible. The major age change was *not* in the consistency with which subjects used their interpretations of conditional statements, but in the actual interpretations. It has been suggested that differences in interpretation reflect differences in the amount of information processing required (Neimark & Slotnick, 1970). A conjunctive interpretation is simplest—both "things" must be present. The biconditional interpretation is more complex since both "things" must be either present or absent. The (truly) conditional interpretation requires that both the presence and absence of each term be considered and that the *order* of the terms also be attended to (*"p, not q"* and *"not p, q"* have quite different status). From middle childhood to adulthood, increasingly complex interpretations are adopted; what does not seem to change much is the consistency with which individuals use their interpretations.

SUMMARY

Cognitive processes exhibit enormous changes from infancy to adulthood. To study cognitive development, researchers often compare the performance of children of different ages; interest lies in the kinds of changes which occur as children grow older rather than in the particular age at which some behavior is exhibited. Although researchers are usually interested in what children are capable of doing, inferring competence from performance is dangerous because the successful performance of any cognitive task involves a number of processes.

Theorizing about cognitive development is dominated by the views of Piaget, who argues that the growing child passes from stage to stage during development, with each stage characterized by a different set of cognitive processes. During the sensory-motor period, the child acquires integrated schemes for dealing with objects and comes to understand that objects continue to exist when they are no longer in view. The concrete operations period is characterized by the child's development of internalized, reversible operations which can be applied to attributes of objects to solve problems. The period of formal operations, which an adult may not necessarily complete, is characterized by truly hypothetical thinking as found in formal logic and scientific reasoning. The distinct cognitive structures associated with each stage are best considered as the end products of a gradual developmental process.

Cognitive development is jointly determined by the biological characteristics of the individual and the type of environment in which the person grows. While the environment must provide the experiences necessary for development, many cognitive processes will develop in any of a variety of environments. The rate of development is neither biologically predetermined nor completely responsive to environmental manipulations. Cognitive growth results from the individual's interactions with the environment, a process consisting of the organism's accommodation to the kinds of environmental information available and its assimilation of that information into existing cognitive structures. Because each interaction results in only slight changes in cognition, major developments are likely to require many interactions and thus fairly long time periods.

Children remember better as they grow older, for several reasons. Older children and adults are better able to focus their attention on the material to be remembered than younger children. In addition, younger children tend not to use spontaneously such effective mnemonic strategies as rehearsal and organizational schemes, although they can be taught to use them to advantage. The use of effective strategies might depend on how much an individual knows about how memory operates, and younger children know far less about memory than older children and adults.

The acquisition of language has often been emphasized as a uniquely human accomplishment. However, language development is not isolated from general cognitive development. The young child encounters spoken language as a part of the total environment and uses nonlinguistic information in trying to make sense of what people are saying. Young children have usable concepts for which they later learn the names. Children typically understand more about language than is apparent in the speech they themselves produce. As language development proceeds, children appear to move from a receptive phase to a more productive phase; this transition appears to depend on the development of cognitive skills which are not well understood at this time.

Performance on conceptual tasks undergoes marked changes with development. Many aspects of concepts which are obvious to adults are slowly acquired by children over a considerable period of time. During infancy and early childhood, children come to understand that an object remains the same object when some aspects of its appearance are changed. Considerable attention has been paid to the conservation of quantitative aspects of objects, which typically occurs during middle childhood. During this period, children develop the understanding that changing the shape of, say, clay, does not change the amount of clay. Quantitative conservation is a two-step process, however: it applies first to a single object and only later to a comparison of two objects. Research has shown that the difficulties which children have in conserving quantitative concepts stem in part from memory failures but also from paying excessive attention to irrelevant or partially relevant attributes of objects.

When formal reasoning tasks are given to individuals of different ages, clear differences in performance are typically observed. Yet these findings do not necessarily mean that people become "more logical" as they develop. Younger and older children, for example, appear to have the same basic understanding of the meaning of "cause," but younger children perform more poorly because they have greater difficulty in detecting regular relations between events when distraction is present. Similarly, young children have been found to be just as consistent as adolescents in dealing with propositions. However, the younger children interpret the propositions in different and simpler ways, thus making more responses which are considered errors by adult standards.

chapter eleven

SOLVING LIFE'S PROBLEMS WITH COGNITIVE PSYCHOLOGY

outline

THIS BOOK HAS TAKEN US on a long and sometimes difficult journey. We have seen how the human information-processing system converts environmental information to a form which permits the execution of mental operations. After perceptual registration of information, the following processes usually occur. First, the information is held veridically for some brief period of time in sensory memory. Very rapidly, however, the information must be matched somehow with the subject's knowledge of the world, presumably retrieved from long-term memory. This matching process is what we know as pattern recognition, that is, the comprehension and interpretation of the current situation, or at least that part which has been selected for focal attention. We have seen how meaningful information is then used consciously for a variety of purposes. Information that is acted upon almost immediately requires little processing and as a consequence is quickly forgotten, that is, lost from short-term memory. Other items of information may be rehearsed or recirculated so as to persist through a time delay for later use. Finally, the third mode involves rehearsing and processing so as to make the information more durable and to assimilate it into the rest of our knowledge of the world. In general, information is used for purposes of making decisions about how to react to the world. Very often, those decisions require going beyond the information given. Thus, based on what we perceive, human beings produce a variety of sophisticated behavioral products, among which are the formulation of reasonable inferences, the attainment and use of concepts, and the acts of problem solving and creativity.

Our presentation of this material has been relatively abstract, scientific, and theoretical. The reader may well wonder whether the results of this basic research have any application at all to the real world. We believe the answer to that question is yes. As yet, however, there have been relatively few applications. This, of course, is partly attributable to the relative newness of the field of cognitive psychology. Nonetheless, some applications have been made and others are fairly predictable for the immediate future. We shall discuss a sample of these applications in the following pages.

Our sample can conveniently be divided into four areas of application. Under implications for other professions, we discuss some real and possible uses of cognitive psychology in the practice of law and in commercial advertising. Regarding public safety, we consider the problems people have perceiving and understanding emergency instructions and road signs. Educational applications are perhaps the most prominent in cognitive psychology and, to illustrate, we review some possible guidelines for improving memory, reading ability, and comprehension of lecture and textual material. Finally, we consider the clinical implications of cognitive psychology, summarizing some very recent work on the thought processes of schizophrenic patients.

IMPLICATIONS FOR OTHER PROFESSIONS

THE LAW

THE ROLE OF EXPECTATIONS.   One fall afternoon in the late 1950s a hunting party of five men started out to shoot some deer. While driving through a soggy field, their car became stuck in the snow. Two of the men left for a nearby farmhouse to seek help, while the others remained near the car. Unknown to those by the car, one of the two men on his way to the farmhouse decided that two men were not needed for that job, and that he would let his friend go on while he tried to find a deer or two. The man forged through the field and ended up on the other side of the car from the farmhouse. One of the men who had stayed by the car saw something moving and remarked, "That's a deer, isn't it?" to which his friend agreed. The first man shot at the deer, apparently successfully, since the deer pitched forward and uttered a cry. The men heard that cry as the cry of a deer, and fired another shot. A third shot brought the deer to the ground for good, whereupon the men ran toward it. Only then did they see that it was not a deer they had shot, but—tragically—it was their companion. (Sommer, 1959).

Set or expectation clearly played a role in this episode, just as it can in the perception of an ambiguous laboratory stimulus. The hunters who eagerly scanned the landscape for a deer perceived the moving object as a deer. "In my thoughts and my eyes, it was a deer," remarked one of the men at the court case arising from the incident. Yet a policeman testified that when he later observed a man under the same conditions, knowing it was a man, he perceived the object as a man. Again, an expectation.

A cognitive psychologist was asked to testify at the trial. He gave a description of how a person's past experience will affect his perception of the world. The psychologist based his testimony on published research concerning the role of needs and expectations. We have already reviewed some of the relevant research in Chapter 3. Recall the experiment by Allport and Postman (1958), who asked subjects to take a brief look at a drawing of several people on a subway train, including a black man who was holding nothing and a white man who was holding a razor, and then to describe the scene to another subject who had not seen it. The typical report relayed by the last of several subjects in succession had the black man holding the razor. This result is due to expectancy; in our society there is a greater expectation that a black man will carry a razor than a white man.

The role of expectations can also be seen in the results of an experiment by Bruner and Postman (1949). These investigators showed subjects a display of playing cards for a few seconds and asked them to report the number of aces of spades in the display (see Figure 11-1). After a brief glance, most subjects reported that they saw three aces of spades. Actually, there were five, however two of them were colored red. People are used to black aces of spades; when they see something that is red, they apparently dismiss it immediately, without careful inspection. Occasionally a subject would give a "compromise response," such as calling the red spade "purple" or "rusty black." In other words the subjects occasionally remembered the color in such a way as to make it more in keeping with, or nearer to,

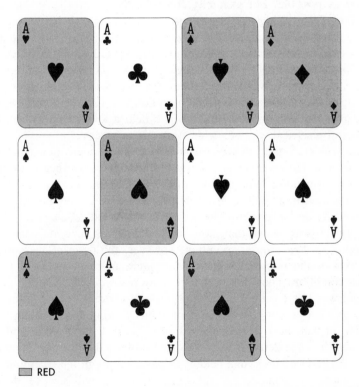

◻ RED

FIGURE 11-1. Glance briefly. How many aces of spaces did you see? Most people report seeing three, whereas actually there are five. (From results by Bruner & Postman, 1949. Figure from R. Buckhout. Eyewitness testimony. Copyright *Scientific American, Inc.,* 1974, *231*(6), p. 25.) All rights reserved.

normal expectations about what colors go with what suits. This classic experiment shows the important role that prior experience or expectancy has on what we perceive and recall.

It becomes important to ask whether or not the experimental situations are exact analogues of the natural conditions to which we attempt to generalize. For instance, do the laboratory manipulations of set or expectation correspond to the expectations experienced by a hunter who shoots a man, mistaking him for a deer. Do the manipulations of stress in a research setting correspond to the stress experienced by the victim of a mugging? For the most part our attitude toward generalizing from laboratory settings to natural situations is optimistic. We assume that the feelings and experiences of a subject in a laboratory situation will be at least similar to those of a person in his natural environment. However, we recognize that the two situations are far from identical.

Some psychologists have attempted to make their laboratory research as realistic as possible. For example, Johnson and Scott (1976) sought to study the effects of high or low arousal on a person's ability to remember the details of an incident he had witnessed. In the high arousal condition the witness, a naive subject who innocently waited alone in a reception room for an experiment to begin, overheard an increasingly acrimonious interaction between two people in the next room. The altercation ended with one of the two bursting into the reception room shouting, "He wouldn't let me go," and exiting. His hands, which held a knife, were covered with blood, and electrical wires dangled from his upperarm.

The witness in the low arousal condition also waited alone in the reception room. However, in this condition the witness overheard a dull and routine conversation between two individuals in the next room. One of them appeared momentarily with grease on his hands, holding a pen. He remarked, "Too bad the machine broke," and exited.

Overall, it was shown that more information was accurately recalled in the high than low arousal condition; however, the descriptions and identifications of the man leaving the room were more accurate in the low arousal condition. There are probably many reasons why the description of the man was less accurate in the high arousal condition. One is that most of the subjects spent a good deal of their viewing time looking at the weapon; in fact, nearly all of the subjects recalled the weapon and could describe it in some detail. The low arousal subjects did not pay much attention to the pen that their man held as he passed through the reception room. Other aspects of this study, although important, will not be discussed further. One should note, however, the great lengths that the experimenters went to in order to create a laboratory situation in which genuine stress was felt by their subjects. You might wish to consider the problems of ethics engendered by this kind of experiment. For example, was there a threat of physical or psychological harm to subjects? How should subjects be debriefed after such an experience?

IDENTIFICATION OF CRIMINALS.   As we have seen, at least one factor, namely stress, affects a person's ability to describe and identify people he or she has seen before. This factor may have played a role in the plight of Assistant District Attorney, William Schrager, whose car stalled one night in Queens, New York (*Time,* April 2, 1973). Two policemen saw Schrager near his car, behaving "suspiciously" and so they approached him. They noticed that he fit the description of a man being sought in connection with a series of sexual assaults, and when he failed to produce identification, they took him to the police station. Schrager was then placed in several lineups, usually with policemen who were bigger than he was. To his horror, he was identified by four women who claimed that he had molested them. Fortunately, a similar-looking postman soon confessed to some of the crimes with which Schrager had been charged, and Schrager was released from custody. Schrager's only "crime" was that he happened to look like someone who had a penchant for molesting women. A similar set of circumstances occurred in the cases of Lawrence Berson and George Morales, who happened to look like a gypsy cab driver named Richard Carbone. Carbone was eventually convicted of a number of crimes for which the other two had been charged.

The experience of a witness in a lineup is similar to the experience of a subject in a recognition memory experiment. In the memory experiment, a subject may first be presented with a list of stimuli (for example, a list of words or objects). Later, he may be presented with a different set of stimuli from which he must choose the one(s) he saw before. In a lineup, the witness is presented with a set of people, one of whom is the police suspect, and he is asked to recognize the person he saw committing the crime. Obviously, the composition of a lineup is extremely important. If the lineup has only two people in it, the witness has a 50 percent chance of picking out the suspect simply by guessing. With three people, the suspect has a 33 percent chance of being chosen by the witness. Thus, there should be a reasonable number of people in the lineup so that if a witness were merely guessing he would have only a small probability of picking out the suspect. Furthermore, the witness must have the opportunity to respond, "None of these."

It is also important that the people in the lineup other than the suspect be similar in appearance to the suspect. If this is not the case, the witness may be able to reject all of the other characters in the lineup as implausible and to pick the suspect by default. This is analogous to presenting a subject with a list of words and giving the following recognition test: 4, 9, horse, 781. Clearly, the subject can choose the correct response by default.

FIGURE 11–2. Lineup similar to the one used in a small town in Michigan to test a witness who had described a black assailant.

This may seem like a trivial point, but it was apparently not appreciated by at least one policeman who formed a lineup like the one in Figure 11-2. The lineup was used to test a witness to a crime who had described the suspect as being a black male. The witness identified the black member of the lineup. When asked why he created this particular lineup, the policeman claimed that the crime had been committed in a small town with hardly any blacks and he wanted a lineup that was "representative" of the town. Much of what psychologists have learned about recognition memory tests could be applied to the construction of lineups. Properly constructed lineup tests could then be fairly used to provide evidence of when a witness recognizes a suspect, and to exonerate the suspect when the witness does not.

COMMERCIAL ADVERTISING

If you lived in Los Angeles, you might one evening find yourself invited to a plush 400-seat Sunset Boulevard theater known as "Preview House." This is the home of a service called Audience Studies Incorporated (ASI), which tests commercials and shows to determine whether they should be released nationally. Your evening might begin by viewing a 30-year-old "Mister Magoo" cartoon, which you would evaluate using a sophisticated device. The device is a dial marked "very dull, dull, normal, good, very good," which you can adjust any number of times while watching the show. The Magoo show is simply for making sure that the audience is reacting "normally" to what is being presented. After Magoo, you might be shown a series of commercials, each of which you would evaluate using the same dialing device. Audience reactions are automatically tabulated, by computer, into a chart showing a commercial's moment-by-moment peak spots and lulls. Separate charts are also computed for men versus women, and for various age categories, since advertisers usually like to know these things. These response data are then supplemented by written questionnaires and oral interviews. Finally, some respondents are permitted to enter the ASI "grocery store" with coupons they can use for purchasing various items in stock. ASI's composite evaluation thus predicts not only what people will remember from a commercial but what effects a commercial will have on people's attitudes and their buying behavior.

Among other results, the techniques used by ASI reveal that people remember things about commercials that were never expressed in those commercials. This is to be expected from all we have been saying about the normal human information-processing system. Let us backtrack a moment to the psychological laboratory.

Recall that Bartlett (1932) presented his subjects with complex stories to be remembered, and found that subjects often included information not presented in the original stories, while deleting other information that had been presented. For example, a subject might have actually read, "That Indian has been hit," but recalled it as either "An Indian was wounded by an arrow" or "An Indian was shot." In other words, the subjects themselves supplied additional information about how the Indian was hit even though this was not actually presented to them. Over 40 years later, researchers were able to observe the same inference-making behavior. Subjects in one study heard a passage about a person named John who was pounding a nail in order to fix a bird house and later falsely recognized a statement suggesting that John was using a hammer to fix the bird house. The original passage said nothing about a hammer; John could have been using his shoe. But subjects recalled a "hammer" that they themselves had supplied (Johnson, Bransford, & Solomon, 1973).

The Federal Trade Commission, the main government body charged with regulating advertising, explicitly forbids advertisers from making false assertions about a product; to do so would make them liable for misrepresentation and could result in a costly legal battle. However, some advertisers manage to design commercials without making manifestly false assertions, yet in such a way as to cause viewers to come up with false inferences. If people remember these inferences as statements of fact, advertisers can still achieve their goal without subjecting themselves to prosecution. Do people remember inferences as fact? This issue was studied in a recent experiment by Richard Harris (Harris & Monaco, 1978) who presented mock commercials like the following:

"Wouldn't it be great," asks the mother, "if you could make him cold-proof? Well, you can't. Nothing can do that. (Boy sneezes.) But there is something that you can do that may help. Have him gargle with Listerine Antiseptic. Listerine can't promise to keep him cold-free, but it may help him fight off colds. During the cold-catching season, have

him gargle twice a day with full-strength Listerine. Watch his diet, see he gets plenty of sleep, and there's a good chance he'll have fewer colds, milder colds this year."

Subjects who listened to this and other mock commercials had to report on the claims made for each product. Every subject tested on the mock Listerine commercial believed that gargling with the antiseptic would help prevent colds. This occurred despite the use of disclaimers and hedges such as "can't promise" and "may help." The message from Harris' work is clear: People remember their inferences as if they were fact. He further found that this occurs even when people are explicitly *warned* about the pitfalls of interpreting implied advertising claims as asserted fact. The experiment used 120 subjects who heard a list of 20 mock commercials and afterwards were asked to evaluate a list of 40 statements of product claims as true, false, or of indeterminate truth value. Half the subjects received introductory instructions explicitly warning them about implied advertising and encouraging them to watch out for it. The warning began:

"As you listen to these commercials, be careful that you do not interpret implied information as fact. Some people, including advertisers trying to sell products, will not state a claim directly as asserted fact but rather will only strongly imply that the particular claim is true. You may infer that the advertiser has said something about his product which in fact he has only suggested, but he has suggested it in such a way that it is very easy for you to naturally, obviously, and normally expect the claim to be true."

Extensive examples were then given, and finally the subjects were tested. With a delayed test (given after all 20 mock commercials were presented), the warning had no effect at all. Subjects still evaluated implications as if they were true assertions (Harris, Teske, Bruno, & Hall, 1976).

It has been argued that effective advertising must have a *unique selling proposition* (Reeves, 1961). In other words, the product must claim benefits that its competitors do not offer. But a product's "uniqueness" need not be explicitly asserted in order for it to be "read into" a commercial. Take the example of an advertising campaign generated for Schlitz Brewery (Mayer, 1958) which used the slogan "washed with live steam." The slogan referred to the fact that Schlitz used a steam bath to wash the bottles before they were filled with beer. But "washing with live steam" was the standard industry-wide procedure, used at every brewery! The advertisement never explicitly stated that the process was unique to Schlitz, yet clearly it implied this uniqueness, with remarkably successful benefits to Schlitz.

So we are faced with the problem that certain kinds of advertising messages might imply information that is not literally true. A problem arises in that not all messages are potentially deceptive for all people. If a message misleads 50 percent of the people, should it be expressly forbidden? What if it misleads only 20 percent? What if only 5 percent? These are very difficult decisions that the Federal Trade Commission grapples with daily.

CONTRIBUTIONS TO PUBLIC SAFETY

EMERGENCY INSTRUCTIONS

When you were younger, you probably participated in fire drills at your school. Bells sounded and teachers instructed students about where to go and what to do. Despite the fact that this was actually a complex information-processing situation, the teacher probably did not spend much time determining which words to use to best convey the message. Rather he or she probably just did and said what "felt right."

Psychologists have recently become more analytical about instructions. They are now beginning to ask about the best way to present information to a person so that it will be comprehended quickly and easily and the subject will act upon it errorlessly. This becomes exceedingly important in emergency situations where people must react without delay.

Two projects are relevant to this discussion of messages. The first (File & Jew, 1973) is a study of airline passengers who were presented with emergency landing instructions while in an airport awaiting the call of their holiday flight. They were approached by an experimenter and, if they agreed to participate, were told that they would be presented with instructions concerning the procedure to be adopted following an emergency in flight. They were asked to try to remember as much as possible, and told that they would be given five minutes to write down all the details they could recall.

The passage used was about 200 words long, containing 25 details, and was closely based on the actual instructions used by the airline. Some subjects were presented with only affirmative statements while others were presented with negative statements. For example, the affirmative group might be given the first set of instructions, while the negative group received the second.

1. Extinguish cigarettes. Remove all sharp objects from your person. When using the slides, remove your shoes, straighten your legs and place hands on knees.
2. Do not leave cigarettes lighted. Do not leave any sharp objects on your person. When using the slides do not keep your shoes on, do not bend knees nor fail to place hands on knees.

The investigators found that performance was significantly worse when the instructions were in the negative than when they were in the affirmative.

This result agrees with the earlier laboratory work of Mehler (1963) who showed that in a rote-learning task subjects recalled active affirmative sentences better than those involving negatives.

Our second example involves emergency instructions in a high-rise office building (Keating & Loftus, 1977). Serious fires in high-rise buildings are unfortunately not rare enough. For example, in January, 1970, a fire in the Conrad Hilton hotel in Chicago claimed two lives and hospitalized 36 people. That same year, a fire in the 50-story New York Plaza building killed two people and injured 30 while causing almost 10 million dollars worth of damage (Sharry, 1974). The important question is, What types of instructions are most effective in eliciting desired responses during emergencies?

Take the case of the 37-floor Seattle Federal Building. Before this building was finished, the basic hardware of a fire-safety system was installed and several important decisions were made. For example, officials decided that total evacuation of the building would be dangerous as well as impractical; instead "area evacuation" was recommended, which meant that during fires only the affected and adjacent floors of the building would be evacuated. The evacuation plan required the use of a public-address component capable of broadcasting pre-recorded taped directions to communicate with building occupants who might be affected by a fire.

FIGURE 11–3.   In the Seattle Federal Building, psychologists designed the emergency messages use to communicate with people in case of a fire or other emergency.

Psychologists were called upon to help design the messages. Relying on basic research to guide them, the following message was designed to communicate with occupants of the 12th floor should a fire erupt there:

(Female voice) *"May I have your attention please. May I have your attention please."*
(Male voice) *"There has been a fire reported on the 12th floor. While this report is being verified, the building manager would like you to proceed to the stairways and walk down to the 10th floor. Wait on the 10th floor for further instructions. Please do not use the elevators, as they may be needed. Please do not use the elevators, but proceed to the stairways."*

Several aspects of the message should be noted. First, the message is introduced by a female voice, and the instructions themselves are delivered by a male voice. Research suggests that switching from a female to a male voice will be noticed even when people are not really paying attention (Cherry, 1953; Cherry & Taylor, 1954).[1]

Note that the message tells the occupants (1) exactly what has happened, (2) what they are to do, and (3) why they should not use the elevators. All essential instructions are stated twice: two times it is pointed out that the occupants should proceed to the stairways, that the 10th floor is the place to go, and that the elevators should not be used. Numerous research studies have shown that repetition facilitates understanding and recall.

One further application of research: The message contains relatively common words. The reason for this decision is that empirical studies have revealed that words that are used commonly in the language are also more easily understood (Howes, 1957). This point has been included in one authoritative source, the *Human Engineering Guide to Equipment Design* (1972), which states "other things being equal, the more frequently a word occurs in everyday usage, the more readily it is correctly identified when transmitted over a speech communication system" (p. 219). These, then, are a few of the decisions that were made by the psychologists working on these messages, along with the rationale for these decisions. It should be evident from these illustrations that the possibilities are infinite for the use of psychological research in the naturalistic environments involving communication of instructions.

[1] One might reasonably ask why a male voice did not introduce a female, since Cherry's work shows that the switch is noticed in both directions. The reason the psychologists decided on their plan is that, at this stage in our society, males are stereotypically looked to as the ones who take charge in an emergency. Relying on this stereotype, however unjustified it may be, a male voice was recommended for most of the directional delivery.

Anyone who has driven an automobile through an unfamiliar city knows the confusion that road signs can generate. At first, the route you wish to take is clearly marked and moments later you are hopelessly lost—a sign has misled you, or there was no sign where there should have been, or you failed to see a sign that would have pointed you in the right direction. These occasions are truly frustrating, though understandable in terms of what we know about the human organism's ability to process visual information. Indeed, it is entirely possible that making effective use of theory and research from cognitive psychology might allow our city traffic engineers and highway designers to provide a system of signs that would minimize problems of this sort.

PROCESSING LIMITS. The human organism has a "limited channel capacity." We can focus our attention and process only a fraction of the amount of information that the environment provides. As George Miller (1956) has so effectively argued, we deal with only seven (plus or minus two) items of information at any given time. In the rapidly changing environment presented to the automobile operator, most information cannot be processed at all. So what is the operator aware of? How does he select from what is available?

For one thing, a driver probably gets, at best, but a single glance at each road sign. Those signs that he does look at are registered, briefly, as we know, in sensory memory. Thus, he has access to the information he has seen for at least some short time beyond stimulation. This is fortunate, for it takes time to process registered information depending on how much there is of it. Spoken language constitutes an analogous example: To understand it, speech must not be accelerated beyond six words per second (which is, of course, faster than most people can talk). Similarly, a sequence of words or of pictures flashed before the eyes will be incomprehensible at rates faster than six per second. It simply takes that much time (and usually more) for the information to "sink in" and become understood. It is, of course, possible to see things without processing them to the level of understanding. We do this all the time, thank goodness, for otherwise we might be overwhelmed by the amount of information available to us from the environment. To understand a given aspect of the environment, such as a sign, however, requires further processing, beyond mere registration of the information. Incidentally, it is interesting to note that the eyes themselves manage this problem of processing time by a controlled rate of fixations at about three per second.

It should be noted that two factors are operative on whether a person

---

[2] This section is based on a technical report written by Mary C. Potter (1972). The authors wish to thank Dr. Potter for her generous permission to use this report.

will understand a sequence of visual events—the time that each is in view *and* the characteristics of the preceding and following events. If you catch a glimpse of a sign followed by a view of a long blank wall, your chances of seeing, recognizing, and understanding the sign are much greater than if it was followed by another sign or some other form of visual confusion. As we know from the studies of visual masking, succeeding stimuli can erase the iconic representation we must often rely on in order to process the information from a transitory stimulus. If another sign comes along immediately, it masks the icon, leaving us with no record of what had been seen previously. Thus, it seems plausible to make the following recommendations. The speed of one's travel down the street must be governed both by the number of signs that need to be fixated in order to understand an instruction and by the time characteristics of the human processing system. Signs that are critical to all travelers such as route markers, posted speed limits, and the like should be separated from other signs which offer potential masks by a sufficient distance so as to allow for complete processing of the icon.

SELECTIVE ATTENTION. Have you ever been to a cocktail party and tried to attend selectively to a single speaker in the midst of many surrounding conversations? Selective attention allows us to process the target message for its meaning or content. In other words, we can comprehend what is being said by a particular person despite a variety of equally loud competitors. We use this ability to focus attention on a single channel while driving, for example, to watch for route markers to the interstate highway. We actually key in certain physical characteristics shared by these markers, just as we key in specific physical characteristics of a speaker's voice as a guide to his or her message.

It is well known, however, that surrounding messages are not completely blocked out; instead they are attenuated and are monitored at some level not as deep as primary messages. We have reviewed a variety of experiments in support of this fact. For example, if the listener's name is mentioned in one of the surrounding conversations, the listener usually recognizes it, indicating that more than just the auditory noise of surrounding conversations gets through to his central processor. Likewise, in the case of signs. We search for a particular type of sign, say, the one that marks the route. Nonetheless, other signs will break into awareness, depending upon their physical and semantic characteristics. A bright or moving sign, for example, or one that has particular meaning, may impinge upon our attention. One would notice a sign that had his or her name on it. Even while searching for route markers we might notice a restaurant sign if we were hungry. Thus, there is a degree of competition for focused attention.

According to Neisser, information is processed in two ways. Upon initial input, a broad, relatively indiscriminate, somewhat primitive process takes in a large quantity of information simultaneously. This is a preattentive process roughly corresponding to our dim awareness of a multiplicity of things going on around us which we are not really concerned about. Most of this material, according to Neisser, is simply forgotten as soon as it disappears from sensory memory. A small part of it, however, achieves our focal attention and gets a detailed analysis. This is the information that leads to comprehension and to memory. Thus, a small change in a familiar sign might go unnoticed for months, although you "see" the sign every day. Finally, on some occasion when your mind is momentarily blank, you look at the sign and comprehend for the first time that it no longer says "Fred's Fresh Fish" but rather "Fred's Fresh Fruits."

When one searches for a particular sign the principles of visual search apply. Basically, what this means is that the sign will be found more quickly and more accurately to the extent that it is discriminable from its surroundings or context. But there is a tradeoff. The very attributes that make a sign detectable, such as its dissimilarity from other signs, make it a strong competitor for attention and thus a potent distractor when the search is for a different sign.

MEMORY. Pictures are easier to remember than words. Thus, when the situation calls for remembering a particular sign, as for example, the sign of a drug store you wish to return to, it is probably better if the sign contains a pictograph rather than merely the name. Pictures and scenes cannot be rehearsed in the same sense as words, so perhaps it is fortunate that they are relatively easy to remember. Yet even pictures take time to be fixed in memory. One experiment found that, although pictures can be seen clearly and understood when shown at a rate of four per second, recognition memory for those pictures, only a few minutes later, is poor (Potter & Levy, 1969). Since the eyes fix on a new place about three times a second, even things that you just looked at a minute or two ago may not look familiar as you glance again. Thus, whether a picture will be remembered depends very much on the total time spent looking at it. The number of different occasions that it is seen is also an important factor. You are more likely to remember a face or a sign that you see for 10 seconds on six different occasions than one that you look at for 1 minute without interruption, other things being equal. Remembering, of course, means different things. Recalling something, that is, bringing it into mind on demand, is usually far more difficult than recognizing something as familiar when you see it again. You can probably recognize the sign of the store you are looking for when you see it, even after just one visit. But it may take many visits before you can describe it clearly to someone else.

Making a sign memorable means making it fit in easily with things we already know. Indeed, as we have seen in earlier chapters, most of what we learn is really a matter of accommodating new material to existing memorial or organizational structures. Thus, in the construction of a sign, it is well recommended that you (1) make the sign at least in part pictorial, (2) make it fit the situation which it is designed to represent, and (3) make it meaningful in the sense that it fits in with things the individual already knows. Thus, we might recommend that Fred construct his message in the form of a bowl of fruit, perhaps along the lines shown in Figure 11-4.

APPLICATIONS TO EDUCATION

READING

Right now, you are engaged in one of the most complex and fascinating cognitive, information-processing activities one can imagine. From the marks on this page, you are extracting and constructing meaning, quickly and possibly automatically. Reading might be the most important cognitive skill people in a modern society develop. Over the years, many

FIGURE 11–4.

attempts have been made to find the "best" method of reading and of reading instruction—without a great deal of success. Recently, however, cognitive scientists have begun to analyze the processes involved in reading, using methods like those employed in the study of other cognitive activities. While we are still quite far from a complete understanding of reading, some interesting findings and ideas have emerged from this effort.

CHARACTERISTICS OF SKILLED READING. It is important to recognize that "reading" refers to a number of component skills, which can change in kind and content with practice. People "read" differently depending on whether they are scanning a page to find the score of a baseball game, relaxing with a novel, skimming a magazine article to grasp the general idea, or studying for an important examination. Furthermore, for the skilled reader, reading just seems to happen, in marked contrast to the beginning reader who might proceed one step at a time.

Several important changes are known to take place as reading skill develops. Particular processes, such as recognizing a letter, identifying a word, or retrieving the meaning of a word, are accomplished increasingly more accurately and more rapidly. LaBerge and Samuels (1974) have emphasized that fluent reading depends on rapid, automatic processing. The stress on automatic processing rests squarely on the notion that a person has a limited capacity for (consciously) processing information. If a person must devote attention to a lower-level process, for example, identifying a word, fewer resources are available for higher-level semantic processing. Thus it is not at all unusual for a beginning reader to work rather laboriously through material on a word-for-word basis, reaching the end of a sentence with little or no idea of its overall meaning. LaBerge and Samuels suggest that the development of automaticity should receive greater emphasis in reading instruction. Thus, they recommend that practice on a subskill should continue until a reasonable level of automaticity can be demonstrated. Only when the lower-level skill is fully automatic will enough processing capacity be available for the next developmental level. Ordinary reading instruction emphasizes accuracy, which tends to make students work slowly to avoid errors. LaBerge and Samuels suggest that automaticity is so important that students should be deliberately encouraged to engage in rapid processing even if doing so means that a few more errors are made during practice.

Skilled reading is a highly integrated activity, and it seems that normal and poor readers differ in degree of integration of subskills at every point in reading development. Guthrie (1973) compared normal and poor readers on a variety of subskills. In terms of reading comprehension, both groups were at the second-grade level, but the normal readers were second graders (average age of 7 years) while the poor readers averaged 9 years of age. Guthrie examined performance of these groups on such tasks as pronouncing words with long or short vowels, pronouncing consonant clusters (*sp, th*) or nonsense words (*kif*), all based on visual presentation, as well as "opposites," in which the child had to select from visual alternatives to match spoken items. The difference between the two groups was *not* so much in terms of achievement on any single subtest but rather in terms of the patterns of scoring across tests. For the normal readers, performance across tests was highly correlated—the various subskills developed in an interdependent fashion. In contrast, performance levels across tests for poor readers were more independent. In effect, the poor reader suffers from mismatched subskill development and inadequate integration of subskills.

In addition to perfecting and organizing component processes, acquiring reading skill can allow a person to eliminate certain steps in extracting meaning from the written symbol. Consider the following example. Young children are able to respond to most common objects before they acquire the appropriate spoken labels. Subsequently, they learn the connection between an object and a picture of it or its spoken name. At that point, a child has a meaning which can be accessed when, for example, a real table, a picture of a table, or the spoken word *table* is encountered. Getting the meaning of a *printed* word, which is what is required in reading, involves, at the beginning level, an extra skill, called phonological encoding. Skilled readers, however, can retrieve meaning directly from the visual information; phonological encoding is not necessary and therefore meaning is arrived at in a more direct fashion. Over years of practice, the phonological step simply drops out of the reading process.

LEARNING TO READ.   At this point, a first-grade teacher might be moved to comment, "Well, you've convinced me (as if I needed it) that becoming a skilled reader is a great idea, but what about beginning readers? Where and how do you start?" Fair questions. While research on reading is not nearly sufficient to devise the "ideal" method for reading instruction, researchers feel that useful guidelines are becoming available. For example, consider the question of what unit to start with. The smallest unit seems to be the individual letter, so perhaps one should begin with lots of work on identifying individual letters, learning "the sound that each letter makes," before going to larger units. This does not appear to be a good idea (Gibson, 1975). People don't read letter by letter. If you read this way, you would be unable to make *any* sense out of the following

T—e q—ck br—wn d—g r—c—d p—st th— cl—msy k—tt—n.

Emphasizing letters in isolation can be misleading because letters occur in contexts and combinations in printed language. The English language has certain correspondences between the rules for spoken and written material, but the rules are not simple letter–sound relations. Consider the sound of *t* in such words as *cat, the,* and *motion.* Clearly, the "*t* sound" is not constant but varies with context. Training must adequately represent such variability. Thus a child who is taught to pronounce *bad, bat, pan, pat* will have more trouble when encountering *bit, bite, pin, pine* than one who is initially trained with *man, mane, fat, fate.* Fortunately, the latter, variable training seems to be no more difficult (Ackerman, 1973).

Perfetti and Hogaboam (1975) studied the relation between reading comprehension and single-word decoding. Comprehension tests were used to identify good and poor readers in both the third and fifth grades; all subjects were given the task of pronouncing visually presented "words," which included words of high and low frequency and pronounceable non-words such as *krip.* The researchers were interested in how long it would take students to begin their pronunciation. As shown in Figure 11-5, there was only a slight difference between good and poor readers for high-frequency, familiar words. The good readers were much faster, however, when low-frequency words and non-words were presented. It took relatively little time for anyone to begin pronouncing familiar words because the students simply knew how to pronounce them, as "whole items." Low-frequency words and non-words were treated differently, however, and depended more on what the student knew about spelling-sound rules. The data indicate that good readers were better able to use such knowledge *automatically.* As Perfetti and Hogaboam, as well as Samuels and LaBerge point out, the fact that poor readers must devote more effort to decoding words means that they will have less processing capacity available for comprehension.

One popular method used in teaching beginning reading is the "whole-word" method, which may be contrasted with methods stressing spelling-sound correspondence rules. The weakness of the whole-word method is that, having learned to pronounce a number of words as separate items, the student has learned little or nothing that will help in decoding new words (Gibson, 1975). It has been stated with justification that whole-word training produces poor readers.

HYPOTHESIS BEHAVIOR AND READING. Printed language has many structural constraints which, if used properly, can aid reading. Spelling rules define allowable sequences and provide constraints. In addition, there are statistical redundancies which can provide clues. Within words, some letter combinations occur more often than others, and certain letters are more likely to be found in some locations than others. Good readers are more sensitive to such constraints, which has been shown by having readers scan letter sequences to determine if a target letter was or was not included. The

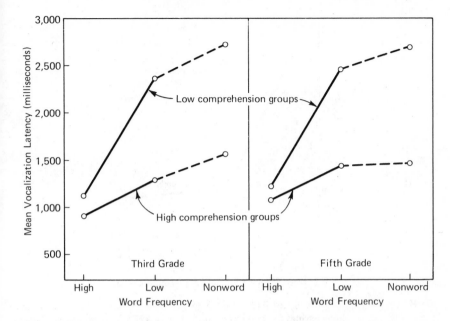

FIGURE 11–5. Pronunciation latencies of good and poor readers for words and nonwords. (From Figure 1 in Perfetti & Hogaboam, 1975. Reprinted by permission of the author and American Psychological Association.)

sequences were either words (such as *seldom*), non-words with the letters in likely positions (*somled*), or non-words in unlikely positions (*sdelmo*). Good readers scan structured sequences (*seldom, somled*) much faster than poor readers; with unlikely sequences (*sdelmo*), good and poor readers do not differ much at all (see Figure 11-6). Good readers seem more sensitive to structural constraints, even with novel materials (Mason, 1975). Responding to such constraints allows a reader to process material more rapidly—eventually, automatically—and frees attention for comprehension.

Let's look closer at exactly what is involved in using constraints. The reader must in some way form and test hypotheses about future information. That information can be about letters and letter sequences yet to appear in a word or about words that will occur later in a sentence. It is important to encourage beginning readers to adopt such a hypothesis-testing approach. First graders who are instructed to look for spelling patterns in training materials show better transfer than those who receive no special instructions or those who are told what the spelling patterns are (Gibson, 1975). Samuels, Dahl, and Archwamety (1974) found that substituting hypothesis training for a part of regular reading instruction for poor readers in the third grade was very helpful. Their training procedure is inter-

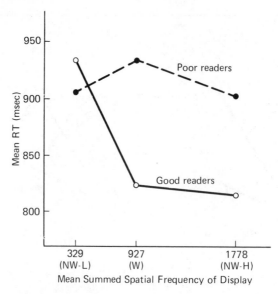

FIGURE 11–6. Mean time to decide that a target letter is not included in a six-letter string, for good and poor readers. (NW-L = non-word, letters in unlikely positions; W = word; NW-H = non-word, letters in likely positions). (From Figure 1 in Mason, 1975. Reprinted by permission of author and American Psychological Association.)

esting in the sense that it required no single correct answer. Rather, the students were trained to make sensible predictions. For example, the student might be asked to complete a sentence like "My mother sleeps on her _____," with any sensible answer accepted. The training also stressed *rapid* responding. Hypothesis training resulted in both faster word recognition and better scores on a comprehension test, compared either to no special training or to extensive practice on rapid word recognition.

While we still have much to learn about basic processes in reading, useful guidelines have emerged. It is important to identify the component processes in reading, since comprehension suffers if any subskill is inadequately developed. Students need to learn about the structural aspects of printed language in such a way that the skills they acquire will transfer to new materials and allow automatic processing. From the beginning, students should be encouraged to develop an active, hypothesis-testing approach to reading.

PROCESSING INFORMATION IN TEXTBOOKS AND LECTURES

College students are all too familiar with textbooks and lectures. To a large extent, students lack control over the conditions under which they read, listen, and learn because they neither write the textbooks nor give the lectures. There are steps, however, that students can take to facilitate their learning from both of these sources of information.

Basically the students' task is to extract the "right" information from the text and to learn it well enough to perform successfully on tests given some time after reading. We can assume that college students have automated lower-level reading skills of the type discussed in the last section and can devote full attention to text comprehension. Still, it appears that the "average student's" study habits could be improved. While there are no magical methods for becoming an outstanding student, research findings do provide some helpful suggestions.

EXTRACTING INFORMATION FROM TEXTS. Poor grades are often attributed to inadequate study—the student who reads a chapter just once is unlikely to learn much. Yet, if left strictly to their own devices, students don't seem to improve much from repeatedly reading course material. Crouse (1974) allowed students to study material until they felt ready to take a test and to repeat the study-and-test cycle up to a total of five tests. The students showed virtually no improvement as a function of repeated study.

Students also underestimate how much they can learn from a text. In one study, students were given material to read and told that they would be tested on it; some students were told to read so that they would "do their best" on the test, while others were told to read so that they could score 90 percent correct on the test. Students given the higher goal both thought they would and really did score higher on the test, as shown in Table 11-1. Those given the higher goal studied longer when length of study time was optional, but the higher goal instructions also led to better performance when study time was controlled, indicating that setting the higher goal led in some sense to better processing of the material (LaPorte & Nath, 1976).

Learning from a text can be improved if the reader engages in appropriate activities before and after reading. Acquisition of text information is aided by utilizing those cues that provide advance information about the

TABLE 11–1. PERCENT CORRECT: SUBJECTS' ESTIMATES AND TEST SCORES. (FROM DATA IN TABLE 2, LAPORTE & NATH, 1976.)

Goal	Estimated Before Reading	Estimated After Reading	Test Performance
90% Correct	64%	58%	56%
"Do your best"	47%	38%	40%

content of the material (Glaser & Resnick, 1972). Such cues will be present in varying degrees from one text to another, and even from section to section, but there are some organizing cues that appear in any text. Before reading a chapter, a student would be well advised to examine the chapter outline and the chapter summary (if provided). Skimming the chapter, attending to section and paragraph headings, will also provide an idea of the structure of the material. Such activities prior to reading give the student a context for the material and provide some attention-directing clues. Similar ideas apply to reading smaller sections such as paragraphs—most paragraphs contain a sentence, often but not necessarily the first, which reasonably summarizes what the paragraph is about.

If a passage has been read through once, what can be done to improve learning and retention of the material? We have seen that merely reading it again probably will not help much, assuming, of course, that the first reading was an honest effort. A technique which does increase subsequent test performance is having students formulate questions about the material they have read. The student might ask himself questions, or work with another student, taking turns asking and answering questions about the material. In either case, students do better on those test items that relate to material studied via the question-answer technique (Frase & Schwartz, 1975). The trick is to construct (ask, answer) questions to cover as much of the material as possible and also to form networks among ideas presented in different places (sentences, paragraphs within a section) rather than merely to "parrot" textual material in a rote-learning manner. Generally, integrative questions have been found to facilitate retention more than simpler, rote-learning questions (Rickards & DiVesta, 1974).

EXTRACTING INFORMATION FROM LECTURES. Lectures present students with an information-processing task considerably different from reading a textbook. Whereas a textbook can be read at one's own pace, reviewed if desired, and need not be read exactly as ordered, a lecture occurs once with information presented at the rate chosen by the lecturer and with little or no opportunity for repetition. Of course, tape recording a lecture provides a student with a partial record (minus visual information) and some opportunity for review. However, for most students, comprehending a lecture presents a considerably more difficult information-processing task than reading a text over the same material.

What can students do to get more out of lectures? Overall, the students might have to educate the lecturer, subtlely of course. It has been found that, if students are given an idea of what they are expected to learn from a lecture before it begins, they do in fact learn more from it (Royer, 1977). If a lecturer does not spontaneously provide such advance information, students should for their own sakes ask for it—a couple of minutes properly spent at the beginning will make the lecture more useful to the students.

Note taking is the typical method of dealing with lectures. Look in on the typical lecture class and you will see most students diligently, perhaps feverishly, taking notes. Is all this effort worthwhile? It depends. Taking notes on what has been said and listening to what is being said compete for a person's limited resources for processing information. Rather than trying to listen and take notes "at the same time," it is better for students to listen for a time and then have a brief "blank period" in which to take notes (Aiken, Thomas, & Shennum, 1975). If a lecture proceeds too quickly and continuously, the lecturer could be asked to provide a few moments of silence on occasion in order that notes can be recorded. One might view the student who asks a lecturer to repeat something as committing a truly benevolent act—not only is the repetition useful for memory and comprehension, but also those students who do not need the repetition have an opportunity to catch up on note taking.

Note taking is a useful activity if (and perhaps only if) the notes are reviewed prior to taking a test. It might plausibly be suggested that the *act* of note taking itself is beneficial because it *could* result in deeper, more elaborate processing of the lecture material. This might not happen, however, especially if notes are largely verbatim records of lecture content. Students who take notes, possibly rewrite them in their own words, *and* most certainly review them prior to a test do score higher than either those who take no lecture notes or those who take notes but do not review them (Carter & Van Matre, 1975). Reviewing notes before a test obviously provides some repetition of the information in the notes and, in effect, shortens the retention interval for that information. In addition, reviewing notes might promote memory retrieval of lecture information not in the notes.

A sense of humor is positively regarded in our society. Lecturers often try to inject humor into their lectures, and students seem to like humorous lectures and lecturers. A little humor can have social benefits, but one might wonder whether humorous lectures are better or worse than serious lectures with respect to learning. Overall, injecting humor seems to have little impact on students' performance. Kaplan and Pascoe (1977) compared several versions of a lecture on personality theory and personality assessment. One version was serious; in a corresponding "lighter" version, humorous examples were used to illustrate the main concepts of the lecture; in a third version humorous comments were interjected that did not bear directly upon the concepts under discussion. The use of humorous examples of concepts tended to result in better test performance on questions related to those concepts but poorer performance on the remaining items. In terms of total test performance, the different versions were equivalent. These results suggest that a lecturer can effectively use humor to direct students' attention to important points in a lecture and to induce deeper processing of the target material. Doing so does not necessarily lead to better overall learning of lecture material, however.

Getting your instructors to cooperate in providing you with good lecture-learning opportunities will probably require tact and subtlety. The direct approach might work but runs the risk of offending an insecure lecturer who resents "being told how to teach by a student." One could try a less direct method such as leaving a memo titled "Suggestions to lecturers" in the instructor's mailbox, but mailboxes are constantly filled with memoranda, many of which are ignored. Since virtually everyone pays attention to presents, perhaps the best approach would be to give your instructors brand-spanking new copies of this book with a card cleverly placed in the appropriate pages.

POST-QUESTION: Why did the authors suggest giving your instructors a copy of this book? (After getting past "to sell more books," review the material to arrive at another answer).

IMPROVING MEMORY

Much of cognitive psychology today is the study of human memory. We have seen how theorists have analyzed memory into its sensory, short-term, and long-term components. We have taken note of the episodic, the semantic, and the procedural character of memory content. This enterprise is beginning to reveal both the structural and the functional aspects of human memory. It is fair to ask, at this point, whether anything in the information that has been uncovered through basic research can be applied to improve human memory. While it would be a misrepresentation to say that there is nothing left to be found out, it is nonetheless true that recommendations about memorizing can presently be made with confidence.

In an earlier day, we might have recommended repetition and rehearsal as the main tools for fixing a fact in memory. More recent evidence suggests, however, that rehearsal itself may not be sufficient to transfer an experience into long-term memory (Craik & Watkins, 1972). The current evidence suggests that deep and elaborate processing is what is required. To make something stick, you must truly understand it. To understand it is to make it fit in with what you already know. Therefore, if a memory is to last, it must somehow be integrated with one's current knowledge of the world.

How, in fact, can this be accomplished? There are certain well-known techniques that are effective, some of which we use without being aware of them. For example, you remember the number of days in each month by taking advantage of the mnemonic device of rhyming: "Thirty days hath September . . ." But there are more general and more easily used procedures. Suppose, as a classroom assignment, you have to remember a large number of pairs of items. For example, you might need to remember the basic products of each of several countries, the definitions of concepts in physics, or the English equivalents of words of a foreign language. One method you might use is based on imagery. Atkinson and Raugh (1975) examined an interactive imagery technique as a means for facilitating the acquisition of Russian vocabulary. They instructed subjects first to associate the spoken Russian word with an English word that sounded like it (or sounded like part of it). For example, the Russian word *zvonok,* meaning bell, is pronounced something like "zvahn-oak," with the emphasis on the last syllable. The Russian word for building (*zdanie*) is pronounced "zdawn-yeh," with the emphasis on the first syllable. The subject is told to form a mental image of the spoken word interacting with its English translation. In the case of bell, the subject might imagine a large oak tree with little brass bells for acorns. In the case of building, one could imagine the pink light of dawn reflected in the windows of a tall building.

While the method may seem a little awkward at first, it is easily mastered and used with great efficiency. Atkinson and Raugh found this technique to be highly effective, yielding a test score of 72 percent correct in comparison to 46 percent correct for a control procedure. In other studies, this imaginal elaboration method has been shown to improve recall by as much as 100 to 150 percent and it becomes increasingly more effective with larger sets of materials to be remembered and with longer retention intervals.

Similar success has been observed by having subjects weave a story around a list of items to be remembered. The narrative method is probably effective because the learner must provide an overall theme (derived from his semantic memory) for organizing the critical words.

An even more familiar organizational technique is provided by what is known as the method of loci. This method works by relating items to be remembered not to one another but rather to a standard list of familiar locations. The method of loci has been known since the time of the great Greek orators, who used it as a means of memorizing long and elaborate speeches which, at the time, for lack of materials, could not be written. To use the method of loci, you must first establish a list of images of places which are familiar to you, such as the distinctive locations you would visit while walking through your own house. You must be able to visualize clearly and to recite the different locations on your list without error. To learn any new set of items, you simply take a "mental walk" through your list of loci, placing successive items in your imagination at successive locations along the route. You should connect the items to their locations by visualizing some interaction between the item and something salient in each location. Then, when you need to recall the items, you simply take another mental walk along the route and "observe" the items that have been deposited there.

Again, the description sounds awkward. It would appear as if one is memorizing more than he really needs to. But the proof of the pudding is in the eating and experimental results demonstrate that the method of loci is a highly effective technique for remembering long lists. One man who developed the method of loci to a fine art was Luria's memory expert, S., whom we mentioned in Chapter 1.

The number of loci can be expanded more or less indefinitely according to your needs. Alternatively, the same loci can be used over and over again to learn new lists of items. No particular difficulty seems to be created by such multiple usages so long as you are interested primarily in the most recent set of items. But even if the same set of loci is used repeatedly for different lists, there is still a substantial advantage over any procedure which does not use this or a comparable organizational procedure. You might also recall that human memory is quite at ease in dealing with chunks of information. It is possible to connect not just a single item but a collection of items which can be grouped in some way with each locus.

Only a modest amount of what we do learn and remember in everyday affairs consists of things such as shopping lists or English equivalents of foreign words. For the most part we are not interested in verbatim learning but rather in comprehension and learning for substance. Lest our examples be misleading, we should note that mnemonic devices are valid for substance learning also. As we know, a written text can be analyzed into a collection of associated concepts or propositions (Kintsch, 1974). When we talk about learning the gist or the substance of something, we mean that the *ideas* in the material have been acquired, though not necessarily the word-for-word text. Human beings seem to reduce text automatically to a conceptual structure. This is part of what we learn when we learn how to read for understanding. The concepts contained in textual material are like individual items. They can be retained by connecting them with loci or by imposing some other organizational system. This, after all, is how the great Greek orators remembered their speeches—not word-for-word, but according to the sequence of concepts to be communicated. Thus, these memory techniques are probably much more general than they may appear on the surface.

There are those who have argued that skills in memorization ought to be taught early, just as skills in reading and writing are taught. Our educational system demands that students learn a lot of facts. We constantly use our reservoir of facts in daily life. Systematically applying the knowledge that we now have about learning and memory techniques should improve the skills of children so that fact memorizing becomes a less time-consuming process. By the strategic use of memory techniques, we should be

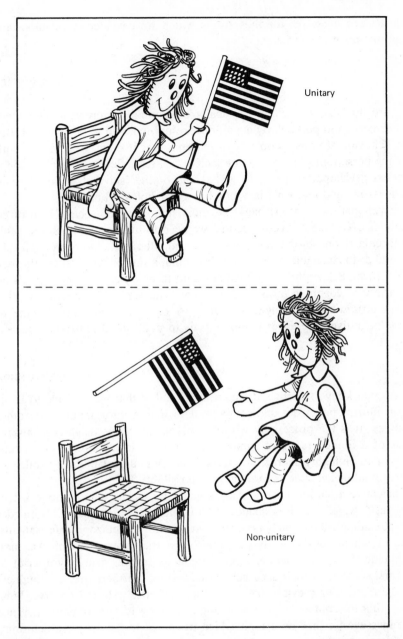

Unitary

Non-unitary

FIGURE 11–7. Imagery facilitates memory. If you can picture three (or more) words, for example, *doll, flag, chair,* when they are first presented, you will remember them better in the future. Imaging the words in an interactive or unitary form helps even more, because, in this case, if you remember one word, the image helps to generate the remaining words.

able to free ourselves for those tasks which we consider more important than just plain memorizing.

We are not all alike, either physically or mentally. Individual differences in behavior, and particularly cognition, are normal, and to be expected. But the behavior of some people is so extreme that it creates problems, both for the person and for the rest of society. Extreme deviance in behavior is labeled psychopathological, to make note of the fact that there is something wrong and that what is wrong has a psychological basis.

Psychopathology is perhaps the most important of society's unsolved problems. To take corrective action, we need to understand its bases. Schizophrenia is one broad category of psychopathology. Although there are several distinguishable types of schizophrenia, a single theme carries through all of them. Schizophrenic individuals tend to be different from normals on a variety of cognitive tasks, and as a consequence, schizophrenia is often characterized as a "thought disorder." A close examination of some of these cognitive differences might help us to understand schizophrenia better.

As you know, selective attention is an ability that we all have to focus upon information from one source and to ignore information from other sources. It is the process by which a person maintains heightened awareness of a limited range of stimulation. Because schizophrenic individuals appear to be highly distractible, several theories suggest that they suffer an attentional deficit. Let us examine this possibility.

Selective attention is commonly studied by means of a dichotic listening task, which requires shadowing of one of two messages. Schneider (1976) administered such tasks to two groups of schizophrenic patients, one of which was basically paranoid [3] and the other of which was not. Schneider found that neither schizophrenic group was generally inferior to normal subjects in their accuracy of shadowing. Furthermore, the loudness of the distracting message had no differential effect. He did observe, however, that the content of the distracting message was quite important. When the message touched on a topic which pertained to the subject's delusions, performance on the shadowed message decreased substantially. This outcome is not unlike Moray's (1959) observation of normal individuals in similar situations. The content of the secondary message is not completely

[3] Paranoia is characterized by personal beliefs that are clearly unfounded, grandiose, persecutory, hallucinatory, or bizarre.

filtered out. Some of its meaning passes into the system. When the secondary message is highly personalized, it demands more attention, in normal and in schizophrenic individuals, and therefore shadowing suffers.

Schneider interpreted his results to imply that the attentional mechanisms of schizophrenic individuals are not impaired. The finding that delusional schizophrenics make a significant number of errors when they are presented with personalized distractions merely indicates that delusional schizophrenics allocate more effort to these stimuli than do other individuals with different or no delusions. Other investigators (for example, Korboot & Damiani, 1976) have reported, however, that individuals who have repeatedly been hospitalized (chronic schizophrenia) do exhibit a slowness of mental processes which becomes apparent when shadowing at a high rate of item presentation is required.

SHORT-TERM MEMORY

Unlike the case with selective attention, there is considerable evidence showing that schizophrenics have some kind of memory impairment. For example, Oltmanns and Neale (1975) showed that external distractors are effective in reducing the memory span of schizophrenic patients when the material to be remembered is of sufficient length. Distractors seem to interfere with some process which is required for efficient performance with longer strings of verbal material. Normal subjects, as we know, tend to organize stimulus input into chunks, if at all possible, because chunks can be stored and recalled as single items. For short messages, such coding strategies are not necessary, but they become increasingly more important with length of message. According to Oltmanns and Neale, the schizophrenic patient's ability to organize sensory input into manageable chunks of information is somehow limited.

The isolation of such a specific deficit in schizophrenia provides a useful clue to the origin of gross, clinical symptomatology. Schizophrenic patients often complain about an inability to concentrate on long messages or sentences. A message might, for lack of organization, become just a string of words when it gets too long. This is consistent with the Oltmanns and Neale finding and leads these authors to suspect that internally generated distractions (intruding thoughts) might interfere with the patient's use of organizational processes.

COMPREHENSION AND RECALL

SYNTACTIC STRUCTURE. Do schizophrenic patients have difficulty using the structure of the language to understand a message? Carpenter (1976) asked schizophrenic and normal subjects to listen to strings of disconnected words, whole sentences with clicks imbedded before, in or after a clause break, and a passage of connected discourse. During designated test pauses, subjects wrote down as many words as they could recall and indicated the location of clicks within recalled sentences. Schizophrenic subjects did not differ from the normal group in the proportion of recall attributable to syntactic structure. Further, all subjects showed the same amount and kind of migration of clicks in the direction of syntactic boundaries. As far as comprehension of the material was concerned, there was no difference between schizophrenics and normals. Thus, schizophrenic subjects do tend to organize verbal material according to clause boundaries.

But schizophrenics were poorer in overall recall than normals. The problem, once again, appears to be a matter of distractibility. There was some suggestion that even the minor distractions generated by clicks were sufficient to interfere with the storage of materials. Furthermore, Carpenter's subjects frequently reported the intrusion of irrelevant thoughts prior to or during recall.

CATEGORIES.   Syntactic structure is only one means of organizing verbal material. Larsen and Fromholt (1976) studied schizophrenics' use of categorical organization. Normal and schizophrenic subjects were required to establish a stable organization for 25 unrelated words through repeated, self-paced sorting into self-determined categories. Subsequently, they were asked to recall the words. Schizophrenics required more trials to complete the sorting tasks but, once this was achieved, they recalled as many words in as orderly a manner as normal subjects. Further, the two groups did not differ with respect to the organizational structure in the sortings. According to Larsen and Fromholt, the results do not support the assumption that deficient retrieval operations contribute to the recall deficit of schizophrenics. They are consistent, however, with the hypothesis of a mnemonic organizational deficiency in schizophrenia. These authors argue that a single presentation of materials is probably not sufficient for schizophrenics to impose a stable organizational scheme. Unlike normal individuals, they require many trials to achieve such stability. The instability in their organizational scheme then is what underlies the often observed recall deficit.

RECALL VS. RECOGNITION.   As we have noted in earlier chapters, there is a difference between recall and recognition tests of memory. Because the correct items are made available in a recognition test, the subject's task is primarily a decisional one—that is, Was this item on the original list or not? In contrast, recall, at least according to some theories, requires the subject first to *search* his memory for possible items and then to *decide* as to the list membership of each. There is empirical evidence that speaks to this distinction between processes involved in recall and recognition. Recall performance is directly related to both the imagery value and the categorizability of items in the original list. Recognition, however, is affected only by imagery and not by whether the items fall into categories. These data have been taken to imply that, for normal subjects, imagery affects decision processes while categorizability affects search.

Using recall and recognition tests, Traupmann (1975) compared normal control subjects with two types of schizophrenic patients, a process or *chronic* group, who had suffered repeated, prolonged psychotic episodes and hospitalizations and a reactive or *acute* group, who had no long history of disturbance. Both groups performed identically on recognition tasks; categorizability of words apparently did not affect performance, but imagery did. From this we can conclude that the decision processes primarily involved in recognition are intact in schizophrenic patients. For controls and reactive schizophrenics, both imagery and categorizability affected recall performance. Neither variable influenced the recall of process schizophrenics, however. The implication is that process schizophrenia is associated with a memory search deficit. Because search is assumed to be based in part on the organization of information in memory, measures of organization such as clustering should provide additional evidence on that possibility. In contrast to the reactive group, process schizophrenics showed only limited clustering of recall items. The data thus demonstrate, once again, that certain types of schizophrenia are associated with a failure to impose organizational schemes on incoming information.

Broen (1973) theorizes that process schizophrenics adopt the strategy of limiting stimulus input by artificial means so as to avoid being overtaxed by a flood of stimulation. It is possible that such an avoidance strategy precludes active processing of information and prohibits the quality of organization necessary for efficient recall. Unorganized information might be of sufficient strength to be recognized, since even process schizophrenics performed adequately on the recognition tasks. The depth of processing required for recall, however, is not typically achieved by these individuals.

DISTRACTION: THE BASIS OF SCHIZOPHRENIC DEFICIT

These empirical studies lead us to the following conclusions about schizophrenia. On the positive side, there is no loss of ability to comprehend speech or to attend selectively. There is, however, an overall memory deficiency. The memory loss is primarily attributable to an inability to impose normal organizational schemas on input material. It is not that the schizophrenic individual is incapable of these schemas, for given sufficient time, the schizophrenic can bring them into play. The problem is that, for one reason or another, these schemas are not as readily used by schizophrenics as they are by normal individuals.

The bulk of the evidence suggests that the reason for the schizophrenics' inability to adopt organizational schemas for input material is their susceptibility to distraction. Distractions are particularly noticeable in individuals who suffer from delusions and/or repeated psychotic episodes. In these cases, distractions that can be ignored by normals and by other schizophrenics intrude, as highly personalized messages do for normals. They attract a sufficient amount of the schizophrenic's attentional capacity to slow his/her processing of the primary message; under these circumstances, higher levels of processing are simply not possible. The schizophrenic seems, upon observation, periodically to "tune out" in response to no obvious external cue. The tuning out process suggests a protective mechanism against a state of information overload (Broen, 1973). In a complex task, even the distraction provided by a simple or neutral stimulus as a click might be sufficient. Where the demands are less intense, relatively neutral external stimulation is probably ineffective, but, even in these cases, a highly personalized distractor can draw attention away from the primary task.

Most interference or distraction is provided not by external cues but by internally generated stimulation (Karboot & Damiani, 1973). Bourne, Justesen, Abraham, Beeker, Brauchi, Whitaker, and Yaroush (1977) have shown that, in a conceptual rule-learning task where there are no time constraints on the subject, external stimulation, in the form of irrelevant variations in the stimulus material, has no effect whatsoever on the ability of process schizophrenics to abstract complicated rules. Severity of disturbance does relate to overall performance. Mildly disturbed chronic patients perform on rule-learning problems essentially the way normal individuals of comparable education and intelligence do, but highly disturbed individuals appear to be totally incapable of abstracting a logical rule, even though they can deal successfully with the specifics of any individual concept illustrating that rule. Evidence collected in this study points to a correlation between amounts of internally generated, intruding thought, and severity of schizophrenic experience. The more disturbed individuals were indeed distracted, but less by external stimulation than by thoughts which arise internally from their own intrapsychic past.

COMMENTS

What was discussed here is a sample of studies using the techniques of modern cognitive psychology aimed at understanding the psychological deficit that underlies schizophrenia. There is more research that could be summarized. For example, the methods of concept formation have been used to pinpoint the psychological effects of localized brain damage (Pishkin & Burn, 1971). Moreover, Sirota, Schwartz and Shapiro (1976) have shown that biofeedback training for relevant physiological responses can serve as an effective behavioral strategy for reducing anxiety and unwarranted fear reactions. What we have sampled is sufficient to make our point, however. Psychopathology is a major problem facing society and individuals within society. To reduce the incidence of psychopathology, we must know more about the underlying mental processes. The business of identifying those processes is well underway. The success that contemporary cognitive techniques have had in this regard bodes well for corrective action in the future.

FINAL COMMENT

We hope these examples are sufficient to illustrate the ways in which current work in cognitive psychology is finding its way into the real world. Human beings have both profited and suffered, in significant ways, from our growing knowledge in physical science of how energy and matter are structured and processed. Out of this knowledge we have built grand machines that warm and cool, that roll and fly, that compute and communicate. The human mind has been more resistant than the physical world to scientific analysis. The mind has been slow to give up its secrets to those who research it. But, in the past 20 years, answers have been forthcoming. Through research in cognitive psychology, we are beginning to understand how the mind works and, as we do, to see increasingly broad uses for this knowledge.

The examples of applied cognitive psychology discussed in this chapter have been simple, limited, and imprecise. That's the way it is at the present time. But as our scientific knowledge accumulates, the applications should become increasingly more common, clear, and valuable. What has been done so far is a promising start. We look for even greater contributions in the future. We hope that at least some of you who have read this book will be among those responsible for the next generation of work in applied cognitive psychology.

REFERENCES

ABELSON, R. P. *Does a story understander need a point of view?* Paper prepared for the Workshop on Theoretical Issues in Natural Language Processing. Massachusetts Institute of Technology, June, 1975.

ACKERMAN, M. D. Acquisition and transfer value of initial training with multiple grapheme-phoneme correspondences. *Journal of Educational Psychology,* 1973, *65,* 28–34.

ADAMS, J. A. *Learning and memory: An introduction.* Homewood, Ill.: Dorsey Press, 1976.

AIKEN, E. G., THOMAS, G. S., & SHENNUM, W. A. Memory for a lecture: Effects of notes, lecture rate, and informational density. *Journal of Educational Psychology,* 1975, *67,* 439–444.

ALLIK, J. P., & SIEGEL, A. W. The use of the cumulative rehearsal strategy: A developmental study. *Journal of Experimental Child Psychology,* 1976, *21,* 316–327.

ALLPORT, G. W., & POSTMAN, L. J. The basic psychology of rumor. In *Readings in social psychology, 3rd ed.,* E. E. Maccoby, T. M. Newcomb, & E. L. Hartley, (Eds.). New York: Holt, Rinehart, & Winston, 1958.

ANDERSON, B. F. *Cognitive psychology.* New York: Academic Press, 1975.

ANDERSON, J. R. *Language, memory, and thought.* Hillsdale, N.J.: Lawrence Erlbaum, 1976.

ANDERSON, J. R., & BOWER, G. H. *Human associative memory.* Washington, D.C.: V. H. Winston & Sons, 1973.

ANISFELD, M., & KNAPP, M. E. Association, synonymity, and directionality in false recognition. *Journal of Experimental Psychology,* 1968, *77,* 171–179.

ANTHONY, W. S. Learning to discover rules by discovery. *Journal of Educational Psychology,* 1973, *64,* 325–328.

ATKINSON, R. C., & RAUGH, M. R. An application of the mnemonic keyword method to the acquisition of a Russian vocabulary. *Journal of Experimental Psychology: Human Learning and Memory,* 1975, *104,* 126–133.

ATKINSON, R. C., & SHIFFRIN, R. M. Human memory: A proposed system and its control processes. In *The psychology of learning and motivation: Advances in research and theory*, Vol. 2, K. W. Spence & J. T. Spence (Eds.). New York: Academic Press, 1968.

ATKINSON, R. C., & SHIFFRIN, R. M. The control of short-term memory. *Scientific American*, 1971, *225*, 82–90.

ATTNEAVE, F. Transfer of experience with a class-schema to identification-learning of patterns and shapes. *Journal of Experimental Psychology*, 1957, *54*, 81–88.

AUSTIN, J. L. *How to do things with words.* London: Oxford University Press, 1962.

BACH, E., & HARMS, R. T. (Eds.) *Universals in linguistic theory.* New York: Holt, Rinehart, & Winston, 1968.

BAHRICK, H. P., & BOUCHER, B. Retention of visual and verbal codes of the same stimuli. *Journal of Experimental Psychology*, 1968, *78*, 417–422.

BARTLETT, F. C. *Remembering: A study in experimental and social psychology.* New York: The Macmillan Co., 1932.

Begg, I., & Denny, J. P. Empirical reconciliation of atmosphere and conversion interpretations of syllogistic reasoning errors. *Journal of Experimental Psychology*, 1969, *81*, 351–354.

BERLIN, B., & KAY, P. *Basic color terms: Their universality and evolution.* Berkeley: University of California Press, 1969.

BERLYNE, D. E. Attention. In *Handbook of perception*, Vol. 1, E. C. Carterette and M. P. Friedman (Eds.). New York: Academic Press, 1974.

BEVER, T. G. The integrated study of language behavior. In *Biological and social factors in psycholinguistics*, I. Morton (Ed.). Cambridge, Mass.: Logos Press, 1971.

BJORK, R. A. Short-term storage: The ordered output of a central processor. In *Cognitive Theory*, Vol. 1, F. Restle, R. M. Shiffrin, N. H. Castellan, H. R. Lindeman, & D. B. Pisoni (Eds.). Hillsdale, N.J.: Lawrence Erlbaum, 1975.

BORING, E. G. *A history of experimental psychology.* New York: Appleton-Century-Crofts, 1950.

BOURNE, L. E., JR. Learning and utilization of conceptual rules. In *Concepts and the structure of memory*, B. Kleinmuntz (Ed.). New York: John Wiley, 1967.

BOURNE, L. E., JR. Knowing and using concepts. *Psychological Review*, 1970, *77*, 546–556.

BOURNE, L. E., JR. An inference model of conceptual rule learning. In *Theories in cognitive psychology*, R. Solso (Ed.). Washington, D.C.: L. Erlbaum and Associates, 1974.

BOURNE, L. E., JR., DODD, D. H., GUY, D. E., & JUSTESEN, D. R. Response-contingent intertrial intervals in concept identification. *Journal of Experimental Psychology*, 1968, *76*, 601–608.

BOURNE, L. E., JR., EKSTRAND, B. R., & DOMINOWSKI, R. L. *The psychology of thinking.* Englewood Cliffs, N.J.: Prentice-Hall, Inc. 1971.

BOURNE, L. E., JR., GUY, D. E., DODD, D. H., & JUSTESEN, D. R. Concept identification: The effect of varying length and the information components of the intertrial interval. *Journal of Experimental Psychology*, 1965, *69*, 624–629.

BOURNE, L. E., JR., JUSTESEN, D. R., ABRAHAM, T., BEEKER, C., BRAUCHI, J. T., WHITAKER, L. C., & YAROUSH, R. A. Limits to conceptual rule-learning in schizophrenic patients. *Journal of Clinical Psychology*, 1977, *33*, 324–334.

BOURNE, L. E., JR., & O'BANION, K. Conceptual rule learning and chronological age. *Developmental Psychology*, 1971, *5*, 525–534.

BOURNE, L. E., JR., & RESTLE, F. A mathematical theory of concept identification. *Psychological Review*, 1959, *66*, 278–296.

BOUSFIELD, W. A. The occurrence of clustering and the recall of randomly arranged associates. *Journal of General Psychology*, 1953, *49*, 229–240.

BOUSFIELD, W. A., COHEN, B. H., & WHITMARSH, G. A. Associative clustering in the recall of words of different taxonomic frequencies of occurrence. *Psychological Reports*, 1958, *4*, 39–44.

BOWER, G. H. How to . . . . uh . . . remember! *Psychology Today*, 1973, 63–70.

BOWER, G. H. Mental imagery and associative learning. In *Cognition in learning and memory*, L. Gregg (Ed.). New York: John Wiley, 1973.

BOWER, G. H., & CLARK, M. C. Narrative stories as mediators for serial learning. *Psychonomic Science*, 1969, *14*, 181–182.

BOWER, G. H., & TRABASSO, T. Reversals prior to solution in concept identification. *Journal of Experimental Psychology*, 1963. *66*, 409–418.

BOWER, G. H., & TRABASSO, T. Concept identification. In *Studies in mathematical psychology*, R. C. Atkinson (Ed.). Stanford, Calif.: Stanford University Press, 1964.

BOWER, G. H., & WINZENZ, D. Comparison of associative learning strategies. *Psychonomic Science*, 1970, *20*, 119–120.

BRAINERD, C. J. Judgments and explanations as criteria for the presence of cognitive structures. *Psychological Review*, 1973, *79*, 172–179.

BRAINERD, C. J. The role of structures in explaining cognitive development. In *The individual and society*, Vol. 1, K. F. Riegel & J. Meecham (Eds.). The Hague: Mouton, 1975.

BRAINERD, C. J., & HOOPER, F. H. A methodological analysis of developmental studies of identity conservation and equivalence conversation. *Psychological Bulletin*, 1975, *82*, 725–737.

BRANSFORD, J. D., & FRANKS, J. J. Abstraction of linguistic ideas. *Cognitive Psychology*, 1971, *2*, 331–350.

BRANSFORD, J. D., & JOHNSON, M. K. Contextual prerequisites for understanding: Some investigations of comprehension and recall. *Journal of Verbal Learning and Verbal Behavior*, 1972, *11*, 717–726.

BRANSFORD, J. D., & JOHNSON, M. K. Consideration of some problems in comprehension. In *Visual information processing*, W. G. Chase (Ed.). New York: Academic Press, 1973.

BRIGGS, G. E. Retroactive inhibition as a function of the degree of original and interpolated learnings. *Journal of Experimental Psychology*, 1957, *53*, 60–67.

BROADBENT, D. E. The role of auditory localization in attention and memory span. *Journal of Experimental Psychology*, 1954, *47*, 191–196.

BROADBENT, D. E. *Perception and communication*. New York: Pergamon Press, 1958.

BROEN, W. E., JR. Limiting the flood of stimulation: A protective deficit in chronic schizophrenia. In *Contemporary issues in cognitive psychology*, R. L. Solso (Ed.). Washington, D.C.: V. H. Winston & Sons, 1973.

BROWN, J. Some tests of the decay theory of immediate memory. *Quarterly Journal of Experimental Psychology*, 1958, *10*, 12–21.

BROWN, R. Reference in memorial tribute to Eric Lenneberg. *Cognition*, 1976, *4*, 125–153.

BROWN, R., & MCNEILL, D. The "tip of the tongue" phenomenon. *Journal of Verbal Learning and Verbal Behavior*, 1966, *5*, 325–337.

BROWN, R. W. How shall a thing be called? *Psychological Review*, 1958, *65*, 14–21.

BROWN, R. W. *Social psychology*. Glencoe, Ill.: The Free Press, 1965.

BROWN, R. W., & LENNEBERG, E. H. A study in language and cognition. *Journal of Abnormal Social Psychology*, 1954, *49*, 454–462.

BRUCE, D., & CROWLEY, J. J. Acoustic similarity effects on retrieval from secondary memory. *Journal of Verbal Learning and Verbal Behavior*, 1970, *9*, 190–196.

BRUNER, J. S., GOODNOW, J. J., & AUSTIN, G. A. *A study of thinking*. New York: John Wiley, 1956.

BRUNER, J. S., & POSTMAN, L. On the perception of incongruity: A paradigm. *Journal of Personality*, 1949, *18*, 206–223.

BUGELSKI, B. R. Words and things and images. *American Psychologist*, 1970, *25*, 1002–1012.

BURKE, R. J. A comparison of two properties of hints in individual problem solving. *Journal of General Psychology*, 1969, *81*, 3–21.

BURKE, R. J., MAIER, N. R. F., & HOFFMAN, L. R. Functions of hints in individual problem solving. *American Journal of Psychology*, 1966, *79*, 389–399.

CARMICHAEL, L., HOGAN, H. P., & WALTER, A. A. An experimental study of the effect of language on the reproduction of visually perceived forms. *Journal of Experimental Psychology*, 1932, *15*, 73–86.

CARPENTER, M. D. Sensitivity to syntactic structure: Good vs. poor premorbid schizophrenics. *Journal of Abnormal Psychology*, 1976, *85*, 41–50.

CARROLL, J. B. (Ed.). *Language, thought, and reality, selected writings of Benjamin Lee Whorf*. Cambridge, Mass.: MIT Press, 1956.

CARTER, J. F., & VANMATRE, N. H. Note taking versus note having. *Journal of Educational Psychology*, 1975, *67*, 900–904.

CERASO, J., & PROVITERA, A. Sources of error in syllogistic reasoning. *Cognitive Psychology*, 1971, *2*, 400–410.

CHAPLIN, J. P., & KRAWIEC, T. S. *Systems and theories of psychology*. New York: Holt, Rinehart, & Winston, 1974.

CHAPMAN, I. J., & CHAPMAN, J. P. Atmosphere effect re-examined. *Journal of Experimental Psychology*, 1959, *58*, 220–226.

CHASE, W. G., & CALFEE, R. C. Modality and similarity effects in short-term recognition memory. *Journal of Experimental Psychology*, 1969, *81*, 510–514.

CHASE, W. G., & SIMON, H. A. Perception in chess. *Cognitive Psychology*, 1973, *4*, 55–81.

CHERRY, E. C. Some experiments on the recognition of speech with one and two ears. *Journal of Acoustical Society of America*, 1953, *25*, 975–979.

CHERRY, E. C., & TAYLOR, W. K. Some further experiments on the recognition of speech with one and two ears. *Journal of Acoustical Society of America*, 1954, *26*, 554–559.

CHOMSKY, N. *Syntactic structures.* The Hague: Mouton, 1957.

CHOMSKY, N. *Current issues in linguistic theory.* The Hague: Mouton, 1964. (Also in *The structure of language: Readings in the philosophy of language,* J. A. Fodor & J. J. Katz (Eds.). Englewood Cliffs, N.J.: Prentice-Hall, Inc., 1964.)

CHOMSKY, N. *Aspects of the theory of syntax.* Cambridge, Mass.: MIT Press, 1965.

CHRISTENSEN, P. R., GUILFORD, J. P., & WILSON, R. C. Relations of creative responses to working time and instructions. *Journal of Experimental Psychology*, 1957, *53*, 82–88.

CLIFTON, C., JR., & ODOM, P. Similarity relations among certain English sentence constructions. *Psychological Monographs*, 1966, *80*, No. 613.

CLIFTON, C., JR., & TASH, J. Effect of syllabic word length on memory-search rate. *Journal of Experimental Psychology*, 1973, *99*, 231–235.

COFER, C. N. Constructive processes in memory. *American Scientist*, 1973, *61*, 537–543.

COLLINS, A. M. A spreading-activation theory of semantic processing. *Psychological Review*, 1975, *82*, 407–428.

COLLINS, A. M., & LOFTUS, E. F. A spreading-activation theory of semantic processing. *Psychological Review*, 1975, *5*, 85–88.

COLLINS, A. M., & QUILLIAN, M. R. Retrieval time from semantic memory. *Journal of Verbal Learning and Verbal Behavior*, 1969, *8*, 240–247.

COLLINS, A. M., & QUILLIAN, M. R. Does category size affect categorization time? *Journal of Verbal Learning and Verbal Behavior*, 1970, *9*, 432–436.

COLLINS, A. M., & QUILLIAN, M. R. Experiments on semantic memory and language comprehension. In *Cognition in learning and memory*, L. W. Gregg (Ed.). New York: John Wiley, 1972a.

COLLINS, A. M., & QUILLIAN, M. R. How to make a language user. In *Organization of memory*, E. Tulving & W. Donaldson (Eds.). New York: Academic Press, 1972b.

CONANT, M. B., & TRABASSO, T. Conjunctive and disjunctive concept formation under equal information conditions. *Journal of Experimental Psychology*, 1964, *67*, 250–255.

CONRAD, C. Cognitive economy in semantic memory. *Journal of Experimental Psychology*, 1972, *92*, 49–54.

COOPER, L. A., & SHEPARD, R. N. Chronometric studies of the rotation of mental images. In *Visual information processing*, W. G. Chase (Ed.). New York: Academic Press, 1973.

CRAIK, F. I. M., & LOCKHART, R. S. Levels of processing: A framework for memory research. *Journal of Verbal Learning and Verbal Behavior*, 1972, *11*, 671–684.

CRAIK, F. I. M., & WATKINS, M. J. The role of rehearsal in short-term memory. *Journal of Verbal Learning and Verbal Behavior*, 1973, *2*, 598–607.

CRAIK, F. I. M., & WATKINS, M. J. The role of rehearsal on short-term memory. *Journal of Verbal Learning and Verbal Behavior,* 1972, *11,* 671–684.

CROUSE, J. H. Acquisition of college course material under conditions of repeated testing. *Journal of Educational Psychology,* 1974, *66,* 367–372.

DALE, P. S. *Language development: Structure and function.* Hinsdale, Ill.: Dryden Press, 1972.

DANIEL, T. C. Nature of the effect of verbal labels on recognition memory for form. *Journal of Experimental Psychology,* 1972, *96,* 152–157.

DARWIN, C. J., TURVEY, M. T., & CROWDER, R. G. An auditory analogue of the Sperling partial-report procedure: Evidence for brief auditory storage. *Cognitive Psychology,* 1972, *3,* 255–267.

DEESE, J. *The structure of associations in language and thought.* Baltimore: Johns Hopkins, 1965.

DEWEY, J. *How we think.* Boston: Heath, 1910.

DODD, D. H., KINSMAN, R., KLIPP, R., & BOURNE, L. E., JR. Effects of logic pretraining on conceptual rule learning. *Journal of Experimental Psychology,* 1971, *88,* 119–122.

DOMINOWSKI, R. L. The effect of pronunciation practice on anagram difficulty. *Psychonomic Science,* 1969, *16,* 99–100.

DOMINOWSKI, R. L. Effects of solution familiarity and number of alternatives on problem difficulty. *Journal of Experimental Psychology,* 1972, *95,* 223–225.

DOMINOWSKI, R. L. Reasoning. *Interamerican Journal of Psychology,* 1976, in press.

DOMINOWSKI, R. L., & EKSTRAND, B. R. Direct and associative priming in anagram solving. *Journal of Experimental Psychology,* 1967, *74,* 85–86.

DOMINOWSKI, R. L., & JENRICK, R. Effects of hints and interpolated activity on solution of an insight problem. *Psychonomic Science,* 1972, *26,* 335–338.

DOMINOWSKI, R. L., & WETHERICK, N. E. Inference processes in conceptual rule learning. *Journal of Experimental Psychology: Human Learning and Memory,* 1976, *2,* 1–10.

DOUGLASS, H. J., & BOURNE, L. E., JR. Chronological age and performance on problems with repeated presolution shifts. *Developmental Psychology,* 1971, *4,* 329–333.

DUNCAN, C. P. Response hierarchies in problem solving. In *Thinking: Current experimental studies,* C. P. Duncan (Ed.). Philadelphia: Lippincott, 1967.

DUNCAN, C. P. Storage and retrieval of low-frequency words. *Memory and Cognition,* 1973, *1,* 129–132.

DUNCKER, K. On problem-solving. *Psychological Monographs,* 1945, *58,* 5, (Whole No. 270).

DYER, J. C., & MEYER, P. A. Facilitation of simple concept identification through mnemonic instruction. *Journal of Experimental Psychology: Human Learning and Memory,* 1976, *2,* 489–496.

EKSTRAND, B. R. To sleep, perchance to dream (about why we forget). In *Human memory: Festschrift in honor of Benton J. Underwood,* C. P. Duncan, L. Sechrest & A. W. Melton (Eds.). New York: Appleton-Century-Crofts, 1972.

ERICKSON, J. R. Hypothesis sampling in concept identification. *Journal of Experimental Psychology,* 1968, *76,* 12–18.

ERICKSON, J. R. A set analysis of behavior in formal syllogistic reasoning tasks. In *Theories in cognitive psychology: The Loyola symposium,* R. L. Solso, (Ed.). Potomac, Md.: Lawrence Erlbaum, 1974.

ERICKSON, J. R., ZAJKOWSKI, M. M., EHMANN, E. D. All-or-none assumptions in concept identification. *Journal of Experimental Psychology,* 1966, *72,* 690–697.

ESTES, W. K. The cognitive side of probability learning. *Psychological Review,* 1976, *83,* 37–64.

EVANS, S. H., & EDMONDS, E. M. Schema discrimination as a function of training. *Psychonomic Science,* 1966, *5,* 303–304.

FISHMAN, J. A systematization of the Whorfian hypothesis. *Behavioral Science,* 1960, *5,* 323–339.

FILLENBAUM, S. Memory for gist: Some relevant variables. *Language and Speech,* 1966, *9,* 217–227.

FINDLAY, A. *A hundred years of chemistry,* 3rd ed. London: Duckworth, 1965. Reprinted by permission of the author and Gerald Duckworth & Co., Ltd.

FLAGG, P. W., POTTS, G. R., & REYNOLDS, A. G. Instructions and response strategies in recognition memory for sentences. *Journal of Experimental Psychology: Human Learning and Memory,* 1975, *1,* 592–598.

FILE, S. E., & JEW, A. Syntax and the recall of instructions in a realistic situation. *British Journal of Psychology,* 1973, *64*(1), 65–70.

FLAVELL, J. H. *The developmental psychology of Jean Piaget.* Princeton, N.J.: Van Nostrand, 1963.

FLAVELL, J. H. Stage-related properties of cognitive development. *Cognitive Psychology,* 1971, *2,* 421–450.

FLAVELL, J. H. *Cognitive development.* Englewood Cliffs, N.J.: Prentice-Hall, Inc., 1976.

FODOR, J., & BEVER, T. The psychological reality of linguistic segments. *Journal of Verbal Learning and Verbal Behavior,* 1965, *4,* 414–420.

FODOR, J. A., BEVER, T. G., & GARRETT, M. F. *The psychology of language.* New York: McGraw-Hill, 1974.

FRAISSE, P., & PIAGET, J. (Eds.). *Experimental psychology: Its scope and method, VII. Intelligence.* New York: Basic Books, 1969.

FRANKS, J. J., & BRANSFORD, J. D. Abstraction of visual patterns. *Journal of Experimental Psychology,* 1971, *90,* 65–74.

FRASE, L. T., & SCHWARTZ, B. J. Effect of question production and answering on prose recall. *Journal of Educational Psychology,* 1975, *67,* 628–635.

FREEDMAN, J. L., & LOFTUS, E. F. Retrieval of words from long-term memory. *Journal of Verbal Learning and Verbal Behavior,* 1971, *10,* 107–115.

FREEMAN, G. L. Mental activity and the muscular process. *Psychological Review,* 1931, *38,* 428–447.

GAGNÉ, R. M., & SMITH, E. C., JR. A study of the effects of verbalization on problem solving. *Journal of Experimental Psychology,* 1962, *63,* 12–18.

GARDNER, R. A., & RUNQUIST, W. N. Acquisition and extinction of problem-solving set. *Journal of Experimental Psychology,* 1958, *55,* 274–277.

GARNER, W. R. *The processing of information and structure.* New York: John Wiley, 1974.

GARRETT, M., BEVER, T., & FODOR, J. The active use of grammar in speech perception. *Perception and Psychophysics,* 1966, *1,* 30–32.

GARRETT, M., & FODOR, J. Psychological theories and linguistic constructs. In *Verbal behavior and general behavior theory,* T. R. Dixon and D. L. Horton (Eds.). Englewood Cliffs, N.J.: Prentice-Hall, Inc., 1968.

GELMAN, P. Conservation acquisition: A problem of learning to attend to relevant attributes. *Journal of Experimental Child Psychology,* 1969, *7,* 67–87.

GHOLSON, B., LEVINE, M., & PHILLIPS, S. Hypotheses, strategies, and stereotypes in discrimination learning. *Journal of Experimental Child Psychology,* 1972, *13,* 423–446.

GIBSON, E. J. Trends in perceptual development: Implications for the reading process. *Minnesota Symposium on Child Psychology,* 1974, *8,* 24–54.

GIBSON, E. J. Theory-based research on reading and its implications for instruction. In *Toward a literate society: The report of the Committee on Reading of the National Academy of Education,* J. B. Carroll & J. S. Chall (Eds.). New York: McGraw-Hill, 1975.

GILHOOLY, K. J., & FALCONER, W. A. Concrete and abstract terms and relations in testing a rule. *Quarterly Journal of Experimental Psychology,* 1974, *26,* 355–359.

GINSBURG, H., & KOSLOWSKI, B. Cognitive development. *Annual Review of Psychology,* 1976, *27,* 29–61.

GLANZER, M., & CUNITZ, A. R. Two storage mechanisms in free-recall. *Journal of Verbal Learning and Verbal Behavior,* 1966, *5,* 351–360.

GLASER, R., & RESNICK, L. B. Instructional psychology. *Annual Review of Psychology,* 1972, *23,* 207–276.

GLASS, A. L., & HOLYOAK, K. J. Alternative conceptions of semantic memory. *Cognition,* 1975, *3*(4), 313–339.

GLEASON, H. A., JR. *An introduction to descriptive linguistics.* New York: Holt, Rinehart, & Winston, 1961.

GLUCKSBERG, S., & WEISBERG, R. W. Verbal behavior and problem solving: Some effects of labeling in a functional fixedness problem. *Journal of Experimental Psychology,* 1966, *71,* 659–664.

GOLDIN-MEADOW, S., SELIGMAN, M. E. P., & GELMAN, R. Language in the two-year-old. *Cognition,* 1976, *4,* 189–202.

GRAY, J. A., & WEDDERBURN, A. A. I. Grouping strategies with simultaneous stimuli. *Quarterly Journal of Experimental Psychology,* 1960, *12,* 180–184.

GREENO, J. G. The structure of memory and the process of solving problems. In *Contemporary issues in cognitive psychology,* R. L. Solso (Ed.). Washington, D.C.: V. H. Winston & Sons, 1973.

GRONIGER, L. D. Mnemonic imagery and forgetting. *Psychonomic Science,* 1971, *23,* 161–163.

GROSSMAN, L., & EAGLE, M. Synonymity, antonymity, and association in false recognition responses. *Journal of Experimental Psychology,* 1970, *83,* 244–248.

GUTHRIE, J. T. Models of reading and reading disability. *Journal of Educational Psychology*, 1973, *65*, 9–18.

HAGEN, J. W., JONGEWARD, R. H., JR., & KAIL, R. V., Jr. Cognitive perspectives on the development of memory. In *Advances in Child Development and Behavior*, Vol. 10, H. Reese (Ed.). New York: Academic Press, 1975.

HAMMERTON, M. A case of radical probability estimation. *Journal of Experimental Psychology*, 1973, *101*, 252–254.

HARRIS, C. S., & HABER, R. N. Selective attention and coding in visual perception. *Journal of Experimental Psychology*, 1963, *65*, 328–333.

HARRIS, P. L. Development of search and object permanence during infancy. *Psychological Bulletin*, 1975, *82*, 332–344.

HARRIS, R. J., & MONACO, G. E. The psychology of pragmatic implication: Information processing between the lines. *Journal of Experimental Psychology: General*, 1978, *107*, 1–22.

HARRIS, R. J., TESKE, R. R., BRUNO, K. B., & HALL, F. H. Memory for pragmatic implications in commercial advertising. Paper presented at Fifth Annual Conference on New Ways of Analyzing Variation in English. Georgetown University, October, 1976.

HARRIS, R. J., TESKE, R. R., & GINNS, M. J. Memory for pragmatic implications from courtroom testimony. *Bulletin of the Psychonomic Society*, 1975, *6*, 494–496.

HAVILAND, S. E., & CLARK, H. H. What's new? Acquiring new information as a process in comprehension. *Journal of Verbal Learning and Verbal Behavior*, 1975, *13*, 512–521.

HAYGOOD, R. C., & BOURNE, L. E., JR. Effects of intermittent reinforcement of an irrelevant dimension and task complexity upon concept identification. *Journal of Experimental Psychology*, 1960, *60*, 371–375.

HAYGOOD, R. C., & BOURNE, L. E., JR. Attribute- and rule-learning aspects of conceptual behavior. *Psychological Review*, 1965, *72*, 175–195.

HEBB, D. O. Concerning imagery. *Psychological Review*, 1968, *75*(6), 466–477.

HEIDER, E. R. Universals in color naming and memory. *Journal of Experimental Psychology*, 1972, *93*, 10–20.

HEIDER, E. R., & OLIVIER, D. C. The structure of the color space in naming and memory in two languages. *Cognitive Psychology*, 1972, *3*, 337–354.

HEISE, D. D. Semantic differential profiles for 1000 most frequent English words. *Psychological Monographs*, 1965, *79*, No. 8.

HELSABECK, F., JR. Syllogistic reasoning: Generation of counterexamples. *Journal of Educational Psychology*, 1975, *67*, 102–108.

HENLE, M. On the relation between logic and thinking. *Psychological Review*, 1962, *69*, 366–378.

HERMAN, D. T., LAWLESS, R. H., & MARSHALL, R. W. Variables in the effect of language on the reproduction of visually perceived forms. *Perceptual and Motor Skills*, 1951, *7*, 171–186 (Monograph).

HIEW, C. C. The acquisition and generalization of a general strategy in conceptual rule learning. Unpublished Ph.D. thesis, University of Colorado, 1973.

HOWES, D. H. On the relation between the intelligibility and frequency of occurence of English words. *Journal of Acoustical Society of America*, 1957, *29*, 296.

HULL, C. L. Quantitative aspects of the evolution of concepts. *Psychological Monographs* (Whole No. 123), 1920.

Human engineering guide to equipment design. Washington, D.C.: U.S. Government Printing Office, 1972.

HUNT, E. What kind of computer is man? *Cognitive Psychology*, 1971, *2*, 57–98.

HUNT, E. B., & HOVLAND, C. I. Order of consideration of different types of concepts. *Journal of Experimental Psychology*, 1960, *59*, 220–225.

HUNTER, I. M. L. Mental calculation. In *Thinking and reasoning*, P. C. Wason & P. N. Johnson-Laird (Eds.). Middlesex, England: Penguin Books, Ltd., 1968. Reprinted by permission of author and Penguin Books, Ltd.

JACOBS, R. A., & ROSENBAUM, P. S. *Readings in English transformational grammar*. Waltham, Mass: Blaisdell, 1970.

JACOBSON, E. Electrophysiology of mental activities and an introduction to the psychological process of thinking. In *The psychophysiology of thinking*, F. J. McGuigan & R. A. Schoonover (Eds.). New York: Academic Press, 1973.

JAMES, W. *The principles of psychology.* New York: Henry Holt & Co., 1890.

JENKINS, J. G., & DALLENBACH, K. M. Obliviscence during sleep and waking. *American Journal of Psychology*, 1924, *35*, 605–612.

JOHNSON, C., & SCOTT, B. Eyewitness testimony and suspect identification as a function of arousal, sex of witness, and scheduling of interrogation. Presented at the meeting of the American Psychological Association, Washington, D.C., September, 1976.

JOHNSON, D. M., & JENNINGS, J. W. Serial analysis of three problem-solving processes. *Journal of Psychology*, 1963, *56*, 43–52.

JOHNSON, D. M., PARROTT, G. R., & STRATTON, R. P. Production and judgment of solutions to five problems. *Journal of Educational Psychology Monograph Supplement*, 1968, *59*, No. 6, Part 2.

JOHNSON, M. K., BRANSFORD, J. D., & SOLOMON, S. K. Memory for tacit implications of sentences. *Journal of Experimental Psychology*, 1973, *98*, 203–205.

JOHNSON-LAIRD, P. N., & WASON, P. C. A theoretical analysis of insight into a reasoning task. *Cognitive Psychology*, 1970, *1*, 134–148.

KAGAN, J. Do infants think? *Scientific American*, 1972, *226*, 74–82.

KAHNEMAN, D., & TVERSKY, A. Subjective probability: A judgment of representativeness. *Cognitive Psychology*, 1972, *3*, 430–454.

KAHNEMAN, D., & TVERSKY, A. On the psychology of prediction. *Psychological Review*, 1973, *80*, 237–251.

KAPLAN, R. M., & PASCOE, G. C. Humorous lectures and humorous examples: Some effects upon comprehension and retention. *Journal of Educational Psychology*, 1977, *69*, 61–65.

KATZ, A. N., & PAIVIO, A. Imagery variables in concept identification. *Journal of Verbal Learning and Verbal Behavior*, 1975, *14*, 284–293.

KATZ, J. J., & FODOR, J. A. The structure of semantic theory. *Language*, 1963, *39*, 170–210.

KATZ, S. Role of instructions in abstraction of linguistic ideas. *Journal of Experimental Psychology*, 1973, *98*, 79–84.

KATZ, S., ATKESON, B., & LEE, J. The Bransford-Franks linear effort: Integration or artifact? *Memory and Cognition*, 1974, *2*, 709–713.

KEATING, J. P., & LOFTUS, E. F. Vocal alarm systems for high-rise buildings— A case study. *Mass Emergencies,* 1977, *2,* 25–34.

KEENAN, J. M., & KINTSCH, W. The identification of explicitly and implicitly presented information. In *The representation of meaning in memory,* W. Kintsch, (Ed.). Hillsdale, N.J.: Lawrence Erlbaum, 1974.

KELLAS, G., MCCAULEY, C., & MCFARLAND, C. E., JR. Developmental aspects of storage and retrieval. *Journal of Experimental Child Psychology,* 1975, *19,* 51–62.

KINTSCH, W. Models for free recall and recognition. In *Models of human memory,* D. A. Norman (Ed.). New York: Academic Press, 1970.

KINTSCH, W. *The representation of meaning in memory.* Hillsdale, N.J.: Lawrence Erlbaum, 1974.

KLAHR, D., & WALLACE, J. G. An information processing analysis of some Piagetian experimental tasks. *Cognitive Psychology,* 1970, *1,* 358–387.

KOPP, C. B., SIGMAN, M., & PARMELEE, A. H. Longitudinal study of sensory-motor development. *Developmental Psychology,* 1974, *10,* 687–695.

KORBOOT, P. J., & DAMIANI, N. Auditory processing speed and signal detection in schizophrenia. *Journal of Abnormal Psychology,* 1976, *85,* 287–295.

KOSSLYN, S. M. Information representation in visual images. *Cognitive Psychology,* 1975, *7,* 341–370.

KREUTZER, M. A., LEONARD, S. C., & FLAVELL, J. H. An interview study of children's knowledge about memory. *Monographs of the Society for Research in Child Development,* 1975, *40* (1, Serial No. 159).

KUHN, D. Inducing development experimentally: Comments on a research paradigm. *Developmental Psychology,* 1974, *10,* 590–600.

KULPE, O. Versuche über Abstraktion. *Berlin International Congress of Experimental Psychology,* 1904, pp. 56–58.

LABERGE, D., & SAMUELS, S. J. Toward a theory of automatic information processing in reading. *Cognitive Psychology,* 1974, *6,* 293–323.

LANE, D. M., MCDANIEL, J. R., BLEICHFELD, B. E., & RABINOWITZ, F. M. Toward the specification of hypothesis domains and Einstellung. *Journal of Experimental Psychology: Human Learning and Memory,* 1976, *2,* 489–496.

LANZ, D., & STEFFLRE, V. Language and cognition revisited. *Journal of Abnormal Social Psychology,* 1964, *69,* 472–481.

LAPORTE, R. E., & NATH, R. Role of performance goals in prose learning. *Journal of Educational Psychology,* 1976, *68,* 260–264.

LARSEN, S. F., & FROMHOLT, W. Mnemonic organization and free recall in schizophrenia. *Journal of Abnormal Psychology,* 1976, *85,* 61–65.

LEMAY, E. H. Anagram solutions as a function of task variables and solution word models. *Journal of Experimental Psychology,* 1972, *92,* 65–68.

LENNEBERG, E. H. A probalistic approach to language learning. *Behavioral Science,* 1957, *2,* 1–12.

LENNEBERG, E. H. On explaining language. *Science,* 1969, *164,* 635–643.

LENNEBERG, E. H., & ROBERTS, J. M. *The language of experience: A study in methodology.* Memoir 19, Indiana University publications in Anthropology and Linguistics, 1956.

LEVINE, M. Hypothesis behavior by humans during discrimination learning. *Journal of Experimental Psychology,* 1966, *71,* 331–338.

LEVINE, M. The latency-choice discrepancy in concept learning. *Journal of Experimental Psychology,* 1969, *82,* 1–3.

LEVINE, M. *A cognitive theory of learning.* Hillsdale, N.J.: Lawrence Erlbaum, 1975.

LOFTUS, E. F. Activation of semantic memory. *American Journal of Psychology,* 1973, *86,* 331–337.

LOFTUS, E. F., & PALMER, J. C. Reconstruction of automobile destruction: An example of the interaction between language and memory. *Journal of Verbal Learning and Verbal Behavior,* 1974, *13,* 585–589.

LOFTUS, E. F., & ZANNI, G. Eyewitness testimony: The influence of the wording of a question. *Bulletin of the Psychonomic Society,* 1975, *5,* 86–88.

LOFTUS, G. R., & LOFTUS, E. F. The influence of one memory retrieval on a subsequent memory retrieval. *Memory and Cognition,* 1974, *3,* 467–471.

LORAYNE, H., & LUCAS, J. *The memory book.* New York: Ballantine Books, 1974. (Published in paperback by Stein and Day Publishers, New York, 1975.)

LURIA, A. R. *The mind of a mnemonist.* A little book about a Vast Memory. Trans. from Russian by Lynn Solotaroff. New York: Basic Books, Inc., Publishers, 1968.

MACNAMARA, J. Cognitive basis of language learning in infants. *Psychological Review,* 1972, *79,* 1–13.

MAIER, N. R. F. The behavior mechanisms concerned with problem solving. *Psychological Review,* 1940, *47,* 43–53.

MAIER, N. R. F., & BURKE, R. J. Influence of timing of hints on their effectiveness in problem solving. *Psychological Reports,* 1967, *20,* 3–8.

MALMO, R. B. *On emotions, needs, and our archaic brain.* New York: Holt, Rinehart, & Winston, 1975.

MALTZMAN, I. Thinking: From a behavioristic point of view. *Psychological Review,* 1955, *66,* 367–386.

MANDLER, G. Organization and memory. In *The psychology of learning and motivation,* Vol. 1, K. W. Spence & J. T. Spence (Eds.). New York: Academic Press, 1967.

MANSKE, M. E., & DAVIS, G. A. Effects of simple instructional biases upon performance in the unusual uses test. *Journal of General Psychology,* 1968, *78,* 25–33.

MARKMAN, E. M., & SEIBERT, J. Classes and collections: Internal organization and resulting holistic properties. *Cognitive Psychology,* 1976, *8,* 561–577.

MARTIN, E. Verbal learning theory and independent retrieval phenomena. *Psychological Review,* 1971, *78,* 314–332.

MASON, M. Reading ability and letter search time: Effects of orthographic structure defined by single-letter positional frequency. *Journal of Experimental Psychology: General,* 1975, *104,* 146–166.

MASON, M., & KATZ, L. Visual processing of nonlinguistic strings: Redundancy effects and reading ability. *Journal of Experimental Psychology: General,* 1976, *105,* 338–348.

MASSARO, D. W. *Experimental psychology and information processing.* Chicago: Rand McNally, 1975.

MAX, L. W. An experimental study of the motor theory of consciousness: IV.

Action-current responses in the deaf during awakening, kinesthetic imagery, and abstract thinking. *Journal of Comparative Psychology,* 1937, *24,* 301–344.

MAYER, M. *Madison Avenue, U.S.A.* New York: Harper & Brothers, 1958.

MAYER, R. E., & GREENO, J. G. Structural differences between learning outcomes produced by different instructional methods. *Journal of Educational Psychology,* 1972, *63,* 165–173.

MAYER, R. E., STIEHL, C. C., & GREENO, J. G. Acquisition of understanding and skill in relation to subjects' preparation and meaningfulness of instruction. *Journal of Educational Psychology,* 1975, *67,* 331–350.

McGEOCH, J. A. *The psychology of human learning.* New York: Longmans, Green & Co., 1942.

McGUIGAN, F. J., & SCHOONOVER, R. A. (Eds.). *The psychophysiology of thinking.* New York: Academic Press, 1973.

McKOON, G., & KEENAN, J. M. Response latencies to explicit and implicit statements as a function of the delay between reading and test. In *The representation of meaning in memory,* W. Kintsch (Ed.). Hillsdale, N.J.: Lawrence Erlbaum, 1974.

MEEHL, P. E., & ROSEN, A. Antecedent probability and the efficiency of psychometric signs, patterns, or cutting scores. *Psychological Bulletin,* 1955, *52,* 194–216.

MEHLER, J. Some effects of grammatical transformations on the recall of English sentences. *Journal of Verbal Learning and Verbal Behavior,* 1963, *2,* 346–351.

MELTON, A. W., & IRWIN, J. M. The influence of degree of interpolated learning on retroactive inhibition and the overt transfer of specific responses. *American Journal of Psychology,* 1940, *53,* 173–203.

MEYER, D. E. On the representation and retrieval of stored semantic information. *Cognitive Psychology,* 1970, *1,* 242–300.

MEYER, D. E. Long-term memory retrieval during the comprehension of affirmative and negative sentences. In *Studies in long-term memory,* R. A. Kennedy & A. L. Wilkes (Eds.). London: Wiley, 1975.

MILLER, G. A. The magical number seven, plus or minus two: Some limits on our capacity to process information. *Psychological Review,* 1956, *63,* 81–97.

MILLER, G. A. A psychological method to investigate verbal concepts. *Journal of Mathematical Psychology,* 1969, *6,* 169–191.

MILLER, G. A., & JOHNSON-LAIRD, P. N. *Language and perception.* Cambridge, Mass.: Belknap Press (Harvard), 1976.

MILLER, P. H. Attention to stimulus dimensions in the conservation of liquid quantity. *Child Development,* 1973, *44,* 129–136.

MILLER, S. A. Nonverbal assessment of Piagetian concepts. *Psychological Bulletin,* 1976, *83,* 405–430.

MILNER, B. The memory defect in bilateral hippocampal lesions. *Psychiatric Research Reports,* 1959, *11,* 43–52. Reprinted by permission of the author and American Psychiatric Association.

MILNER, B. Amnesia following operation on temporal lobes. In *Amnesia,* C. W. M. Whitty & P. Zangwill (Eds.). London: Butterworth and Company, 1966.

MILLWARD, R. B., & SPOEHR, K. T. The direct measurement of hypothesis sampling strategies. *Cognitive Psychology*, 1973, *4*, 1–38.

MOELY, B. E., OLSON, F. A., HALWES, T. G., & FLAVELL, J. H. Production deficiency in young children's clustered recall. *Developmental Psychology*, 1969, *1*, 26–34.

MOERK, E. L. Piaget's research as applied to the explanation of language development. *Merrill-Palmer Quarterly of Behavior and Development*, 1975, *21*, 151–169.

MORAY, N. Attention in dichotic listening: Affective cues and the influence of instructions. *Quarterly Journal of Experimental Psychology*, 1959, *11*, 59–60.

MORAY, N. *Listening and attention*. Baltimore, Md.: Penguin Books, 1969.

MORGAN, C. S. A study in the psychology of testimony. *Journal of the American Institute of Criminal Law*, 1917, *8*, 222.

MURRAY, H. G., & DENNY, J. P. Interaction of ability level and interpolated activity (opportunity for incubation) in human problem solving. *Psychological Reports*, 1969, *24*, 271–276.

MURDOCK, B. B., JR. Serial order effects in short-term memory. *Journal of Experimental Psychology Monograph Supplement*, 1968, *76* (*Part 2*), 1–15.

MURDOCK, B. B., JR. *Human memory: Theory and data*. Potomac, Md.: Lawrence Erlbaum, 1974.

NEIMARK, E. D. Intellectual development during adolescence. In *Review of Child Development Research*, Vol. 4, F. D. Horowitz (Ed.). Chicago: University of Chicago Press, 1975.

NEIMARK, E. D., & SLOTNICK, N. S. Development of the understanding of logical connectives. *Journal of Educational Psychology*, 1970, *61*, 451–460.

NEIMARK, E. D., & WAGNER, H. Information-gathering in diagnostic problem solving as a function of number of alternative solutions. *Psychonomic Science*, 1964, *1*, 329–330.

NEISSER, U. Changing conceptions of imagery. In *The Function and nature of imagery*, P. W. Sheehan (Ed.). New York: Academic Press, 1972.

NEISSER, U., & KERR, N. Spatial and mnemonic properties of visual images. *Cognitive Psychology*, 1973, *5*, 138–150.

NEISSER, U., & WEENE P. Hierarchies in concept attainment. *Journal of Experimental Psychology*, 1962, *64*, 640–645.

NELSON, K. Some evidence for the cognitive primacy of categorization and its functional basis. *Merrill-Palmer Quarterly of Behavior and Development*, 1973, *19*, 21–39.

NELSON, K. Concept, word, and sentence: Interrelations in acquisition and development. *Psychological Review*, 1974, *81*, 267–285.

NEUMANN, P. G. An attribute frequency model for the abstraction of prototypes. *Memory and Cognition*, 1974, *2*, 241–248.

NEUMANN, P. G. Visual prototype formation with discontinuous representation of dimensions of variability. Unpublished Ph.D. dissertation, University of Colorado, 1975.

NEWELL, A., & SIMON, H. A. *Human problem solving*. Englewood Cliffs, N.J.: Prentice-Hall, Inc., 1972.

NORMAN, D. A. *Memory and attention*, 2nd ed. New York: John Wiley, 1976.

NORMAN, D. A., & BOBROW, D. G. On data-limited and resource-limited processes. *Cognitive Psychology,* 1975, *7,* 44–64.

NORMAN, D. A., & RUMELHART, D. E. *Explorations in cognition.* San Francisco: W. H. Freeman, 1975.

OLTMANNS, T. F., & NEALE, J. M. Schizophrenic performance when distractors are present: Attentional deficit or differential task difficulty? *Journal of Abnormal Psychology,* 1975, *84,* 205–209.

ORNSTEIN, P. A., NAUS, M. J., & LIBERTY, C. Rehearsal and organizational processes in children's memory. *Child Development,* 1975, *46,* 818–830.

OSGOOD, C. E. The nature and measurement of meaning. *Psychological Bulletin,* 1952, *49,* 197–237.

OSGOOD, C. E. A behavioristic analysis of perception and language as cognitive phenomena. In *Contemporary approaches to cognition.* Cambridge, Mass.: Harvard University Press, 1957.

OSHERON, D. N., & WASOW, T. Task-specificity and species-specificity in the study of language. *Cognition,* 1976, *4,* 203–214.

PAIVIO, A. *Imagery and verbal processes.* New York: Holt, Rinehart, & Winston, 1971.

PAIVIO, A. Perceptual comparisons through the mind's eye. *Memory and Cognition,* 1975, *3*(6), 635–647.

PALERMO, D. S., & MOLFESE, D. L. Language acquisition from age five onward. *Psychological Bulletin,* 1972, *78,* 409–428.

PAVLOV, I. *Conditioned reflexes.* London and New York: Oxford University Press, 1927.

PERFETTI, C. A., & HOGABOAM, T. Relationship between single word decoding and reading comprehension skill. *Journal of Educational Psychology,* 1975, *67,* 461–469.

PETERSON, C. R., & BEACH, L. R. Man as an intuitive statistician. *Psychological Bulletin,* 1967, *68,* 29–46.

PETERSON, L. R., & PETERSON, M. J. Short-term retention of individual verbal items. *Journal of Experimental Psychology,* 1959, *58,* 193–198.

PETERSON, M. J., MEAGHER, R. B., JR., CHAIL, H., & GILLIE, S. The abstraction and generalization of dot patterns. *Cognitive Psychology,* 1973, *4,* 378–398.

PIAGET, J. *The psychology of intelligence,* trans, by M. Piercy & D. E. Berlyne. London: Routledge, 1950.

PIAGET, J. *Genetic epistemology.* New York: Norton, 1970.

PICK, A. D., FRANKEL, D. G., & HESS, V. L. Children's attention: The development of selectivity. In *Review of child development research,* Vol. 5, E. M. Hetherington (Ed.). Chicago: University of Chicago Press, 1975.

PISHKIN, V., & BURN, J. M. Concept identification in the brain-damaged: Intertrial interval and information complexity. *Journal of Abnormal Psychology,* 1971, *77,* 205–210.

POLICH, J. M., & SCHWARTZ, S. H. The effect of problem size on representation in deductive problem solving. *Memory and Cognition,* 1974, *2,* 683–686.

POSNER, M. I., GOLDSMITH, R., & WELTON, K. E., JR. Perceived distance and the classification of distorted patterns. *Journal of Experimental Psychology,* 1967, *73,* 28–38.

POSNER, M. I., & KEELE, S. On the genesis of abstract ideas. *Journal of Experimental Psychology*, 1968, *77*, 353–363.

POSNER, M. I., & KONICK, A. F. On the role of interference in short-term retention. *Journal of Experimental Psychology*, 1966, *72*, 221–231.

POSTMAN, L., & PHILLIPS, L. W. Short-term temporal changes in free-recall. *Quarterly Journal of Experimental Psychology*, 1965, *17*, 132–138.

POSTMAN, L., & STARK, K. Role of response availability in transfer and interference. *Journal of Experimental Psychology*, 1969, *79*, 168–177.

POSTMAN, L., STARK, K., & FRASER, J. Temporal changes in interference. *Journal of Verbal Learning and Verbal Behavior*, 1968, *7*, 672–694.

POSTMAN, L., & UNDERWOOD, B. J. Critical issues in interference theory. *Memory and Cognition*, 1973, *1*, 19–40.

POTTER, M. C. How people see signs. Ashley, Myer, Smith Technical Report, October, 1972.

POTTER, M. C. Short term conceptual memory for pictures. *Journal of Experimental Psychology: Human Learning and Memory*, 1976, *2*, 509–522.

POTTER, M. C., & LEVY, E. I. Recognition memory for a rapid sequence of pictures. *Journal of Experimental Psychology*, 1969, *81*, 10–15.

PYLYSHYN, Z. W. What the mind's eye tells the mind's brain: A critique of mental imagery. *Psychological Bulletin*, 1973, *80*(1), 1–24.

RAPHAEL, B. *The thinking computer: Mind inside matter.* San Francisco: W. H. Freeman, 1976.

REBER, A. S. What clicks may tell us about speech perception. *Journal of Psycholinguistic Research*, 1973, *2*, 286–287.

REBER, A. S., & ANDERSON, J. R. The perception of clicks in linguistic and nonlinguistic messages. *Perception and Psychophysics*, 1970, *8*, 81–89.

REED, S. F., ERNST, G. W., & BANERJI, R. The role of analogy in transfer between similar problem states. *Cognitive Psychology*, 1974, *6*, 435–450.

REED, S. K. Pattern recognition and categorization. *Cognitive Psychology*, 1972, *3*, 383–407. Reprinted by permission of author and Academic Press, Inc.

REED, S. K., & FRIEDMAN, M. P. Perceptual vs. conceptual categorization. *Memory and Cognition*, 1973, *1*, 157–163. Reprinted by permission of author and Psychonomic Society Press.

REEVES, R. *Reality in advertising.* New York: Alfred A Knopf, 1961.

REITMAN, J. S., & BOWER, G. H. Storage and later recognition of exemplars of concepts. *Cognitive Psychology*, 1973, *4*, 194–206.

RESTLE, F. The selection of strategies in cue learning. *Psychological Review*, 1962, *69*, 329–343.

REVLIS, R. Representation and set size in syllogistic reasoning. Paper given at the annual meeting of the Psychonomic Society, November, 1973.

REZNICK, J. S., & RICHMAN, C. L. Effects of class complexity, class frequency, and pre-experimental bias on rule learning. *Journal of Experimental Psychology: Human Learning and Memory*, 1976, *2*, 774–782.

RICKARDS, J. P., & DIVESTA, F. J. Type and frequency of questions in processing textual material. *Journal of Educational Psychology*, 1974, *66*, 354–362.

RIPS, L. J. Inductive judgments about natural categories. *Journal of Verbal Learning and Verbal Behavior*, 1975, *14*, 665–681.

RIPS, L. J., SHOBEN, E. J., & SMITH, E. E. Semantic distance and the verification of semantic relations. *Journal of Verbal Learning and Verbal Behavior,* 1973, *12,* 1–20.

RONNING, R. R. Anagram solution times: A function of the "Rule-out" factor. *Journal of Experimental Psychology,* 1965, *69,* 35–39.

ROSCH, E. Universals and cultural specifics in human categorization. In *Cross-cultural perspectives on learning,* R. Breslin, W. Lonner, and S. Bochner (Eds.). London: Sage Press, 1974.

ROSCH, E. H. Natural categories. *Cognitive Psychology,* 1973, *4,* 328–350.

ROSCH, E. H. Cognitive representations of semantic categories. *Journal of Experimental Psychology: General,* 1975, *104,* 192–233.

ROSCH, E. H., & MERVIS, C. B. Family resemblances: Studies in the internal structure of categories. *Cognitive Psychology,* 1975, *7,* 573–605.

ROSCH, E. H., MERVIS, C. B., GRAY, W. D., JOHNSON, D. M., & BOYES-BRAEM, P. Basic objects in natural categories. *Cognitive Psychology,* 1976, *8,* 382–439.

ROSENZWEIG, M. R., BENNETT, E. L., & DIAMOND, M. C. Brain changes in response to experience. *Scientific American,* 1972, *226,* 22–29.

ROYER, P. N. Effects of specificity and position of written instructional objectives on learning from a lecture. *Journal of Educational Psychology,* 1977, *69,* 40–45.

RUMELHART, D. E., LINDSAY, P. H., & NORMAN, D. A. A process model for long-term memory. In *Organization of Memory,* E. Tulving & W. Donaldson (Eds.). New York: Academic Press, 1972.

RUNDUS, D. Analysis of rehearsal processes in free-recall. *Journal of Experimental Psychology,* 1971, *89,* 63–77.

RUNDUS, E., & ATKINSON, R. C. Rehearsal processes in free-recall: A procedure for direct observation. *Journal of Verbal Learning and Verbal Behavior,* 1970, *9,* 99–105.

RYBASH, J. M., ROODIN, P. A., & SULLIVAN, L. F. The effects of a memory aid on three types of conservation judgments. *Journal of Experimental Child Psychology,* 1975, *19,* 358–370.

SACHS, J. Recognition memory for syntactic and semantic aspects of connected discourse. *Perception and Psychophysics,* 1967, *2,* 437–442.

SACHS, J. S. Memory in reading and listening to discourse. *Memory and Cognition,* 1974, *2,* 95–100.

SAFREN, M. A. Associations, sets, and the solution of word problems. *Journal of Experimental Psychology,* 1962, *64,* 40–45.

SAMUELS, S. J., DAHL, P., & ARCHWAMETY, T. Effect of hypothesis/test training in reading skill. *Journal of Educational Psychology,* 1974, *66,* 835–844.

SAVIN, H. S., & PERCHONOK, E. Grammatical structures and the immediate recall of English sentences. *Journal of Verbal Learning and Verbal Behavior,* 1965, *4,* 348–353.

SCANDURA, J. M. Role of higher order rules in problem solving. *Journal of Experimental Psychology,* 1974, *102,* 984–991.

SCHEERER, M., ROTHMANN, E., & GOLDSTEIN, K. A case of "idiot savant": An experimental study of personality organization. *Psychological Monographs,* 1945, *58,* Whole No. 269.

SCHNEIDER, S. J. Selective attention in schizophrenia. *Journal of Abnormal Psychology,* 1976, *85,* 167–173.

SCHWARTZ, S. H. Modes of representation and problem solving: Well evolved is half solved. *Journal of Experimental Psychology,* 1971, *91,* 347–350.

SCHWELLER, K. G., BREWER, W. F., & DAHL, D. A. Memory for illocutionary forces and perlocutionary effects of utterances. *Journal of Verbal Learning and Verbal Behavior,* 1976, *15,* 325–337.

SHANTEAU, J. Averaging versus multiplying combination rules of inference judgment. *Acta Psychologica,* 1975, *39,* 83–89.

SHARRY, J. A. South America burning. *Fire Journal,* 1974, *68,* 23–33.

SHEPARD, R. N., & METZLER, J. Mental rotation of three-dimensional objects. *Science,* 1971, *171,* 701–703.

SHIFFRIN, R. M. Short-term store: The basis for a memory system. In *Cognitive theory,* Vol. 1, F. Restle, R. M. Shiffrin, N. J. Castellan, H. R. Lindman, & D. B. Pisoni (Eds.). Hillsdale, N.J.: Lawrence Erlbaum, 1975.

SHIFFRIN, R. M., & GARDNER, G. T. Visual processing capacity and attentional control. *Journal of Experimental Psychology,* 1972, *93,* 72–82.

SHIFFRIN, R. M., & GEISLER, W. S. Visual recognition in a theory of information processing. In *Contemporary issues in cognitive psychology: The Loyola symposium,* R. L. Solso, (Ed.). Washington, D.C.: V. H. Winston & Sons, 1973.

SHIFFRIN, R. M., & GRANTHAM, D. W. Can attention be allocated to sensory modalities? *Perception and Psychophysics,* 1974, *6,* 190–215.

SIEGLER, R. S. Defining the locus of developmental differences in children's causal reasoning. *Journal of Experimental Child Psychology,* 1975, *20,* 512–525.

SIEGLER, R. S., & LIEBERT, R. M. Effects of contiguity, regularity, and age on children's causal inferences. *Developmental Psychology,* 1974, *10,* 574–579.

SIMON, H. A. What is visual imagery: An information processing interpretation. In *Cognition in learning and memory,* L. W. Gregg, (Ed.). New York: John Wiley, 1972.

SIMON, H. A. The functional equivalence of problem solving skills. *Cognitive Psychology,* 1975, *7,* 268–288.

SIMON, H. A., & REED, S. K. Modeling strategy shifts in a problem-solving task. *Cognitive Psychology,* 1976, *8,* 86–97.

SINGER, M. A replication of Bransford and Franks' (1971) "The abstraction of linguistic ideas." *Bulletin of the Psychonomic Society,* 1973, *1,* 416–418.

SIROTA, A. D., SCHWARTZ, G. E., & SHAPIRO, D. Voluntary control of human heart rate: Effect on reaction to aversive stimulation: A replication and extension. *Journal of Abnormal Psychology,* 1976, *85,* 473–477.

SKINNER, B. F. *Verbal behavior.* New York: Appleton-Century-Crofts, 1957.

SLOVIC, P., & LICHTENSTEIN, S. Comparison of Bayesian and regression approaches to the study of information processing in judgment. *Journal of Organizational Behavior and Human Performance,* 1971, *6,* 649–744.

SMITH, E. E. Theories of semantic memory. In *Handbook of learning and cognitive processes,* Vol. 5, W. K. Estes (Ed.). Hillsdale, N.J.: Lawrence Erlbaum, 1976.

SMITH, E. E., SHOBEN, E. J., & RIPS, L. J. Structure and process in semantic memory: A featural model for semantic decisions. *Psychological Review,* 1974, *81,* 214–241.

SOLI, S. D., & BALCH, W. R. Performance biases and recognition memory for semantic and formal changes in connected discourse. *Memory and Cognition,* 1976, *4,* 673–677.

SOMMER, R. The new look on the witness stand. *Canadian Psychologist,* 1959, *8,* 94–99.

SPERLING, G. The information available in brief visual presentations. *Psychological Monographs,* 1960, *74,* 1–29.

SROUFE, L. A., & WATERS, E. The ontogenesis of smiling and laughter: A perspective on the organization of development in infancy. *Psychological Review,* 1976, *83,* 173–189.

STEFFLRE, V., VALES, V. C., & MORLEY, L. Language and cognition in Yucatan: A cross-cultural replication. *Journal of Personality and Social Psychology,* 1955, *4,* 112–115.

STERNBERG, S. High-speed scanning in human memory. *Science,* 1966, *153,* 652–654.

STERNBERG, S. Two operations in character-recognition. Some evidence from reaction-time measurements. *Perception and Psychophysics,* 1967, *2,* 45–53.

STERNBERG, S. The discovery of processing stages. Extensions of Donder's method. *Acta Psychologica,* 1969, *30,* 276–315.

STRATTON, R. P., & WATHEN, K. E. Thinking of a word under instructional constraints. *Psychonomic Science,* 1972, *28,* 97–99.

TAPLIN, J. E. Evaluation of hypotheses in concept identification. *Memory and Cognition,* 1975, *3,* 85–96.

TAPLIN, J. E., STAUDENMAYER, H., & TADDONIO, J. L. Developmental changes in conditional reasoning: Linguistic or logical? *Journal of Experimental Child Psychology,* 1974, *17,* 360–373.

THEIOS, J., SMITH, P. G., HAVILAND, S. E., TRAUPMANN, J., & MOY, M. C. Memory scanning as a serial self-terminating process. *Journal of Experimental Psychology,* 1973, *97,* 323–336.

THOMAS, J. C., JR. An analysis of behavior in the hobbits-orcs problem. *Cognitive Psychology,* 1974, *6,* 257–269.

THOMAS, W. I. *Primitive behavior.* New York: McGraw-Hill, 1937.

THORNDIKE, E. L. Animal intelligence. *Psychological Monographs,* 1898, Whole No. 8.

TITCHENER, E. B. *Lectures on the elementary psychology of feeling and attention.* New York: Macmillan, 1908.

TOWNSEND, J. T. Some results concerning the identifiability of parallel and serial processes. *British Journal of Mathematical and Statistical Psychology,* 1972, *25,* 168–199.

TRABASSO, T., & BOWER, G. H. *Attention in learning.* New York: John Wiley, 1968.

TRAUPMANN, K. L. Effects of categorization and imagery on recognition and recall by process and reactive schizophrenics. *Journal of Abnormal Psychology,* 1975, *84,* 307–314.

TREISMAN, A. M., & DAVIES, A. Divided attention to ear and eye. In *Attention and performance IV,* S. Kornblum (Ed.). New York: Academic Press, 1973.

TULVING, E. Episodic and semantic memory. In *Organization of memory*, E. Tulving & W. Donaldson (Eds.). New York: Academic Press, 1972.

TULVING, E., & PEARLSTONE, Z. Availability versus accessibility of information in memory for words. *Journal of Verbal Learning and Verbal Behavior*, 1966, *5*, 381–391.

TULVING, E., THOMSON, D. M. Retrieval processes in recognition memory: Effect of associative context. *Journal of Experimental Psychology*, 1971, *87*, 116–124.

TULVING, E., & THOMSON, D. M. Encoding specificity and retrieval processes in episodic memory. *Psychological Review*, 1973, *80*, 352–373.

TVERSKY, A., & KAHNEMAN, D. Belief in the law of small numbers. *Psychological Bulletin*, 1971, *76*, 105–110.

TVERSKY, A., & KAHNEMAN, D. Availability: A heuristic for judging frequency and probability. *Cognitive Psychology*, 1973, *5*, 207–232.

UNDERWOOD, B. J. Retroactive and proactive inhibition after five and forty-eight hours. *Journal of Experimental Psychology*, 1948, *38*, 29–38. (a)

UNDERWOOD, B. J. "Spontaneous recovery" of verbal associations. *Journal of Experimental Psychology*, 1948, *38*, 429–439. (b)

UNDERWOOD, B. J. Proactive inhibition as a function of time and degree of prior learning. *Journal of Experimental Psychology*, 1949, *39*, 24–34.

UNDERWOOD, B. J. Interference and forgetting. *Psychological Review*, 1957, *64*, 49–60.

UNDERWOOD, B. J. Forgetting. *Scientific American*, reprint 482, 1964.

UNDERWOOD, B. J. Attributes of memory. *Psychological Review*, 1969, *76*, 559–573.

WASON, P. C. On the failure to eliminate hypotheses—a second look. In *Thinking and reasoning*, P. C. Wason & P. N. Johnson-Laird (Eds.). Baltimore: Penguin, 1968.

WASON, P. C., & JOHNSON-LAIRD, P. N. *Psychology of reasoning: Structure and content*. Cambridge, Mass.: Harvard University Press, 1972.

WATKINS, M. J., & WATKINS, O. C. Processing of recency items for free-recall. *Journal of Experimental Psychology*, 1974, *102*, 488–493.

WERNER, H., & KAPLAN, E. Development of word meaning through verbal context: An experimental study. *Journal of Psychology*, 1950, *29*, 251–257. Courtesy of Journal Press.

WETHERICK, N. E. On the representativeness of some experiments in cognition. *Bulletin of the British Psychological Society*, 1970, *23*, 213–214.

WHITE, R. M., Jr. Relationship of performance in concept identification problems to type of pretraining problem and response-contingent post-feedback intervals. *Journal of Experimental Psychology*, 1972, *94*, 132–140.

WHORF, B. L. *Language, thought, and reality: Selected writings of Benjamin Lee Whorf*, J. B. Carroll (Ed.). New York: John Wiley, 1956.

WICKENS, C. D. Temporal limits of human information processing: A developmental study. *Psychological Bulletin*, 1974, *81*, 739–755.

WICKENS, D. D. Encoding categories of words: An empirical approach to meaning. *Psychological Review*, 1970, *77*, 1–15.

WICKENS, D. D. Some characteristics of word encoding. *Memory and Cognition*, 1973, *1*, 485–490.

WILLIAMS, J. P. From basic research on reading to educational practice. In *Basic studies on reading,* H. Levin & J. P. Williams (Eds.). New York: Basic Books, Inc., 1970, pp. 263–277.

WOHLWILL, J. F. The age variable in psychological research. *Psychological Review,* 1970, *77,* 49–64.

WOLLEN, K. A., WEBER, A., & LOWRY, D. H. Bizarreness versus interaction of mental images as determinants of learning. *Cognitive Psychology,* 1972, *2,* 518–523.

WULFF, F. Über die Veränderung von Vorstellungen. *Psychologische Forschung,* 1922, *1,* 333–373.

WUNDT, W. *Grundzüge der physiologischen Psychologie.* Leipzig: Engelmann, 1874.

ZADEH, L. A. Fuzzy sets. *Information and Control,* 1965, *8,* 338–375.

ZADEH, L. A. Quantitative fuzzy semantics. *Information Science,* 1971, *3,* 159–176.

AUTHOR
INDEX

SUBJECT
INDEX